ROUTLEDGE LIBRARY EDITIONS:
IMMIGRATION AND MIGRATION

Volume 4

ASIA'S POPULATION PROBLEMS

ASIA'S POPULATION PROBLEMS

With a Discussion of Population and Immigration in Australia

Edited by
S. CHANDRASEKHAR

Routledge
Taylor & Francis Group
LONDON AND NEW YORK

First published in 1967 by George Allen & Unwin Ltd

This edition first published in 2023
by Routledge
4 Park Square, Milton Park, Abingdon, Oxon OX14 4RN

and by Routledge
605 Third Avenue, New York, NY 10158

Routledge is an imprint of the Taylor & Francis Group, an informa business

British Library Cataloguing in Publication Data
A catalogue record for this book is available from the British Library

ISBN: 978-1-032-31713-7 (Set)
ISBN: 978-1-032-36729-3 (Volume 4) (hbk)
ISBN: 978-1-032-36833-7 (Volume 4) (pbk)
ISBN: 978-1-003-33402-6 (Volume 4) (ebk)

DOI: 10.4324/9781003334026

Publisher's Note
The publisher has gone to great lengths to ensure the quality of this reprint but points out that some imperfections in the original copies may be apparent.

Disclaimer
The publisher has made every effort to trace copyright holders and would welcome correspondence from those they have been unable to trace.

ASIA'S POPULATION PROBLEMS

With a Discussion of Population and Immigration in Australia

EDITED BY
S. CHANDRASEKHAR

London
GEORGE ALLEN & UNWIN LTD
RUSKIN HOUSE MUSEUM STREET

FIRST PUBLISHED IN 1967

PRINTED IN GREAT BRITAIN
in 11 *on* 12 *point Times Roman*
BY UNWIN BROTHERS LIMITED
WOKING AND LONDON

Dedicated by the Editor
to
Shrimathi Indira Gandhi
Prime Minister of India
With affection and admiration

N
0 700
Scale of Miles
U. S. S. R
A S I A
Ulan Bator
MONGOLIAN PEOPLES REPUBLIC
Amur
Kurilskie Is.
Peking
CHINESE PEOPLES REPUBLIC
CHINA
Hwang Ho
Yangtze
Seoul
KOREA
Tokyo
JAPAN
AFGHANISTAN
PAKISTAN
Lahore
Delhi
Ganges
Brahmaputra
Salween
Mekong
Karachi
INDIA
Dacca
Calcutta
BURMA
Hanoi
LAOS
VIETNAM
Taiwan
PACIFIC OCEAN
Bombay
Madras
Rangoon
THAILAND
Bangkok
Saigon
Manila
PHILIPPINE ISLANDS
Colombo
CEYLON
MALAYSIA
Borneo
Singapore
Padang
Sumatra
INDONESIA
NEW GUINEA
Java
INDIAN OCEAN
AUSTRALIA
Brisbane
Perth
Murray
Sydney
Melbourne
TASMANIA
Hobart
E.G.M.

PREFACE

THE idea for this volume of essays on Asian and Australian population problems arose at an International Seminar on Asian Population Problems organized by the World Assembly of Youth held at Monash University, Melbourne, Australia, in December 1963. Youth delegations from fourteen Asian nations, besides the host country, participated in the Seminar. All the youth delegations, with diverse professional interests, presented papers on the population problems of their respective countries from youth's point of view.

The World Assembly of Youth did me the honour of inviting me to preside over the Seminar and deliver the keynote address. The papers and proceedings of the Seminar revealed the need for a book of scholarly essays on Asian population problems written by specialists—demographers, economists and sociologists—and designed for both the expert and the lay reader. Hence this volume.

While population problems in general have been discussed for at least two centuries, it is only in recent years, particularly the last two decades since the termination of the Second World War, that the problem has received serious attention from both the academic and the political world. Such demographic problem areas as China, India, Japan and Latin America have naturally received considerable attention from the point of view of their need for national policies of population limitation. With the emergence of Asian countries as independent states and with their efforts to promote economic development, the population question, and its role in the overall progress of the developing countries, has become a major, live, and public issue.

Population facts and policies, apart from affecting an individual's happiness and security and a nation's economic and social advancement, have come to play an important role in international relations. A proper understanding of demographic trends and an effort to solve population problems through democratic and positive policies in the context of the total economic picture of various countries are a necessary pre-condition to lessening international tensions and promoting peace. Therefore, this volume aims at not only supplying significant population facts and figures behind the problem, but also providing the general national, economic and political framework of each country against which certain current international demographic attitudes, approaches and policies may be understood. Thus the book is designed to meet the needs in this area of both the student of social sciences as well as of international affairs.

I am indebted to all the contributors who readily acceded to my request to write essays specially for this volume in the midst of their other preoccupations. I am particularly thankful to Dr. Kenneth Rivett of the University of New South Wales and Professor William Petersen of the University of California, Berkeley, for their help in various ways.

My thanks are due to Robert Lang and Miss Evelyn Huston of the University of California Library at Riverside for help with books and documents and Mrs Donna Lippert and Miss Darlene Myers for their secretarial assistance.

And I am particularly grateful to Mr Charles Furth who has taken more than ordinary interest in bringing out this book.

S. CHANDRASEKHAR

University of California
Riverside, California
January 1966

CONTENTS

page

PREFACE

1. Asia's Population Problems and Solutions 7
   THE EDITOR
2. Communist China's Demographic Dilemma 48
   S. CHANDRASEKHAR
3. India's Population: Fact, Problem and Policy 72
   S. CHANDRASEKHAR
4. Japan's Population Problem 100
   THOMAS O. WILKINSON
5. Indonesia's Population Problem 119
   EVERETT HAWKINS
6. Pakistan's Population Problem 146
   ANWAR IQBAL QUERISHI
7. Malaysia's Population Problem 165
   J. C. CALDWELL
8. Taiwan's Population Problem 189
   WILLIAM PETERSEN
9. Australia's Population 211
   ROBERT HORN
10. Asian Migration—An Australian Failure? 235
    ANTHONY CLUNIES ROSS
11. A Proposal for Change in Australia's Immigration Policy 256
    KENNETH RIVETT

APPENDICES

1. Demographic and Economic Data for Asian Countries 277
2. Marriage Law in the People's Republic of China 282
3. India's Planning Commission on Population Problems and Family Planning 287
4. Eugenic Protection Law in Japan 298
5. Australia's Immigration Act 300

ABOUT THE CONTRIBUTORS 304

INDEX 307

CHAPTER 1

ASIA'S POPULATION PROBLEMS AND SOLUTIONS

BY S. CHANDRASEKHAR

INTRODUCTION

ASIA, perhaps the oldest of the continents, is in a geopolitical sense the centre of the world. Geographically Europe is her annex, Africa her sub-continent and Australia her island.

That geographical Asia, which includes the Soviet Union, is the largest continent, is well known, though this fact does not always convey an idea of its real immensity. Extending from the icebound regions of the Arctic Circle to the sunny islands of the Tropics, Asia is more than a million miles larger than the area of North and South America combined.

Asia claims extremes in elevation, temperature and rainfall. Both the highest and lowest elevations, from towering Mount Everest, 29,141 feet high, to the low Dead Sea, 1,297 feet below sea level, are in Asia. Extremes in climate are also not wanting. Asia has some of the lowest and highest recorded temperatures for any inhabited place in the world. It has extremes in rainfall as well. Both the wettest and the driest places in the world—Assam and Northern Siberia—belong to Asia. Asia has some of the most impressive mountain ranges as well as some of the largest river systems in the world. The mountain ranges stretch across from west to east constituting a veritable 'roof of the world' with the lofty Himalayas and the commanding Tibetan plateau, about 16,000 feet above sea level, almost in the centre of the continent. The Ob, Yenisei and the Lena rivers in the north, when they are not frozen, flow into the Arctic. The Huang Ho or the Yellow River, now gradually being brought under control, flows into the Yellow Sea, while the Yangtze Kiang or the Blue River meanders sluggishly into the East China Sea. And while North India is the gift of the Indus, the Ganges and the Brahmaputra, South India is watered by the Godavari, the Krishna and the Cauvery rivers—all save the Indus flowing into the Bay of Bengal.

Although Nature has not distributed minerals and other raw materials equally over the globe, Asia is blessed with a variety of natural resources. But much of these are unexploited and even unexplored, resulting in relatively little industrialization, particularly if the Soviet Union is excluded from Asia.

In view of the considerable differentials in latitudes and the consequent climatic variations, Asian vegetation varies all the way from tundra mosses in snowy Siberia to the luxurious verdure of tropical Ceylon and South India. Despite the considerable pressure of population in many regions in Asia, less than 15 per cent of the total available land has been brought under cultivation. Much of the continent is either too arid or dry, too cold or mountainous for successful human settlement and agricultural development.

While it is probable that man originally entered the cosmic scene in Asia—it is the home of the oldest fossil man, *Sinanthropus Pekinensis*—it is not only the cradle of earliest human civilization but also of some of its oldest cultures—those of the Sumerians, the Indians and the Chinese.

Asia is also the birthplace of all the great religions: Hinduism, Buddhism and other offshoots in India, Judaism, Christianity and Islam in south-west Asia, Confucianism and Taoism in China, and Shintoism, if it may be called a religion, in Japan. And of the many cultures evolved by various national-ethnic groups, some in Asia have proved dominant, coming down to this day continuous and unbroken with a tradition stretching back more than 5,000 years. While several comparable complex cultures and civilizations have risen in other parts of the world, the tradition of continuity and persistence in the face of internal dissensions and external onslaught is nowhere so marked as, for instance, in India and China.

And last, geographical Asia extends over eighteen million square miles or one third of the earth, and shelters about two billion people, or nearly two thirds of the world's population of about 3·3 billion (in 1965). If the Soviet Union is excluded from Asia, as it is in this volume, Asia claims only a little more than half, about 56 per cent, of the world's population. This huge population of more than a billion and a half is confined to a fifth of the total world area. These people are made up of hundreds of ethnic groups with an extraordinary variety of language and religion, custom and tradition, belief and outlook.

Of all the Asian problems: achieving political integrity and stability, establishing free and representative governments, ensuring economic advancement and social progress and encouraging modernization and a scientific outlook, perhaps the most basic and challenging is the population problem—finding resources for the adequate support of Asia's teeming millions. The problem involves not only the man–land and man–resources ratio but also the application of the available science and technology to man's life on this planet.

Many questions about Asia's demographic problems can be raised. Who are these people? Where do they live? How do they make a living? What are their beliefs and attitudes towards marriage, children and life in general? How are their numbers increasing? Can they be assured of a better standard of living? What of their neighbours? What of their future? It is the aim of this and the following essays to attempt to answer these questions in the light of the available facts and figures, of the existing difficulties and problems, and of the various policies and solutions which have already been proposed and attempted.

FACTS

Growth of World Population

The growth of Asia's population may be viewed against the growth of the world's population as a whole. In 1965 the total world population passed the 3·3 billion mark (three thousand million). It has been increasing at a faster rate during the last fifty years, particularly during the last two decades, than ever before in recorded human history.

According to some 'guestimates' there were probably no more than ten to fifteen million people in the whole world at the end of the Stone Age (*circa* 5000 BC). By the beginning of the Christian era the population had probably increased to about 250 million. By AD 1650 the number rose to about 500 million, and a century later, in 1750, to about 695 million. In 1850 the total population passed the billion mark and became 1,091 million. If the evolution of both life and man on this planet is assumed to have taken two billion years, then human population increased to one million in a period of about two billion years. In other words, it took mankind the entire period of recorded time down to the early nineteenth century to reach a population of one billion. In other words, from the emergence of man on the cosmic scene it took more than a million years for his numbers to reach a billion.

The subsequent increase in world population has been dramatic and can be expressed in several ways. It took only a century to add the *second* billion. It took a little over thirty years to increase the world population to *three* billion. Viewed from the beginning, on the assumption that there were some 250 million people in the world at the time of Christ, it took some sixteen centuries for this number to double—a very slow rate of increase. But it took only two centuries for the next doubling. And the *next* doubling needed only eighty years! Thus it took man many thousands of years to multiply to a billion and a half but it took only a little less than half a century to double that number—an incredible and unprecedented rate of increase.

Today more than a hundred and thirty million babies are born every year and some 65 million persons of all age groups die, leaving a net annual addition of some 65 million to the existing population of more than 3·3 billion. This means a daily increase of 177,500 to the existing population. And at the current rate of increase the present population is likely to double in less than forty years. The world might well have between 6 and 7 billion people by AD 2000.

If the same rate of growth continues, it is possible for this planet to have 12 billion people in seventy years and well over 25 billion people by the year AD 2065, a hundred years from now. Thus 'viewed in the long-run perspective, the growth of the earth's population has been like a long thin powder fuse that burns slowly and haltingly until it finally reaches a charge and then explodes'.[1]

Growth of Asia's Population

Of the world's 3·3 billion people, Asia, as we have seen, claims over one half, and these billion and a half people are confined to about a fifth of the total world area. Table 1 gives the growth of Asia's population from 1650 to 1960.

TABLE 1. *Growth of Asia's Population (in millions)*

Year	1650	1750	1800	1850	1900	1950*	1960†
Asia's population	327	475	597	741	915	1,360	1,612
Total world population	545	728	906	1,171	1,608	2,400	2,901
Percentage of Asia's population to world total	60·0	65·2	65·9	63·3	56·9	56·7	55·6

Source: The figures for 1650 to 1900 are Carr-Saunders' estimates.

* *Demographic Year Book* (New York, United Nations, 1960), p. 118.
† Estimate for mid-year 1959 population.

From the demographic point of view, Asia claims the two largest countries in the world: Communist China with about 750 million (if her published 1953 census and her birth and death rates between 1953 and 1963 are assumed to be reasonably correct) and India with a present population of 500 millions (according to the 1961 census India's population was 434 million). These two countries alone account for more than a billion people. Only three other countries in Asia are of importance from the point of view of population numbers—Indonesia, Pakistan and Japan. There are some forty-five countries and territories in Asia. Table 2 presents their area, latest census population, 1964 mid-year population estimate, the annual rate of increase and their density.

The populations of most of the Asian countries are increasing at the rate of between 2·5 and 3·5 per cent per annum. That is, Asians today are increasing faster than Europeans (this was not true of the past) thanks to the belated health revolution which has brought a dramatic and definitive decline in the death rates. And since Asia's population is a young one from the point of view of age composition the potential for rapid growth is great. At the current rate of increase, in 1980, only fifteen years from now, Asia will add another one billion to the already existing population of a billion and a half. By AD 2000 Asia may have to take care of more than 60 per cent of the total world population—an enormous increase she can hardly afford in the light of her present overall depressing standard of living and at the current meagre rate of her economic development.

Density and Distribution

What are some of the major demographic characteristics of Asia, or at least of certain large Asian countries? It is nearly impossible to generalize about so vast an area, with such a long and chequered history, with such a variegated economic and cultural evolution and such a variety of social patterns. In almost everything Asia provides both extremes. However, certain predominantly near-common features and near-identical major trends can be mentioned, although at the outset it must be pointed out that Japan, modernized and Westernized, and Israel, almost a European enclave on Asian soil, are the two well-known exceptions to many Asian generalizations.

There are several methods of calculating density of human settlement. A simple and crude index is to indicate the number of people per square mile or square kilometre. Of course, this does not take into consideration whether the available area consists of mountains or marshes, lakes or deserts, cultivated or pasture land. But while the refined index is more meaningful, unfortunately accurate figures for many Asian countries are simply not available, and where they are, comparability is made difficult for want of uniform definitions of such concepts as semi-arid land, or land which is part of the year under and the rest of the year out of water, etc. Although further refinement can be effected when density is expressed as so many people per so many square feet of living space, when millions live in shacks that appear and disappear with irritating frequency, and when many sleep on pavements, this kind of calculation can become meaningless.

Asia and Europe are the two most densely populated continents in the world, though Asia is perhaps slightly more overcrowded than Europe. Despite the fact that nearly 80 per cent of the Asian population is rural (on the criteria of agricultural occupation and small settlements) the density per square mile in some Asian countries is considerably higher than the density in some thickly populated European countries.

In terms of continents, the density of Asia is sixty-four per square mile while that of Europe is sixty-three. The density of the Soviet Union, North America and South America, is ten while the comparable figures for Africa and Oceania are nine and two. As for countries, while in the United States of America the density per square mile is about fifty,

TABLE 2. *Population, Area, Rate of Growth and Density of Asian Countries*

Country	Latest census date	Latest census population	1963 mid-year estimate in population in thousands	1964 mid-year population estimate in thousands	Annual rate of increase percentage	Area in sq. km.	Density in 1963
Aden	1955	138,441	225	—	3·1	194	1,160
Afghanistan	—	—	14,900	15,227	2·8	657,500	23
Bahrain	1965	182,203	160	—	2·8	598	268
Bhutan	—	—	700	—	1·9	47,000	15
Brunei	1960	83,877	93	—	3·7	5,765	16
Burma	1941	16,823,798	23,735	24,229	—	678,033	35
Cambodia	1962	5,740,115	5,700	—	—	181,035	33
Ceylon	1963	10,624,507	10,625	10,965	2·5	65,610	162
China (Mainland)	1953	582,603,417	646,530 (1958)	—	—	9,561,000	—
China (Taiwan)	1956	9,367,661	11,696	12,070	3·5	35,961	325
Cyprus	1960	577,615	589	587	1·1	9,251	64
Hong Kong	1961	3,133,131	3,592	3,692	4·7	1,032	3,481
India	1961	435,511,606	460,490	471,627	2·3	3,046,232	151
Indonesia	1961	96,318,829	100,045	—	2·3	1,491,564	67
Iran	1956	18,954,704	22,182	22,860	2·4	1,648,000	13
Iraq	1957	6,339,960	6,885	7,004	1·6	448,742	15
Israel	1961	2,183,332	2,376	2,475	3·5	20,700	115
Japan	1960	93,418,501	95,899	96,906	0·9	369,661	259
Jordan	1961	1,706,226	1,827	—	2·9	90,185	20
Korea (North)	—	—	10,700	—	2·2	120,538	89
Korea (South) Republic of Korea	1960	24,989,241	26,868	27,633	2·8	98,631	273

Kuwait	1965	468,000	388	426	10·7	16,000	23
Laos	—	—	1,925	—	2·4	236,800	8
Lebanon	—	—	2,200	—	3·0	10,400	212
Macau	1960	169,299	172	—	−0·1	16	10,750
Malaysia: Malaya	1957	6,278,758	7,607	7,810	3·2	131,313	58
Malaysia: Sabah	1960	454,421	490	507	—	76,115	6
Malaysia: Sarawak	1960	744,529	799	820	—	125,206	6
Maldive Islands	1963	93,293	93	—	1·9	298	312
Mongolia	1963	1,018,800	1,019	—	3·2	1,535,000	1
Muscat and Oman	—	—	565	—	0·5	212,380	3
Nepal	1961	9,387,661	9,700	—	—	140,798	69
Pakistan	1961	93,831,982	98,612	100,762	2·1	946,719	104
Philippines	1960	27,087,685	30,241	31,270	3·2	300,000	101
Qatar	—	—	55	60	6·6	22,014	2
Ryukyu Islands	1962	883,122	915	—	1·7	2,196	417
Saudi Arabia	—	—	6,600	—	1·9	2,253,300	3
Sikkim	1961	162,189	167	—	2·2	7,107	23
Singapore	1957	1,445,929	1,775	1,820	3·2	581	3,055
Syria	1960	4,565,121	5,251	5,399	4·2	185,180	28
Thailand	1960	26,257,916	28,835	29,700	3·0	514,000	56
Trucial Oman	—	—	111	—	5·2	83,600	1
Turkey	1960	27,754,820	30,256	31,118	2·9	780,574	39
Viet Nam (North)	1960	15,916,955	17,800	—	3·4	158,750	112
Viet Nam (South)	—	—	15,317	—	3·4	170,806	90
Yemen	—	—	5,000	—	2·6	195,000	26

Source: *Demographic Yearbook, 1964* (New York, United Nations, 1965.)

it is 700 in Taiwan and 650 in Japan. The densities of India and Pakistan are 384 and 225 respectively. If regions and provinces within nations are considered, the density is much higher in East Pakistan, where a majority of Pakistanis live, than in West Pakistan. Kerala in India has 1,125 people per square mile and West Bengal comes close with 1,031 per

---

From the points of view of area and population the Asian countries can roughly be grouped into four categories as follows:

TABLE 3. *Asian Countries in the order of their Population Size*

Country	Population in millions (1964–5)
Group I (100 millions and over)	
Communist China	740
India	480
Indonesia	103·0
Pakistan	100·7
Japan	96·9
Group II (between 50 and 20 million)	
The Philippines	31·2
Turkey	31·1
Thailand	29·7
South Korea	27·6
Burma	24·2
Iran	22·8
Group III (between 20 and 10 million)	17·8
Viet Nam (North)	
Viet Nam (South)	15·3
Afghanistan	15·2
Taiwan	12·0
Ceylon	10·9
North Korea	10·7
Group IV (below 10 million)	
Malaysia	8·8
Iraq	7·0
Saudi Arabia	6·6
Cambodia	6·0
Syria	5·3
Yemen	5·0
Hong Kong	3·3
Israel	2·4
Lebanon	2·2
Laos	1·9
Singapore	1·8
Jordan	1·8
Mongolia	1·0

Source: *Demographic Yearbook, 1964* (New York, United Nations, 1965).

square mile. Java in Indonesia comes in between with 1,050 per square mile. The meaning of this crowding in terms at least of the health of the people will be considered elsewhere in this essay.

Agrarian Economy

Asia's population is predominantly rural and consequently agrarian. All the Asian countries from Arab Western Asia to Indonesia, with the single possible exception of Japan, are dependent on traditional and near-primitive agriculture for the meagre livelihood of a majority—70 to 80 per cent—of their population. The man–land ratio is so adverse and the pressure of population on the soil so great that agriculture is by and large more a pathetic and sentimental way of life than a successful business or commercial proposition. Despite some sprawling, unplanned urbanization in almost every Asian country, between 70 and 80 per cent of the population is dependent on the soil for a livelihood. Hunger, particularly in Communist China, and to a steadily lessening extent in India, is almost endemic.

The problems of Asian agriculture are well known—too well known to need any pointed discussion. In some parts of the continent the outmoded feudalistic land revenue system gives little right and consequently little incentive to the tiller of the soil. Variations of absentee landlordism and the share-cropping system, with all their drawbacks, still continue in some regions. The farmer, because he is illiterate, is shut out from the world of enlightenment; he is ignorant of all that may be called modern scientific agriculture. He is often in poor health, largely the result of his insanitary and unhygienic rural environment, poor diet and the want of adequate—or often any—rural medical aid. He is permanently in debt and he has little or no resources to improve himself, his livestock or land. He is usually in the grip of the usurious village moneylender, unless the government or the co-operative society can give him ready credit. Such social and religious obligations as festivals, marriages and funerals involve him in irrational, unnecessary and uneconomic expenditure which he can ill-afford. And last, no matter what his resources, unwanted children keep arriving at regular intervals, depressing his already poor level of living.

As for his land, both pressure on the limited area and the laws of inheritance have conspired to make it a fragmented and subdivided bit of a plot, uneconomic in size to become a successful agricultural proposition. From year to year the cultivator is dependent upon the availability of good seed, natural manure or chemical fertilizer, seasonal rainfall or government irrigation water—factors usually beyond his control. Then he has problems of pest control, soil erosion, storage and marketing. It is true that in recent years the governments in most Asian countries have become dedicated to improving the general welfare of the farmer, but the pace of reform and the measure of improvement have been slow due to paucity of resources as well as cultural and institutional resistance. As for Asian communist countries where agrarian reforms have been revolutionary, the long-range outcome for both the peasants and production has been near disastrous. The peasant lost his freedom and initiative and the land refused to obey Marxist dialectics. On the whole, the problem of food—adequate nutrition in quantity and quality—for the people, even for the primary producer, continues to be a major problem in many Asian countries.

Literacy and Education

As for literacy and primary education, more than half the world lives in unlettered darkness, and Asia's share of these illiterates is disproportionately high. The illiteracy rates range from 70 per cent in India to 30 per cent in Japan. Leaving aside the adult illiterates, all the Asian countries find it impossible to provide educational resources to catch up with the birth rate. Their governments are simply unable to provide trained teachers and textbooks, school buildings and equipment to take care of the children reaching school-going age every year.

And with predominant illiteracy the problems of running democratic governments where they exist, increasing agricultural and industrial productivity, promoting health and inculcating the family planning habit become all the more intractable.

The ability to run a democracy or any kind of representative popular political institution implies a high degree of literacy and widespread education. There is no doubt that all the governments of the developing Asian nations attach immense importance and significance to the role of education in all their various plans of national development. This is true despite the fact that they are able to expend only a small share of their limited resources on education. While Asia has been the seat of great intellectual and philosophic quest and attainment in the past, a vast majority of the Asian population remains illiterate today for a variety of political and economic reasons. But it should not be forgotten that education was the privilege of a small *élite* even in Europe until the advent of the industrial revolution. While universal literacy and basic education are really products of the twentieth century, Asia apparently will have to wait for another half a century to achieve this minimum requisite of modern civilized existence.

Public Health

The Asian countries within the tropics and sub-tropics have severe public health problems. Apart from diseases (such as tuberculosis, venereal diseases, etc.) which they have in common with temperate and advanced countries, there are purely tropical diseases that claim heavy mortality and morbidity. Millions continue to suffer from such debilitating maladies as Malaria, Hookworm, Trachoma, Yaws, Filariasis and Leprosy. Although reliable statistics on the incidence of mortality and morbidity for the following diseases in all Asian countries are not available, tens of thousands suffer from one or more of these diseases, sometimes simultaneously, in many parts of Asia. A selected list of these diseases and their possible control through now known (if not fully available) programmes, is presented in Table 4.

TABLE 4. *Diseases and Public Health Control Programmes*

Immunization or vaccination	Control or eradication of disease-carrying insects	Control of human wastes	Prophylaxis or clinical treatment
Smallpox	Malaria	Hookworm	Yaws
Typhus	Typhus	Schistosomiasis	Malaria
Whooping Cough	Plague	Roundworm	Leprosy
Poliomyelitis	Encephalitis	Cholera	Tuberculosis
Typhoid Fever	Filariasis	Amebiasis	Syphilis
Tuberculosis	Onchocerciasis	Dysentery	Bejel
Influenza			Pinta
Cholera			Trachoma
Plague			
Yellow Fever			

Source: U.S. Senate Report of the Committee on Government Operations: *The Status of World Health*, 86th Congress, April 10, 1959, p. 58.

The important role of public health in the eventual solution of Asian population problems has not received adequate attention. The relation between public health development (the virtual eradication of some diseases and the containment of others) and the pressure of population on the limited available resources is obvious. The resulting population pressure is due more to the decrease in the death rate than to any rise in the birth rate. The current population explosion is also the result of overall agricultural development and increase in transportation facilities which have nearly eliminated famine in many parts of the world. And yet, from an overall, long-range point of view, there is paradoxically enough an urgent need for an enormous improvement in the public health sector of the economies of almost all Asian countries.

This paradox needs some elucidation. The beginnings of a revolution in public health are visible all over Asia. The improvements in health services and environmental sanitation, the eradication of epidemics, the use of antibiotics and the availability of other wonder drugs, DDT spraying, BCG vaccination, the services of trained midwives, the overall assistance of the World Health Organization, the Colombo Plan and American technical aid, particularly in malaria eradication—all have combined to produce a welcome and long overdue improvement in the health and longevity of people who, for decades, were denied the benefits of the modern health revolution which the advanced nations have been enjoying for nearly half a century. But this revolution in Asia's public health is producing another result: an unwelcome and alarming increase in population numbers that is outstripping the demographers' most pessimistic predictions.

The other side of the paradox is that Asia and other underdeveloped countries are not really spending a large enough share of their national income on ensuring better health standards and services. The result is that in these very underdeveloped countries where large population increases are threatening the already low living standards, the high incidence of disease continues to be one of the major deterrents to increased economic productivity. While much is being done today compared to conditions existing about half a century ago, much more needs to be done. Controllable and curable diseases still rob millions of man hours in Asia from the field and factory, home and office, leading not only to sapped human lives but to tremendous loss in the nations' productivity.[2]

In this connection the question has been raised of the relationship between the prevention of disease and overall economic productivity. The relation between a healthy population living and working in a hygienic and sanitary environment and the overall productivity and economic growth of the community is direct and obvious, though the precise relation between improved health and economic productivity cannot be established with any statistical accuracy. But a healthy farmer or industrial worker can naturally work harder and produce more food and commodities respectively. In the long run a healthy population generates a far higher standard of living than a population with a high incidence of morbidity.

And yet most Asian countries spend disproportionately little upon the promotion of health. In most underdeveloped countries the portfolio of health is given to a relatively unimportant person who does not usually enjoy cabinet rank. And the Health Ministry usually receives less funds than other ministries. The Asian countries are aping the West in this, but the advanced countries in the West have solved most of their basic health problems such as hygiene, sanitation and water supply and can afford to relegate the subject of health to a junior minister.

Further, in some quarters an unconscious and unexpressed feeling probably persists that any significant expenditure on health will only make matters worse. But it must be pointed out that improved public health must be an end in itself; this is one place where means and ends should not be balanced. Alleviation of physical suffering, prolongation of life and postponement of death, despite their undesirable demographic consequences, must be pursued for purely humanitarian and compassionate reasons. It is theoretically true that when resources are scarce, choices must be made, among alternative forms of investments, which are likely to yield the highest dividends. But 'it must be granted that health is an indivisible good, the consumption of which increases the quantity available for all. There are few, if any, better investments than in such a commodity.'[3]

As Dr Stephen Enke sums up, 'It is possible to invest in human

TABLE 5. *Numbers of Inhabitants per Physician in Some Asian Countries*

Country	Population per physician
Afghanistan	58,000
Burma	29,000
Ceylon	4,700
China (Mainland)	8,700
India	5,000
Iran	4,500
Iraq	5,600
Japan	940
Jordan	6,200
Korea (South)	3,500
Lebanon	1,300
Malaya	7,300
Mongolia P.R.	2,400
Pakistan	15,000
Saudi Arabia	24,000
Syria	4,600
Thailand	6,900
Turkey	2,300
Viet Nam (South)	22,000

Source: 'Medicine Comes to Yemen', *Abbottempo*, Vol. 1, No. 3, September 1963, Interspan, London.

capital and obtain very high rates of return. Education and health expenditures may enormously increase the productivity of those who are gainfully employed. Nor are public medical expenditures necessarily limited to improving health and therefore reducing the death rate. Given political support and establishment of necessary clinics, resources can also be used to reduce births and thereby prevent rapid population growth. If the object of development is to raise income per head without adversely affecting income distribution, supplementary programmes for increasing education, improving health, and reducing births are all needed. It may yet be discovered that the economics of labour quality and population control have a much greater potential than ordinary capital investment for purposes of economic development. And as these investments in human capital and welfare will ordinarily be made by governments or not at all, the opportunity costs of public sector investments in industry may be too high to be met. Perhaps, as a very general rule, private investment should be in physical capital and public investment should be in human capital.'[4]

Per Capita Income

Asia, with about 18 per cent of the world's land surface and 55 per cent of the world's total population, receives only about 12 per cent of the

TABLE 6. *Estimates of Per Capita Income for Asian Countries in U.S. Dollars for 1962*

Country	Per capita income in U.S. dollars
Afghanistan	70
Burma	59
Cambodia	115
Ceylon	136
China (Taiwan)	154
India	81
Indonesia	85
Iran	211
Iraq	192
Israel	940
Japan	556
Jordan	200
Korea (South)	83
Kuwait	3,000
Lebanon	411
Malaysia	296
Nepal	56
Pakistan	78
Philippines	128
Saudi Arabia	167
Thailand	100
Turkey	209
Viet Nam (South)	94

Source: *Estimates of Gross National Product*. Statistics and Reports Division (Washington, D.C., Agency for International Development, 1964).

world's total income. The per capita income of a vast majority of Asians is below the poverty line. It ranges between $56 (US dollars) in Nepal to $3,000 in Kuwait. (Kuwait's total population in mid-1962 was 0·4 million.) This range of income is in striking contrast to the per capita incomes of $2,974 for the United States of America, $2,011 for Canada, $1,482 for the United Kingdom and $1,616 for New Zealand. This low income is both the cause and consequence of the poor levels of consumption in the underdeveloped countries in Asia.

The table opposite presents the per capita incomes of certain Asian countries for which the latest data are available.

Age Composition

An examination of the age structure of the populations of those Asian countries for which reliable age statistics are available[5] reveals that Asia's population, particularly in the developing countries, is predominantly young.

On the whole, roughly two persons in every five are under fifteen

TABLE 7. *Age Structure of the Populations in Selected Asian Countries*

Country	Year	Age (percentage distribution) all ages	under 15 years	15–19 years	60 years and over
Burma	1960	100	41·3	53·5	5·2
Cambodia	1959	100	44·7	51·3	4·0
Ceylon	1961	100	40·7	54·0	5·3
China (Mainland)	1953	100	35·9	59·7	4·4
China (Taiwan)	1960	100	45·1	50·7	4·2
India	1961	100	41·1	54·1	4·8
Indonesia	1961	100	42·1	53·8	4·1
Iran	1956	100	42·2	52·2	5·6
Japan	1960	100	30·0	61·1	8·9
Korea (Republic)	1960	100	43·3	51·4	5·3
Malaya	1957	100	43·8	51·6	4·6
Sabah	1960	100	43·5	52·6	3·9
Sarawak	1960	100	44·5	50·3	5·2
Pakistan	1961	100	44·5	49·5	6·0
Philippines	1960	100	45·7	50·0	4·3
Thailand	1960	100	43·2	52·2	4·6
United Kingdom	1960	100	22·8	60·0	17·2
United States	1960	100	31·1	55·7	13·2

Source: Based on national census data and U.N. publications.

years; about 55 per cent belong to the age group 15–59; and about one in twenty is sixty years or over. This has two undesirable consequences. One is that the number of dependants per adult is relatively large. For the economy as a whole the number of gainfully employed is disproportionately small in relation to the two unproductive groups who are dependent on them—children and old people. Secondly, in view of Asia's current birth rate, the age structure is favourable to ensure large additions in the future to the existing massive population.

Sex Ratio

The most simple and universal measure of sex distribution in any population is the sex ratio—the number of males per 1,000 females[6]—

which is normally the product of past fertility, mortality and migration.

It is popularly supposed, on the basis of insufficient evidence, that more males than females are conceived. In almost all countries of the world, more male than female babies are born. In advanced industrialized countries where maternal mortality is low and where girl babies receive as much care as boy babies, the male death rates are higher than female death rates at every stage. The numerical excess of males at birth is gradually reduced until females outnumber males in the older age groups, for males have higher mortality throughout life due to occupational and other hazards.

Some Asian countries, particularly India, Ceylon, Pakistan and a few predominantly Muslim countries, have a high sex ratio in the sense that there is a greater number of males at successive age groups, even though in a few groups females predominate at birth. This adverse sex ratio in Asia has led to some controversy over the reasons behind this phenomenon.

In some Asian countries, the current social attitudes are held to be responsible for the differential mortality rates of the sexes after birth. Writing about India's sex ratio in 1946, the present writer observed:

'The social attitudes in the country are such that a girl is sometimes looked upon as a liability, whereas a boy is welcomed as an asset. This attitude arises out of certain obscurantist factors inherent in the Indian socio-economic order. So a rural girl in her infancy is treated with a wholesome neglect—neglect nevertheless. Care and attention in her upbringing, especially when beset by infantile ailments, are conspicuously absent . . . .'[7]

Early marriages, if not quite child marriages, worsen the initial balance of births in favour of male babies; the reason for this is high maternal mortality. After the early reproductive years, the sex ratio is very much in favour of males in those Asian countries where women have not been completely emancipated.

The relevance of the social factor in this connection finds some support in pre-Communist China. The sex ratio in China, or rather of the population in the Kumming Lake region, is apparently comparable to the Indian situation. Unlike India, China has more female than male births. But the female infants lose their numerical superiority in a few years as they grow up and the sex ratio becomes favourable to males for apparently the same reasons that operate in India and some other Asian countries.

It is possible that the sex ratio is in a sense both the cause and effect of the role and status of women in Asian society, and the result of the overall attitude of any society towards the female sex.

Role and Status of Women

The impact of the role and status of women (or to put it differently, women's emancipation or the lack of it) on Asian population problems has for some strange reason received little attention in demographic literature. The reason behind this may be both the want of a precise definition of 'emancipation' and the difficulty in measuring the impact in any exact quantitative terms.

This subject embraces a variety of such questions as the legal and political status of women, the differing roles of the two sexes in home, polity and society, and the existing general attitudes towards women, marriage, family and children, separation, divorce, family size and planned parenthood. There are also such factors as women's right to receive education, to hold property and to seek all forms of paid employment on an equal basis with men. What complicates the situation further is that the entire picture is constantly changing. Even in the so-called agrarian, conservative, tradition-bound societies, women's role and status was never rigidly fixed and unchanging; on the contrary, it has been flexible and dynamic and the last quarter of a century has witnessed near-revolutionary changes in Asia and elsewhere. Therefore, general-

TABLE 8. *Sex Ratio (Number of Males per 1,000 Females) in Selected Asian Countries*

Country	Year	Males per 1,000 females
Burma	1953	1,040
Cambodia	1959	998
Ceylon	1961	1,115
China (Mainland)	1953	1,076
China (Taiwan)	1960	1,044
India	1961	1,063
Indonesia	1961	973
Iran	1956	1,036
Japan	1960	964
Korea (Republic of)	1960	1,002
Malaysia:		
Federation of Malaya	1957	1,065
Sabah	1960	1,086
Sarawak	1960	1,019
Nepal	1961	969
Pakistan	1961	1,111
Philippines	1960	1,018
Thailand	1960	1,004
United Kingdom	1960	936
United States	1960	971

Source: United Nations, *Demographic Yearbook, 1961*, and national census data.

izations become difficult and almost impossible when it is found that in a relatively homogeneous Asian nation certain segments are more 'modernized', 'Westernized' or 'emancipated' than others. Certain groups in an Asian country may be more advanced in their mores than some groups in an occidental society, from which presumably a certain amount of inspiration for this change comes. Here there is also a semantic problem. Some sophisticated Asians dislike the term 'Westernization' for it implies that certain desirable basic changes in Asian mores are the product of Western political and economic influence and contact. They prefer the term 'modernization' which is independent of geography.

Asia's present-day overall demographic dilemma arising out of a welcome decrease in the death rate unaccompanied by a matching decline in the birth rate might not be what it is today in Arab–Muslim and Hindu Asia but for the relatively backward position that the majority of ordinary women have come to occupy in the social economy. Such social attitudes and institutions with a quasi-religious and traditional sanction as early marriage, the near-universality of marriage for females, the inauspicious nature of infertility and the unwanted barren woman, the desire for male children, the social ban on widow remarriage, the lack of economic independence for single women, the want of prolonged education, training and professional careers for women, the unhappy plight of the widow, divorcee and separated woman —all these have a direct and major influence on the age at marriage for girls, the length of the reproductive period, the size of the family, the sex composition, female morbidity, longevity and mortality.

It is obvious that the emancipation of Asian women, in the economic, legal and political sense, can basically alter the magnitude of the Asian population problem. For then, conceivably women themselves would decide when and whom they would marry, whether they would be homemakers or career women or both and when and how many children they would choose to bear and rear. Almost all Asian children would then be wanted, and few would be an unplanned accident.

Today, the available evidence reveals that Asian women, by and large, have higher mortality rates than males. In the West, native-born females invariably have a higher expectation of life than males. (For instance, the white, native-born female in the United States of America is perhaps the most indestructible of all creatures.) But this is not so in Asia, with the possible exceptions of Israel and Japan. The infant mortality rate in most of Asia is nearly five times as high as rates in advanced, northwestern Europe. In some areas the infant mortality rate is higher for female than for male babies.

The relation between the want of purposeful education for women and social emancipation and these depressing demographic facts need not be laboured. It is to be hoped that the whole question of women's role and status as it impinges on the total demographic situation will begin to receive more attention than it has in the past all over Asia, at least in the relatively progressive Asian countries where anti-natalist population policies have been formulated in the last two decades.

High but Declining Death Rates

The tremendous increase in the world's population and particularly the population of Asia in recent years is due in large measure, as we have mentioned earlier, to man's increasing control over disease and death. The effectiveness of death control is not uniform the world over, for, while the death rate in the Soviet Union and most countries of North-west Europe is about 10 per 1,000, the rates in Asia are relatively high—about 30 to 35 per 1,000 in Burma and Nepal, 20 in Thailand, 15 in India and Indonesia, and about 10 in Ceylon and 9 in Japan.

However, during the last decade and more the death rates in many Asian countries have begun to decline. In Ceylon, for instance, between 1945 and 1955, the death rate was cut by more than 40 per cent; in India within a few years by 33 per cent. What is more, once underground drainage, potable water supplies, modern conservancy measures, and up-to-date preventive, diagnostic, and curative medical services are made available, the death rates in even the most underdeveloped Asian countries will register even more dramatic declines.

The Infant Mortality Rate, which is considered a sensitive index of a community's level of living and total cultural milieu, is also declining in many Asian countries. While in north-western Europe, Canada and the United States of America, the Infant Mortality Rate is between 20 and 25 per 1,000 live births, the rates in Asian countries, which were considerably above 100 before the Second World War, have dropped in recent years to 98 in India and Indonesia, 67 in Ceylon, 41 in Japan, 35 in Taiwan, and 33 in Israel. The rates are still high in Burma and the Philippines, about 150 and 110 respectively. Even the lower Asian rates are uncivilized and there is room for considerable further decline. However, it must be remembered that in some parts of Asia the rates were between 150 and 200 only twenty-five years ago.

High and Stationary Birth Rates

The average world birth rate during 1955–60 was estimated to be about 35 per 1,000 population. On a continental basis, Africa has the highest estimated birth rate of 45 per 1,000. Asia, which has the next highest birth rate, has an overall rate of about 40 per 1,000.

Within Asia the birth rates range from 46·2 per 1,000 in the Federation of Malaya, 40 in India, 37 in Burma and Pakistan, and about 35 in Ceylon and Thailand, to 17 in Jordan and 10 in Lebanon. Regionally during the last decade the birth rates have ranged between 42 per 1,000 in West Asia to 35 in East Asia.

Thus with a definitive decline in the death rate and a high and near stationary birth rate, the survival rate is high, yielding huge net annual additions to the existing population. For instance, the population of India alone increased by more than 77 millions during the last decade, 1951–61.

However, within this decade, a few countries like Taiwan, South Korea and perhaps India may start to register slight declines in the birth

TABLE 9. *Vital Statistics for Selected Asian Countries (1964–5)* (Where data are available)

Country	Crude birth rate per 1,000	Crude death rate per 1,000	Infant mortality rate	Expectation of life at birth Males	Expectation of life at birth Females
Afghanistan	45–53	—	139·2	—	
Burma	47–53	33–37	128·1	—	
Ceylon	35·8	8·5	52·8	59 (for both sexes)	
China (Mainland)	—	—	—	—	
China (Taiwan)	36–39	6·1	26·4	60 (for both sexes)	
India	39–40	21–23	81·0	41·89	40·55
Indonesia	40–46	19–23	74·5	—	
Iran	42–48	23–27	—	—	
Iraq	47–51	—	—	—	
Israel	24·6	6·2	26·2	70·88	73·01
Japan	17·2	7·0	20·4	67·21	72·34
Korea (South)	39–43	11–13	58·2	—	
Malaysia	40·9	8·6	56·7	54 (for both sexes)	
Nepal	46–54	34–40	—	—	
Pakistan	43–46	16–17	—	—	
Philippines	44–48	—	72·8	—	
Thailand	40–44	19–21	44·7	—	
Viet Nam (South)	40–48	—	35·7	—	

Sources: *Demographic Yearbook, 1965* (New York, United Nations, 1965), also various National Statistical Yearbooks.

rates. The total population numbers, of course, are bound to increase but the net annual additions to the existing populations may not be so large. If the large-scale acceptance of the new contraceptive device, the intra-uterine device (IUD), spreads to the countryside and is adopted by millions of young women, then the beginning of the decline in the birth rate may be in sight before the end of this decade.

II

ASIA'S POPULATION PROBLEMS

Asian culture and civilization were fundamentally untouched by the West up to the end of the eighteenth century, though 300 years earlier a sea route to India had been discovered. European rivalries for Asian goods, and eventually European expansionism and imperialism, led to the political subjugation and consequent economic exploitation of Asia. Some Asian countries lost their freedom entirely; others, like China and Thailand, enjoyed a spurious sovereignty; and all were subject to strong economic, political and cultural pressures from the West. In short, they had no genuine political or economic independence.

The present-day population problems of Asia are partly a legacy of European imperialism. The balance sheet of Western colonialism in Asia is a mixed one. When Asia lost her political freedom she lost with it all chances of rapid economic development as her raw materials were taken off to feed the hungry new machines in Europe, while the manufactured products were dumped on Asian markets with the aid of preferential tariffs, siphoning off the available purchasing power. But, on the other hand, Europe brought a measure of peace, if the term can be interpreted as the sum total of averted internal wars, democratic political institutions and, in the case of Great Britain, even a measure of moral idealism. Above all, a modicum of health and hygiene, modern science and technology came to Asia. The abolition of internecine struggles and wars and the near control of epidemics and famines through sanitation and transportation brought down the high death rate. But at the same time political expediency prevented the European imperialist nations from interfering seriously with the indigenous cultural mores conducive to a high birth rate and a large family. And thus with a declining death rate, a high birth rate, and an arrested agrarian economy without any industrialization, Asia began to add relatively large numbers to her existing population. The result was increasing poverty. The seeds of Asia's current population explosion were unwittingly sown more than a century ago by well-meaning British, Dutch and French administrators!

Now Asia is politically free. But political freedom without economic advancement and social progress is largely meaningless. Therefore almost all Asian countries have embarked today upon planned economic development. And they are finding that the greatest single obstacle to rapid economic betterment is runaway population growth. The net annual addition of millions of mouths to the existing large population base nullifies much of the national efforts towards a higher level of living. Thus the basic economic and social problem in Asia is really demographic.

The United Nations in their *Report on World Social Situation* sum up the three major ways in which rapid population growth in the developing and underdeveloped countries adversely affect their economic and social development.

'First, it can increase the pressure of population on land that is already densely settled and so retard increases in the productivity of agricultural labour. This effect is seen not only in countries where nearly all the cultivable land is now occupied but also in many underdeveloped countries where the density of agricultural population in the cultivated areas is high, although large amounts of potentially productive land lie unused because of land ownership systems, lack of capital or techniques to exploit available land, or for other reasons.

'Second, accelerating population growth can aggravate the problem of capital shortage, which is one of the most important obstacles to economic development of nearly all underdeveloped countries. The faster the population grows, the larger the share of each year's income which must be invested in increasing the stock of productive equipment merely to maintain the existing level of equipment per worker. The larger the investments required for this purpose, the smaller the share of annual income that will be available either to raise the level of current consumption *per capita*, or to make investments which would increase the productivity and permit higher levels of consumption in the future.

'While in a well-developed dynamic economy the demand for such capital investments may serve as a stimulus to continuing economic growth, the case of the underdeveloped countries, with their narrow margin of income over subsistence needs, is different. For most of them it is difficult to save and invest enough from their meagre annual income to permit economic development to proceed at a satisfactory pace, even without rapid population growth. It is true that if these countries can industrialize and better utilize their human as well as their natural resources, some of them, at least, will undoubtedly benefit in the long run from a substantially larger population. But even where a large population would be advantageous in the long run, economic progress will be hindered, if numbers increase so rapidly as to put an excessive strain upon the economy.

'Third, the high birth rates of the underdeveloped countries create a heavy load of dependent children for the working population . . . the percentages of children under 15 years of age in the less developed countries of Asia, Africa, and Latin America are generally in the order of 40 per cent or more of the total population, while the range of this ratio in the European countries is from about 20 to 30 per cent. The difference is the consequence of the higher birth rates in the former areas. The necessity of supporting so many children puts the workers of the underdeveloped countries at an added disadvantage in their efforts to save and invest for economic development. It also complicates the problem of providing the children with the education that is essential for social and economic advancement in the long run.'[8]

III

ECONOMIC AND DEMOGRAPHIC POLICIES

All the Asian countries—free and Communist—are dedicated to the task of liquidating poverty, raising the general standard of living and evolving ultimately some kind of a welfare state. Almost every country, particularly those which regained their political freedom after the Second World War, have drawn up plans—Five-, Six-, Seven- or Ten-Year Plans—for overall economic and social development. They have taken an inventory of available resources—natural, human, monetary, managerial and technological—have set up targets on the basis of priorities of the countries' pressing needs, and are doing their best to achieve their objectives.

But these countries are faced with assets as well as liabilities. Natural and financial resources are limited. While there is a large reservoir of labour, it is largely illiterate, unskilled and untrained. Capital goods and technical know-how are wanting.

Nevertheless, many Asian countries have embarked on economic development on the more or less conventional lines of stepping up agricultural production and industrializing the economy as far as possible. If the political and ideological aspect of the subject (that is, under what political system a developing country can advance fastest—Communism and centralized totalitarian planning as in Mainland China, a mixed economy as in India, or free enterprise as in Japan) is ignored, the basic economic problem in Asia becomes one of pooling all the available resources, material and human, and allocating them according to planned priorities to yield maximum returns to a large majority of the population.

Attempts to accomplish this have been made in most developing countries by rehabilitating backward agricultural systems and embarking on policies of rapid and large-scale industrialization.

Agricultural Development

Agriculture in most Asian countries, as pointed out already, is characterized by near-primitive methods of farming and fragmentation of land (which renders mechanization impossible, even granting that the necessary capital for machinery is available); lack of irrigation and consequently either dependence on the uncertain deluge of the rains or drought—all this leading to uneconomic holdings and to an excessive dependence by the majority of the people on the land for a meagre living.

The rehabilitation and modernization of agriculture in the developing nations must involve a radical departure from traditional agricultural methods and effect a marriage between science and agriculture. What is needed is a silent social revolution in the countryside where the peasant is educated to live in ecological harmony with his land, animals and environment, through all the persuasive communication channels available today. Once this formidable task is done, Asian agriculture will cease to be a pathetic and sentimental way of life and become a successful economic proposition. Then the surplus population that has been trying to eke out a low level of living from the overcrowded soil can be siphoned into urban factories producing much needed goods and services. This means industrialization.

Industrialization

Every developing country looks upon industrialization as an infallible cure to its mass poverty. In some areas, the basic requisites for large-scale industrialization, namely raw materials, capital resources, technological know-how, skilled labour and a market are available to a greater or lesser degree. In some countries the lack of capital resources and technical know-how pose serious problems. But thanks to the aid offered by the United Nations and its various specialized agencies, the Colombo Plan, the United States of America, the Soviet Union, the United Kingdom and other advanced countries, these countries are able to close some of the gaps.

The developing countries hope that such a policy of rapid and large-scale industrialization, bringing idle men and machines, latent resources and the available technology together, will start a beneficent chain reaction of more and better jobs and higher incomes, resulting in greater demand for necessary goods and services, thereby increasing levels of consumption and eventually increasing employment and production to meet these demands.

Most of these nations, irrespective of their political and economic ideologies, are thus involved in some planned effort at economic and social development. They are in a hurry for they want to catch up with the advanced and affluent nations in as short a time as possible.

But the biggest barrier in the path of the rapid economic development of several Asian countries is not just their relatively large populations but, what is worse, their rapid rate of population increase. The additions to national income generated by both these approaches—agricultural improvement and industrialization—have been more than swallowed up by the increasing number of new mouths. It is in this context that particular population policies—in terms of migration possibilities and the widespread practice of family planning should be examined. While it is true that economic policies are also to some extent demographic policies, policies with major demographic ends in view can be formulated and adopted by governments to achieve such objectives as higher or lower birth rates or rates of population increase or decrease.

Asian Emigration

What about Asian emigration as a factor in Asian economic development and as a solution to Asian population problems? It may be stated at the very outset that the population problems of Asian countries are so large that they cannot be solved through emigration. This does not mean that they do not need emigration outlets or that emigration would not be of some help. There has been a great deal of discussion on this subject and a vast amount of literature is available.[9] The difficulties are many. There are few emigration outlets for people from overpopulated Asian countries because of ethnic and cultural prejudices; and in the countries which might be willing to receive Asian immigrants there may not be jobs available for them. Then there is the expenditure involved in the transportation of immigrant families, the problem of taking care of them (all the necessary social services) until they can find suitable employment or otherwise stand on their feet, and last but not least, the problems inherent in their eventual cultural and physical assimilation.

Asian emigration, and by and large emigration in general, has usually been the product of acute pressure of one kind or another such as compelling poverty, political tyranny or religious persecution. People do not just pick up their belongings and move bag and baggage to a foreign country to settle there permanently, forsaking all the familiar sights, smells and sounds of their homeland, without very strong motivation. And, since Asians are amongst the most stay-at-home people in the world, only the worst kind of pressure has made and can make them move.

Of course, in terms of poverty and low living standards, the pressure to migrate is ever present. The 'push' mechanism of distress, hunger and famine is almost always there. Emigration, unlike water, flows whenever possible, from countries of low standards of living to countries with better opportunities and higher standards of living. But, if would-be emigrants never leave their homes, it is because there is no 'pull' mechanism and no country ready to receive them.

Unfortunately, although the relatively 'empty' lands like Australia, Brazil, Canada and even parts of Africa, are most willing to receive Europeans—especially emigrants from such countries as the United Kingdom where there is no great population pressure and no particular need for emigration outlets—Asians, who desperately need emigration openings, are unwelcome. This unjust imbalance in the availability of effective emigration opportunities perpetuates the traditional denial to Asians of emigration possibilities that has been going on for three hundred years. In fact, the Europeans have not only denied Asians access to new lands, until only a decade and a half ago they occupied and exploited much of the Asians' and Africans' native habitat.

Today, now that the means of 'death control' are available to them, it is the Asian populations which are increasing rapidly. But it should not be forgotten that during the last 300 years, between 1650 and 1950, while the world as a whole was increasing about four-fold, the Europeans increased about seven-fold. They emigrated to and settled in the empty lands of Canada, the United States, Latin America, Australia and New Zealand. For instance, the number of European emigrants to the new continents in a single century, 1815–1914, has been estimated at more than 60 million, 20 million of whom came from the British Isles alone. In addition, they conquered, colonized and settled in the cooler areas of Asia and Africa, and where they could not settle, they exploited the countries and peoples with rare greed.

It is obvious that today emigration from Asia on the lines of the European emigration of the eighteenth and nineteenth centuries is clearly ruled out. All the virgin and vacant lands have been taken over, and it would be impossible to find emigration outlets for some 20 to 30 million surplus Asians a year. And, even if there were countries willing to receive them, the cost of transporting and settling such vast numbers of emigrants would be next to impossible, though perhaps not quite as expensive as a stockpile of atom bombs or putting a man on the Moon or racing to Mars.

What has been the direction of inter-Asian and intercontinental migration in the past? Within Asia, the Japanese emigrated to Korea (now Communist North Korea and free South Korea), Manchukuo (now part of Communist China), Taiwan (now Nationalist China), Thailand, Burma, Malaya, Indonesia and the Philippines. The Chinese, mostly from the southern and coastal provinces, emigrated to practically every country in south-east Asia, but primarily to the four nations constituting the former Indo-China, to Malaya, Thailand, Indonesia, the Philippines, Borneo and, of course, Hong Kong, Macao and Taiwan. Indians emigrated to Ceylon, Burma and Malaya.

Beyond Asia, the Japanese emigrated largely to Hawaii, Canada, the continental USA, Brazil and the Union of South Africa; the Chinese to Hawaii, the USA, Canada and Central America; the Indians to East Africa, South Africa, the Fiji Islands, Canada and the United States of America.

But though Asians have migrated to distant countries, the total of emigrants does not add up to a large number. The total number of

Japanese settled abroad is about a million, the number of overseas Chinese is less than fifteen million, and the Indians abroad about six million. All the other Asians overseas number about half a million.

Voluntary Migration

The difficulties concerning planned international migration under the auspices of governments or governmental agencies, and emigration on a large scale, irrespective of the auspices under which it may be carried out, have been referred to. But emigration from the point of view of a single individual or an individual family may be different. Considerations of whether emigration solves a country's population problem or not, do not deter an individual emigrant. All he knows is that opportunities for a decent living are extremely limited and that, should he emigrate to a relatively rich, opportunity-filled country such as Canada or the USA, his lot would be better.

If he and his family are able to emigrate, the chances are that they will move into comfortable and perhaps affluent circumstances. Thus emigration can help one family. His native country need not support him and the pressure on limited resources is lessened by at least one family. From his old country's point of view, this may be a drop of relief in an ocean of distress, but from the individual emigrant's standpoint, he has been saved from hunger and humiliation. This kind of individual and voluntary emigration is going on every day between Asian countries and from Asia to the West. But the total number of emigrants involved is negligible.

Of course, some countries, whatever their record in the past, just do not admit Asian immigrants. A blatant, if curious, example is that of South Africa. The South African Whites, who have taken over the country from the Natives, do not permit Asians as immigrants today. And while every country must have the theoretical right to decide upon the composition of her population, it is a strange anomaly that the Whites, themselves immigrants to a non-white country, should deny others the right of migration on the basis of colour or culture.

Here is the issue that is basic to the entire problem—race prejudice and colour discrimination. So much has been said and written on this agonizing problem of our day and yet relatively so little has been accomplished, that one wonders whether man is really capable of reason. If only we could bring to the White man the elementary, scientific, anthropological knowledge, that all men are brothers under the skin, how much more civilized and peaceful the world would be!

Once the 'White' countries can be persuaded to accept Asian immigrants they could be put on some quota basis as the USA has done so far, though the present American system of receiving immigrants will change in a few years for the better in the light of her recent legislation on this subject. Australia, for instance, would be happier and more secure, situated as she is close to Asia, if she would admit Asian immigrants on the same basis as she does Europeans. The excuses she gives for not doing so are being assailed by some progressive Australians themselves. In this connection, Dr Kenneth Rivett's thoughtful paper in this volume deserves careful reading.

The second major problem is one of fair treatment to the new immigrants once a country has admitted alien elements into its population. These immigrants, as long as they satisfy the law on the subject (unless the law itself is discriminatory) must be treated as one hundred per cent citizens and as an integral part of the country's population. The denials and discriminations heaped upon the Negroes (forced immigrants at that) in the United States after nearly three centuries of residence and toil, and the treatment meted out to Asians in South Africa after a century of domicile, are striking and painful examples of extraordinary prejudice, discrimination and injustice.

What is needed is a non-official international body, above and beyond ethnic differences which could work to raise the status of minorities to wanted instead of rejected groups. Whether it is the question of Jews in Europe, the Negroes in the United States, the Orientals in Canada, or the minorities in the Asian countries themselves, the majority communities must learn to treat the minorities in a fair and just fashion and give them every opportunity for assimilation. Tolerance is not enough. What is needed is acceptance. This implies the right to vote, own property and live in an area one can afford, choose one's occupation on the basis of training and merit, marry the person one loves, travel to any place, eat in any public restaurant, educate one's children at the school of one's choice, etc.

Thirdly, the immigrant community must be helped to adjust to the relatively new ways of the receiving country. Even where total prejudice against the immigrant community is absent, the difficulties in learning a new language, new manners and imbibing new mores, are hard enough. Here a great deal can be accomplished in promoting harmony and accelerating assimilation if the 'peculiar' ways of the immigrants can be looked upon with friendship, sympathy and understanding.

And last is the provision of certain social services to the newcomer, who may come on his own without any particular sponsorship or relatives or friends to receive him, or a suitable job awaiting him. The role of any organization that can call on him and welcome him, help him to find suitable accommodation, commend him to sympathetic friends, and above all satisfy his spiritual needs, can be a vital one.

All these problems are common to migrants, all over the world, irrespective of their national, ethnic or religious origin. It must, however, be accepted that these common problems are more acute with Asian or African migrants, especially when they go to countries alien to their cultural milieu.

There are also difficult problems connected with inter-Asian migration—not perhaps as acute as when people of different or conflicting cultures meet, but problems nevertheless. The Indians in Ceylon and Malaya, the Chinese in Thailand and Indonesia, the Koreans in Japan and the Japanese in Okinawa and the Philippines have their own problems of citizenship rights, trade privileges, linguistic conflicts, etc.

In any plan to help migrants, top priority must be given to refugees because they are forced migrants and not refugees by choice. While the Tibetans and the people of South Vietnam are the latest batch of uprooted humanity in Asia, there have been others since the cessation of the Second World War. As a result of partition India received some seven million Hindu refugees from Pakistan and some 4·5 million Muslim refugees went to Pakistan from India. While most of these refugees have been settled and rehabilitated by their respective governments, considerable work in raising the level of living of these people still needs to be done.

Besides these, there are about a million refugees in South Korea from the North, and nearly the same number from Mainland China in Hong Kong and other areas; there are Arab refugees from Israel in Egypt and other countries and the refugees from the current fighting in South Viet Nam—and the economic and political status of these people is far from satisfactory.

It is unfortunate that, while the European refugees of the Second World War have been settled in such countries as the United States of America, Canada, Australia, the United Kingdom, Brazil, Israel, Turkey and Sweden, etc., Asian refugees have nowhere to go beyond overcrowded Asia where opportunities for economic advancement are so severely limited. An international, non-governmental and non-partisan body needs to be set up to explore the possibilities of certain advanced and relatively thinly populated countries such as Australia, Canada and Brazil accepting Asian refugees and other voluntary emigrants on a fairly large scale.

In brief, a policy of assisted, planned and selective emigration from Asia to thinly settled but advanced countries could have a decisive, and highly desirable effect on Asian relations with other nations. Apart from the moral position of thinly populated, prosperous countries in a distressed and overcrowded world, those who oppose international migration as a threat to their high standards of living or to their cultural or 'racial superiority' may be actually losing an opportunity to raise that standard further, in that they are promoting an atmosphere of international distrust and suspicion in which neither the particular dominant ethnic group nor culture can progress and succeed unhampered.

The difficulties inherent in such a policy of Asian emigration, as already observed, are not to be minimized. Nor will such emigration solve, it must be repeated, the population problems of Asia. But it is contended that such emigration will generate tremendous goodwill towards the 'White' nations, and the emotional and psychological relief to Asia will be out of all proportion to the actual economic and demographic relief involved.

The plea for emigration rights for Asians does not mean that the sending countries should not control their birth rates. On the contrary, only those countries which are making serious efforts to promote family planning should have priority in sending emigrants to any immigrant-receiving country.

Family Planning

All the major Asian countries, as we have noted, have embarked on policies of planned economic development of one kind or another. These policies primarily involve efforts to rehabilitate and modernize agriculture, to increase food production and to industrialize their economy to maximize as far as possible their per capita incomes.

Some Asian countries, including at times the Communist ones, despite occasional ideological protests, have now realized that in an underdeveloped economy, the hard-won slow growth in the national income tends to be eaten up by the large increase in the population, leaving per capita income and consumption levels almost as low as before. That is, most Asian countries are demographically running so fast that they are almost forced to stand still economically. India's example is fairly typical. Her national income increased by some 40 per cent while her per capita income by only 19 per cent during the period of her first two Five-Year Plans (1951–61). Therefore, some Asian countries have included programmes of fertility control in their overall plans for economic development. Thus, family planning has come to occupy a relatively important place in the economic plans of certain Asian countries. It is true that not all Asian countries have realized the importance of the problem, for the nature and magnitude of the population problem varies from country to country—all the way from Communist China to Israel and Yemen. However, the Asian countries can be grouped under four broad categories on the basis of their governments' attitude toward planned parenthood:

(1) The governments that are not only officially committed to family planning but have embarked upon policies designed to reduce fertility.

Japan, India, Pakistan, Ceylon and South Korea may be included in this category.

(2) The governments that believe in the need for family planning, at least in theory, although they have not taken any official steps to control fertility. Some of these countries do permit and often encourage voluntary agencies with financial support to carry on family planning work. Indonesia, Taiwan, Malaysia, Hong Kong and Singapore may be included in this category.

(3) The case of the government of Communist China is almost unique. They are torn between pro-natalist Marxist ideology and anti-natalist Malthusian economic necessity. Her birth control policies are on and off, depending upon the existing national economic weather. Even when they do adopt family planning measures they are always for 'health, leisure and study' and never for economic reasons.

(4) The governments that are either opposed or indifferent to family planning. The countries other than those already mentioned may be grouped under this category. Many of these countries are small and lack active women's and other voluntary organizations and the governments are perhaps more indifferent and uninformed than opposed to family planning.

The population policies of certain Asian governments, even if they are not designed or designated as such, and the people's attitudes towards population control, deserve only a brief examination here, for the various essays in this volume go into this question in some detail.

Five major Asian nations—Japan, India, China, Indonesia and Pakistan—have attempted to implement national population policies with varying degrees of success.

Japan was faced with a desperately serious population problem at the end of the Second World War, what with the loss of her empire and the repatriation of her overseas nationals. Actually population pressure was a serious problem for Japan before the last war and was one of the major factors that turned her into a belligerent nation. In 1948, with a war-shattered economy, Japan had to support some 78 million on an area the size of the state of California. To meet this situation, Japan passed in 1948 the Eugenic Protection Law which 'authorizes voluntary and even compulsory sterilization in certain cases, the public sale of contraceptives which had hitherto been forbidden, and the performance of abortion in the event that continued pregnancy or parturition is likely to harm the mother's health on account of physical or economic reasons'. Japan thus reversed her pre-Second World War, pro-natalist population policy. Till recently, officially a million (and unofficially about two million) abortions were performed in Japan every year. Japan's population increased from 78 million in 1947 to 93·3 million in 1957. But the total number of births fell from 2·7 to 1·6 million during the same period. That is, Japan's birth rate dropped from 34 per 1,000 in 1947 to 17 in 1957. The country's birth rate was halved in ten years.

With her high literacy and educational levels, disciplined national consciousness and adequate medical resources (more than 763 health centres in 1960) Japan has been able to reduce her birth rate through the drastic and costly method of induced abortion.

India, where the problem is not as pressing as in Japan, embarked on an official policy of population control in 1951 when the Government Planning Commission was set up. The Government realized that a rapidly growing population in an underdeveloped agrarian country like India is more a hindrance than a help in raising the nation's standard of living, for with a high birth rate every increase in national effort was being used up to maintain the existing low standard of living.

But unfortunately, non-Catholic, secular India lost nearly a decade foolishly experimenting with the safe period or rhythm method of birth control because of the Gandhian ideology of the then Minister of Health. (Mahatma Gandhi was opposed to scientific contraception.)

Today, the Government of India has taken a progressive stand on this question and is in favour of all mechanical, chemical and surgical methods of family planning. It has been found, however, that under backward rural conditions conventional contraceptives are not successful as they require a clinical consultation, some knowledge of the physiology of reproduction and a relatively high level of living. Indian experience shows that sterilization or surgical methods of permanent conception control (vasectomy for fathers and salpingectomy for mothers) is really the answer to effectively curb population growth. Therefore today several states of the Indian Union have embarked on a programme of subsidized voluntary sterilization in addition to popularizing intra-uterine devices.

A rough calculation shows that India's birth rate can be halved if about five fathers or mothers out of every thousand of the total population undergo sterilization. India's vital statistics are none too reliable but the latest statistics show that the death rate is definitely declining while the birth rate is stationary at a high level, yielding a net annual addition of some twelve million to the existing population. It is to be hoped that India can stabilize her population at no more than about 550 to 600 millions.

As for Communist China, her population today is about 750 million if her published statistics are accurate and reliable and not padded as some of her production figures are. Among all the underdeveloped countries, China has been the *locus classicus* of the Malthusian dilemma. But when the Communists conducted the country's first census and discovered that the mainland's population in 1953 was around 583 million, they apparently found the figures an occasion for jubilation. However, in 1957 the plight of the economy, and particularly the food situation, was so bad that the country became a surprising convert to family planning. For nearly two years an intensive and unconventional campaign in favour of birth control was waged all over the country through all the available mass media. But at the end of 1958 the country reversed its stand on ideological grounds. Marx won, Malthus was overthrown and the traditional Communist dogma that over-population is a vicious figment of the bourgeois imagination asserted itself.

Now for the last two years China is again in some economic difficulties particularly with her food supply, and talk of birth control and late marriages is being heard. The pressure of China's population numbers coupled with an aggressive Communist ideology and a regimented totalitarian economy may portend disaster in the long run for China's own economy, the security of south-east Asia and the peace of the world.

Indonesia, with an area of 569,000 square miles, has to support more than 100 million people. Indonesia's population problem is in a sense regional and not national. The density on the main island of Java is very high, whereas many outer islands are relatively sparsely populated. Java contains about one-eleventh of the area of Indonesia but about two thirds of the entire population. While the land in the outer islands is probably less fertile than that in Java, it is good enough to carry many millions. So even before Indonesia became free, emigration of peasant families to Sumatra and Borneo was organized, but the cost per settler was high and the Javanese farmer was not too willing to migrate to neighbouring underdeveloped islands. In recent years there has been some talk of pursuing the schemes of settlements in other Indonesian islands but nothing substantial has come of it. Apart from the theoretical schemes of redistributing the Indonesian population among the various islands, the government has given no thought to any policy of population control, possibly on the assumption that there is plenty of land in the country as a whole.

Now that Indonesia has gained from the Dutch the western half of New Guinea, now called West Irian, her land problem is not acute. This region has an area of 180,000 square miles and an estimated population of some 750,000. If Indonesia can successfully colonize West Irian with the Javanese, Indonesia's population problems can be said to be solved.

As for other Asian countries, Pakistan, with a population of about 95 millions, has embarked, under President Ayub Khan, on a policy of population control. Birth control clinics have been opened in both wings of the country but the Muslim masses have not been attracted to them as yet. Ceylon is also officially in favour of population control but determined government efforts are not visible. Taiwan, Hong Kong and

Singapore have active voluntary family planning associations which are doing useful work with some government encouragement.

On the other hand, Burma, Thailand and Israel, for reasons best known to their governments, consider themselves under-populated or at any rate free from population pressure. The levels of living in these countries, with the possible exception of Israel (which is more European than Asian), are not particularly high in relation to other Asian countries and there is no reason to suppose that their per capita incomes would increase if there were more people.

Conclusion

This volume is confined largely to an examination of the problems of the big five Asian countries (China, India, Indonesia, Pakistan and Japan). The reason behind this choice is that these countries are faced with acute problems and any reasonable solutions to them will promote the welfare of millions of people. This does not mean, it need hardly be added, that the smaller Asian nations are unimportant or that they are not confronted with any problems. It is hoped that a second volume will cover the population problems of other Asian nations.

Therefore, no attempt has been made to explore the demography of every Asian country. An initial difficulty with certain small Asian countries is lack of comparable data. While nations like India and Japan have considerable official and non-official demographic literature of a fairly sophisticated nature, areas such as Communist China and Arab Western Asia have only meagre, and that not up-to-date, official data. Afghanistan, for instance, has not yet embarked on a decennial census. There are other regions where even basic vital statistics are difficult to come by. And yet some effort must be made to understand the population dynamics of these nations.

As for population policies, some countries more than others have exhibited a lively awareness of the importance and role of the population factor in their national plans for economic development. Hence the policies of controlling the birth rate in such countries as Japan, India, Pakistan, South Korea and Taiwan. Certain other Asian governments have remained, by and large, indifferent to family planning, presumably on the assumption that they do not have a population problem of any serious proportions. Nevertheless, certain voluntary agencies like women's groups and family planning associations in these countries have been able to carry on some amount of planned parenthood work for health and economic reasons.

While the official national population policies are rightly dedicated to the task of lowering the birth rates, some groups, usually the small, educated elite as distinguished from the uneducated masses, have looked beyond the frontiers of Asia for personal or family demographic relief and economic betterment. Here their attention has been directed to advanced and affluent countries like Canada, the United States of America and the United Kingdom which permit Asian immigrants, although in limited numbers. Some Asians have looked to nearby Australia, but largely in vain, for she is the only major thinly populated country with a relatively high level of living that does not permit permanent Asian immigrants. Australia's present and prospective demographic position and her overall immigration policy deserve a careful and objective examination in the light of Asian population problems and policies. Hence the three informative essays on Australia in this volume. Dr Kenneth Rivett's concluding essay shows that this question is engaging the attention of all thoughtful Australians and that a way out along progressive lines, friendly to Asian needs and sentiment, is perhaps possible in the near future.

In conclusion, the solution to Asia's population problems lies as much in population control as in economic and social development. The latter is often a necessary prerequisite to the implementation of the former. While every Asian country is trying to develop its agricultural resources and industrialize its economy as much as possible, only a few countries, as already pointed out, are trying to curb their population growth.

However, the successful and widespread implementation of planned parenthood implies not only a reasonable standard of living but more important, women's social and economic emancipation. Once the women of Asia are liberated from apathy and ignorance, and some education, in the fundamental and liberal sense of the term, becomes widespread for all the people in Asia, a new awareness of the dignity and worth of the individual is bound to dawn.

And last, no Asian country can develop her resources and raise her levels of consumption without substantial aid from the rich Western nations. Such aid should not be confined to agricultural and industrial development alone but must extend to all the available 'know-how' on health, hygiene and family planning. In the long run, Asia must be enabled to lower both her birth and death rates to civilized levels. When every Asian woman delivers two babies instead of the five or six she delivered before, and when every Asian farmer grows two ears of corn where one or none grew before, Asia's demographic and economic problem can be solved. A relatively rich and stable Asia is bound to have beneficient repercussions even on the affluent West, for prosperity, like peace, is one and indivisible.

NOTES

1. Kingsley Davis, 'The World Demographic Transition', *The Annals* of the American Academy of Political and Social Science, January 1945, p. 2.
2. See J. George Harrar, 'Making the Most of Human Resources', *Journal of Public Health*, March 1965.
3. Anthony M. M. Payne, 'The Role of Health Today in Social and Economic Development', *Journal of Public Health*, March 1963.
4. Stephen Enke, *Economics for Development* (Englewood Cliffs, N.J., Prentice Hall, 1963), pp. 414–15.
5. *Compendium of Social Statistics—Statistical Papers, Series K, No. 2* (New York, United Nations, 1963). See Table 2, pp. 31–47.
6. The definition of 'sex ratio' needs to be standardized. In the United Kingdom (and consequently in some parts of the Commonwealth) it is defined as 'the number of females per 1,000 males'. But in the United States it is defined as 'the number of males per 1,000 females'. The present writer is inclined to consider the American definition more scientific because the use of females as the denominator is more consistent with other demographic reasoning, particularly concerning fertility.
7. S. Chandrasekhar, *India's Population: Fact and Policy* (New York, John Day, 1946), p. 34.
8. *Report on World Social Situation* (New York, United Nations, Department of Economic and Social Affairs, 1957), p. 127.
9. For a discussion of the problem from an Asian point of view, see S. Chandrasekhar, *Hungry People and Empty Lands* (London and New York, 1955). Third edition.

BIBLIOGRAPHY

Chandrasekhar, S., *Hungry People and Empty Lands* (London, Allen and Unwin, 1955). Third edition.

'An Indian Demographer Looks at the World', *UNESCO Courier* (Paris), November 1949.

'Population Problems and International Tensions', *International Social Science Bulletin* (Paris, UNESCO, 1949).

'Population Growth, Socio-economic development and Living Standards,' *International Labour Review*, June, 1954.

'Population Problems of Asia', *Population Review*, Vol. 7, No. 1, January, 1963.

'World Population Growth and Desert Reclamation', *Population Review*, January and July 1965.

Borgstrom, Georg, *The Hungry Planet* (New York, The Macmillan Company, 1965).

Buss, Claude A., *Asia in the Modern World* (New York, The Macmillan Company, 1965).

Cowan, C. D. (Ed.), *The Economic Development of Southeast Asia* (London, Allen and Unwin, 1964).

Cressey, George B., *Asia's Lands and Peoples* (New York, McGraw-Hill Book Co., 1963). Third edition.

Hauser, Philip (Ed.), *Urbanization in Asia and the Far East* (Chicago University Press, 1957).

International Labour Office: *International Migration: 1945–47* (Geneva, 1959).

May, Jacques M., *The Ecology of Malnutrition in the Far and Near East* (New York, Hafner, 1961).

Panikkar, K. M., *Asia and Western Dominance* (London, Allen and Unwin, 1954). Fourth edition.

PEP: *World Population and Resources* (London, Allen and Unwin, 1955).
Robbins, John, *Too Many Asians* (New York, Doubleday, 1959).
Spencer, Joseph E., *Asia East by South* (New York, Wiley, 1954).
Thompson, Warren S., *Population and Peace in the Pacific* (The University of Chicago Press, 1946).
Population and Progress in the Far East (The University of Chicago Press, 1959).
United Nations: *The Determinants and Consequences of Population Trends* (New York, 1953).
Foetal, Infant and Early Childhood Mortality (New York, 1954), 2 volumes.
Population Growth and the Standard of Living in Underdeveloped Countries (New York, 1954).
Report on World Social Situation (New York, 1957).
The Future Growth of World Population (New York, 1958).
Demographic Yearbook (New York, 1964).
Wint, Guy (Ed.), *Asia: A Handbook* (London, Anthony Bond; New York, Frederick A. Praeger, 1966).

CHAPTER 2

COMMUNIST CHINA'S DEMOGRAPHIC DILEMMA

BY S. CHANDRASEKHAR

CHINA, with an area of more than three and a half million square miles (3,657,765) occupies a dominant position in east Asia as the world's third largest country. The Soviet Union leads the world with 8,597,000 square miles, followed by Canada with 3,843,144 square miles. China is followed by the United States and Brazil with 3,615,210 and 3,286,170 square miles respectively.

China's position on the Asian mainland is such that she borders on practically all the mainland nations of south Asia. Only western Asia is beyond her frontiers. While Afghanistan, India, Nepal, Bhutan, Burma, Laos and North Vietnam are China's direct southern and eastern neighbours, she borders on the north and west on North Korea, Mongolian People's Republic and the Soviet Union.

In another sense, China's frontiers with these countries are more nominal than real, for she is isolated by great physical barriers. On the east and south she is washed by the wide expanse of the Pacific Ocean. On the west she is girded by the world's highest plateau, 'the roof of the world'. On the north, between China and the Soviet Union, lies the sovereign Mongolian People's Republic, hardly a buffer state since it is modelled after the Soviet Union and is, by and large, historically a product of the Soviet and Chinese manoeuvres for security. And along the north-west stretch a thousand miles of deserts of cold sand. On the north-east the Sino-Soviet border is clearly defined by the great Amur River and its tributaries, the Ussuri and the Argun. Similarly, the Yalu and Tumen rivers constitute the frontier between China and North Korea.

In the south, China borders on India, Nepal and Bhutan along the mighty and rugged mountain barrier of the Himalayas. The Chinese frontier with India is disputed, though the available historical evidence is in favour of the traditional Indian borders. Further east the frontier passes along the mountain terrain north of Laos and North Vietnam to the Gulf of Tonkin. Thus China stretches from the Gobi desert to the Gulf of Tonkin, from Tibet to North Korea. China, like India and unlike the Soviet Union and the United States, stretches from north to south; from the Amur river to south of Hainan, the distance of about 2,500 miles.

Earlier Population Estimates

While China has some of the oldest population (household) records in the world, maintained for purposes of taxation, conscription of military manpower, police and administrative needs, her total population numbers, before the Communist take-over, have always been a question of some speculation. The reasons are obvious. The absence of a strong central government and the consequent want of political stability, the large land area and difficult terrain, an admittedly large population, a lack of adequate communications and transportation system and the low level of overall development were some of the major reasons that prevented China from conducting a nation-wide census in the past. During the first quarter of this century three inconclusive attempts at the counting of the Chinese population were made by the governments then in power. Estimates of China's total population, however, were not lacking. The United Nations (1949) estimate of 450 million was taken as a representative figure for working purposes, until the Communists carried out their 'first modern census' of China in 1953 and came up with the figure of 582·6 million as the total population of the Chinese mainland.

Population Statistics in Communist China

A student of Communist Chinese statistics is confronted with several difficulties. To begin with, in almost all Communist countries, statistics, be they demographic, economic or social, are not freely and fully published for public consumption. Communist governments appear to be rather secretive about all data pertaining to life, labour and wealth, and this seems to be particularly true of China.

When the Chinese do publish statistics they suffer from two basic drawbacks. One is their inaccuracy. The information-gathering agencies are new; there are not enough well-trained statisticians and the average citizen does not possess the statistical consciousness to furnish the questioner with accurate information. The administrative mechanism has not had long experience and the lack of adequate communication channels and transport difficulties add to the total problem.

The second drawback is the ideological bias of Chinese statistics. They are highly coloured by propaganda, and figures on production, for instance, may be padded to satisfy immediate political demands. Official statistics are often contradictory and the sources themselves do not even agree. Therefore, the inaccuracy and inadequacy of Chinese statistics result from both human and ideological factors. (On the other hand, non-Chinese sources, such as they are, may be biased in the opposite direction.)

During the last five years the Chinese authorities have ceased to publish several statistical series altogether. Apparently they want to guard themselves against external attack and exposure as poor and misleading statisticians. For instance, it is not known for certain whether or not a second national census that was due in 1963 was ever conducted. If they did take a census in 1963, no one has heard of its results. Therefore the problem is one of what is available and what is acceptable.

As a recent carefully documented review of China points out: 'The problem is one of what is knowable. Statistics in Communist China are at best inadequate, at worst, dangerously misleading because avowedly a tool of the state. And statistics are too dull a tool for crisis management. The Chinese Communists cut off the publication of statistics when the failure of the Great Leap Forward began to be apparent. Presumably, they wished to conceal the extent of their failures, but perhaps also they began to realize the extent to which they had been misled by their own statistical illusions. The information black-out started in 1958 and became virtually complete in 1960. One now feels as though he were trying to photograph a black cat in a dark room.'[1]

The 1953 Census

The People's Republic of China announced on November 1, 1954 that it had conducted the 'first scientific census' of China in 1953 and that the population of the mainland on June 30, 1953 was 582·6 million.[2] This figure includes an allowance for an estimated 8,397,477 persons who lived in outlying frontier areas who were not counted. There was also, according to official reports, a 0·1 per cent under-enumeration of the total population. Though this census was the first all-China census, it had certain features markedly different from a modern, conventional census. It was not a direct count but a by-product of the national elections to the All-China People's Congress.

Secondly, instead of the census enumerator visiting the homes, the heads of households were asked to register and furnish details at certain locations. Thirdly, the schedule was limited to only four questions of habitual residence, age, sex and ethnic identity.

Density of Population

Despite China's large population, the density of about 150 persons per square mile appears to be low, but this is natural in view of the enormous area of the country. But this low density as well as the large area are deceptive because much of China's land area is useless and the population numbers are distributed very unevenly. A great part of China's land is mountainous and rugged and parts are even inaccessible. It has been estimated that about 65 per cent of the land mass consists of high mountain ranges and plateaus, about 10 per cent of hills, 15 per cent of river basins and only about 10 per cent of fertile plains. In fact, an overwhelming majority of the population is concentrated on this 10 per cent of cultivated land and the consequent density in the central and maritime provinces is quite high.

If a line were drawn from Yunnan province in the south-west to Heilungkiang province in the north-east, China would be divided into two natural geographic regions. The western region (excluding Tibet and the Chamdo area) would consist of some 40 per cent of land area and less than 5 per cent of the country's total population. The eastern region, on the other hand, covers some 58 per cent of the total land area and supports about 95 per cent of the total population.

Age Composition

The age statistics of China's population has always posed a problem. The 1953 census elicited the citizen's actual age (age at last birthday) computed on the basis of the census date of June 30th. This presented certain minor complications as the traditional Chinese method of expressing one's age is different from the general Western method based on the Gregorian calendar. As there is no commonly accepted uniform calendar year in China, a conversion table was devised, on the basis of which age in completed years was calculated.

Of the total population, the 0–4, 5–9 and 10–17 age groups constituted 15·6, 11·0 and 14·5 per cent respectively. That is, the 0–17 age group formed 41·1 per cent of the total population. The age groups 18–49 and 50 and above were 45·4 and 13·5 per cent of the total population. S. K. Tai points out, 'In terms of the three types of Sundbaerg's divisions, the population of new China may be regarded as between the progressive type and the stationary type and appears to be a youthful and propitious population. The youth group of 16 years and under constitutes about 39 per cent of the total population'.[3]

Sex Composition

Of the total population directly surveyed and registered, 297,553,518 persons were males constituting 51·82 per cent, and 276,652,422 persons were females constituting 48·18 per cent. The sex ratio was in favour of males; there were 107·7 males per every 100 females.

Table 1 gives the sex ratio of China's (1953) population at different age groups.

These figures support the common assumption in China—and it has been the experience of some other Asian countries as well—of the sex ratio being in favour of males. In the past, the chances of survival of a female infant in China between 0–5 years were not as favourable as those of a male infant. Female infanticide was not unknown and the practice of abandoning female infants during famines, floods and other calamities was widely prevalent. The cultural mores favoured the male infant. These have now undergone a considerable change, and the change

TABLE 1. *Sex Ratio at Various Age Groups*

Age group	Sex ratio (Number of males per 100 females)
At birth	104·9
1–2	106·2
3–6	110·0
7–13	115·8
14–17	113·7
18–35	111·5
36–55	106·8
56 and over	86·7

is reflected in the sex ratio of infants under three years. That the sex ratio becomes increasingly unfavourable to the female in the higher age groups is noteworthy; the heritage of the past is in evidence in the higher age groups.

Rural–Urban Ratio

The census defined 'a rural area as a place with a population of 2,000 persons and less and also a place where the population was more than 2,000 but where 50 per cent of the total were peasants or otherwise engaged in agriculture'.[4] The rest of the population was classified as urban. According to this definition, 86·74 per cent of the 1953 population was rural and 13·26 urban.

It is not known for certain whether this 1953 rural–urban ratio is true of China's population today (1966). Statistics on rural–urban and inter-provincial migration are not available. However, some fragmentary evidence on the internal movement of population during the last dozen years is available, and according to this evidence, there have been three major shifts of population: (1) The Communist Government has seriously pursued a policy of reclaiming sparsely populated virgin lands in the northern and western provinces. This policy was based primarily on the need for increased food production and a desire for depopulating certain cities, like Shanghai, where the people in the light of their past history were not particularly enthusiastic about Communist ideology. (2) There have been certain minor migratory movements of labour to the new industrial locations. Major heavy industries have been created or moved near the source of raw materials and away from coastal areas which may be vulnerable to enemy attack. Much of this migration was from nearby crowded rural areas. (3) And last, the Communists have pursued a deliberate policy of diluting the minority areas with Han people. Despite the Government's assurances of religious freedom and the cultural autonomy of ethnic minorities, the Chinese Communists are not happy at the thought of some border areas being inhabited predominantly by the minority groups. Their loyalty to the Communist regime is not taken for granted. They are afraid that both the Soviet Union and India might foment disaffection among the minority peoples in Sinkiang (Chinese Turkestan) and Tibet and the Chamdo area against the Chinese Government. Hence the large-scale settling of Han people in these areas. The Tibetans, for instance are becoming an ineffectual minority in their own land.

All these three migratory movements have contributed to the spatial redistribution of the Chinese population and its rural–urban composition. While the direction of this migration is more or less known, no precise information on its volume is available.

Ethnic Minorities

China is a land of many ethnic groups or 'nationalities' as they are called in the official census. In non-Communist language they are religious and tribal minorities who may or may not be ethnically different from the Han majority of the Chinese population.

The Hans, who constitute the largest nationality, numbered in the 1953 census 547·2 millions or nearly 94 per cent of the total mainland population. The other minority nationalities total 35·3 millions or 6 per cent of the total population. These 35 million people belonging to some fifty minority groups are concentrated primarily in the south-west and north-west of China. The major minority groups and their numerical strength are as follows: Mongolian, 1·4 million; Hui, 1·3; Tibetan, 2·7; Uighur, 3·6; Miao, 2·5; Yi, 3·2; Chuang, 6·6; Puyi, 1·2; Korean, 1·1; Manchu, 2·4; and others, 6·7.[5]

Vital Statistics

Prior to the present regime, China had no regular nationwide, vital registration system. Periodically certain Chinese and foreign agencies made some attempts, largely unsuccessful, to collect vital statistics for such small areas as a village or a town. The last such attempt was made by Professor Ta Chen who carried out a census and vital registration for a small area in the Kunming Lake Region in 1942.

When the Communists came to power in 1949, they initially resorted to the conventional and misleading vital statistical rates bequeathed by the Koumingtang regime. But about the time of the 1953 census, vital statistical registration was organized on a near-national basis. An official in every village was made responsible to the People's Council for the registration of all births and deaths at the *hsiang* level. At the town and city level vital registration became the responsibility of the police, and a parent or some other responsible member of each family has to report all vital occurrences to them. All this is demanded by the Vital Registration Law passed in January 1952 by the National People's Congress.

It is not known whether the system is nationwide and complete or whether the figures are accurate. Apparently the figures are not published for public consumption. As already mentioned, vital statistical data have strange strategical value in most Communist countries and the fact that they are not published does not necessarily mean that the government does not have the figures for their own use.

Birth and Death Rates

On the basis of the 1953 census-registration the Government announced that the Chinese birth rate and death rate were 37 and 17 per thousand respectively. Official birth and death rates are available up to 1957 but for some reason no population statistics have been published after that year or if they have, the author is not aware of them.

The following table gives the crude birth and death rates for the Chinese mainland for 1952–57.

TABLE 2. *Crude Birth and Death Rates in Communist China, 1952–57*[6]

Year	Birth rate	Death rate	Natural increase (Birth rate minus death rate)
1952	37	18	19
1953	37	17	20
1954	38	15	23
1955	35	12·4	22·6
1956	32	11·4	20·6
1957	34	11	23

Source: S. Chandrasekhar, 1961, p. 3. The death rate for 1954 has been changed on the basis of later evidence.

While no official statistics have been released for recent years (1958–65) such fragmentary and indirect evidence as is available shows that while birth rates have increased, death rates have declined, resulting in a natural increase rate of more than 2 per cent. Thus, China has been adding somewhere between 15 and 17 millions every year to her already existing massive population.

Two questions may be raised here. Are these birth and death rates reasonably near or representative of the actual present birth and death rate in China? The factors that generally affect the birth rates in China, or for that matter in any other country, are peaceful conditions (in the sense of absence of war), satisfactory levels of food consumption, minimum levels of public hygiene and environmental sanitation and the absence of epidemics, the availability of medical services, the practice of contraception, individual and official attitudes towards family size and the overall cultural mores. We know today that China is enjoying peaceful internal conditions, that China's traditional filth has been more or less cleaned up, and that there is a growing network of preventive and curative health and medical services. The food situation has varied through these eighteen years (1948–66) from adequate to meagre rations from the point of view of individual health needs. As for contraception, the vacillating official policy has led to poor and ineffective attempts to restrict the size of the family. In the light of all this, the birth rate may be assumed to be around 35 per thousand with 40 as the upper limit. It is true that the registered birth rates of some Chinese communities overseas range between 40 and 45 per thousand but these communities are relatively affluent and there is no official propaganda—however halting and half-hearted—in favour of birth control among them.

The death rate of 11 per thousand or even lower appears to be on the low side for a country like China. It may be pointed out that while vital registration may not be accurate and complete in China today, the general trend in most underdeveloped countries is that deaths have a better chance than births of being registered for the simple reason that there is a body to be buried. Secondly, there is evidence from such developing countries as Ceylon and India that death rates respond dramatically to DDT spraying, BCG vaccination and general antibiotics. In fact such elementary reforms as the supply of potable water to everyone and the hygienic disposal of human wastes can lead to a definitive decline in the death rate in a short period. There is no doubt that a large number of disease-carrying mosquitoes and flies, rats, and other rodents have been destroyed and the incidence of such traditional scourges as cholera, smallpox and typhus has been considerably reduced. Perhaps today the meagre food rations are the only major contributing factor to the death rate. Both malnutrition and under-nutrition lower resistance to disease and render recovery from illness slow. Even here, it would be untrue to say that a large number of Chinese are starving to death. China is buying an enormous amount of wheat from the free world to stave off famine.

On the whole, those like the present writer who had the opportunity of seeing China before and after the Communist take-over, can testify to the enormous, sustained and largely effective attempts of the Communists to clean up the country and are inclined to believe that the death rate has come down. Of course, one cannot be certain how low the actual death rate is today, for reasons already mentioned.[7]

Therefore, in the absence of official published data and in the light of what is known of factors affecting both birth and death rates, it may be reasonable to assume that the birth rate may be about 33 or 35 per thousand and the death rate about 11 or 12 per thousand; yielding about a 2·2 per cent annual increase. If anything, this rate of increase may be an underestimate.

Marriage Law Reforms

Before the Communists came to power the universality of the married state had been a well-known feature of the Chinese social scene. So had been the institution of concubinage, so widely practised and persistent that it was recognized in Chinese domestic law. Concubinage, which amounted in practice to polygamy, was abolished by the Communists with no great effort, and today monogamy has become the law of the land. In sexual morals, the Chinese Communists have become, if anything, puritanical.

In April 1950 the new Marriage Law was promulgated. The law (see Appendix No. 2) has numerous provisions but only a few can be referred to here.

Marriage, for the first time in the nation's long history, has been made a civil contract and not a religious ceremony. Secondly, unlike in the past, marriages must be registered, which is the condition of legitimacy. The procedure is defined as follows:

'. . . for the registration of marriage: first both parties, the man and the woman, shall go in person, either to the man's or woman's city, village, etc., of residence to fill in the application form at the registry. After the application form is filled, bring it to the police station to get it endorsed. After that, both parties shall each take the Pre-nuptial Health Examination form to the appointed hospital for examination. If there is no physiological defect or disease, if all the procedures mentioned are complied with and if they are proved in conformity with Article 3 and Article 5 of the Law, registration may be granted. Moreover, they are subject to the approval of the local people's government before marriage certificates are obtainable.'

A desirable feature of this directive is the compulsory pre-marital medical examination of the prospective couple. But the permits by the police and the local people's government may involve bureaucratic delays unless the bride and groom are acceptable to the Party. Another welcome feature is embodied in Article 4 which raises the age of consent from 18 to 20 for males and from 16 to 18 for females.

As for the rights and duties of husband and wife, Article 8 stipulates:

'Husband and wife are in duty bound to love, respect, assist and look after each other, to live in harmony, to labour for production, to care for the children, to strive jointly for the welfare of the family and the building up of a new society.'

In brief, several fetters of the past on individual freedom in the choice of partners have been removed. Marriage based on arbitrary and compulsory arrangement by parents or senior members of the family as well as those by purchase or gifts are no longer permitted. The social barriers against a widow's remarriage have been removed and divorce has been made relatively easy. Children born out of wedlock have the same rights as legitimate children. Thus Chinese marriage law has been brought up to date and in consonance with practice in advanced Communist countries like the Soviet Union.

What is likely to be the effect of the new law on the country's population problem? The institution of marriage has become even more widespread under the Communists than it was before. The marriage rate is possibly higher today than it was in earlier years, despite the Government's efforts to encourage couples to postpone their marriages in recent years.

Present Population and Future Growth

Perhaps the most important question in China's demography today is her population size and the prospects of her future growth. The Chinese

TABLE 3. *Estimates of Communist China's Population: 1949–65*[9]

Year	Year-end population estimate in millions	Population increase over preceding year: Millions	Per cent
1949	541·7	—	—
1950	552·0	10·3	1·90
1951	563·0	11·0	1·99
1952	574·8	11·8	2·10
1953	588·0	13·2	2·30
1954	601·7	13·7	2·33
1955	614·7	13·0	2·16
1956	627·8	13·1	2·13
1957	349·5	21·7	3·46
1958	662·9	13·4	2·06
1959	675·2	Year-end population projected from 1958 at 2·2 per cent per year from 1957 population as base.	
1960	690·1		
1961	705·3		
1962	720·8		
1963	736·7		
1964	752·9		
1965	769·5		

government under normal circumstances ought to have conducted their second decennial census in 1963 or 1964, but is not known for certain whether they have and, if they have, why they have not published the results.[8]

As presented in Table 3, the year-end population was around 663 million, and various Chinese official publications in recent years have referred to China's population variously as 600, 650 and 750 millions. If China's annual rate of growth is assumed to be around 2 or 2·2 per cent it is possible that her population has increased by at least a hundred million between 1958 and 1965. If this assumption is valid, her present 1965 year-end population must be about 750 million.

What is likely to be the pattern of the future growth of China's population? An adequate answer is dependent upon a variety of factors relevant to her population policy, now and in the years ahead. Such evidence as is available on China's current birth control policy and her economic potential suggests that her population growth is not likely to be checked short of a major global war waged on Chinese soil or unprecedented economic distress and famine.

The Problem

What are the implications of China's population size and the rate at which it is growing? Seven hundred and fifty million people growing at a 2 to 2·5 per cent rate per annum, adding some fifteen million every year—the limitations this imposes on the economy are obvious. The basic problem is feeding, clothing and housing this enormous existing population as well as the prodigious yearly additions to it.

While a large population has certain advantages, the remarkable decline in infant and childhood mortality rates has enormously increased the number of dependents in relation to the total working population. Between 35 and 40 per cent of China's total population are children below 15 years of age. This is a disproportionately large dependency ratio for any underdeveloped economy.

China's tireless efforts to industrialize her economy imply capital formation at a rate faster than her population growth. Here reliable statistics are scanty, but the available evidence shows that China is expending a large share of her productive effort just to keep up with the growth of population. This situation, which prevails in any underdeveloped country based on a market economy, is true of China only up to a point, however. The advantage of a totalitarian economy is that its total production and distribution can be mobilized and directed to stipulated goals of economic, social and political development. Totalitarian economic planning, like a 'command' or war economy, can manipulate the entire economic resources and the people's value system towards specific ends—like replacing butter with guns. Everyone can admire several specific Chinese accomplishments but no one can question the alternatives that have been foregone. But despite these basic advantages of a Communist economy, China has found her population size and its rate of growth more of a problem than an advantage in her present stage of socio-economic and technological development.

Hence her concern with an ante-natal population policy, however meandering and wavering it has been in actual execution.

Population Policy

Any attempt to understand Communist China's vacillating population policy must keep in view four inescapable, if rather contradictory, approaches to the problem. First is the traditional Chinese view of the question of family size. Both Confucius and Mencius, master and disciple, have extolled the virtues of a large family and filial piety. Classical Chinese thought, much as thought elsewhere in Asia, was very much in favour of a large population. Their ethics, morals and philosophy were all pro-natalist and countless quotations which are a familiar part of the people's mores supported this view.

According to Confucius, to die without offspring is one of the three greatest unfilial acts. To Mencius, 'There are three things which are unfilial, and to have no posterity is the greatest of them. . . . It is man's first duty to ensure the continuity of the male line of succession. Man is envied for the number of descendants in the male line who will walk in his funeral train. Grandchildren and still more grandchildren, are counted as special blessings of heaven.' And the folklore revealed the wisdom of the time with the proverb, 'Grain is stored against famine just as sons are brought up against old age.' Thus, through the ages, the Chinese married early and produced as many children as possible, preferably sons. The plurality of wives (including concubinage), the universality of the married state, the extended family, the low status accorded to women and a high death rate—all conspired to yield a high birth rate and relatively large families. It must be remembered that Confucius, custom and tradition directed the lives of the people and no emperor could change them.

The second factor is what may be called 'the chamber of commerce' attitude. Every ethnic group feels that it is a chosen one and there can never be too many of them. Every community would like to be a bigger and better entity in the world. More people means more tax payers, more demand from more consumers, more soldiers, and more followers of the revealed religion, etc. This feeling is not particularly Chinese but universal. So the Chinese can be excused when one of them exclaims, 'Six hundred million! . . . cause for us to rejoice, excellent news for all the peoples on the side of democracy and peace . . .'[10] When this patriotic outburst is viewed against the background of China's traditional feelings of superiority and their middle kingdom attitude, their population policy becomes a little more intelligible. Whether the average Chinese citizen is a Malthusian or a Marxist, there is a certain latent pride that he belongs to an ethnic group that constitutes almost a fourth of mankind.

The Communists relished this 'the bigger the better' approach during the early years of the political consolidation of their regime. E. Stuart Kirby points out, 'Playing up the size of the population was also used by the regime as a domestic morale booster. By stressing that China alone accounted for one quarter of the world's population, and all the Communist countries together for one third, the regime encouraged popular belief that the national strength of Communist China in particular, and the international strength of the 'socialist camp' as a whole, were such that the enemies of Communism must necessarily fear to attack. Very possibly also, such statements reflected a natural psychological urge to emphasize China's importance within the Communist bloc, where, in terms of population at least she is by far the leading power, outnumbering the Soviet "big brother" by some three to one.'[11]

The third is the Malthusian approach. For nearly a century and a half every writer on China has held up that country as an excellent example of the Malthusian theory. Did not Malthus say that there is a tendency for the human race to constantly increase and to press upon subsistence. Subsistence, he said, only increases in arithmetical ratio while population leaps forwards in a geometrical ratio. But he also pointed out that the unequal race was counteracted in either one of two ways which he called positive and preventive checks. The positive checks contributed to an increase in the death rate while preventive checks to a decrease in the birth rate. Since the Chinese have been increasing so fast and pressing on the limited resources, the positive check of famine, floods and epidemics had to intervene and kill off people. It has been calculated that China experienced more than 1,828 famines in some part of the country or the other between the years 108 BC and AD 1911, or about a famine a year!

And some thirty years ago, when China, in the throes of a severe and widespread famine, appealed to the International Red Cross for relief, they declined to help on the ground that the International Red Cross was designed to meet national *emergencies*, and that famine in China was *not* an emergency but a chronic state of affairs! This cynical attitude was, of course, based essentially on facts, but the verdict rankled in the minds of those Chinese who gave thought to such matters. The Chinese have been hearing of their Malthusian predicament so long that they may be forgiven if they are sick of Malthusianism, old and new.

And last is the Marxist approach. It is interesting to recall Marx's well-known comment on Malthus's Essay on the *Principle of Population*. He wrote:

'An utter baseness of mind, a baseness which only a priest can afford, is characteristic of Malthus . . . Malthus, indeed! This scoundrel draws from the premises already established by science (and *stolen* by him in every case) only such conclusions as are *agreeable* to the aristocracy for use against the bourgeoisie and to both of them for use *against* the proletariat . . . Malthus sets out to prove that "the greatest part of the sufferings of the lower classes of society is attributable exclusively to themselves and that the principal and most permanent cause of poverty has little or no relation to forms of government, or the unequal division of property; and that as the rich do not in reality possess the power of finding employment and maintenance for the poor, the poor cannot, in the nature of things . . ." In his conclusion—manipulated to suit the purposes of the propertied classes—Malthus attempts to attribute poverty and unemployment to the excessively rapid reproduction of the working classes. Malthus refers to an alleged natural law, according to which the population increases in geometrical progression, and the means of subsistence in arithmetical progression, leading to population pressure which is therefore independent of the social system.'[12]

In short, 'while under the capitalist system growth of production means growth of the wealth of the exploiting minority, accompanied by the impoverishment of the working masses, both relative and absolute, under socialism production is developed for the benefit of society as a whole namely in the interest of meeting the expanding material and cultural requirements of all the members of society, and increased production means a steady improvement of living conditions.'[13]

To the Chinese Communists, the Malthusian theory of overpopulation and poverty is simply irrelevant in a socialist society. Labour is the sole source of value. A large labouring population—the proletariat—represents a creative and productive class. And as there is no minority group of capitalists to rob the working class of the fruits of production, all the product will go to the working people. The more working people, the more production, which, with equal distribution (without any share for capitalist parasites) guarantees a rise in the people's (all workers) level of living.

Communist Chinese leaders have been exposed to all these four approaches to their country's population problems. It is perhaps understandable if they are not able to precisely demarcate the area of truth in all these explanations as a basis for formulating a positive, definitive and unwavering population policy for China. The fact that both Malthusian and Marxist approaches at certain stages of a country's development are not completely devoid of truth might also be the source of confusion in Communist China's thinking on the precise objectives of a population policy. A careful perusal of current Chinese thinking on this subject gives one the impression that the Communist leaders are not only torn between the traditional Chinese desire for a large population on the one hand, and the compelling economic need of achieving a smaller optimum population. Perhaps the fact that in a 'command' Communist economy and society there need be no unemployment persuades the Chinese to adopt, in the last analysis, the Marxist approach to their population problem.

Initial Official Reaction to Population Numbers

While the reactions of the world at large to the Chinese disclosure of the magnitude of their total population was a mixture of surprise, shock and scepticism, the initial official Communist reaction was one of jubilation. On November 1, 1954, commenting on the census results, Pai Chien-hua, the chief census official, observed.

'The existence of over 600,000,000 people is the source of wealth of our great country and the basis of its socialist reconstruction. . . . In the People's Democracies, man is the most precious form of capital, the master of his fate, the conscious creator of his own happiness . . . under the reactionary Koumingtang Government, bad material conditions coupled with social and public insecurity led to a high death rate and a low rate of natural increase. . . . After the liberation, the rate of natural increase rose considerably owing to the restoration and development of production, the improvement of the people's material conditions, and the progress in medicine and hygiene.'[14]

It is interesting to note that this pro-natalist and anti-Malthusian attitude was voiced even earlier, on April 25, 1952, when *Jen-min Jih-pao* condemned birth control as being simply 'a means of killing the Chinese without shedding blood'.

The Great Debate on Birth Control

However, the official attitude on the desirability of a large population began to slowly change from late 1954. The first session of the People's Congress, held in Peking in September 1954, witnessed the beginnings of the great debate on China's population problems and the need or otherwise for birth control. As even the so-called public debates on national questions are usually started with the Party's permission, it is reasonable to infer that the Government—and the Party which runs the Government—felt the need to disseminate information on birth control for a variety of reasons. The major reason was the unsatisfactory food situation in 1954, bordering on quasi-famine conditions in certain provinces.

It was Deputy Shao Li-tzu[15] who first publicly raised the issue of birth control before the Congress and set the ball rolling. In his speech Shao Li-tzu made it clear that there was no population problem in China in the conventional, bourgeois, capitalistic sense, and his plea for birth control had nothing to do with decadent, outmoded, reactionary Malthusian doctrines. His plea for introducing birth control measures was for the protection of the health of Chinese mothers and children. He pointed out that 'a big population is a good thing, but there should be certain limits to it when there are many difficulties'.[16] This cautious Government-approved statement was followed by speeches by several other deputies on similar lines as Deputy Shao's. In the newspapers several writers began to point out the difficulties inherent in a large population in the context of China's economic underdevelopment. The subject of population growth and family planning began to be explored from various points of view.

As a result of this continuing debate the state council issued a directive to the Ministry of Public Health to educate the broad masses on the need for practising birth control—both 'contraception and artificial expulsion (induced abortion)'. In response to the directive, the Ministry formulated measures concerning birth control and submitted them to the Government for approval. These measures were more or less on the lines adopted by other Communist countries. Among others covering several birth control devices, the following rules concerning abortion were laid down:

'Abortion is permitted in all cases where medical science considers the prolongation of pregnancy to be unwise, where births occur at too close intervals, where a mother with a baby of only four months old becomes pregnant again and has difficulty in feeding her baby. In all these cases, surgically assisted abortion is permitted, but it must be carried out on the request and with the consent of the two parents concerned, on the presentation of a medical certificate and with the approval of the responsible authorities of the organizations to which the two parties belong. If the abortion is requested for reasons of study, special or too heavy work, all requests for surgical intervention must first be certified and supported by the director of responsible organizations and approved by the medical service.'[17]

The next step was nationwide discussion of birth control. On December 27, 1954 Liu Shao-chi, one of the big five in China, next only to Mao Tse-tung and now Head of the State, convened a conference to discuss the problems relating to birth control. The association of Liu Shao-chi with birth control at that moment revealed to the people how serious and earnest the Government was on the question. As a result of this conference, the Second General Office of the State Council 'designated the responsible officials of the competent departments to organize research groups for the discussion of contraception problems'.[18]

During the two years, 1956 and 1957, the campaign for birth control began to gather momentum and numerous articles, inspired and otherwise, on the Chinese population problem, the need for a fresh look at the Marxist view of population and the compelling necessity for contraception, began to appear in the Chinese press. Madam Li Te-chuan, the Minister for Public Health, declared (on June 18, 1956) in her report to the third session of the National People's Congress that the birth control propaganda should be intensified all over the country under the direction of the Party and the Government. By the end of 1956 birth control received the final seal of ideological respectability when Prime Minister Chou En-lai declared that the Health Ministry should adopt effective birth control measures 'to protect women and children and bring up and educate our younger generation in a way conducive to the health and prosperity of the nation'.[19]

In all this great propaganda, it must be pointed out, the argument that family planning would promote the country's economic development was invariably rejected. All pleas for birth control were prefaced with strong denunciations of the Malthusian view. The reasons for family planning were always for the better health of the mothers, better education of the children, more leisure for study and the desire of young women to be free to work to increase national production.

Dr Ma-Yinchu and his Thesis[20]

When the Chinese Government decided to 'suspend' the campaign for birth control in 1957, a controversy on the population problem which started earlier between avowed Chinese Communists and non-party scholars continued for several months. A major contributor to this controversial debate was Dr Ma-Yinchu. His rise and fall, his theoretical contribution, and his subsequent denunciation constitute an intriguing episode in any discussion of contemporary China's population problems.

On July 3, 1957, Dr Ma-Yinchu, President of Peking University, and an economist and scholar of some repute (with a Ph.D. from Columbia University) delivered a written statement before the Fourth Session of the First National People's Congress in Peking on 'A New Theory of Population'. Dr Ma's thesis was that China's massive population was a serious barrier to the country's rapid economic growth. 'The consumption expenditure is enormous and much national income cannot be saved for capital formation. Hence, the urgent need to bring the growth of Chinese population under control in order to lower the ratio of current consumption to capital formation. He went on to add, and perhaps here overstepped the official line, that unless birth control measures were taken, rapid industrialization would involve denial of consumer goods to the people. And a disappointed and frustrated people might rise against the Government as the Poles and Hungarians had done.[21]

At first the speech presenting this paper was apparently ignored, or at any rate it received no particular comment, and the author continued to enjoy his scholarly reputation as well as his academic position. But a few months later a virulent campaign was launched against him as a rightist and a Malthusian by the party faithful. Daily newspapers, political and economic periodicals, women's magazines and trade union journals all joined the fray. Many people did not know what the offending thesis was but denunciation was the official line and everyone attacked him. This was an extraordinary procedure, for the Party and the Government had been very much in favour of birth control only a few months earlier. Dr Ma had little chance to reply or explain his theory. And the upshot of the attack was that he was dismissed from the presidency of the university.

Birth Control Policy Reversal and Present Position

Until the middle of 1958, a nationwide birth control policy was pursued with fanfare and vigour. Two factories to manufacture contraceptives were established in Canton and Shanghai. Several exhibitions on birth control were opened in urban areas. Countless posters proclaimed the need for family planning. The radio, film, press, platform and musicals were pressed into service to disseminate birth control information. Birth control clinics were opened in most cities. And teams of doctors were sent to the countryside to teach the peasants of the need for and actual techniques of limiting family size. It was almost made a party mandate to the cadres.

But in the summer of 1958 without any explanation the campaign for birth control was suddenly called off. This reversal or postponement coincided with the now discredited 'great leap forward' campaign and the introduction of the famous and now largely discarded Communes. All over the country one heard a bewildering new song that China was not only not overpopulated but actually underpopulated in view of the endless tasks of socialist reconstruction. The problem now changed to one of severe manpower shortage. Now the women had to be liberated from domestic chores to work in the fields and factories. Hence the Communes.

What are the real reasons behind this sudden reversal? No one knows for certain but the present writer speculated in 1959 as follows:

'Several explanations have been advanced by foreign observers for this sudden reversal of policy. The Chinese themselves have never explained why their birth control policy was reversed, but the most plausible explanation according to many observers is that a sudden shift in population policy became necessary because the impression had gained ground that the nationwide birth control drive implied that Peking was incapable of delivering the goods. It invited, in other words, a vote of no confidence in Communism. It is surmised, therefore, that in order to bolster complete confidence in the economy and persuade the people that a heaven on earth could be constructed within decades, Peking decided to abandon the 1957 campaign to control fertility and revert to the *laissez-faire* policy of allowing the population increase.'[22]

It is possible that the Chinese authorities expected bumper crops in the next few years as a result of the Communes. But on the contrary, a variety of natural and man-made factors contributed to serious agriculture failures for the next three years. China had to expend her meagre foreign exchange to import large quantities of wheat from Canada and Australia. But the population began to increase and the Communes which could not grow more food were virtually abandoned. In 1962 voices were again raised in favour of birth control. The current campaign, if it can be called one, in favour of small families is subdued. Young men and women are being exhorted to postpone their marriages, and when married, limit their children to two. It is doubtful whether this policy is leading to a reduction in the nation's birth rate.

It must, however, be pointed out here that Communist China did not resort to a Marxist pro-natalist policy when she reversed her birth control campaign. Birth control information and supplies have been available on request through a decade and a half.

The latest (1964–6) Chinese official attitude on family planning can be gathered from an interview Edgar Snow, the American journalist, was given by Chou En-lai on January 23, 1964. In the course of the interview, Snow raised the question of sterilization as a solution to China's population problem and received the following answer:

"Snow: Recently I read in the Chinese press an interview between you, Premier Chou, and a factory worker, a husband and father of two children, who had been sterilized to avoid further increase. Is that practice now widely fostered?

Premier Chou (laughing): I'm afraid your question will give people the impression that I am a Marxist who advocates having no offspring. This is of course absurd. What you referred to was something I said on a specific occasion. We do believe in planned parenthood, but it is not easy to introduce it all at once in China and it is more difficult to achieve in the rural areas, where most of our people live, than in the cities. The first thing is to encourage later marriages. The years 20 to 30 are very important to mental and physical development—years when scientific and artistic growth often occur most rapidly. Among various means of planned parenthood, sterilization is only the last and only applies to those already burdened by too many children. (*Newly married couples are advised to try to limit their offspring to two. Among party members the small state subsidy for help in child support is limited to two children—as has been true at least since 1960.*—E. Snow.) Sterilization is practised in many countries of the world, but heretofore mainly on women, not men. That not only imposed inequality on women but what is more, as I have been told by many doctors, sterilization is simple and harmless for men while more complicated for women. However, in China, which has just freed itself from semi-feudalism, there is great resistance among men to the practice of sterilization to curtail excessive reproduction. Others are likely to say that such a man has been castrated; he has become a eunuch!

That is why I was particularly interested in encountering a factory worker who had subjected himself to sterilization. It happened that Chen Yi and I were visiting a factory where we found that a great many workers were encumbered by large families. Then I came upon a woman worker holding a child in her arms (*nursing mothers in China often place their infants in factory crèches during working hours, where they visit and care for them intermittently.* E. S.). I asked her how many children she had, she replied she had two, and then I asked if she approved of family planning. When she replied that her husband had been sterilized, I asked to meet him and discovered he was a deputy manager of the plant. He had simply decided that it was a good means and had adopted it; his factory superiors were not even aware of it. (*The magazine article referred to quoted the father as saying that sterilization had in no way impaired his health and his normal married life continued satisfactorily.* E. S.)"[23]

Communism, Population Pressure and War

During the past decade and a half, China has emerged from a century and more of national chaos and decline, civil war and foreign invasion to become almost a major power. Should the new China be welcomed into the community of nations or is she to be debarred from the civilized world as a growing threat to peace in Asia? The attempt to answer this important question must take into consideration several factors.

First, China is a big country in area. It is true that much of her land is useless from the point of view of agricultural development but she can settle people in the arid west with the aid of modern technology. While all big countries are not necessarily powerful, it is difficult in modern times for a small country to become a great power.

Her bigness would be an asset in case of any external aggression against her frontiers. A strong, industrialized and militarized Japan could not conquer China during her eight-year war (1937–45) because China was too large and she could always fight in depth. But this asset can also become a liability, for she has far-flung frontiers and a long coastline to defend. As she borders on many countries, she is also vulnerable to attack from more than one direction.

Secondly, China has the largest population of any country in the world. Here the question of the relation between population size and national power arises. It is obvious that a nation of teeming millions is not necessarily a powerful nation, if a majority of the millions do not have the basic, irreducible, minimum needs of human existence—food, clothing, housing, education, health services, etc.

But on the other hand, the correlation between total population numbers and national power stems from the size of the labour force. It has already been pointed out that China, from the point of view of her age pyramid, is a young nation. The latest available data revealed that the magnitude of the labour force is quite large. Under a centralized, totalitarian economy, a large population can become a formidable force as it can be directed to any desired end.

Another consideration is the military aspect of the population problem. The creation of a sizeable defence force—army, navy and air services and the ancillary personnel—demands people of a particular age group with adequate training and necessary skills. A large army, for instance, is possible only where there is a large population from which men of a required age group and the necessary physical condition can be drawn. A vast defence force can be raised and maintained, given a certain level of technical knowledge and equipment; and although in the next war the importance of the role of massive manpower may be doubtful, numbers can be used as a threat to encroach upon neighbouring territories.

Thirdly, China today is more industrialized than she was in 1949. Next to Japan and India she is the most industrialized Asian country and she may perhaps surpass them in the future. She has a wide range of raw materials brought to light through recent geological surveys, capital goods built with Russian help, a large reservoir of semi-skilled manpower and a backward but slowly changing technological base. These prerequsites are likely to accelerate the rapid and large-scale industrialization of China.

And fourth is China's atom bomb. It is true that the explosion of a simple atomic device does not make her a nuclear power. One does not know whether her first atomic explosion was merely a status symbol or the beginning of a serious nuclear pile. Students of this question wonder whether China at her present level of development can afford to keep up with the West's nuclear armament race and whether she can develop a modern delivery system. But China does not need ICBM's to put an atom bomb on Taiwan, South Vietnam or India. While China may seem like a poor boy from a starving family with an expensive firecracker to impress his neighbours, she has become the first Asian member of the exclusive nuclear club.

The last factor is China's disturbing orthodox Marxism which apparently cannot permit the possibility of the co-existence of conflicting political ideologies. She believes that nationalist, non-Communist Asian countries are really colonial, hanging on the apron strings of Western imperialist nations. She feels impelled with the zeal of a new convert to export the gospel according to Saint Marx to Asian and African countries. She seems to labour under the illusion that she is destined once again to become the Middle Kingdom of Asia, if not of the world. She seems to forget that Asia did not fight a relentless war for a century to throw off European imperialism in order to fall prey to another and even more depressing form of exploitation.

Will a strong and united China, rapidly industrialized and mechanized and with a growing fighting force be a source of aggression in the future? Will she, with the economic and political system she embraces, use her population numbers as a pretext for a demand for *Lebensraum*? Is China's rape of Tibet and aggression against and illegal occupation of India's frontier territory merely the beginning of a more serious threat to the territorial integrity and peace of south-east Asia?

It is obvious from all that the Communist Chinese leaders have been saying and doing since they came to power that they are motivated by two major objectives. The first is to build China into a strong nation on the basis of an industrial economy and military might. The second objective is the penetration and subversion of the south-east Asian countries. This she is trying to do with propaganda and when possible through the support of local national Communist parties.

It is reasonable to believe that no matter what Communist China does in the next decade, her population numbers will certainly be an important factor in the decisions she makes. China's traditional desire for expansion, Communist ideology, and population pressure are an alarming combination.[24] In a sense, China's population is Asia's problem.

NOTES

1. Wu, Yuan-li, Francis P. Hoeber, *et al.*, *The Economic Potential of Communist China* (Menlo Park, Calif., SRI, 1963), p. 2.
2. For an account of the census drama, see S. Chandrasekhar, *China's Population: Census and Vital Statistics* (Oxford University Press, 1961). Second edition. (Hereafter cited as Chandrasekhar, 1961).
3. S. K. Tai, *The 1953 Population Census of China* (Calcutta, Indian Statistical Institute, 1956), mimeographed.
4. S. Chandrasekhar (1961), p. 49.
5. For a brief discussion of the Chinese Communist attitude towards their minorities, see John DeFrancis, 'National and Minority Policies', *The Annals* of the American Academy of Political and Social Science, September 1951.

6. S. Chandrasekhar, 1961, p. 3. The death rate for 1954 has been changed on the basis of later evidence.
7. S. Chandrasekhar, *Red China: An Asian View* (New York, Praeger, 1964). Fifth impression. (Hereafter cited as Chandrasekhar, 1964), pp. 9–10.
8. Mrs Joan Robinson, a British economist who visited China in 1964, writes: 'But the census (which has not yet been published) seems to have shown a disturbingly high rate of growth of population. A propaganda campaign is going on for family planning and later marriage.' (She implies that a second census *was* taken.) 'What is New in China?', *Eastern Horizon* (Hong Kong), January 1965.
9. 1949–57—Official estimates and 1958—unofficial estimate. S. Chandrasekhar, 1961, p. 58, and Wu, Yuan-li, *et al.*, *The Economic Potential of Communist China* (1963), p. 16.
10. Wang, Ya-nan, *Marxist Population Theory and China's Population* (in Chinese) (Peking, 1956).
11. E. Stuart Kirby, 'Peiping's Growing Dilemma—Population', *Problems of Communism* (Washington, DC), March–April 1958.
12. Summarized from *Capital* (Moscow, 1957), Vol. 4, Part 2, pp. 110–11.
13. I. Pisarev, *The Population of the USSR* (Moscow, The Progress Publishers, 1963), p. 27.
14. Pai Chien-hua's statement in *Jen-min Jih-pao*, November 1, 1956.
15. *People's Daily*, Peking, September 19, 1954.
16. See S. Chandrasekhar, 'China's Population Problems' in *Contemporary China* (Hong Kong University Press, 1960), Vol. III, pp. 22–3.
17. *Kwang-ming Jih-pao*, Peking, December 19, 1956.
18. S. Chandrasekhar, *op. cit.*
19. S. Chandrasekhar, *op. cit.*
20. The material here is drawn from my earlier writings on this subject. For a full discussion, see S. Chandrasekhar (1964), pp. 122–68.
21. Ma-Yinchu, 'A New Theory of Population' in *Current Background* (Hong Kong), No. 469, July 27, 1957.
22. S. Chandrasekhar (1960), p. 27.
23. *The New York Times*, February 3, 1964.
24. Georg Borgstrom writes: 'Will China advance further toward the vast expanses of Siberia? Is this the true reason for strained relations between her and the Soviet Bloc? In his memoirs, Reynaud, former Prime Minister of France, gave an account of a conversation he had with Khrushchev. The latter brought up his favourite subject, the reunification of Germany, and asked outright why it was that the West was so keen to have a United Germany. Reynaud replied: "Because within twenty-five years you will have a billion Chinese to deal with." For several minutes Khrushchev was speechless, then he changed the subject. "But I am sure that he understood what I meant," Reynaud adds.'

    In a speech that President Charles de Gaulle made in November 1959, he said: 'The Soviet Union, so endowed with land, mines, factories, and other riches, now stands face to face with the yellow hordes of China, innumerable, impoverished, unswerving and ambitious. They are casting their eyes upon the open expanses of Siberia, where one day they intend to spread.' Georg Borgstrom, *The Hungry Planet* (New York, Macmillan Co., 1965), p. 119.

BIBLIOGRAPHY

Aird, John S., 'The Size, Composition, and Growth of the Population of Mainland China', *International Population Statistical Reports* (Washington, DC, US Bureau of the Census, Series P-90, No. 15, 1955).

Chandrasekhar, S., 'Mao's War with the Chinese Family: Remaking China's Traditional Patterns of Society', *The New York Times Magazine*, May 17, 1959.

'China's Population Problems: A Report', *Population Review* (Madras), July 1959, pp. 17–38.

'The Human Inflation of Red China', *The New York Times Magazine*, December 6, 1959.

'China's Population Problems', in E. S. Kirby (Ed.) *Contemporary China* (Hong Kong, University Press, 1960), Vol. III, pp. 10–40.

'China's Population is Asia's Problem', *The Hindu* Sunday edition (Madras), May 28, 1961.

'Red China's Population', *Atlantic Monthly*, December, 1961.

China's Population: Census and Vital Statistics (London; Oxford University Press, 1961). Second edition.

Communist China Today (London, Asia Publishing House, 1964). Fourth revised edition.

Red China: An Asian View (New York, Praeger, 1964). Fifth impression, Chapter X on 'China's Population Problems'.

Hu, Chang-tu, *et al.*, *China: Its People, Its Society, Its Culture* (New Haven, Conn., HRAF Press, 1960).

Chen, Ta, 'New China's Population Census of 1953 and Its Relations to National Reconstruction and Demographic Research', *Bulletin de l'Institut International de Statistique* (Stockholm, 1957), Vol. 36, No. 2.

Cressey, G. B., *Land of the 600 Millions—A Geography of China* (New York, McGraw Hill, 1956).

Emerson, John Philip, 'Population Increases and Manpower Utilization in Mainland China', A paper presented at the Annual Meeting of the Association of Asian Studies, March 28, 1961.

Ho, Ping-ti, *Studies on the Population of China, 1368–1953* (Cambridge, Mass., Harvard University Press, 1959).

Kirby, E. Stuart (Ed.), *Contemporary China* (Hong Kong University Press, 1957–65), Annual Volume.

Li, Choh-Ming, *The Statistical System of Communist China* (Berkeley, The University of California Press, 1962).

Pressat, Roland, 'La Population de la Chine et son economie', *Population* (Paris), October–December 1958.

Scott, J. C., *Health and Agriculture in China* (London, Faber, 1952).

Snow, Edgar, *The Other Side of the River: Red China Today* (New York, The Random House, 1962).

Tien, H. Y., 'Birth Control in Mainland China: Ideology and Politics', *Milbank Memorial Fund Quarterly*, July 1963.

Ullman, Morris B., *Cities of Mainland China: 1953 and 1958. International Statistical Reports* (Washington, DC, US Bureau of the Census, Series P-95, No. 59, 1960).

Wu, Yuan-li, Francis P. Hoeber, and Mabel M. Rockwell, *The Economic Potential of Communist China* (Menlo Park, Calif., Stanford Research Institute, 1963), 3 volumes.

Wu, Yuan-li, *The Economy of Communist China: An Introduction* (New York, Praeger, 1965).

Yang, C. K., *A Chinese Village in Early Communist Transition* (Cambridge, Mass., The Technology Press, 1959).

CHAPTER 3

INDIA'S POPULATION: FACT, PROBLEM AND POLICY

BY S. CHANDRASEKHAR

I

THE FACTS

Introduction

LOCATED on a vast 'tongue-shaped promontory that juts southwards from the continent of Asia', India is well marked off from the rest of Asia by mountains and seas, stamping the country with an undeniable geographical unity as well as isolation. The country is bounded by the snow-capped Himalayas in the north, and, tapering southward, by the Bay of Bengal on the south-east and the Arabian sea on the south-west. On the east a series of mountain ranges separates India from independent Burma. To the east also lies East Pakistan, surrounded by the Indian territories of West Bengal, Assam and Tripura. On the north-east, besides independent Nepal, lie the two states of Sikkim and Bhutan, attached to India by special treaties and as such considered part of India. West Pakistan and Afghanistan border India on the north-west. In the south, the Gulf of Munnar and the Palk Strait separate India from independent Ceylon. The Andaman and Nicobar Islands in the Bay of Bengal and the Laccadive, Minicoy and Amindivi Islands in the Arabian Sea are parts of India's territory. India has a land frontier 9,425 miles long and a coastline of 3,535 miles.

With an area of 1·2 million square miles (about a third of the area of the continental United States excluding Alaska), India stretches about 2,000 miles from Kashmir in the north to Cape Comorin in the south and about 1,850 miles from Assam in the east to Gujarat in the west. The country lies entirely in the northern hemisphere and extends between latitudes 8° and 37° and longitudes 68° and 97°.

India's Population Growth

In the world today India ranks second in population numbers (Communist China tops the list) and seventh in land area. Today she claims about 15 per cent of the world's population on 2·4 per cent of the world's land area. Although India is only about two fifths the size of the continental United States, she shelters about two and a half times the United States population.

Before the growth of India's population is examined it should be pointed out that Indian census figures and particularly vital statistics are somewhat defective. Despite the great efforts made by the Government of India, the data continues to be unreliable and the series over a period of years must be taken more as revealing trends and less as exact statements.[1]

The population of undivided India, according to a rough estimate, was about 130 million in AD 1600.[2] During the next two and a half centuries (1850) the numbers, according to several rough estimates, increased to about 150 million[3] as high birth rates were nearly matched by high death

TABLE 1. *Growth of India's Population: 1891–1961*

Census year	Population in millions (adjusted to the present area)	Increase or decrease in millions	Percentage variation during the preceding decade
1891	236·7	—	—
1901	236·3	−0·4	−0·20
1911	252·1	15·8	5·73
1921	251·4	−0·7	−0·31
1931	279·0	27·6	11·01
1941	316·7	37·7	14·22
1951	361·1	44·4	13·31
1961	439·2	78·1	21·50

Source: *Census of India, 1951, Part 1-A* and *Census of India, 1961, Paper 1, 1962.*

rates. Several factors contributed to the slow increase, among them the wars the European imperialist nations waged against the people of India as well as the wars between Indian rulers for political supremacy. These eighteenth-century wars contributed to extreme political instability, famines and epidemics resulting in heavy mortality. However, with the establishment of British rule and the restoration of a measure of internal peace in the sense of averted wars, and the setting up of a skeleton of health and medical services, the population began to grow slowly up to the turn of the twentieth century and rapidly after 1921.

The first and incomplete census of the sub-continent was taken in 1871–2 and 206 million people were counted. In 1881 the second and relatively complete census for the same area yielded 256 million. Both these census figures represent more approximations than exact figures. The third and complete decennial census was taken in 1891 and from this year the series are more or less reliable.

The growth of population for 1891 to 1961 is summarized in Table 1.

In 1891, as shown in Table 1, India's population (adjusted to the present area) was 236 million. In 1921, three decades later, the population had increased to 251 million—only a 15 million increase in 30 years because of epidemics and famine. During this period cholera and plague took an annual toll of a million deaths and an estimate puts India's loss during the world-wide influenza epidemic of 1918–19 at about 60 million. During the next thirty years, 1921–51, the population increased not by another 15 million but by 110 million. And during the last single decade, 1951–61, the population increased by 78·1 million. In mid-1965 India's population was estimated to be about 475 million.

It must be remembered that the last decade's increase of 78 million is more than the entire population of any country in Europe, with the exception of the Soviet Union, or of any country in Latin America. India's total population today (though only second largest in the world) equals that of 55 states of Africa and Latin America put together.

What are the factors behind this great increase in numbers? To begin with, India in 1951 had a large population and even a small and nominal rate of increase would have yielded an impressive decennial addition. But the 21·5 per cent rate of increase is not small and the addition of 78 million was unexpected. An explanation of the country's population growth is to be found in the nation's relatively high and rapidly declining death rates. These in themselves are products of such demographic features as age and sex composition.

Age and Sex Composition

Age and sex are the two basic biological characteristics of a population that exercise considerable influence on the various aspects of the composition and structure of a population. The importance of the age composition is obvious. A person's age is the decisive factor in such questions as the age at which a person can or must enter school, enter the labour force, exercise the franchise, get married, retire from work, and so on. The age structure has direct repercussions on the death and marriage rates, the economic and occupational composition of a population and certain cultural and social activities of a community.

According to the 1961 census, 40·2 per cent of the total population was in the 0–14 age group, 47·9 per cent in the 15–49 and 11·9 per cent in the 50 and over age groups. Thus young and more fecund people predominate in India's population. This means that a relatively large burden rests on the productive active population and that population numbers are bound to increase at an even higher rate than they have in the past.

As for the sex ratio, it has equally important socio-economic bearings. The sex ratio, which is affected by past fertility, mortality and migration, plays an important role in determining the birth and death rates of a community. Females have a lower death rate than males because nature has equipped them better to meet disease (biologically it is man and not woman who is the weaker vessel) and because males are usually in more hazardous occupations. If the females, therefore, constitute less than half the total population, the crude death rate will be affected unfavourably. Secondly, the sex ratio affects both the marriage rate and the number of legitimate births. Thirdly, an adverse sex ratio, in the sense of relative scarcity of females, may sometimes lead to prostitution and other social problems. It is paradoxical that a society which cannot provide mature brides for all its marriageable males can spare women for professional prostitution.

The sex ratio of a population varies from year to year, and from region to region. It is determined not only at conception but also by selective death rates at various stages, by war, occupational distribution, migration, migration differentials and socio-cultural attitudes towards the role of either sex in society.

The sex ratios at conception, birth and maturity, are known respectively as primary, secondary and tertiary but data on primary ratio are not available. Since normal meiosis leads to the production of x-bearing and y-bearing sperm in equal number, one would expect that the chances are equal that any particular child conceived would be a girl or a boy. Yet the secondary sex ratio is invariably high—that is an excess of male births. This appears true of India. It might appear that this inequality in favour of males is the product of greater mortality of female embryos. But the truth apparently is the opposite for more male than female foetuses are likely to be lost in advanced pregnancy. According to some biologists 'the ultimate explanation would seem to be that natural selection is operating on the sex ratio in a rather interesting way, to produce an equality of the sexes at maturity'.[4]

The sex ratio in India (which is defined by the Indian census as 'the number of females per 1,000 males' after the definition adopted in the United Kingdom and unlike that in the United States where it is 'the number of males per 100 females') for the last six census years (1901 to 1961) was as follows: 963, 953, 940, 934, 947 and 941 females per 1,000 males. The relative scarcity of females or the excessive masculinity of the Indian population has been a significant feature of Indian demography. There is some controversy over this phenomenon. In the absence of reliable statistical and other evidence it is difficult to say whether this adverse sex ratio reveals any genetic trait in the Indian population. Some maintain that it is merely an underenumeration of females. It is probable that it is culturally and socially conditioned selective female mortality rates at infancy and reproductive age groups. Besides the available evidence does not reveal that this imbalance does not occur at birth.

The observations of the 1931 census commissioner of India have been by and large substantiated by the results of the 1951 and 1961 censuses. 'The figures of India's population by sexes show a further continuation of the steady fall in the proportion of females to males that has been going on since 1901. The female infant is definitely better equipped by nature for survival than the male, but in India the advantages she has at birth are probably neutralized in infancy by comparative neglect and in adolescence by the strain of bearing children too early and too often.'[5]

Density and Literacy

Several economic, social and demographic characteristics of India's population are relevant to any serious discussion of the dynamics of

TABLE 2. *Density per Square Mile—India: 1951–61 and Percentage of Literacy in the Indian States: 1961*

State	Density per square mile 1951	1961	Percentage of literacy in 1961 (for all age groups)
Andhra Pradesh	291	339	21·2
Assam	188	252	27·4
Bihar	577	691	18·4
Gujarat	225	286	30·5
Jammu and Kashmir	38	42	11·0
Kerala	903	1,127	46·8
Madhya Pradesh	152	189	17·1
Madras	598	669	31·4
Maharashtra	270	333	29·8
Mysore	261	318	25·4
Orissa	243	292	21·7
Punjab	342	430	24·2
Rajasthan	121	153	15·2
Uttar Pradesh	556	649	17·6
West Bengal	778	1,032	29·3
Union Territories	78	114	—
All India	312	370	24·0

India's population. But for lack of space only a few of the more important aspects can be touched upon here briefly.

As a result of the unprecedented population increase during the 1951–61 decade the density of population per square mile for the country as a whole (including Jammu and Kashmir) increased from 312 per square mile in 1951 to 370 in 1961. The density of the various states of the Indian Union for 1951 and 1961 are presented in Table 2.

Of the sixteen states (including the Union territories) Kerala ranks highest with a density of 1,127 per square mile followed by West Bengal with 1,032 per square mile. Kerala has always been a crowded region and it maintains its status despite a slow rate of natural increase in comparison with other states, and relatively increasing migration from this state to other parts of the Indian Union. West Bengal's difficulties are traceable both to a large natural increase and an almost daily influx of displaced persons, as well as refugees from East Pakistan, Nepal and Tibet and immigrants from other parts of the country, particularly Bihar and Assam. Madras, Bihar and Punjab are relatively less densely populated while the rest of the states have less than 340 per square mile.

According to the 1961 census only 28·3 per cent of the population aged 5 and over were literate (and 24 per cent for all age groups), the test for literacy being the ability to read and write a post card. The corresponding figure for 1951 was 19·2. Thus, the literates have increased but the illiterates have increased much more in view of the great increase in the population over the decade.

Literacy in the rural areas is low, for in 1961 only 23·5 per cent of males and 7·5 per cent of females (15·7 per cent for both sexes) in the rural areas were literate, and the rural population is 82 per cent of the total population of the country. Of the urban population, who have relatively better and more educational opportunities, 31·2 per cent of the males and 22·5 per cent of the females (27·3 per cent for both sexes) were literate. Compared to the earlier census years the gap between male and female literacy levels seems to be widening.

The position of literacy in different age groups shows what a great leeway India has to make up to attain compulsory primary and secondary education. Of all the persons in the 5–19 age group only 54·4 per cent were literate; that is, almost half the total teenage population, largely in the rural areas, have no opportunities of completing either a primary or a high school education.

Among the states, the percentage of literacy for all age groups and both sexes was highest in Kerala with 46·8 followed by Gujarat and Madras with 30·5 and 31·4 respectively. Literacy rates are lowest among the Hindi-speaking states of Uttar Pradesh, Madhya Pradesh and Rajasthan. A comparison of the literacy levels among the states between 1951 and 1961 shows that Madras has scored the highest increase (9·4 per cent) while Bengal registered the least increase (5·1 per cent).

Rural–Urban Ratio

Though India continues to be a predominantly agricultural and rural country, the urban proportion of the total population has been slowly increasing from 11 to 18 per cent between 1901 and 1961[6] as shown in Table 3. The rate of growth of urban population has been quite slow from 1881 to 1941 but during the last two decades the tempo of urbanization has been relatively increased. It is interesting to note that during the last census decade the rate of urban growth has been greater than that of the rural population. Three factors possibly account for the rapid growth of the urban population for the period 1941–61. The traditional rural exodus caused by the economic rural 'push' mechanism has been stepped up by the gradual industrialization of urban India, the greater natural increase of urban population contrary to general expectation,

TABLE 3. *Percentage Increase of India's Rural–Urban Population: 1901–61*

Year	Percentage of population Rural	Urban	Decade	Decennial growth rate Rural	Urban
1901	89·0	11·0	1901–11	6·4	0·3
1911	90·0	10·0	1911–21	−1·3	8·3
1921	89·0	11·0	1921–31	9·9	19·1
1931	88·0	12·0	1931–41	11·8	31·9
1941	86·0	14·0	1941–51	8·8	41·4
1951	83·0	17·0	1951–61	20·6	26·4
1961	82·0	18·0	—	—	—

TABLE 4. *Growth of Cities and Towns: 1901–61*

	SIZE OF POPULATION					
Year	100,000 and above Class I	Between 50,000 and 100,000 Class II	Between 20,000 and 50,000 Class III	Between 10,000 and 20,000 Class IV	Between 5,000 and 10,000 Class V	Less than 5,000 Class VI
1901	27	45	148	422	768	500
1911	25	38	157	390	756	547
1921	28	49	172	398	780	623
1931	32	56	224	484	856	609
1941	49	87	272	553	988	478
1951	74	111	375	670	1,189	638
1961	107	141	515	817	844	266

TABLE 5. *Growth of Selected Indian Cities, 1951–61*

Town	1961 population in thousands	Percent decennial increase
Greater Bombay	4,152	38·7
Calcutta	2,927	8·5
Delhi Corporation	2,062	84·1
Madras	1,729	22·1
Ahmedabad	1,150	37·4
Hyderabad	1,119	9·4
Bangalore	1,094	40·4
Kanpur	895	37·9
Nagpur	644	43·3
Poona	598	24·2
Lucknow	595	33·9
Howrah	513	18·2

and the arrival of the displaced rural Hindu population from West and East Pakistan into Indian cities.

As for towns and cities, in 1961 India had seven cities with a population of a million and more and 107 towns with a population of 100,000 and more. And less than 40 million people lived in these towns and cities. In other words, about a half of the urban population lives in towns of 100,000 or more. The growth of cities and towns between 1901 and 1961 and the growth of selected cities during the last decade are presented in Tables 4 and 5.

Occupational Composition

Perhaps no aspect of a population throws as much light on the economic development of a country as its occupational composition. A comparison of India's working force during the last six census years reveals that the

TABLE 6. *Percentage Distribution of Working Force by Occupation and Sex: 1961 census*

Occupation	Males	Percentage Females	Persons
Cultivators	51·46	55·72	52·82
Agricultural Labour	13·42	23·86	16·71
Mining, Quarrying, Livestock, Fishing, Forestry, Plantations, etc.	3·10	2·00	2·75
Manufacturing—household	4·51	6·82	5·25
Other household industries	1·20	1·03	1·14
Manufacturing—non-household	5·56	1·33	4·22
Construction	1·41	0·41	1·09
Trade and Commerce	5·29	1·37	4·05
Transport and Communication	2·28	0·11	1·59
Other Services	11·77	7·35	10·38
Total	100·0	100·0	100·0

percentage has been steadily declining from 47 in 1901 to 43 in 1961, but the comparability is not strictly valid because of the periodic changes in the definition of the various occupational concepts. However, a comparson of the last two census returns shows how little progress India has registered in the direction of industrialization, judged by the simple test of the percentage of population dependent on agriculture and industry. The occupational composition of the working force (15–59) of India's population reveals that about 70 per cent is engaged in agriculture, despite considerable efforts at industrialization since 1947. What is noteworthy is that despite this large number of people working on the land, the country is chronically deficient in food supply and only 20 per cent of the labour force is absorbed by the secondary and tertiary sectors. In most advanced and industrialized countries the labour force employed in agriculture—which in these countries is a commercial and paying proposition and not a pathetic way of life—is between 5 and 15 per cent. This single index reveals more about the arrested nature of Indian economic development than anything else could. What is obviously needed is an agricultural revolution and apparently something is wrong with the scale of priorities adopted by the Indian planning authorities.

India's High Birth Rate

The average birth rate, on the basis of incomplete data, was estimated to be between 35 and 40 per 1,000 in 1951–61, and apart from fluctuations usual for such a high figure it has not registered any serious decline

TABLE 7. *India's Birth and Death Rates: 1901–61*

	Birth rate		Death rate	
Years	Registered	Estimated	Registered	Estimated
1901–10	40·20	52·4	35·10	46·8
1911–20	36·94	48·1	34·14	47·2
1921–30	34·55	46·4	26·29	36·3
1931–40	34·17	45·2	22·99	31·2
1941–50	27·32	43·0	20·10	30·0
1951–60	29·81	40·0	19·13	22·0

Source: Government of India, Department of Statistics, 1963. The estimated rates for all years except for 1911–20 were calculated on the basis of a quasi-stable population model while for 1911–20 the figure was obtained by the reverse survival method.

during the last few years. And today (1965) the nation's birth rate is around 40 per 1,000.

There are various reasons why India's birth rate continues to be high. There is the well-known feature of the universality of the married state in India. That is, everyone in India sooner or later, usually sooner, gets married. Marriage is not merely a necessary social institution but a quasi-religious duty. As an individual's economic security or emotional maturity are seldom a prerequisite to marriage and as there is no individual choice, by and large, in obtaining a husband or wife, there is no economic or emotional deterrent to marriage. Thus spinsters and bachelors are a rare phenomenon in India and nearly every adult male and female in the country participates in reproduction.

Secondly, early marriages are still the rule in India. True, child marriages have virtually disappeared. But though thirty-two years have elapsed since the Child Marriage Restraint Act (the Sarada Act) was passed in 1929, millions of girls still marry early.[7] In the rural areas nearly 80 per cent of all teenagers are married and the 1951 census enumerated some ten million girls and boys married below the age of consent (18 for males and 14 for females). It has been estimated that the mean age at marriage of Indian females of all religions was 15·6 years according to the data available in the 1951 census.[8]

Thirdly, some relief from population pressure was obtained in the past from an obscurantist feature of the Hindu social scene—the social (not legal) ban on widow remarriage.[9] There are about 25 million widows of all ages (including 'virgin widows') who normally do not marry. Even widowers do not marry widows as a rule. But India is fast changing and, of late, there are some men who are willing to marry eligible and unencumbered widows. This welcome modern trend which negates the traditional custom of banning widow remarriage and with-

TABLE 8. *Infant Mortality Rates in India: 1901–61*
(Quinquennial averages)

Period	Infant mortality rate	Period	Infant mortality rate
1901–6	215	1931–6	174
1906–11	228	1936–41	161
1911–16	204	1941–6	161
1916–21	219	1946–51	134
1921–6	174	1951–6	113
1926–31	178	1956–61	98

drawing these women from participating in reproduction is contributing its small share to the population problem.

And last, there is the absence of any effective, widespread family planning habit among the rural population who constitute some 82 per cent of India's total population. Birth control even in the cities is of such recent origin that it has not yet become a part of the marital mores of the people. All these factors contribute their share to India's high birth rate.

However, the decisive factor behind the growth of India's population is the decline in the nation's death rate. Here again, the country's statistics are none too accurate. But the estimated death rate shows a steady decline from 42·6 per 1,000 in 1901 to 27·4 in 1951 and 16·0 in 1961.

Even more revealing is the decline in the Infant Mortality Rate (that is, the number of infants under the age of one year who die per 1,000 live births in the course of a year) which is a better and more sensitive index of the total public health situation and cultural milieu of the country. The rate has dropped from 232 in 1901 to 98 in 1960. While this rate is considerably higher than those prevailing in advanced Western countries, it represents considerable progress for India.[10]

The child and maternal mortality rates have also registered similar decreases during the last half a century. And the last decade has witnessed a greater decline in the over-all death rate than in the entire preceding fifty years.

This dramatic decline in the death rate has been brought about by the Government's action in various directions: an increase in trained medical and para-medical personnel, DDT spraying, BCG vaccination for tuberculosis, the services of trained midwives, the spread of a modicum of health education and services, American technical aid, particularly in malaria eradication, and the overall assistance of the World Health Organization and the Colombo Plan.

The successful attack on such diseases as malaria and tuberculosis has a kind of cumulative effect which has not been adequately studied in the developing countries. For example, malaria not only kills but leaves

TABLE 9. *Expectation of Life at Birth in India: 1901–61*

Census year	Expectation of life at birth in India		
	Male	Female	Total population
1901	23·63	23·96	23·6
1911	22·59	23·31	22·6
1921	19·42	20·91	19·4
1931	26·91	26·56	26·9
1941	32·09	31·37	32·1
1951	32·45	31·66	42·1
1961	47·00	46·33	46·6

Source: Census of India, 1931, 1951 and 1961.

those victims who do not succumb totally debilitated, unproductive and an easy prey to numerous infections. Therefore malaria eradication not only lowers the death rate, but raises the individual's overall resistance to disease and, what is more, increases the birth rate. In response to all this, not only has the general death rate declined but the expectation of life at birth has increased from 23 years in 1931 to 47·5 in 1961, leading eventually to a rise in the birth rate.

And if all the health and medical projects included in India's Third Five-Year Plan (1961–6)[11] are carried out, the death rate (which is still high compared to certain advanced countries) will register even further declines. While there is no question that all this is extremely welcome from the humanitarian point of view, it is estimated on the assumption of the current rate of annual increase of 2·2 per cent that India's present population of 480 million can reach about a billion in thirty-five years or by about AD 2000.[12]

Of course, a population figure in itself—no matter how many millions—does not mean very much. If India had the necessary resources and technological skills, she could possibly transform the present liability of such massive human numbers into a positive asset. But unfortunately her natural resources, capital, scientific and technological know-how are severely limited in relation to what is needed to raise the very low level of living of her 480 million people.

Another important fact that must be remembered is that to raise a country's level of living a variety of natural resources, not just agricultural production and food, are necessary. While agricultural production can be increased up to a point, land and other natural resources do not increase with the growth of population. We tend to forget the simple fact that the total land area and the natural resources of India and the world are limited and non-renewable entities, irrespective of the number of human beings. Short of emigrating to the Moon or Mars, perhaps theoretical possibilities in the remote future, man today has to look to the finite earth and its limited renewable and non-renewable resources both for his habitat and food supply.

II

THE PROBLEM

From the demographic point of view, the population of any country, whether it be underdeveloped, developing or advanced, can become a problem under certain circumstances.

A nation in the world today may have too many people or too few people. As we are in the midst of a global population explosion, we are apt to forget that there has been and can be such a thing as a problem of underpopulation. There can also be a problem from the point of view of age—that is, when the majority in a population is either too young or too old. When the young and the old age groups are disproportionately large, the burden of supporting these two unproductive ends of the age scale fall on the small percentage of the gainfully employed.

Any aspect of a population's composition can create a serious economic, social or cultural problem for a country under certain circumstances. And, broadly speaking, a population problem can be examined from either the quantitative or the qualitative points of view, or both. However, under present circumstances the question of sheer quantity will continue to be the major problem in most underdeveloped countries.

The qualitative improvement of population—eugenics—can be positive or negative. While societal agreement is not possible on the positive aspect, or the most desirable type of human being, societal agreement on the negative aspect of eugenics is easy and readily available. No argument is needed to prove that our society would do well to reduce the incidence of blindness, deafness, imbecility and various types of mental illness. Every infant has a right to be born healthy in the fullest sense of the term and to grow up into healthy adulthood. Anyone who is familiar with such statistics as are available in India on this question need hardly to be told that the *quality* of India's population needs improvement.

As for quantity, the most desirable population number is the one that permits the maximum production, the highest standard of living, political stability and economic security, and adequate freedom and leisure for the pursuit of cultural values. Theoretically, there is such a thing as an optimum size of population for every country under a particular economic and political system. As Sir Julian Huxley points out, one could not carry on an advanced modern civilization with a population the size of a bushman's tribe, any more than life could evolve the mental powers of a higher mammal in an organism the size of an amoeba. A land animal ten times the weight of an elephant would be biologically extremely inefficient just as a committee of two hundred members would be socially inefficient.[13]

What then should be the quantitative optimum for India? An examination of India's present standard of living in the light of the Government's desire to raise it substantially, shows that the greatest obstacle in the path of overall economic development is the alarming rate of population growth.

The central problem of India's economy is simply poverty or the low level of living of the great majority of the people. It is true that the standard of living of a country is a relative matter and what is a poor level of living in one area may be relative affluence in another area. Therefore, while there may be disagreement on what is an optimum or acceptable level of living for various countries, there cannot be any doubt about the basic minimum of goods and services needed for healthy and purposeful living.

India's Standard of Living

What is the standard of living of the average citizen of India? Technical definitions apart, a standard of living can be simply defined as the level of consumption of the basic requisites of civilized human existence in terms of food, clothing, housing, educational opportunities, health facilities, leisure and certain cultural amenities. Recent and accurate statistics on all these matters are not available but they are not really necessary, for even a casual look at the conditions of life in India show how distressing life is for the average man. While the level of living in general, even in the villages, has improved somewhat since freedom, thanks to India's three Five-Year Plans, it is still far from what the Government and people want it to be.

Food is India's biggest problem. The country suffers from almost perennial hunger. According to a recent United Nations Survey,[14] four out of every five people, or 80 per cent of the three billion people of the world, have never had and will not have in the foreseeable future what an American, Canadian or European family take for granted as a good square meal. And a great majority of the underfed and the unfed live in Asia, particularly China and India. The per capita daily consumption in 1960 in terms of calories was 1,950 in India as against an estimated minimum requirement of 2,300 to 2,500 calories.[15] India wages a daily battle on the food front but she is never out of the woods, and, like China, she seems to alternate between fat and lean years depending upon that unpredictable factor, the monsoon.

The present low food consumption of about 2,000 calories is in striking contrast to the 3,000–3,400 calories consumed in Canada, the United States of America and countries in north-west Europe. Therefore, if the levels of consumption, both in quality and quantity, recommended by nutrition experts are taken into consideration, at least some fifty millions in India suffer from serious malnutrition. Good nutrition is not an end in itself but an effective means to many desirable ends. It not only promotes sound health and lessens morbidity (reducing the nation's medical bill) but increases the nation's productivity and promotes overall physical and mental well-being. Thus the country suffers more than hunger because of her low consumption of food.

As for clothing, thanks to India's tropical climate her needs are not great. Even so, many millions in the country go about semi-naked. The per capita consumption of cotton textiles is less than twenty yards per year despite the fact that India is a major cotton producing and textile manufacturing country. The present level of consumption is low even in the context of the tropical climate and the fact that agriculture is the major occupation.

The housing situation is no better. Barring palaces and mansions, which probably house well under a million people, middle-class housing with certain elementary amenities takes care of the needs of only a minority of our population. A great majority—almost the entire rural population—live in backward and blighted areas from the point of view of minimum amenities and sometimes of even basic necessities. As for urban areas, land has become so valuable and population pressure so intense in the major cities that there is incredible overcrowding with its inevitable consequence of unenviable slums. Here the difficulty is twofold. Not only is housing not increasing sufficiently to meet existing needs, but what is worse, a part of the existing housing is annually lost because of both age and lack of repair. The provision of even low cost housing for the existing population appears to be a formidable problem not to speak of housing for the future population. It is no longer shocking to see people sleeping on the city pavements.[16]

As for literacy and primary education, more than half the world's population lives in unlettered darkness. While Asia claims more than half of the world's population, her share of illiterates is disproportionately high. India's illiteracy rate is about 70 per cent. Leaving aside adult illiterates, the Government is finding it difficult to provide sufficient educational resources to catch up with the nation's birth rate. The supply of trained teachers, textbooks, school buildings and equipment is not adequate to cope with the swelling army of youngsters of school-going age. Sustained literacy (not literates who lapse into illiteracy) is a minimum requisite for the proper exercise of franchise, for predominant illiteracy and successful parliamentary democracy are incompatible.

In brief, while India's agricultural and industrial production have been impressive during the last decade in relation to her position earlier, and advances and improvements are being registered in every sector of the economy year by year, the level of living of a vast majority of India's people continues to be below the poverty line.

In fact, the entire vicious circle starts with incredibly low incomes. The gain in national income is largely eaten up by the unprecedented increase in population numbers. India's total national income, for instance, rose by nearly 40 per cent during her first two Five-Year Plan periods (1951–61) but the per capita income increased by only 19 per cent during the same period. Here again, although the per capita annual income has also increased a little during the last seventeen years of freedom, the present per capita figure of $70.00 still puts India at the bottom of the list of the world's major countries. And the real income and the consumption levels of the average Indian have not increased significantly.[17]

Thus the basic economic problem in India is really demographic. A statement of India's population problem can be summarized as follows: How can India raise the standard of living of her people (and this means more food, goods and services for everybody) and cut down the still relatively high death rate (this means keeping alive more people and taking care of them) when it is so difficult to support the existing population even at a low standard of living, *if the population continues to increase by about twelve million every year*? In other words, demographically India is running so fast that economically, despite all the progress being made, she is almost standing still.

It is obvious that with a slower rate of population growth, along with steadily improving agricultural and industrial production, India's standard of living is bound to rise. But India's economic and demographic experience seems to show that even with slight improvements in living conditions, population numbers tend to increase further. What is more, as levels of living rise and as India becomes modernized her traditional social customs and taboos (such as the ban on the remarriage of widows) are given up, resulting in a temporary rise in fertility. Therefore, in the near future, as India advances materially, her total numbers are bound to increase. This aspect of the question is apt to be forgotten in general discussions of India's population problem.

Since India's alarming increase of some ten million people each year defers or nullifies most programmes for improvement in education, public health, sanitation or rural reconstruction, the need for a national population policy cannot be over-emphasized. It must be based on and balanced between the country's population numbers (present and potential) and the basic irreducible needs of the people on the one hand, and the available resources (developed and latent) within the context of the available technological knowledge on the other.

III

TOWARDS A POPULATION POLICY?

What is a population policy? The size and composition of a nation's population are altered by many factors without deliberate human intention or intervention. The failure of a monsoon, the discovery of a drug, the invention of a machine, the devastation of an earthquake or the advent of war may exercise considerable influence upon births, deaths and migration within a country. However, a population policy is a deliberate effort by a national government to change the size and composition of a country's population through some kind of legislation or governmental directive. Most countries' population policies in the past have been pro-natalist involving cash bonuses to families with a certain number of children or modifying the tax structure in favour of large families, and making available certain social services like maternity benefits, free medical aid and cheap housing to lessen the burden of large families.

A population policy must be democratic and positive and in matters of conscience free from coercion and force. Such a policy seeking to influence fertility, mortality or migration must keep clearly in view both the positive objectives to be attained and the democratic means to be adopted.

There are two well-known views on the question of the relation between the birth rate and the standard of living. One school maintains that once the standard of living is raised, willy nilly the birth rate will tend to fall because the people, having tasted the benefits and pleasures of a higher level of living, would want to retain it at any cost, and hence would have fewer babies. Therefore, according to this view the Government must help to increase over-all agricultural and industrial production and raise the per capita income of the people significantly, and not bother about the birth rate.

The second view contends that a community's low level of living cannot be substantially raised unless the birth rate is reduced because the new arrivals consume the increased production, leaving the community with its old low standard of living, despite increased production. The poor incomes do not leave sufficient savings to be invested to augment further production. The increase in population, including the working population (granting the existence of full employment opportunities) does not normally result in a proportional rise in production.

There is no need to go into the evidence in support or refutation of these two points of view. It is true that such relatively thinly populated countries as Afghanistan or Saudi Arabia can be poor and such thickly populated countries as Belgium and the Netherlands can have a high standard of living. Obviously population is related to production. But the point is that production does not necessarily increase with the increase in population. In recent years it has been found that it is easier to impart techniques of death-control than techniques of increasing productivity in an underdeveloped country. Therefore, in the present circumstances it is difficult to significantly raise the standard of living in India unless the birth rate is drastically cut.

While there are no simple solutions to India's population problems, five solutions are usually advocated to meet the problem of over-population in an underdeveloped economy. They are: (1) scientific agricultural development; (2) large-scale, heavy industrialization; (3) internal migration to ease regional pressures; (4) emigration to foreign countries; and last and perhaps the most important (5) birth control.

Agricultural Development

Through the three Five-Year Plans, India is seriously attempting the first two approaches with partial success, but they are really long-range solutions. Attempts are being made to increase the per capita as well as the per acre productivity in agriculture by adopting various methods. Agricultural production per unit of operation in India is markedly low in comparison, for instance, with Japan, not to speak of any comparison with such advanced countries as Canada and the United States of America.

India has been trying to bring under cultivation land classified as 'cultivable but uncultivated'. This is marginal land but it can be made to yield if large sums are invested in it. This is again a long-range solution, and *for the present*, reclamation of waste land including the arid and semi-arid lands appears to be an uneconomic proposition.

There are numerous problems connected with efforts to raise agricultural production but only one, which has been more or less completely neglected, need be mentioned here. It is the incredible cost of the average Hindu's irrational attitude towards the cow, the monkey and certain other animals. The cost of this obscurantist attitude is enormous and it is to be hoped that some serious thought will be given to this question in the near future.

Large-Scale Industrialization

As for large-scale and heavy industrialization, both the public and private sectors have made considerable progress judged in relation to the level from which they started twenty years ago (1947) and in the context of continuing limitations of financial and technological resources. Industrialization of India is desirable for at least three reasons. First it can contribute to the solution of the problem of the rural unemployed and underemployed by absorbing them into city factories or small rural industries. Secondly, skilled men and complex machines can turn out much needed goods and services on a mass scale, raising both the per capita income and levels of consumption. Thirdly, planned and successful industrialization can eventually spread new urban patterns of living involving prolonged education and training, late marriages and small planned families. Industrialization has led to declining fertility at the beginning in several advanced countries in the past and there is no reason why India should not conform to this experience of the West and Japan.

Internal Migration

The third solution to the population problem is that of internal migration. The people of India are considered 'stay-at-homes' as they do not generally migrate unless they have to. The major reason behind the immobility of the population is the complex structure of Indian society which is fragmented by the criteria of caste, language, religion, province, diet, etc. If anything, since political freedom, these divisive distinctions have not only not disappeared but have in some ways become more rigid, despite the Federal Government's efforts towards what is called 'the nation's emotional integration'. Therefore, the population pressure in one state can hardly be eased by the migration of her people to a neighbouring state, in the present context of an undue emphasis on states' rights.

Indian Emigration

Fourthly, what about Indian emigration to such developed but thinly populated countries as Australia, Brazil and Canada, for instance? There are also relatively empty and underdeveloped regions in Africa and some Pacific islands. Needless to say, all sovereign states have the right to control the size and composition of their populations. And, therefore, in the present international situation no country can have the right to export her surplus population to another country which is unwilling to receive it, no matter how thinly she may be or may appear to be populated. If a country wants more people she has the right to choose the kind of people she wants on the basis of colour, language, religion and culture so that the receiving country may not have to face the problems of assimilation and minorities in the future. So long as any group is not wanted elsewhere and so long as there is discrimination against the nationals of any country who have emigrated to some parts of the world, there is no point in India or any overpopulated country demanding space overseas. This does not, of course, mean that there is no just cause for granting land and immigration opportunities to the over-populated, especially in thinly populated areas where the new immigrants can raise more food and create more wealth. This is for the present a moral problem and moral considerations do not weigh very heavily with modern nations when their national interests appear to be threatened.[18]

Family Planning

And last, family planning. Fortunately, the Government of India, dedicated to the task of promoting a welfare state, has been aware of this problem of population increase almost ever since the country attained independence in 1947. The first tangible official recognition of the problem came with the publication of the First Five-Year Plan which pointed out that 'the objective of stabilizing the growth of population over a reasonable period must be at the very centre of planned development . . . in the circumstances of the country family planning has to be undertaken not merely as a major development programme, but as a nationwide movement which embodies a basic attitude towards a better life for the individual, the family and the community . . . [therefore] the reduction in the rate of growth of the population must be regarded as a major desideratum'.[19] Besides the governmental awareness of the problem, India is fortunate in not having any organized religious opposition to birth control, since India's major religion, Hinduism, is not opposed to it.[20] To achieve this end the Five-Year Plan recommended certain measures for the inculcation of the need and technique of family planning.

Any official effort to promote family planning on a nationwide basis poses an initial problem. The dilemma before India and other underdeveloped countries is that whereas population control is needed not only to increase but check the threatened decline in the already poor living standards of her people, the successful practice of family planning methods requires a far higher general living standard than is the case. A way has to be found to cut through this vicious circle. Hence the search for an ideal and acceptable method of fertility control.

From a biological point of view all fertility control methods may be roughly grouped into four categories. They are (1) abstinence, (2) contraception, (3) sterilization,[21] and (4) abortion.[22] From a sociological point of view both delayed marriages and permanent celibacy may be considered methods of fertility control.

As for these methods, abortion does not appear to be acceptable to an overwhelming majority in India unless certain special circumstances should warrant it. Total abstinence from conjugal relations is not acceptable to the majority in any culture, and to many would constitute a negation of a major objective of marriage. Delayed marriages are a help, but even if the age at marriage were raised as much as a decade the reduction in the number of children born would not be significant. As for contraception there are several methods. The Government of India approached the United Nations and asked the WHO for technical aid to promote its family planning programme in 1950. As certain Catholic member nations of WHO objected to the world body offering scientific contraceptive advice even to non-Catholic countries, and as India's then Health Minister was 'Gandhian' on the birth control question (Mahatma Gandhi opposed contraception and favoured moral restraint for India), WHO's response was to send the late Dr Abraham Stone, America's planned parenthood expert, to India to set up a series of pilot projects to try out the rhythm or safe period method of family planning.

The WHO assignment specifically stated that family planning was to be confined to the rhythm method 'on the assumption that if this method were to prove successful on a large population basis it would represent a simple method for dealing with family planning in India'.[23] The Health Minister felt that this method would not go against the traditions, culture and mores of the Indian people, and in addition it would have the advantage of not requiring any expenditure for supplies.

The Rhythm Method

As a result, five centres were set up in New Delhi, Mysore and West Bengal States where the rhythm method[24] was taught to selected couples. But teaching the safe period to illiterate wives in backward rural conditions raised its own problems. Reliance on the rhythm method implies accurate records and careful calculations of the menstrual cycle and of fertile and infertile days. Some simple techniques therefore had to be developed. Dr Stone and some Indian physicians hit upon the idea of constructing a special necklace of twenty-eight beads, one bead for each day of the menstrual cycle. There were orange beads for the days of menstruation, green beads for the safe, non-conception days, and red beads for the fertile or 'baby' days. The beads were strung for the individual woman on the basis of her menstrual cycle and she was instructed to move one bead daily from one side of the string of the necklace to the other, beginning with the first day of menstruation. During the time that the green beads appeared she was in the safe period and when the red beads came around sexual relations were to be avoided.[25]

When the necklaces of coloured beads were distributed to the women willing to practise family planning no one anticipated how many snags there were going to be in translating this apparently simple device into effective action. After a week the women came to the clinic with the complaint that they could not distinguish the colour of the beads in the middle of the night. An improvement was effected in retaining the colour but changing the shape of the beads into round and square ones: round red beads were unsafe, square green beads were safe. The wife could feel their shape in the night and say 'yes' or 'no' to her husband accordingly. (The question of fluorescent beads was even considered.)

Then some women complained that the beads went both clockwise and anti-clockwise. This was a minor problem, however; a necklace with a safety catch was devised which permitted the movement of the beads in only one direction.

Some women simply forgot to push the beads. Some decided not to wear the necklaces because they didn't want the whole village to know that they were practising family planning. And some mistook the beads for charmed amulets distributed through the courtesy of the Government of India. They thought it was enough to simply push the beads to space or limit their families. Needless to say, the rhythm method failed to bring down the birth rate.

Besides these more bizarre difficulties, there are the well-known biological difficulties inherent in the rhythm method itself. Not only has each individual woman a different cycle, the cycle itself may vary from time to time. When nature deviates from the statistical norm, who can complain?[26]

Diaphragm and Jelly

The setting up of these rhythm method experiments by WHO were not India's first attempts at birth control. In fact, as early as 1928 two distinguished citizens of Madras, one a Justice of the High Court who was the father of ten children and the other a Member of the Governor's Executive Council who was childless, opened a birth control clinic in the city.[27] In 1930 the Government of Mysore opened a birth control clinic in Bangalore and a few years later the Poona Birth Control League was founded.

During the thirties both the All-India Women's Conference at their regular annual sessions and the National Planning Committee appointed by the Congress Party, under the chairmanship of Jawaharlal Nehru, strongly endorsed family planning. So even during those early years scientific contraception was not unknown in India, though it was probably confined to about one per cent of the high-income, educated population.

When the rhythm method failed to show any favourable results the Ministry of Health approved the supply of such modern methods of birth control as sheaths and diaphragms and jellies, which the early clinics had been using all along, for distribution in government hospitals and clinics free to needy mothers.

The difficulties in the use of such conventional Western contraceptives as diaphragms in the backward rural conditions of India can be easily imagined. To begin with a strong motivation is necessary to get the rural mother to a clinic where she can be fitted with a diaphragm. Village dwellings are plagued by unhygienic conditions, insufficient running water and often no readily available water at all, lack of lighting and bathrooms. And predominant illiteracy means that even basic directions on a tube of jelly cannot be read. Backward living conditions apart, the diaphragm and jelly method implies some knowledge on the part of the women of the structure and function of their reproductive organs.

Once after a detailed talk to a large group of rural women, made with the aid of charts and diagrams, a diaphragm was shown and one young woman promptly asked 'Isn't it too *large* to swallow?' The village mind expects contraception in the form of a medicine—a pill or a mixture—to be swallowed once or twice a day to cure fertility. Knowledge of human physiology and reproduction seems to be rare even in towns and cities.

Mothers who have been taught the diaphragm and jelly methods and given free supplies to last for a few months have returned to the clinics within a few weeks complaining that their periods have stopped and the birth control materials didn't work. 'Did you use the diaphragm and jelly as instructed?' 'Yes.' 'Regularly?' 'Yes.'

But on further questioning it was discovered that they forgot sometimes and didn't think it would really matter! The fact that the contraceptives have to be used every time is apparently a problem demanding too much perseverance. And many Indian women have complained after a few attempts at contraception that it is messy and meddlesome, awkward and unaesthetic. Some confess that contraception is just too revolting even for such a desirable purpose as preventing conception.

Foam Tablets

A family planning experiment under government auspices was undertaken in the Punjab where foam tablets were distributed free of cost to all mothers anxious to space or limit the size of their families. The Health Ministry believed that this method was relatively inexpensive and simple to use and the fact that no apparatus was needed was an added advantage. Trained women social workers visited willing mothers at regular intervals with foam tablets. The mothers were asked to insert a tablet up into the vagina prior to intercourse and wait for a few minutes for the tablet to disintegrate, creating a dense foam which would act both as a mechanical and chemical barrier. This experiment also failed in effecting a reduction in the birth rate. Some of the women who failed pointed out on questioning that they had simply forgotten to use the tablets and a few stated, 'I didn't like the taste of the tablets'. It was not ascertained whether the women did not understand what they were to do with the tablets or whether they found it repugnant to use them as instructed.

A decade ago everyone was pleading for a simple oral contraceptive. The magic pill. But now that the pill is here, India has not taken to it, for swallowing twenty pills a month for months on end is expensive. And, expense apart, there will always be women who will forget to take their daily dose. Also the Government feels that the pill has not been tried long enough to be certain that there will be no adverse side effects after prolonged use.

Intra-uterine Device

Another contraceptive, the loop or the intra-uterine coil, a small light plastic or stainless steel device worn by women has recently come into vogue in Europe and the United States. The advantage of this device for a country like India is that it is cheap (it can be produced for less than 3 cents or 10 paise) and can be inserted into the uterus easily by any competent doctor without the use of anaesthetics.

However, in clinical tests in India the coil has been effective in only 80 per cent of the cases. In some instances it proved too uncomfortable; in others it was spontaneously expelled from the body, a fact the woman did not discover until she found she was pregnant. But in the view of medical experts, the real difficulty is that this is only a temporary measure.

Sterilization

Besides a method of family planning that is cheap, harmless, reliable and acceptable to the people who use it, India needs a method of permanent conception control. This means surgical sterilization: vasectomy for fathers or salpingectomy for mothers. In view of the current socio-economic–cultural conditions in India, certainly the most effectiv- method is sterilization. The writer has been pleading for this for nearly two decades.

The advantage of sterilization is that it solves the problem, once and for all, for those couples who have had from two to four children and do not want any more for health, economic or other reasons. Up to now the experience of couples in India shows that after sterilization (preferably of the man for a variety of reasons, not least of which is that the operation is much simpler for a man), husband and wife can enjoy sexual relations with great psychological satisfaction. (In India a written declaration from both husband and wife stating that they do not want any more children is obtained and the irreversible nature of the operation—under normal conditions—is emphasized to them.)

Madras State embarked in 1957 upon a policy of voluntary subsidized sterilization (a free operation plus a bonus of $7.50, and a three- to six-day holiday with pay for government employees) and Maharashtra and Kerala States have followed suit. They have done fairly well.

Of all the methods tried so far, only sterilization has yielded significant results, and a small dent has been made in the high birth rates of these states. So far a little more than a million sterilizations have been performed, mostly on fathers, and the Government hopes to step up the programme in India's Fourth Five-Year Plan (1966–71). About 700,000 of the operations have been performed in government hospitals, the rest by private surgeons.

But India will have to perform three operations per 1,000 of population annually for ten years if the nation's birth rate is to be reduced from 40 to 20.[28]

At first the Federal Government of India was sceptical about this method, but it finally came out in favour of sterilization, and today almost all the sixteen states of the Indian Union have such programmes, although some of these have scarcely got under way. Had India embarked on this policy fifteen years ago with fervour, the country by now could have cut its birth rate by half.

The Future—Motivation

It is late, but not yet too late, to do something concrete about India's runaway population growth. Unfortunately, although today everybody talks about family planning, the country is still waiting for a crash programme. Despite all the debate and discussion, the money and effort, the foreign aid and advice, India's family-planning programme has so far been a failure. No significant decline in the nation's birth rate has been achieved. Only in those areas where the summary method of sterilization has been adopted has even a slight dent in the birth rate been made. While the Government of India as a whole under the leadership of Nehru took a refreshingly courageous attitude on the population question, actual efforts throughout these years of freedom have been half-hearted at best. A variety of problems have been responsible for this failure. There are problems of motivation, methods, money and men.

All the attitude surveys conducted to date show that more than 70 per cent of the mothers and fathers of all castes, religions and income groups are in favour of practising family planning. But this desire is not sufficient motivation to send them to a clinic to learn about a method of family planning and use it rationally.[29] The average Hindu wants sons, an understandable attitude in a country where there is neither Social Security nor old-age pensions, sickness benefits nor unemployment insurance for an overwhelming majority of the population.

Parents have to depend on gainfully employed adult sons for support in their old age. Daughters are 'married off' as soon as possible and it is bad Hindu manners to expect financial aid from daughters or sons-in-law. It is much easier to motivate a couple with three sons in favour of family planning than a couple with four daughters who want to keep trying for a son. If only we could fix the sex of India's babies!

It is true that everyone wants the good things of life. Nobody loves poverty. But it is one thing to aspire to a higher level of living and another to seek persistently the ways of achieving this. Research is needed in this area of motivation in the context of Indian conditions.

As for techniques, India needs a simple method that cannot go wrong. People marry early, and once they have had two or three children, the Government must make every effort to persuade fathers or mothers to undergo sterilization. (It is also desirable to raise the marriage age, but in the absence of prolonged education and training, postponing the age of marriage becomes a formidable problem.)

The Government will also have to spend considerably larger sums than it has spent so far, yet if this results in a relatively small population, it will eventually save money on national food, education and medical bills. One solution would be for the Indian Government to ask the United States Government's permission to use United States counterpart funds (rupees accumulated in India) for promoting sterilization. A cash bonus of 100 rupees (a rupee is worth about 21 cents or a shilling) per vasectomy might do the trick. I have suggested this in Parliament but both Governments are extremely sensitive in this area. Yet in a problem this crucial perhaps we need more action and less sensitivity.

Another problem has been that the subject of population control has been saddled on the Ministry of Health, which has a hundred other pressing problems as it is. The prevention and control of disease, the eradication of filth and the improvement of sanitation and hygiene alone could keep the Ministry busy night and day for the next half century. As Sir Julian Huxley pleaded some time ago, India should create a separate Ministry of Population Control.[30]

A Population Ministry, with sufficient funds at its disposal, could train a large group of dedicated men and women to go into the countryside and convert their underprivileged fellow citizens to the philosophy of small families. Given dynamic leadership—civil servants in a vast bureaucracy usually adjust their attitudes and pace to the Minister in charge—this can be accomplished. Resistance to change is universal but methods must and can be found to overcome it.

With the solution of these four problems, it should be possible to spread the family-planning habit in India within the next crucial decade. As India's Planning Commission puts it, 'Given a sense of urgency and a spirit of dedicated endeavour, it is fully within the capacity of the nation to achieve the goals it has set itself'.[31] If this sense of urgency and spirit of dedication can be created soon, the population problem can be solved. If not, the outlook is gloomy indeed.

NOTES

1. For a discussion of the subject, see S. Chandrasekhar, *Census and Statistics in India* (Chidambaram, Annamalai University Press, 1948). See also S. Chandrasekhar, 'A Note on Demographic Statistics in India', *Population Review*, January 1960, pp. 40–5.
2. W. H. Moreland, *India at the Death of Akbar* (London, 1927), p. 71.
3. J. McCulloch, *Descriptive and Statistical Accounts of the British Empire* (London, 1847), p. 87.
4. G. A. Harrison, *et al.*, *Human Biology* (New York, Oxford University Press, 1964), p. 117.
5. J. H. Hutton, *Census of India, 1931*, Vol. 1, Part 1 (Delhi, Government of India Press, 1933), p. 42.
6. The 1951 and 1961 'urban population' figures are not strictly comparable in view of the change in the definition of 'urban population' adopted by the 1961 census. While the earlier censuses defined an urban area as a community of 5,000 people with pronounced urban characteristics, the 1961 census adopted a more restricted criterion.
7. The Child Marriage Restraint Act (the Sarada Act) was passed in 1929 and made early marriage (males under 18 and females under 14 years of age) a punishable offence. But the legislation is so poorly framed and vital statistical data are so unreliable that it is honoured more in its breach than otherwise. See S. Chandrasekhar, *Population and Planned Parenthood in India* (London and New York, 1961), second edition, pp. 35–6.
8. S. N. Agarwala, *The Mean Age at Marriage as Ascertained from Census Data*, unpublished dissertation, Princeton University, 1957.
9. The Hindu Widow Remarriage Act was passed in 1856, thanks to the agitation of the pioneering Indian social reformer, Iswar Chandra Vidyasagar. But the social ban against widow remarriage continues to operate even after more than a century.
10. See S. Chandrasekhar, *Infant Mortality in India* (London, Allen and Unwin, 1959), *passim.*
11. *The Third Five Year Plan: A Draft Outline* (New Delhi, Planning Commission, 1960), section on health.
12. S. Chandrasekhar, 'A Billion Indians by 2000 AD?', *The New York Times Magazine*, April 4, 1965.
13. Julian Huxley, *Unesco: Its Purpose and Philosophy* (Washington, DC Public Affairs Press, 1947).
14. United Nations, *Report on the World Social Situation* (New York, 1963), pp. 40–50.
15. *FAO Yearbook, 1960* (Rome, 1961), p. 245.
16. See S. Chandrasekhar, 'Population Growth and Housing Needs in India', *Population Review*, January 1957, pp. 12–18. There is also the distressing problem of the pavement dwellers. 'In India, for example, one fifth of the population of Delhi and Ahmedabad, one quarter of the population of Calcutta and over one fifth of the population of Kanpur are reported to be housed in slums or to "lack of housing" altogether.' *1963 Report on the World Social Situation* (New York, United Nations, 1963), p. 171.

17. India's per capita income in terms of US dollars is apt to mislead the foreign reader. It is $70 in terms of the present exchange rate between India and the United States, but in terms of actual purchasing power for Indian-produced commodities and services, the Indian rupee is more equivalent to the American dollar than is the 21 cents or 1s. 6d. which was the official exchange rate before devaluation of the rupee in May 1966. In other words, India's per capita income is really about $334.
18. For a discussion of this topic from the point of view of the underdeveloped and over-populated countries, see S. Chandrasekhar, *Hungry People and Empty Lands* (London, Allen and Unwin, 1955), third edition.
19. *The First Five Year Plan* (New Delhi, The Planning Commission, 1953), p. 23.
20. S. Radhakrishnan, *Inaugural Address to the Third International Conference on Planned Parenthood* (Bombay), *The Eugenics Review* (London), April 1953. See also the Hindu view of population in S. Chandrasekhar, *Population and Planned Parenthood in India* (London, 1961), pp. 69–73.
21. See S. Chandrasekhar, 'One Answer to India's "Population Explosion" ', *The Washington Post*, May 2, 1961.
22. The Government of India (the Ministry of Health) appointed a committee of officials and non-officials in 1965 to examine the question of the legalization of abortion for various reasons. The Report is awaited.
23. Abraham Stone, 'Fertility Problems in India', *Fertility and Sterility* (New York), May–June 1953, p. 213.
24. The long-range biological consequences of the universal adoption of the rhythm method may be self-defeating. There is no tested scientific evidence for this as yet but Professor Garrett Hardin's fears have probably scientific basis. He writes: '*Blessed are the women that are irregular for their daughters shall inherit the earth.* The inheritability of reproductive characteristics is amply proved to us by all God's creatures. Are not women God's creatures?

    'The rhythm method of birth control is, when used by women who have a rhythm, only two and a half times as bad as "artificial" methods, according to the studies of Tietze. But even if it were every bit as good, it would be self-defeating for there would still be those arhythmic women, about one woman in six, for whom the method is meaningless. Compelled by dogma to reject artificial methods, these women would soon outbreed the rhythmic ones. If there is even a tiny hereditary element in their irregularity (as there surely must be), natural selection would then ultimately produce a world populated only by irregular women.

    'Tidings of Darwin should be carried to Rome.' Garrett Hardin, 'A Second Sermon on the Mount', *Perspectives in Biology and Medicine* (Chicago), Vol. VI, No. 3, Spring 1963, p. 370.
25. Abraham Stone, *ibid.*
26. See *Final Report on Pilot Studies in Family Planning* with 36 appendices (New Delhi, World Health Organization (WHO) Regional Office, 1954), 2 volumes.
27. The two Madras pioneers were Sir Justice Vepa Ramesam and Sir P. S. Sivaswamy Iyer.
28. R. A. Gopalaswami, 'How Japan Halved her Birth Rate in Ten Years and the Lessons for India', *Population Review* (Madras), Vol. 3, No. 2, July 1959.
29. About thirty attitude surveys have been conducted so far by a number of Indian scholars. Some of these have been examined in L. G. Reeder and G. B. Krishnamurty, 'Family Planning in Rural India: A Problem in Social Change', *Social Problems*, Autumn 1964, pp. 212–23.
30. Julian Huxley's Introduction to S. Chandrasekhar's *Population and Planned Parenthood in India* (London and New York, 1961), Second edition.
31. *The Third Five Year Plan: A Draft Outline* (New Delhi, Planning Commission, 1960), p. 60.

BIBLIOGRAPHY

Census of India, 1931, Vol. 1. India, Part 1 (New Delhi, Government of India, 1933).

Census of India, 1951. Report, Vol. 1, Part 1A (New Delhi, Government of India, 1953).

Census of India: 1961 Census. Paper No. 1 of 1962. Final Population Totals (New Delhi, Government of India, 1965).

Paper No. 2 of 1963. Age Tables (New Delhi, Government of India, 1963).

Census and Statistics in India (Chidambaram, Annamalai University Press, 1948).

Chandrasekhar, S., *India's Population: Fact and Policy* (New York, John Day, 1951), second edition.

Hungry People and Empty Lands (London, Allen and Unwin, 1955), third edition.

Population and Planned Parenthood in India (London, Allen and Unwin, 1961), second edition.

Infant Mortality in India (London, Allen and Unwin, 1959).

'The Hindu Joint Family' *Social Forces*, March 1943.

'Population Pressure in India' *Pacific Affairs*, June 1943.

'Population Problems of India and Pakistan', *The Eugenics Review*, July 1949.

'Population Problem of India', *Penguin Science News*, No. 13, 1949.

Les Problemes Demographiques Dan L'Inde et Dans Le Pakistan (Paris, Dunod, 1950).

'Prospects of Planned Parenthood in India' *Pacific Affairs*, December 1953.

'Population Growth, Socio-economic development and Living Standards', *International Labour Review*, June 1954.

'The Family in India' *Marriage and Family Living*, November 1954.

'Cultural Barriers to Family Planning in Underdeveloped countries', *The Rationalist Annual*, London, 1956.

'Family Planning in Rural India', *The Antioch Review*, 1959.

'The Unplanned Millions', *The Guardian* India Today Supplement (Manchester), August 15, 1961.

'A Billion Indians by 2000 A.D.?' *The New York Times Magazine*, April 4, 1965.

'Should we Legalize Abortion in India?' *Population Review*, July 1966.

Coale, Ansley J. and Edgar M. Hoover, *Population Growth and Economic Development in Low-Income Countries* (Princeton, Princeton University Press, 1958).

Davis, Kingsley, *The Population of India and Pakistan* (Princeton, Princeton University Press, 1951).

Family Planning Programme: Report for 1962–63 (New Delhi, Directorate General of Health Services, Ministry of Health, 1964).

Gopalaswami, R. A., *Planned Development and Population Growth* (New Delhi, Institute of Applied Manpower Research, 1963).

India, 1964: A Reference Manual (New Delhi, Government of India, 1965).

Papers contributed by Indian Authors to the World Population Conference, Belgrade, August–September 1965 (New Delhi, Office of the Registrar General, 1965).

CHAPTER 4

JAPAN'S POPULATION PROBLEM

BY THOMAS O. WILKINSON

I

THE FACTS

THE JAPANESE nation consists of an island chain located off the eastern coast of Asia. A wide range of climatic conditions characterize the archipelago. Extending from north to south, the principal islands are Hokkaido (78·5 thousand sq. km.), Honshu (230·4 thousand sq. km.), Shikoku (18·8 thousand sq. km.), and Kyushu (41·9 thousand sq. km.). The four main islands which make up the Japanese nation are dominated by great mountainous spines. The limited lowland areas are typically small isolated patches of river- and wave-worked sediments developed in a coastal indentation or in a mountain basin. The largest of these plains which contains the city of Tokyo has an area of only some 13 thousand square kilometres. Being predominantly peripheral, most of the plains have sea frontage. They are seldom continuous along the coast because of frequent interruptions of spurs and larger masses of hardrock hill land that extend to the sea.

At the close of the Second World War Japan was shorn of her extensive Eastern Pacific colonial holdings which had amounted to something over three hundred thousand square kilometres. The four home islands have a total area of 370 thousand square kilometres on which some 94 million Japanese reside. A total density of 253 persons per square kilometre places Japan first in any list of the world's nations ranked by density.

Japan is unique among the countries of Asia in its possession of detailed and comprehensive population statistics covering a significant period of her modern history. The compilation of modern population data is a continuation of the tradition of census taking established by the Tokugawa Shogunate in the eighteenth century. These early censuses make it possible to estimate the base from which Japan's modern population has developed.

The basic sources for modern Japanese population data are the quinquennial censuses conducted since 1920 and prior to that date the various national statistics resulting from compilations of household registers.[1] There are difficulties stemming from differences in definitions, coverage, and classifications in dealing with these data. Two major breaks occur in the data sources: The first appears with the shift from national statistics based upon household registrations to a genuine national census in 1920; the second, brought about by reorganizations of methods and techniques of census taking and reporting, occurs in the comparisons of pre- and post-Second World War materials. In the main, however, the nature of Japanese population structure and development is clear.

Since the institution of the national census in 1920, age, sex, marital status, place of birth, household, and industrial–occupational data are available at least on a ten-year interval, and frequently on a five-year interval basis. Details on duration of marriage, number of children ever born, and place of work-residence are available only for the post-Second World War period, though place of work in a modified form did appear on the 1930 schedule.

Vital statistics until 1947 are available as compilations of household registers under the Cabinet Bureau of Statistics. The Ministry of Health and Welfare has had responsibility in this area since 1947. Post-Second World War vital statistics are based upon periodic summaries of schedules submitted for every registration of a vital event.

A full battery of specialized reporting agencies provides further data on all areas of Japan's modern demographic situation. In addition to a monthly labour force survey, there are censuses of commerce, manufacturing and productivity. Wages and prices, internal and international trade, and household income and expenditures are suggestive of the range and types of statistical data now regularly available for the Japanese population.

Rates and Sources of Population Growth

Analysis of Tokugawa censuses show a relatively stable population of approximately thirty million Japanese at the time of the opening of the country in the mid-nineteenth century. High levels of mortality and widespread infanticide and abortion had held the national population at this level throughout the roughly two hundred and fifty years of Tokugawa rule.

The national population began a steady increase from the initiation of the Meiji Era (1868) with its international intercourse and the consequent industrialization of the country. There were forty million Japanese by 1891, in 1912 the total had reached fifty million, followed by increases to sixty million in 1926, seventy million in 1937, and eighty million in 1947. The repatriation of a significant number of Japanese to the home islands following the close of the Second World War aided an increase to ninety million by 1956. The most recent estimate of November 1964 places the figure at 96·7 million.

The major factor in the growth of Japanese population has been and continues to be natural increase in contrast to the growth of the countries of the West where large-scale immigration and emigration over extended periods of time contributed heavily to population changes. Conversely, the Japanese have historically contributed only slightly to the flow of emigrants into other countries and have received relatively few through immigration into Japan. The Koreans make up the major portion of Japan's currently registered aliens; out of a total alien population of 645,000 (1962), the Koreans account for something over one half million. At the height of Japanese expansion during the late 1930s, only some one million Japanese were outside the home islands and the major portion of these were concentrated in Japanese-held Manchuria.

Japan's Birth and Death Rates

The fluctuations of Japan's vital rates, therefore, become the key to grasping the nature of the nation's population development. Crude birth rates for the period 1900 until the middle of the Second World War show levels of approximately 30 births per 1,000 total population. There was some indication of a decline in fertility during the 1930s but this was more than balanced by a spurt upwards upon the close of the Second World War. Beginning with 1950, however, a steady and consistent decline is evident. In 1961, the crude birth rate reached its lowest point in Japanese history: 16·9, a rate approximately one half that in 1947–9.

The rapid post-war decline in Japanese fertility is most reasonably explained in terms of the nature of the nation's socio-economic development after 1945. Significant industrial urbanization had taken place in Japan prior to the Second World War, but the nature of its influences upon the population as a whole was such that the pressures making for fertility reduction were reduced by the continuation of such elements as a paternalistic labour situation and a heavy reliance upon a traditional family-centred social organization. The recovery from physical and organizational disruptions of the Second World War emphasized, though it did not totally remove, major aspects of these vestiges of a peasant-agricultural past. A broadly-based rise in standard of living occurred, employment practices were modified to incorporate elements of individualism, and an impressive national economic development took place. These among other factors tended to create genuine socio-economic pressures upon traditional fertility values. The pattern familiar to students of Western urban-industrialization of lowered fertility in the face of broadly-based economic development now characterizes Japan.

The pattern of mortality levels in Japan follows much the same form as that of fertility except that the turning point in mortality decrease was earlier. From 1900 to the mid-1920s the crude death rates ranged between 20 and 23 per 1,000 total population, excluding the rise to 27·3 during the world-wide influenza epidemic of 1918. In 1926, for the first time the crude death rate dropped below 20 and it has shown continuous decline since that date. In 1950, the rate fell below 10 for the first time, and 1961 shows a rate of 7·4 deaths per 1,000 total population.

TABLE 1. *Japanese Total Population, Crude Birth and Death Rates and Natural Increases, 1900–62*

Year	Total population (millions)	Crude birth rate*	Crude death rate*	Natural increase
1900†	43·8	32·4	20·8	11·6
1905	46·6	32·5	21·0	11·5
1910	49·2	33·6	21·5	12·1
1915	52·8	34·5	20·7	13·8
1920	56·0	33·7	24·1	9·6
1925	59·7	34·7	21·9	12·8
1930	64·5	33·4	19·3	14·1
1935	69·3	31·6	17·9	13·7
1940	71·9	26·8	17·3	9·5
1943†	72·9	30·9	16·7	14·2
1947†	78·1	34·3	14·6	19·7
1950†	83·2	28·1	10·9	17·2
1955	89·3	21·9	8·7	13·2
1960	93·4	17·7	7·7	10·0
1962†	95·2	17·0	7·5	9·5

* Average annual rate for five years ending with year indicated.
† Rates for single year indicated.

Source: Japan, Office of the Prime Minister, Bureau of Statistics, *Vital Statistics*, 1962, Volume 1, pp. 47 and 85.

The 1963 natural increase for Japan is an annual addition of approximately 10·5 persons per 1,000 total population.

Japan's Urbanization

Concomitant with the increase in total population and expansion of industrialization has come a series of major shifts in internal distribution of population. In 1872 some 6·9 per cent of the total national population was located in 39 cities and towns. The national census of 1960 designated 556 cities containing 63·5 per cent of the total population. The striking trait of this Japanese urban growth was the relative speed with which it was accomplished. From 1889 to 1940, the percentage of Japan's total population in cities of 20,000 or more increased from 9·7 per cent to 37·5 per cent. In approximately fifty years Japan had moved from less than 10 per cent urban to over one third urban.

England and Wales at the time reliable figures become available (1801) already had 16·9 per cent of her population in cities of 20,000 or more. Assuming that it took at a minimum two decades to move from approximately 10 per cent in cities of 20,000 or over to the level she had reached by 1801, England and Wales required roughly eighty years (1780–1860) to match the Japanese level of urbanization. In moving between approximately the same points, the United States took approximately seventy-five years (1850–1925). The urbanization of Germany, however, is roughly comparable in rate to that of Japan; in some fifty-five years (1860–1915) Germany's proportion of total

TABLE 2. *Growth of Japan's Urban Population, 1891–1960*

Year	Population in incorporated cities (thousands)	Percentage increase from last date
1891	3,821	—
1898	5,518	44·8
1903	6,748	22·3
1908	8,227	21·9
1913	8,920	8·4
1920	10,020	12·3
1925	12,823	28·0
1930	15,363	19·8
1935	22,582	47·0
1940	27,494	21·8
1944	29,650	7·8
1945	20,022	−32·5
1950	46,660	133·0
1955	50,288	7·8
1960	59,333	17·9

Sources: *Résumé Statistique de L'Empire du Japon*, Vols. 8–31; *Population Census of Japan, 1955*, Vol. 1; *1960 Population Census of Japan*, Vol. 1.

population in cities of 20,000 or more increased from 10 per cent to 38 per cent.

This rapid urbanization of Japan has meant essentially a continuation of the pattern of city growth whose roots reach well back into her pre-modern period. Of the nation's ten largest cities ranked by size, only Yokohama and Kobe are cities which were primarily created by Japan's modernization. Further, this list of ten largest cities contains the *same* cities from the last decade of the nineteenth century to the present, with one exception: Fukuoka replaces Kanazawa in the decade 1920–30. Yet another means to point up the concentration of Japan's urban population is to note, as Reischauer does,[2] that in pre-Second World War Japan if a line is drawn from Tokyo some 540 miles southward to northern Kyushu, one finds the great bulk of Japan's urban population within forty miles of either side of this line. The 1955 census shows that such a strip still contains all of the cities of one million or more population, fifty-eight of the ninety-eight cities of 100,000 or more, and forty-seven of the 140 cities between 50,000 and 100,000 population. Further, the fifteen prefectures which constitute such a strip contained 75·4 per cent of the population of incorporated cities in 1891, and roughly the same percentage (76·7 per cent) in 1940. With the incorporation of a large number of new cities following the Second World War, the percentage of total cities in this strip has dropped to roughly two thirds. The fact remains, however, that slightly less than one third of Japan's forty-six prefectures have contained two thirds or more of her urban population throughout her modern period.

Not only have Japan's cities increased in size and number, but the nature of her urban structure has as well experienced modification with the recent evolution of the large, multi-nucleated, urban agglomerations termed metropolitan areas. The vast urban complexes of the Tokyo–Yokohama, Osaka–Kobe and Kitakyushu areas match in size and internal functional interdependence the metropolitan developments in the most advanced nations of the West. In 1955, Japan's sixty-three metropolitan areas contained 40·3 per cent of the total national population and approximately two thirds of the total urban population. As in the West, these large urban populations have been experiencing a process of decentralization in the post-Second World War period. The greatest percentage increases within these metropolitan areas during the past three decades have been in the smaller cities peripheral to the large central cities. Several of the central wards of Tokyo actually show resident populations decreasing for the period 1955–60. However, the evidence seems to indicate that, unlike the decentralization familiar to students of Western metropolitan structure, this process in Japan is more frequently creating satellite cities rather than suburbs. The distinction here is between the outlying urban areas which contain a significant proportion of the services and employment for their own populations (satellites) and the area which is primarily dependent upon the central city for these needs (suburbs). Using such indices as commuting, industrial structure, and rate of population change, the Tokyo–Yokohama metropolitan area shows nine satellite cities as against eight suburbs, while Osaka–Kobe shows nine satellites to seven suburbs. The other three major metropolitan areas (Nagoya, Kyoto, and Kitakyushu) with the method of analysis noted have a total of ten satellites but no suburbs. Possible explanations for this divergence in metropolitan development by the Japanese lie in the relative scarcity of private ownership of transportation, the dual productive system to be discussed below, and the frequency of agriculture as a secondary occupation for outlying urban populations.

The urban-industrialization of Japan has made for significant shifts in the major demographic characteristics of the national population. In age structure, occupational–industrial structure, and education the demographic modernization of the nation is clearly visible.

Age Structure

The pattern of fertility–mortality relationships evident during the past half century and especially during the last decade, has had a signal effect upon the age structure of Japan. The average expectation of life has risen consistently in recent decades. For example, males had an expectation at birth of 46·9 years and females, 49·6 years in 1935; the most recent life tables (1962) reveal expectations of 66·2 and 71·2 years respectively for males and females. This, coupled with the recent drop in fertility has produced a visible ageing in the population as a whole. The 24·7 million who were fourteen years of age or younger in 1965 are projected, if current trends continue, to fall to 23·5 million in 1975, 23·2 million in 1985, and 20·3 million in 1995. Concurrently, those sixty-five years of age and older are projected to move from 6·2 million (1965), to 8 million (1975), to 9·7 million (1985), and to 12·6 million (1995). The segment 15–64 years of age will show a corresponding increase with larger and larger proportions in the upper years of this age span.

The speed with which this ageing is taking place is clearly visible in Japan's population pyramid. Children 0–4 years of age made up only 8·4 per cent of the total population in 1960 (males 4·3 per cent and females 4·1 per cent), while those 10–14 years of age were 11·8 per cent (6 per cent males and 5·8 per cent females) which was the highest proportions among these younger age segments holds true in both urban and rural areas, but the urban fertility decreases are significantly ahead of those for the rural areas.

The primary consequence of this rapid ageing of the Japanese population is the shift in the nature of the population dependent upon that segment of the population providing the labour force for the nation. Traditionally, the heaviest dependence has been of young children upon their labouring parents with the relatively few aged being absorbed into the security of a strong family system. As the fertility pattern shifts towards fewer children and mortality improvements make for longer and longer lived older people radical adaptations have to be made in traditionally family-centred methods of providing for the aged.

If ratios of population 0–14 years of age and sixty-five years and over to those 15–64 years of age (that segment providing the preponderance of labour force) are made, the nature of these age shifts can be specified. For every 1,000 population in the age group 15–39 years of age (the younger half of the labour force and also the major portion of the parents with young children) in 1920, there were 973 children under fifteen years of age; in 1960, this ratio had dropped to 713 children under fifteen years of age. The ratio of children under fifteen years of age to the older half of the labour force ages (40–64 years) for 1920 was 1,756 children per 1,000 in the older labour force ages, while the 1960 figure had fallen to 1,362. The ratios of those sixty-five years of age and older to the labour force age segments do not yet show this striking change for the 1920 to 1960 period, but it is to be noted that the labour force age group itself is undergoing a process of ageing which tends to hold these ratios relatively unchanged. However, as larger and larger numbers from the current labour force age groups move into this group sixty-five years of age and over, the ratios can be expected to rise. The net effect of the age structure changes for 1920–60 is an overall decrease in the total dependency ratio (the sum of the 0–14 years and the sixty-five years plus as a ratio over those 15–64 years of age): 716 in 1920 in contrast to 557 for 1960. An upturn in this ratio can be expected, but it will represent a significantly different dependency structure than that of the past.

Occupational–Industrial Structure

The demographic mechanism underlying the modernization of Japan has been the shift of the major focus of her labour force activities away from the agrarian pursuits of the past into the urban-centred industrial activities of the present. It was not until the latter half of the second decade of this century that Japan passed the 50 per cent level of total males employed in non-extractive pursuits; the national census of 1920 gave the official figure as 51·8 per cent. The Second World War interrupted a steady rise in non-extractive employment (64·3 per cent in 1940), but the post-war period saw a rapid recovery and even a surpassing of the pre-war peak: the national census of 1960 placed male non-extractive employment at 74·2 per cent and 56·9 per cent for females.

The broad outline of this industrial transition is visible in comparisons of Japan's industrial structures in 1930 and 1962. Of the approximately thirty million in the labour force in 1930, roughly one half (47·5 per cent) were employed in agriculture–forestry–fishing; this percentage had decreased to 28·8 by 1962. For the first time, the absolute number in these extractive pursuits showed a decrease: in 1930, some fourteen million were so employed; in 1955, though the percentage had dropped to 39·2 per cent, the absolute number showed an increase to fifteen and a half million. In 1962 the 28·8 per cent extractively occupied represented a total of approximately 12·3 million. The manufacturing category was that which absorbed the major portions of this loss in extractive pursuits. The manufacturing labour force in absolute numbers more than doubled in the 1930–62 period, while the percentage increased from 16 to 24 per cent.

By 1962, Japan can be characterized as industrially well into the matured phase of development. Her labour force commitment in the tertiary categories of industry has shown a steady increase, though these increases do not match those in the secondary sector. According to economic plans, the 1962 secondary–tertiary industry relationship of 31·1 per cent/38·8 per cent is projected to move to 32 per cent/44 per cent in 1970 and to 40 per cent/44 per cent in 1980.[3]

The nature of Japan's industrial development has been influenced by

TABLE 3. *Japanese Dependency Ratios, 1920–60*

Age group ratios	1920 Population (thousands)	1920 Ratio per 1,000	1960 Population (thousands)	1960 Ratio per 1,000
0–14 / 15–39	20,203 / 20,760	973·1	28,066 / 39,393	712·5
0–14 / 40–64	20,203 / 11,502	1,756·4	28,066 / 20,611	1,361·7
0–14 / 15–64	20,203 / 32,262	626·1	28,066 / 60,004	467·7
65 / 15–39	2,908 / 20,760	140·1	5,349 / 39,393	135·8
65 / 40–64	2,908 / 11,502	252·8	5,349 / 20,611	259·5
65 / 15–64	2,908 / 32,262	90·1	5,349 / 60,004	89·1
(0–14) (65+) / 15–64	23,111 / 32,262	716·3	33,415 / 60,004	556·9

Source: *Japan Statistical Yearbook, 1963*, pp. 26–7.

two factors: (1) the continuation of a significant element of household-based production with a dependence upon unpaid family workers, and (2) the historical use of female labour force, especially in textiles, as a device for gaining industrial production without major disruptions in the social organization. A number of the salient differences between the emergence of an industrial system in Japan and in Western nations can be accounted for in terms of these two factors.

The development of a so-called dual economic system in Japan is principally the outgrowth of the policies of industrialization followed from the opening of the country in the latter half of the nineteenth century. Government encouragement was lavished upon those industrial segments which could contribute to the build-up of Japan as an international power: shipbuilding, chemicals, railways, and the whole range of heavy industries. Industries primarily oriented towards indigenous consumption production were left to function largely in the traditional home handicraft manner. In this way, the scarce capital and the abundant labour supply, which characterized Japan during the major portion of her modern period, were most efficiently utilized in her industrialization. Only in the post-Second World War period has Japan had to begin to re-orient her industrial system to a tightening labour supply, but there is still clear evidence of the consequences of the nature of her development. For example, from the census of industrial establishments

TABLE 4. *Industrial Structure of Japanese Employment, 1930–62*

Industry	Employed population			
	1930		1962	
	Thousands	Per cent	Thousands	Per cent
Primary	*14,490*	*49·4*	*12,845*	*30·2*
Agriculture and Forestry	13,928	47·5	12,268	28·8
Fishing	562	1·9	577	1·4
Secondary	*5,993*	*20·4*	*13,251*	*31·0*
Mining	314	1·1	481	1·1
Construction	977	3·3	2,531	5·9
Manufacturing	4,702	16·0	10,239	24·0
Tertiary	*8,788*	*30·0*	*16,490*	*38·6*
Wholesale and Retail Trade	4,307	14·7	7,731	18·1
Transportation and Communication	1,289	4·4	2,666	6·2
Services	2,459	8·4	4,814	11·3
Government	733	2·5	1,279	3·0
Unclassified	70	0·2	67	0·2
Total	29,341	100·0	42,653	100·0

Sources: *Population Census of 1930*; *Employment Status Survey*, 1962.

of 1963 we note that there were some 1·9 million workers (7·5 per cent) enumerated as unpaid family workers in a total establishment labour force of 25·7 million. This percentage is even higher for such areas as food–kindred products (10·2 per cent) and miscellaneous products (8·2 per cent). If we move to commercial areas, retail trade in dry goods (20·6 per cent) and food–beverages (32·3 per cent) show significantly high rates. Much the same is true in services where hotel–lodging service and domestic service have rates of 14·2 per cent and 20·5 per cent respectively.[4]

Not only in levels of unpaid family workers, but in size of establishments is this dimension of Japanese industrial structure visible. Of Japan's total industrial establishments in 1954, 79·5 per cent had less than ten employees and these establishments employed 23·2 per cent of the industrial labour force. At the other extreme, only 1·2 per cent of the establishments had 100 or more employees, but these establishments employed 38·5 per cent of the industrial labour force.[5]

Japan's Occupational Composition

Turning now to occupational structure, it is to be noted that a significant portion of Japan's urban-oriented occupational categories are heavily represented in non-urban areas. This is to say that a clear distinction between rural and urban areas in occupational terms is absent. The rurality of significant portions of Japan's non-extractive production is clear. The continuation of household-based productive units and the rural pattern of assuming by-occupations together with traditional agricultural pursuits account for this pattern.

In what could be termed the most urban-oriented occupations, the

TABLE 5. *Japanese Occupational Structure by Place of Residence, 1960*

Occupational category	Per cent of total employed population		
	Total	Urban (*shi*)	Rural (*gun*)
Professional–Technical	4·9	5·7	3·5
Managers–Officials	2·3	3·1	1·1
Clerical and Related	10·4	13·4	5·6
Sales Workers	10·6	12·9	6·8
Farmers, Lumbermen, Fishermen	32·6	18·0	56·5
Mining Workers	0·8	0·6	1·2
Transport–Communications Workers	3·3	3·7	2·6
Craftsmen, Production Workers	28·6	34·3	19·3
Service Workers	6·5	8·3	3·5
Unclassified	0·0	0·0	0·0
Total	100·0	100·0	100·0

Source: *1960 Population Census of Japan*, Vol. 2, Part 4.

professional and technical, the rural or *gun* areas had 3·5 per cent as against 5·7 per cent for the urban or *shi* areas in 1960. At the other extreme, farming–lumbering–fishing, the rural areas show an expected high level, 56·5 per cent, but at the same time urban areas had almost one fifth (18 per cent) in this category. It is clear that one of the major characteristics of Japan's occupational structure is the emphatic interpenetration of the agrarian and the urban-oriented industrial pursuits.

A long history of abundant labour supply has meant that Japan's wage structure has remained relatively skewed to the lower levels of income. However, with the post-Second World War shifts towards a lessening of labour supply (though these shifts are not widespread) the wage structure has undergone some corresponding changes. A comparison of distribution of national income for 1934–36 and 1962 shows clearly the rise in employee compensation and a corresponding fall in proprietor's income. In 1962, 53·3 per cent of national income went to employees with something less than half this percentage (25·7 per cent) going to proprietors. This is in contrast to an employee/proprietor relationship of 38·9 per cent/31·3 per cent for 1934–36. It is still to be noted, however, that relative to the income structure of Western industrialized countries, the Japanese proprietor receives a significantly higher portion than do his employees.

Educational Levels

From the beginning of Japan's modern era intensive efforts have been made to provide educational opportunities for the general population. Attendance of children up to specified levels has been compulsory since the institution of a public educational system. The result has been a level of literacy in Japan which has exceeded that associated with similar levels of development for other areas of the society in industrializing nations. Currently Japanese educational authorities contend that for all practical purposes illiteracy has disappeared from Japan.

In the pre-Second World War Japanese educational system a series of stages existed within the system which channelled students rigidly into the several terminal educational levels. Only the select few were permitted to achieve a college education. Post-Second World War reorganization of this structure now places all students within a single 6–3–3 system. Attendance through junior high school (grade nine) is now compulsory, in contrast to the pre-war six-year requirement. In addition, higher educational institutions are now open to the general public through competitive examinations.

The liberalization of education opportunities in Japan since the close of the Second World War has prompted a significant increase in college and university enrolments: the 1962 college and university students are some five times as numerous as those of 1940. Further, the participation of women in higher education has increased even more rapidly. The 1962 female enrolment approaches seven times that of the 1940 figure.[6]

Though great strides have been made in the educational opportunities of women, the higher levels of university training are essentially confined to the realm of males. In the technical colleges, only 1 per cent of the students are females and in the universities only 15 per cent of those enrolled are females. Only in the junior colleges do the females outnumber the males in enrolment: 69·3 per cent females as against 30·7 per cent for males. The disparity of participation in higher education is clearly reflected in the dearth of females in the upper professional levels. For example, in 1960, male physicians outnumbered female MD's by a ratio of slightly less than ten to one (9·8); among scientific research workers the ratio was 9·4 to one.

In terms of overall educational attainment, however, Japan's record is an impressive one. Only slightly over 2 per cent of her population fifteen years of age and over in 1960 had never attended school, while well over one half the population of these ages had completed junior high school or more. These total figures mask the really startling advances made since the Second World War. For example, 11·6 per cent of Japan's

TABLE 6. *Distribution of Japan's National Income, 1934–36 and 1962*

Income category	Per cent distribution of national income 1934–36	1962
Employees' Compensation	38·9	53·3
Proprietor's Compensation	31·3	25·7
Personal Rental Income	9·0	2·2
Personal Interest Income	9·0	4·2
Corporation Profits	9·0	14·5
Surplus in Government and Public Enterprises	2·8	1·4
Net Income from Abroad	0·0	−0·5
Debt Interest	—	−0·8
Total	100·0	100·0

Source: *Nippon: A Chartered Survey of Japan, 1964*, Tokyo, 1964.

TABLE 7. *Educational Enrolment in Japan by Sex, 1962*

Educational institution	Percentage of total enrolment Males	Females	Total
Kindergarten	51·5	48·5	100·0
Elementary	51·1	48·9	100·0
Lower Secondary	51·0	49·0	100·0
Upper Secondary	51·5	48·5	100·0
Technical College	99·0	1·0	100·0
Junior College	30·7	69·3	100·0
Universities	85·0	15·0	100·0

TABLE 8. *Educational Attainment in Japan by Age and Sex, 1960*

Educational level completed	Percentage of population 15 years of age and over Males	Females	Total
Elementary	41·7	46·0	43·9
Junior High School	19·6	19·0	19·3
Senior High School	20·8	23·5	22·2
Junior College	3·6	1·8	2·7
University and Above	4·8	0·4	2·5
Currently in School	8·6	6·1	7·3
Never Attended and not Reported	1·0	3·3	2·2
Total	100·0	100·0	100·0

Source for Tables 7 and 8: *Education in Japan: A Graphic Presentation*, Ministry of Education, Tokyo, 1964.

males in 1960 between the ages of 25 and 29 years had had university and/or post graduate training. In the ages 20 through 24, there were 10·3 per cent of her males still in educational training, largely college, while 4·2 per cent had already completed training at this level.

II

THE PROBLEMS

The demographic problems facing Japan are essentially those of a maturing urban-industrial system. No longer does the spectre of an overwhelming rate of population increase threaten Japan, but the consequences of a greatly reduced pace of increase do make for future concerns.

A rising general standard of living coupled with increasing average expectation of life is conducive to a trend towards a lowering of the age at which withdrawal from the labour force takes place. This, in addition to a lowered fertility's reducing the rate at which potential labour force is created, means ultimately a reduction in the labour force relative to the population as a whole. The analysis of dependency ratios cited above reveals that currently the falling fertility has served to reduce the dependency of the very young, but significantly little if any change is yet to be seen in the dependency of the aged. If current vital trends continue, however, increasing aged dependency is potentially capable of outbalancing the reduction noted in that of the young. Aged dependency, viewed demographically, has the major disadvantage of representing reduced labour force potential in contrast to youth dependency which can be viewed as a preliminary stage in the development of a major source of future labour force.

Already the consequences of these age shifts are being felt in the Japanese labour market. Tanaka[6] in his recent study of the Tokyo employment structure notes that historically labour supply has exceeded demand in all areas of employment, but that currently the supply is approaching the demand. This is especially true for initial entrants into the labour force, but the closing of the labour supply–demand gap is as well visible at older ages though the rate of closing is not so striking. In the areas of engineering and skilled workers, labour supply is well below that of demand; this situation places a heavy burden upon small businesses which are less able to compete for the services of technicians.

An expanding urban-industrial system such as Japan's requires a constant supply of young, newly-trained technicians not only because of their facility with the latest methods and knowledge but because of their adaptability and relatively lower wage scale. The shrinking of these resources will require significant readjustments in the whole of the industrial system which Japan has historically evolved.

A second major problem area for Japan also stems from her maturation as an industrial society. The growth of her cities has and continues to concentrate larger and larger portions of the population within urban boundaries. In the urban category itself increasing portions of the urban population are further concentrating in the largest of the cities. The result is a mass of problems related to land use, transportation, and utilities for these growing urban concentrations. Efforts are being made in such areas as decentralization of industry and control of migration into the already densely settled cities, but as yet these efforts are uncoordinated and lacking in effective official sponsorship. The solutions to such problems for Japan are hampered not only by this absence of efficient organizational planning efforts, but by the very nature of the geographical environment. Well over one half of the national area is mountainous, leaving a limited area for settlement and cultivation. Inhabitable areas are concentrated principally in seven alluvial plains and these plains are understandably the locations of Japan's major metropolitan developments.

III

POPULATION POLICIES

As measured by all available indices, the relative ease of legalized abortion is the dominant factor in Japanese post-Second World War fertility patterns. Japanese officials are quite clear in their contention that abortion outweighs contraception in the amazing recent drop in reproduction. Okasaki of the Japanese Institute of Population Studies states 'In the final analysis, the strongest brake on Japanese birth rate was contrary to expectation, abortion and not contraception'.[7] As evidence for this conclusion, these officials cite such figures as the contrast of decrease in absolute number of births compared to the year 1949 with the official number of abortions for years following 1949. For example:

Year	Decrease in births from 1949	Official abortions reported
1951	559,000	636,524
1952	692,000	798,193

That abortions outnumber birth decreases in such comparisons argues for an acceptance of the probability that in any given year more than one abortion may have been required to avoid a single birth.

Muramatsu has attempted a more rigorous analysis of the influence of abortion on Japan's fertility by making estimates of (1) potential reproduction without contraception or abortion, and (2) effectiveness of contraception.[8] Contraceptive effectiveness subtracted from the hypothetically pure birth rate, gives an estimated birth rate influenced by abortion. This rate, in turn, is contrasted with actual reported birth rates and the difference is assumed to represent reproduction lost through abortion. Recognizing that his estimates and assumptions are conservative, Muramatsu concludes:

'In summary, it can be stated that the number of live births in 1955 in Japan would have amounted to twice (or more) the number actually registered, if there had been no induced abortion at all. And, the reporting of induced abortions to the health authorities probably included only 50 to 60 per cent of all cases actually performed.'[9]

There is some indication that abortions reached a peak in 1955 and now show some slight decline. This does not necessarily indicate that the continuously declining birth rate is more the result of effective contraception, for eugenic sterilization has shown a considerable increase during the period. Okasaki cites the following sterilization data for the period 1949–56:[10]

Year	Sterilizations	Year	Sterilizations
1949	5,356	1953	31,162
1950	10,792	1954	36,601
1951	15,409	1955	41,273
1952	21,241	1956	42,662

The Japanese experience in rapid fertility decline is instructive on several counts. First, Japanese experience reveals that abortion is more effective than contraception in its present state of practice, even in a population which is relatively highly developed economically and socially. Second, the amazing rate of acceptance of abortion as a means of fertility control in Japan is directly related to the fact that the society presents genuine alternatives to high fertility. This is to say that Japan offers an actual increased standard of living in return for lowered reproduction. Economic development in the post-war period has greatly expanded opportunities for higher income, leisure, and physical comfort; pragmatically the Japanese can experience immediately the consequences of fertility reduction.

Japanese experience argues clearly for recognition of the effectiveness of fertility control policies when they are an integral part of an on-going economic development. The Japanese are not unique in their recognition of the relationship between reduced fertility and higher standards of living. This recognition and the motivation to implement it are widespread in Asia as elsewhere. However, the Japanese do find themselves in a position where the fertility–living standards relationship is an actuality rather than a potentiality. Japanese anti-natal policies run counter to traditional fertility values, but these policies are strengthened by the readily-visible consequences of breaks with tradition. Unlike the vast majority of other Asian populations, Japan has already accomplished an industrial development capable of supporting in pragmatic terms pressures antithetical to traditional values not only in fertility but in all the other major institutional areas of her social organization. The ready availability of legalized abortion and sterilization and contraceptive techniques do not alone account for Japan's fertility reduction. Rather, Japanese experience emphasizes a society-wide development within which these fertility controls can and do take on practical meaning for significant portions of the total population.

Currently Japanese population policy activities are basically public health activities rather than official governmental policies as such. The Eugenic Protection Law of 1940 is the fundamental legal framework within which these activities are carried out. This was liberalized in 1948 and again in 1949 at which time economic factors became acceptable for induced abortion, contraceptive advice and sterilization. In 1952, the legal requirement for the consent of a second physician in induced abortion was dropped.

The more indirect influences upon population control of governmental and quasi-official agencies are significant in any assessment of demographic policies of Japan. Traditional paternalistic patterns in employment and a strong network of family relationships would, for example, tend to support a high fertility level. However, governmental support of and co-operation with widespread industrial development leads inevitably to higher general standards of living. These improvements in the possibilities of higher living standards tend to erode the effects of high fertility supporting traditions. In effect, government economic policies indirectly become factors in population change through the creation of elements conducive to controlled fertility. The post-Second World War legal emancipation of women is yet another government action which tends to contribute to a social context wherein a rational control of fertility is possible.

By the same token, the policies and practices of social welfare agencies have contributed substantially to the decline of mortality among the Japanese. Extensive government and privately sponsored medical plans and intensive public health programmes have served to bring Japan's death rates to the levels of the most advanced nations. For example, the death rate from pulmonary tuberculosis has fallen from a 1935 rate of 191 to 29 per 100,000 population in 1962. Corresponding declines are evident in other acute and communicable diseases.

The demographic development of Japan as a modern, urban-industrial nation offers stimulating clues as to the possibilities inherent in this transition for those nations, Asian and otherwise, currently at an earlier stage of development. This is not to say that Japan is the prototype of non-Western urban-industrialization. Rather, it says that those who are exercising leadership in the modernization of the non-Western nations can in their policy decisions draw upon a vastly expanded range of alternatives.

The Japanese modernization experience adds little, if at all, to the *general* theory of urban-industrialization. The growth of urban areas linked with the introduction of manpower-expanding technologies and production for markets beyond indigenous consumer needs occurred in Japan as the same generalized process had occurred in earlier developing nations. Concomitant with these developments fertility and mortality as well as other vital rates were adapted to meet a new focus for social organization. Once beyond this generalized level, however, Japan's demographic modernization is a unique blending of the demands of a modern technological system with significant and viable modifications of her traditional socio-economic organization. The Japanese experience underscores the conclusion that the nations currently striving for a transition to an urban-industrial modernization need not face the prospect of a total replacement of traditional goals and values by essentially Western socio-economic elements. Modernization, as Japan clearly illustrates, can be accomplished in such a way as to create a new social structure, but with all its newness it can carry the imprint of a unique set of traditional goals and values.

NOTES

1. Irene B. Taeuber and Edwin G. Beal, Jr, 'The Dynamics of Population in Japan', *Demographic Studies of Selected Areas of Rapid Growth* (New York, The Milbank Memorial Fund, 1944), pp. 11–15.
2. Edwin O. Reischauer, *The United States and Japan* (Cambridge, Harvard University Press, 1950), pp. 82–3.
3. The Tsuneta Yano Memorial Society, *Nippon: A Chartered Survey of Japan, 1964* (Tokyo, Kokusei-Sha, 1964), p. 33.
4. Japan, Bureau of Statistics, Office of the Prime Minister, *Japan Statistical Yearbook, 1963* (Tokyo, 1964), p. 62.
5. *Ibid.*, 1955, p. 49.
6. Heikichi Tanaka, 'Features, Tendencies and Changes in Labor Market of Tokyo', *Toshi mondai* (Municipal Problems), Vol. 54, No. 1 (January 1963), pp. 56–66.
7. Quoted by Alfred Sauvy, *Fertility and Survival* (London, Chatto and Windus, 1961), p. 185.
8. Minoru Muramatsu, 'Effect of Induced Abortion on the Reduction of Births in Japan', *Milbank Memorial Fund Quarterly*, XXXVIII, No. 2 (April 1960).
9. *Ibid.*, p. 166.
10. Sauvy, *op. cit.*, p. 186.

BIBLIOGRAPHY

Ishii, Ryoishi, *Population Pressure and Economic Life in Japan* (London, P. S. King and Son, Ltd., 1937).

Japan, Prime Minister's Office, Bureau of Statistics. *Japan Statistical Yearbook* (Tokyo, annually from 1949).

Levy, M. J., Jr., 'Contrasting Factors in the Modernization of China and Japan', *Economic Development and Cultural Change*, 2 (1953).

Parsons, Talcott, 'Population and Social Structure', in Douglas G. Haring, editor, *Japan's Prospect* (Cambridge, Massachusetts, Harvard University Press, 1946).

Penrose, E. F., *Population Theories and Their Application with Special Reference to Japan* (Stanford, California, Stanford University Press, 1946).

Schumpeter, E. B., editor, *The Industrialization of Japan and Manchukuo, 1930–1940: Population, Raw Materials and Industry* (New York, Macmillan Co., 1940).

Taeuber, Irene B., *The Population of Japan* (Princeton, New Jersey, Princeton University Press, 1958).

'Japan's Demographic Transition Re-examined', *Population Studies*, 14 (1960).

and Edwin G. Beal, Jr., 'The Dynamics of Population in Japan', *Demographic Studies of Selected Areas of Rapid Growth*. The Milbank Memorial Fund, New York, 1944.

Wilkinson, Thomas O., 'Family Structure and Industrialization in Japan', *American Sociological Review*, 27 (1962).

The Urbanization of Japanese Labor (Amherst, Massachusetts, University of Massachusetts Press, 1965).

CHAPTER 5

INDONESIA'S POPULATION PROBLEM[1]

BY EVERETT D. HAWKINS

I

THE FACTS

INDONESIA is one of the largest countries in the world with a population of over 105 million in 1965. Its claim to be the fifth largest country, surpassed only by China, India, the Soviet Union and the United States, is based on its 1961 census,[2] which indicated a total population of 97,018,829, exceeding that year's reported figures for Pakistan and Japan, her closest rivals. Pakistan has recently claimed to be the fifth largest. Whether Indonesia be fifth or sixth is not so important as the fact that she is one of the 'big five' in Asia and much larger than any of the other countries in south-east Asia. In fact, Indonesia herself has about 40 per cent of the population of all south-east Asia.

Present Characteristics

As one of the largest countries, with a rapid rate of population increase, she faces major population problems, many of which are recognized fully by only a very few Indonesians. Before discussing these problems and some suggested solutions, such as transmigration, it is important to present pertinent data on population developments to date, in the light of some especially sharp contrasts in the country's demographic picture.

(1) The contrast between Java, Madura, and Bali, which are very crowded, and most of the Outer Islands, which have relatively low population densities, is very striking.

(2) Although the population of Indonesia has grown rapidly since the first general census in 1905, growth rates have varied markedly in recent years, with a 'hollow generation' in the 1940's and a 'baby boom' in the 1950's.

(3) As with other countries in the early stages of a demographic transition, birth rates remain high, while death rates are falling rapidly.

(4) Although over 85 per cent of the population lives in rural areas of 20,000 or less, Indonesian cities are growing faster than the country as a whole, giving the country a distinct 'urban bulge'.

(5) The labour force is still largely made up of peasants, unpaid

family workers, and the unskilled, but 'management courses' flourish in the cities.

(6) The education industry has grown more rapidly since independence than all other industries or the economy as a whole.

Regional Disparities

Indonesia is a huge archipelago made up of five large islands, a score of important ones, and thousands more—some of which are inhabited. The diversity of population density between crowded Java, Madura, and Bali, on the one hand, and relatively empty West Irian, on the other, is enormous (see Table 1). In 1961, Java and Madura accounted for less than 7 per cent of the total land area of 1,904,345 square kilometres, but for almost 65 per cent of the people, or an overall density of 477 per sq. km.; while West Irian had over 22 per cent of the land area, less than

TABLE 1. *Population, Area and Densities by Region, Indonesia, 1961*

Region	Population Total	Population Per cent	Area Sq. km.	Area Per cent	Density persons per sq. km.
Java	62,993,056	64·93	132,174	6·94	477
Sumatra	15,739,363	16·22	473,606	24·87	33·0
Kalimantan	4,101,475	4·23	539,460	28·33	7·6
Sulawesi	7,079,349	7·30	189,035	9·93	37·0
Other Islands	7,105,586	7·32	570,070	29·93	12·5
including					
Bali	1,782,529	1·84	5,561	0·29	321
West Irian	758,396	0·78	421,951	22·16	1·8
Indonesia	97,018,829		1,904,345		51

Source: Central Bureau of Statistics, Census of 1961.

1 per cent of the population and only 1·8 persons per sq. km. The density of Bali is also high, 321, but most of the other island groups are below the Indonesian average of 51, with Sulawesi (Celebes) 37, Sumatra 33, Maluku Islands 11, and Kalimantan (Borneo) 7·6. Thus it will be important in many parts of this chapter to consider the various islands and provinces separately, rather than to lump them together in averages, which in many cases would hide wide disparities. These sharp divergences in density, for example, make for important differences in the degree of urbanization, the supply of labour, and the level of wages. Furthermore, because of their greater numbers the Javanese, who constitute about half the total population, play a key role in the political life of the country.

Indonesia is made up of hundreds of different ethnic and language groups, with cultural, religious, and geographic differences abounding.[3] Although great progress has been made in creating an Indonesian national identity and the use of the Indonesian language has spread widely, regional and ethnic differences cannot be ignored. One of the five basic principles of Indonesian life (*Pantja Sila*) is belief in God, and the country prides itself on religious freedom. It is generally believed that 90 per cent of the people are Moslems, but in Sumatra, Kalimantan, and the northern coast of Java there are many more devout Moslems than in Central and East Java, where most of the people are nominal Moslems, still very much influenced by Hindu and animistic beliefs. In Greater Djakarta, according to the census of 1961,[4] almost 85 per cent of the people claimed to be Moslem, 7·8 per cent were Buddhist and Hindu (including many Chinese), 3·1 per cent were Protestant, 1·7 per cent were Catholic, and over 2 per cent held other religions or none at all. In Bali the Hindu faith is still dominant. There are many Catholics in Flores and Central Java. Protestants are more apt to be concentrated in Ambon, Minahassa, Timor, and around Lake Toba among certain Batak clans. Thus, regional and ethnic differences may be compounded by different religious beliefs.

Growth of Population

Census data on the population of Java and Madura goes back much further than for Indonesia as a whole. In the time from the first census of 1815 (taken by Raffles) to the Indonesian census of 1961, the population of Java and Madura increased fourteenfold, from 4·5 to 63 million (see Table 2). If allowance is made for the possibility of under-enumeration in 1815, Keyfitz believes, 'The increase of Java and Madura was tenfold in a century and a half'.[5] A somewhat less startling figure is the fivefold increase in the century from 1860 to 1961. The greatest expansion in population coincided with the period when the Dutch transformed the agriculture of Java and Madura into a series of commercial crops to supply the West with specialized foods and raw materials for its growing millions and industries. There was some slowing down in the rate of increase until the new burst of population in the 1950s. In the thirty years from 1815 to 1845, the Indonesian population in Java more than doubled, if we can trust the 1815 enumeration. The population increased by about two thirds during the twenty-five years from 1845 to 1870 and again during the thirty years from 1870 to 1900. From 1900 to 1930, however, the increase was less than 50 per cent, while in the thirty-one years from 1930 to 1961, the population increased by over 50 per cent.

The first census for all of Indonesia dates back only to 1905. In the fifty-six-year period from 1905 to 1961, the total Indonesian population increased about 140 per cent. During the twenty-five years from 1905 to 1930, the population rose by a little more than 50 per cent; while in the next thirty-one years it increased almost 60 per cent, in spite of the depression of the thirties and the disruption of war and revolution in the forties. The last burst of population came in the fifties after independence had been won and shows up clearly in the very large percentage of children (over a third of the total population) under ten years of age.

During this fifty-six-year period, the population in the Outer Islands grew more rapidly than that of Java and Madura or Indonesia as a whole, increasing more than 250 per cent, if we can trust the 1905 enumeration of the Outer Islands. During the twenty-five years from 1905 to 1930, the population in the Outer Islands almost doubled, while

TABLE 2. *Population Growth in Indonesia—Java and the Outer Islands*
Census Data 1815–1961

Census year	Indonesians: Java and Madura	Indonesians: Outer islands	Others	Total
1815	4·5			
1845	9·4			
1860	12·5			
1870	16·2			
1880	19·5			
1890	23·6			
1900	28·4			
1905	30·0	9·7	0·7	40·4
1920	34·4	13·9	1·0	49·3
1930	41·7	18·2	1·6	61·5
1961	63·0 (all)	34·0 (all)	—	97·0

Source: 'The Population of Indonesia', *Ekonomi dan Keuangan Indonesia*, Vol. IX, No. 2, February 1956, Appendix D 1, p. 110. Census of 1961.

in the thirty-one years from 1930 to 1961 the population almost doubled again (rising about 87 per cent). These percentage increases are substantially greater than those for Java and Madura, but the absolute increases in the Outer Islands contributed less than half the total growth between 1930 and 1961.

The census data collected during the period of Dutch control separated the population into two groups: Indonesians and others (Chinese, Indians, Dutch, etc.). Such a breakdown has not been presented in the 1961 census, except for Greater Djakarta, where about 96 per cent were Indonesian and 3·5 per cent Chinese, with all other groups too small to be significant. In 1958, 97·6 per cent of the labour force in Java and Madura was estimated to be Indonesian. Professor Skinner estimated that in 1961 there were approximately 2,450,000 Chinese in Indonesia, about evenly divided between Java and the Outer Islands.[6]

In general, international migrations have had little recent effect on the annual rate of population increase in Indonesia. In the fifties and early sixties, the number of persons arriving from and leaving for abroad annually were each about 70,000, except for the large outflow of the Dutch, which reached about 30,000 in 1957, and the 102,000 Chinese who left in 1960.[7]

The Hollow Generation and the Baby Boom

A study of the age and sex distribution of the population, based on a 1 per cent sample of the 1961 census, indicated 1·3 million more females than males out of a total population of 96·3 million (see Table 3). This

TABLE 3. *Population by Sex and Age—Indonesia, 1961*

Age group	Males	Females	Both sexes	Per cent
0– 4	8,461,949	8,580,361	17,042,310	17·7
5– 9	7,683,534	7,639,422	15,322,956	15·9
10–14	4,318,543	3,860,869	8,179, 412	8·5
15–19	3,834,117	3,874,058	7,708,175	8·0
20–24	3,452,362	4,338,603	7,790,965	8·1
25–34	7,333,617	8,542,102	15,875,719	16·5
35–44	5,719,856	5,363,334	11,083,190	11·5
45–54	3,559,007	3,483,325	7,042,332	7·3
55–64	1,897,510	1,850,396	3,747,906	3·9
65–74	795,730	829,027	1,624,757	1·7
75+	377,747	406,609	784,356	0·8
Unknown	59,882	56,869	116,751	0·1
Total	47,493,854	48,824,975	96,318,829*	100·0

* Excludes the estimated population of West Irian (700,000).

Source: *Statistical Pocketbook of Indonesia*, 1963, p. 15.

excludes West Irian, where no census was taken, since it was not then under Indonesian jurisdiction. Only in the 10–14 age group were there substantially more males reported than females. In the 20–34 groups, females were much more numerous, perhaps because more men lost their lives during the Second World War and the Revolution. Furthermore, some Indonesian women in these age brackets may have underestimated their ages, since the 35–55 groups showed more males. In the older established regions such as Java, females exceeded males by 1·4 million out of a total of 63 million (95 males to 100 females). Sumatra and Kalimantan had more males than females, especially in the frontier areas, while in Sulawesi and the other islands females slightly exceeded males.

The sex composition is probably not so notable as the unusual concentration of children under ten years of age, amounting to more than a third of the population (33·6 per cent). In sharp contrast, the group from 10–19—the 'hollow' generation—constitutes less than half that much (16·5 per cent) and less than those in the 20 through 34 bracket.

After comparing figures from Pakistan, the Labour Force Survey for Java and Madura in 1958, and the results of the Indonesian Demographic Survey of 1962, Professor Keyfitz concludes: 'The study of the three sets of data not only broadly confirms the census but permits us to locate somewhat more precisely the moment of change.'[8]

An island-by-island study of the age distribution indicates a higher than average percentage under ten in the Outer Islands (35·7 per cent in Sumatra) and a slightly lower percentage (32·9 per cent) in Java. This is not contrary to expectations, since the population in the Outer Islands is growing more rapidly than in Java. On the other hand, the hollow generation shows up more clearly in Java, as does the lower percentage in the 20–24 group. Conversely, Java has more in the 25–55 bracket than do the other islands. In no case is the number of people 55 and over large, varying around 6·5 per cent.[9]

What accounts for the existence of the 'hollow' generation? Undoubtedly, times were disturbed—the 1940's saw the Second World War and the Japanese occupation, and later came the Revolution and the fight with the Dutch. Food was scarce, families were scattered, marriages were postponed, births fell (some think to as low as 20 per 1,000), and mortality among children rose. In the 1950's times were much more peaceful, there was a reunion of families, reconstruction took place, and rice and other food crops generally increased. Whether the decreasing percentage of children under one (3·3 per cent) and age one (3 per cent) in relation to age two (3·6 per cent) and age three (3·8 per cent) indicates a real downward trend at the end of the decade or merely reflects the manner of reporting the ages of younger children is not clear. It is still too early to tell for sure whether the revolts of 1958, the poor harvests in 1961 and 1964, inflation, and political crises will have a substantial effect on the population, but these items need to be considered in making future projections. Certainly the implications of the baby boom of the fifties must be considered. Roughly speaking, twice as large a group as the hollow generation of the forties will be demanding primary education, advanced education, food, clothing, and shelter. It will mean twice the number of new entrants into the labour force.

High Fertility and Declining Mortality

Reports of births and deaths throughout Indonesia are too incomplete for compiling fertility and mortality figures for the country as a whole, but the records in Java are better. The evidence of the early 1960's points to an average annual crude birth rate of 43 per 1,000, with a death rate of just over 20 and a rate of growth of 21·6. The last is slightly lower in Java (20·4) and slightly higher in the other islands (23·8). These figures might be compared with an estimated fertility rate of over 40 and an estimated annual rate of population increase of 15 in the

1930's and, therefore, with a death rate of over 25. In many years of the forties, the birth and the death rates came closer together, with a reduction in the annual rate of increase to less than 10 per 1,000 or under 1 per cent. Just prior to the census of 1961, the Central Bureau of Statistics used a figure for estimating population increase of 23 per 1,000. The Department of Health, working with data reported by local authorities, used a crude birth rate of 40 and a crude death rate of 17, resulting in an annual increase of 23 per 1,000, or 2·3 per cent a year. This is higher than the minimum assumption of 1·5 per cent or the probable assumption of 2 per cent used by the National Planning Bureau in its projections in the mid-fifties.[10]

Vaino Kannisto, a UN expert assisting the Central Bureau of Statistics, made an intensive study of data (collected in the 1961 census) for children aged 2–6 years and by applying survivorship ratios from UN model life tables developed a whole series of crude birth rates for each of the years 1956 to 1960; they consistently exceeded 40 per 1,000 and were closer to 43 per 1,000.[11] This general figure of 43 was converted to estimated crude birth rates by regions and in urban and rural areas, with a range from 37·4 in urban Java to 45·6 in the rural areas of the other islands (see Table 4).

TABLE 4. *Estimated Crude Birth Rates in Indonesia by Regions, 1961 (per 1,000 persons)*

Region	Urban	Rural	Urban and rural
Indonesia	38·5	43·8	43·0
Java	37·4	42·9	42·0
All other islands	40·9	45·6	45·0

Source: *Population of Indonesia*, p. 32.

From these studies and also from those made in the post-enumeration survey of December 1961 and the Demographic Survey of December 1962 for the same districts, the following estimates were made for 1962:

	Indonesia	Java	All other islands
Crude Birth Rates per 1,000	43·0	42·0	44·9
Crude Death Rates per 1,000	21·4	21·6	21·1
Crude Rate of Growth per 1,000	21·6	20·4	23·8

These rates would result in an increase of population in Indonesia of 2,130,000 in 1962, 1,308,000 in Java and 822,000 in all the other islands. Looking towards the future, the report concludes:

'There are some indications that the fertility level is somewhat lower in urban areas. However, there are no signs as yet as to probable changes in the future course of the overall level of fertility. With respect to mortality it can be safely assumed that the present downward trend will continue in the future.'[12]

Certainly, the *Statistical Pocketbook for Indonesia* for 1963 reported substantial declines in mortality rates in Java, and the 1962 rates reported were considerably below the level of 21·6 estimated above.[13] Also, death rates may drop to 10 to 12 per thousand, as in some other Asian countries. Without any decrease in fertility, this could mean population increases of as much as 3 per cent a year; such a rate has already been recorded in other countries of Asia.

Rural Base and Urban Bulge

Although about 85·2 per cent of her 1961 population lived in rural areas, places with less than 20,000 population, Indonesia has a great many important cities. Urban population is growing faster than rural, as in most countries, primarily because of substantial movement, particularly of young people, from the rural areas to the city. Rapid urbanization and the beginning of suburbanization are characteristics of present-day Indonesia.

The most important internal migration is from the rural areas to the cities, not only to the big ten shown in Table 5, but also to the middle-sized cities and the smaller ones as well. Using 1930 as a base of 100, the big city increases range from 226 to 583, while total population in 1961 had risen to only 158. Some of the cityward movement may be temporary, but studies made in Java, comparing place of residence with place of birth indicate movements almost entirely from rural areas to the towns and cities, rather than the reverse. The extensive shortage of village land in Java is one explanation. The city offers better housing, more public utilities, higher levels of education, more entertainment and better wages and salaries. Ambitious men make their names in politics and business in the city. At times of disturbance in rural areas, such as during the Darul Islam raids, families have moved to the city for protection. Despite the great flight of city people to the villages during the struggles with the Dutch (1945–49), the reverse flow since seems to have been too strong to leave any significant trace of the movement from urban to rural areas during the Revolution. Further, rice injections in the cities have even encouraged people in rural areas to flock to the cities in times of bad crops, as in the early months of 1964.

Some figures are available from the 1961 census for Greater Djakarta, which sustained one of the most rapid rises in population and by far the largest in absolute numbers. Only 51 per cent of the 1961 population of 2,906,533 were born in Djakarta, and about half of these were babies and small children under five years of age. About 41 per cent were born in other parts of Java, the greatest portion, 26·9 per cent, coming from West Java, which, with the Java Sea on the north, surrounds Greater Djakarta. About 3·9 per cent were born in Sumatra, 1 per cent in Sulawesi, 0·5 per cent in Kalimantan, 1·1 per cent in foreign countries, and the balance in other islands (or unknown).

The migration to Djakarta was very high amongst young people, especially those from 15–34 years of age. Taking males, who are a bit more mobile, the picture is very clear. Two thirds to four fifths of the

TABLE 5. *Population Growth in the Largest Cities of Indonesia, 1930, 1952, 1961 (in 1,000's)*

	1930	1952	1961	1961 per cent of 1930	1961 per cent of 1952
Djakarta	533·0	1,635·2	2,973·1	558	182
Surabaja	341·7	900·0	1,007·9	295	112
Bandung	166·8	679·5	972·8	583	143
Semerang	217·8	330·4	503·1	231	152
Medan	76·6	254·4	479·1	625	188
Palembang	108·1	237·6	475·0	439	200
Makasar	84·9	265·3	384·2	453	145
Surakarta	163·0	—	367·6	226	—
Malang	86·6	—	341·4	394	—
Jogjakarta	136·6	244·4	312·7	229	128

Source: *Statistical Pocketbook of Indonesia, 1957,* and also *1963.*

boys up to fourteen years of age were born in Djakarta, but for the 15–19 group the proportion drops to 37 per cent, and for the 20–34 group it is about 27 per cent. As age goes up further the percentage born in Djakarta rises slowly to 48·3 per cent of those seventy-five and over. Furthermore, 40·7 per cent of Djakarta's population is in the 15–34 age bracket, compared to only 32·6 per cent for the rest of Indonesia. Djakarta is the place for young people to come for education, politics, and employment. The movement of young people to the other cities has also been recorded in earlier sample surveys.[14]

Differences between rural and urban fertility rates have already been noted. Movements to the city may cause some reduction in fertility rates, but for a long time to come the rural population will greatly exceed the urban.

Labour Force

This rural–urban split is also important in studying the labour force composition. In rural regions 81 per cent of the labour force is engaged in agriculture, fishing, or forestry, while in the urban areas over 85 per cent are engaged in industry, construction, commerce, transportation, and services. The 1961 census showed only 36 per cent of the population in the labour force, but sample studies indicate that if part-time women workers in rural areas were included, as in Thailand, for example, the percentage would be much higher. In 1961, the total labour force was reported at 34·6 million, or 54·1 per cent of a total population ten years of age or over of 64 million (see Table 6), including 79·8 per cent of the

TABLE 6. *Relation between Total Population and the Labour Force in All Indonesia—1961 Census*

Total Population excluding W. Irian	96·3 million
—Children 0–9 years old	32·3
Population 10 years and over	64·0
—Still in school 10 and over	6·4
—Home-Houseworkers (mostly women, 18·5)	19·5
—Others	3·5
Labour Force 10 and over	34·6
—Unemployed	1·9
Working Labour Force	32·7 million

Source: Census of 1961

males, but only 29·4 of the females. The reasons for the relatively small number in the labour force are the low percentage of women reported in the rural work force by the census of 1961, the peculiar age distribution already discussed, and the increasing percentage going on to middle schools, technical institutes and universities, thus entering the labour force at a later age.

In 1958 a Labour Force Sample Survey was made in Java and Madura[15] which can be compared with the Census of 1961 to show the rates of male and female participation in the labour force, in both the rural and urban areas. (See Table 7.) The most striking difference between the

TABLE 7. *Labour Force in Rural and Urban Areas as a Percentage of Population in Java and Madura, 1958, 1961*

	1958			1961		
	Rural	Urban	Total	Rural	Urban	Total
Male	57·12	49·25	56·05	53·9	49·9	53·2
Female	43·09	19·67	39·67	19·7	19·4	19·7
Total	49·93	34·31	47·77	36·4	34·5	36·1

Source: Labour Force Sample Survey of 1958. Census of 1961.

two sets of figures lies in the participation rates for rural women. The 1958 figure given was 43·09 per cent (i.e. 10·6 million), while in 1961 the number reported was only 19·7 per cent, or 5·4 million. The difference between the two figures is largely due to the fact that a much broader definition of labour force participation was used in 1958 than in 1961. Unlike the census, the 1958 survey included all those in the rural areas who had had a job or part-time occupation at any time in the year preceding the survey. Female participation in rural areas was usually high, but it is largely part-time, seasonal and unpaid. The partial exclusion of this category in 1961 was the primary reason for the lower total figure of only 36·1 per cent as compared to 47·8 per cent in the labour force in Java, since there was no substantial difference in the

TABLE 8. *Number and Percentage of Population in the Labour Force by Age and Sex in Indonesia, 1961 (in millions)*

Population		Labour force			
		Males		Females	
Age	Number	Number	Per cent	Number	Per cent
0–4	17·0	—	—	—	—
5–9	15·3	—	—	—	—
10–14	8·2	1·0	22·6	0·6	15·6
15–19	7·7	2·6	66·7	1·2	30·6
20–24	7·8	3·0	87·2	1·2	27·4
25–34	15·8	6·9	94·4	2·3	27·3
35–44	11·1	5·5	96·8	1·8	33·3
45–54	7·0	3·4	95·6	1·4	39·8
55–64	3·7	1·7	89·6	0·7	39·1
65–74	1·6	0·6	78·0	0·3	31·5
75+	0·8	0·2	61·7	0·1	20·3
Unknown	0·1	0·05	82·2	0·04	53·2
Totals	96·3	25·0	52·7	9·6	19·6
Totals 10 and over	64·0	25·0	79·8	9·6	29·4

Source: Census of 1961.

other groups. This undoubtedly affected the low percentage for the country as a whole.

If the figures reported by the Census of 1961 were adjusted to reflect the 47·8 per cent participation rate found in the Sample Labour Force Survey in Java in 1958, thus including a large number of part-time rural workers, especially women, the total labour force would have been about 45 million in 1961, or close to 50 million in 1965. This method gives a relatively high figure, since the population 15–55 years of age is not increasing as rapidly as the population under fifteen. On the other hand, inflation has made it necessary for more wives and children to seek full- or part-time ways of earning money to eke out a living for the family.

The second reason for the low percentage of the total population in the labour force lies in the birth patterns of the last two decades, especially in the baby boom of the 1950's and the hollow generation of the 1940's. (See Table 8.) The children aged from 0–9 years, born in the baby boom from 1951 to 1960, number 32·3 million, or over a third of the population, while those from 10–19 years, born in the period of struggles with the Japanese and the Dutch number only 15·9 million (16·5 per cent). The teenagers who entered the labour force by 1961 were a small group, only half the size of the 0–9 group too young to enter the labour force, and smaller than the group in their twenties which had already entered it. This age distribution would continue to depress the percentage of the total population in the labour force for at least the first half of the sixties. The youthfulness of the present Indonesian population will soon cause many changes and will necessitate many adaptations in the economy and the society. The baby boom of the early fifties has already become the primary school bulge, and from 1967 to 1971 it will double the numbers of new entrants into the labour force. Completing the twenty-year cycle, by 1971 or earlier these new labour force entrants will themselves be marrying and setting off a new baby boom of even greater proportions.

Unemployment figures reported by the Census of 1961 amounted to only 1·9 million or 5·4 per cent of the labour force, with 4·8 per cent reported for males, and 5·4 per cent for females. Unemployment was very high (over 20 per cent) among teenagers, both boys and girls, while it tapered off among the 20–24 group and was only 1 or 2 per cent for those aged 25–54. In fact, over 70 per cent of the reported unemployment was sustained by those under twenty-five, indicating, it would seem, the difficulty young, unsettled people experience in finding ways to earn a living.

In both Java and the rest of Indonesia, reported percentages of unemployment were substantially greater in the urban (8·5 per cent) than in the rural areas (4·9 per cent). It is not surprising therefore to find the highest unemployment rate in Djakarta, 7·4 per cent (6·4 per cent males and 11·3 per cent females).[16]

Indonesia, like other developing countries, not only has unemployment, but also a vast amount of underemployment. It was estimated that in 1958 in Java there was a great difference in employment in agricultural work during the peak and slack seasons as follows:[17]

Peak season	Slack season
7·37 million worked 7 hours and over per day	0·47 million
7·10 million worked 4–6 hours and over per day	4·72 million
1·27 million worked 1–3 hours and over per day	8·12 million

Using these data the Labour Force Sample Survey estimated that there was an underemployment rate of one third in agriculture in 1958. Over 11 billion man-hours were lost in that year.

In the country as a whole in 1961, as well as in Java in 1958 and 1961, the labour force participation of those ten years of age and older in rural areas was higher, 55·4 per cent, compared with only 47·1 per cent in the urban areas. A smaller difference exists in the relationship between the labour force and the total population, 36·5 per cent (rural) and 32·8 per cent (urban), respectively. With the exception of Sulawesi, the Outer Islands had higher labour participation rates than Java or than the average for Indonesia. The range by province was greater for women

TABLE 9. *Industrial Classification of the Indonesian Employed* Labour Force, 1930 and 1961*

	1930 Census	1961 Census				
	Total	Total	Rural	Urban	Java	Other islands
0 Agriculture, forestry, fishing	68·9	71·9	81·0	11·7	68·0	79·4
1 Mining		0·3	0·2	0·5	0·1	0·5
2 Manufacturing, 3 industry	10·5	5·7	4·1	15·9	6·8	3·5
4 Construction	—	1·8	0·1	5·9	2·0	1·3
5 Electric Power etc.	—	0·1	0·1	0·8	0·1	0·2
6 Commerce	6·2	6·7	4·6	20·5	7·8	4·7
7 Transportation	1·5	2·1	1·0	9·7	2·3	1·8
8 Services	3·4	9·5	5·9	33·1	11·0	6·6
Others and unknown	9·5	1·9	2·0	1·9	1·9	2·0

* Includes many self-employed.
Source: Census of 1961.

than for men. Jogjakarta had a high of 45 per cent of the women over ten in the labour force[18] while Sulawesi had only 17·9 per cent. On the other hand, Jogjakarta had the lowest percentage of males, 72·4 per cent, and East Java the highest, 83·2 per cent.

That Indonesia is still predominantly rural is demonstrated by the 1961 census figures, which show that agriculture was still the occupation of over 70 per cent of the total labour force, while manufacturing, commerce, and services together accounted for only 21·9 per cent. These three groups, however, accounted for almost 70 per cent of the urban labour force (see Table 9).

The total included in the industrial classification of the labour force in the census of 1930 was 20·7 million, as compared with 32·7 in the employed labour force in 1961—about a 60 per cent increase. Contrary to expectation, a comparison of the two sets of census data shows a slightly higher percentage in agriculture in 1961 than in 1930. (See

Table 9.) Some estimates made in the 1950s indicated somewhat lower percentages in agriculture then than in 1930.[19] The real situation may be that other types of employment in the modern sector are not able to provide sufficient new jobs for the growing population, so that people must remain in agriculture, forestry, and fishing. The decline in percentage in manufacturing tends to bear out this point even if mining, construction, and power are added to manufacturing in the 1961 figures to make it more comparable to the 1930 census. Commerce and transportation show moderate percentage increases and services, including the Government, the most substantial. Actually, some of this may not be a real increase because of the large percentage in the 'other' category in 1930. The fact that Indonesia has not moved more of its people out of the primary occupations into the secondary industries and the services is probably a reflection of the depression of the thirties, the war and revolution of the forties, and the lack of rapid growth in the fifties. Some lack of movement might also be because agriculture, forestry and fishing are so much more important in the other islands (79·4 per cent) than in Java (68 per cent), and they have been increasing in population more rapidly than Java. In all the other industrial classifications except mining, Java has higher percentages in the labour force than the other islands.

Indonesia has a relatively small base of professional and administrative personnel—only about 5 per cent, even in the capital city of Djakarta in 1961. Unfortunately, the Census of 1961 has not published figures for the whole country so the Labour Force Study in Java in 1958 must be used. (See Table 10.) There was a marked difference in 1958 between the rural areas of Java, with only 1·3 per cent professional and administrative personnel, and the urban areas, with 7·6 per cent. The contrast was also great among the clerical and sales employees. In 1956 the Ministry of Labour made a study of one million employees in larger firms and found 1·5 per cent were owners and managers, 5 per cent administrative and welfare staff members, 30·4 per cent skilled workers and 63·1 per cent unskilled and semi-skilled workers. In the country as a whole, the percentage of unskilled and semi-skilled would probably be greater.

One other way to classify the labour force is by status. In Java in 1958 the workers and salaried employees were only 32·5 per cent of the total, the self-employed 31 per cent and the unpaid family workers 29 per cent. Employers totalled 7·5 per cent. In rural Java, the percentage for paid workers was slightly lower and the other categories higher. In the urban areas and in Djakarta in 1961, about two thirds were workers or salaried employees with a substantial number of self-employed, but fewer unpaid family workers and employers (see Table 11). It seems certain that as Indonesia becomes more urbanized and modernized, the percentage of the labour force who are employees and are paid wages or salaries will rise, and that the percentage of self-employed and unpaid family workers will be substantially reduced; this has been the pattern in more developed countries.

TABLE 10. *Occupational Classification of the Labour Force in Java, 1958, and in Djakarta, 1961*

	Java rural 1958 per cent	Java urban 1958 per cent	Djakarta 1961 per cent
0 Professional	0·71	4·20	3·0
1 Administrative	0·54	3·44	2·0
2 Clerical	0·54	10·69	12·0
3 Sales	12·28	26·71	20·0
4 Farmers	70·56	4·20	48·0
5 Miners	0·17	—	0·2
6 Transport Workers	1·17	6·87	12·0
7, 8 Craftsmen and other workers	8·94	26·33	28·0
9 Services	3·80	16·41	15·0
10 Not classified	1·19	1·15	3·0

Source: Labour Force Sample Survey, 1958. Census of Djakarta, 1961.

TABLE 11. *Status of the Labour Force in Java, 1958, and in Djakarta, 1961*

	Java rural 1958	Java urban 1958	Java Total 1958	Djakarta Total 1961
Employers	8·10	2·67	7·5	1·9
Self-employed	31·19	29·39	31·0	23·0
Wage and salaried workers	29·10	63·36	32·5	67·1
Unpaid family workers	31·61	4·58	29·0	1·7
Other	—	—	—	6·3
Total	100·0	100·0	100·0	100·0

Sources: Labour Force Sample Survey in Java and Madura, Tables 10, 22. Census of 1961, DCI. Djakarta Raya, p. 38.

Illiteracy, Education, and Training

Indonesia has been rapidly expanding its whole educational programme from the first grade through the universities, but the demand seems to outrun the supply. No province feels respectable unless it has at least one university faculty, and most expect many more. The Government has also carried on a large adult education programme to combat illiteracy, and by 1961, 13½ million certificates had been awarded.[20] Big ceremonies were held to declare certain cities or regions free from illiteracy, and in 1965 President Sukarno declared the whole of Indonesia to be literate.[21] Indonesians like to stress that the literacy rate was only 7 per cent at the end of the Dutch régime.

The Census of 1961 pointed to real progress in the reduction of illiteracy: 46·7 per cent of the people ten years of age and over were able to read and write.[22] The highest rate of literacy (72·1 per cent) was in the 10–14 age group, educated entirely since independence. The figures thereafter decreased steadily to 14·9 per cent in the 65–74 group. Males had a higher literacy rate, 59·8 per cent, than females, who had only 34·1 per cent. Urban dwellers were 50 per cent more literate (66·6 per cent) than rural people (43 per cent). Sumatra had much the highest rate of literacy (56·6 per cent), exceeding Java (45·5 per cent) and the other islands (38·8–45 per cent). Thus, the sections of the population in which literacy must be pushed are among females, the people in the rural areas (especially in the islands other than Sumatra), and those in the older age brackets.

The great increase in literacy among the younger people has come about largely because of the growth in the number of pupils attending schools, who by 1951–52, after the recovery from the difficulties of war, revolution, and reconstruction, surpassed those in attendance in the pre-war period. By 1961 the census showed that 22·5 million people, about 35 per cent of the total population ten years of age and over, had had three or more years of primary school.[23] This meant that 41·5 million had never gone to school, or had gone only to a religious school, or had less than three years of primary education. As might be expected, most of these people (over 37 million) lived in rural areas, and the difference in educational attainment between males and females was also great (see Table 12).

TABLE 12. *Percentage of Population Ten Years and over by Level of Education attained in Indonesia, 1961*

	Males			Females		
	No school	Primary (Grade 3)	Higher	No school	Primary (Grade 3)	Higher
Urban	28·8	54·9	16·3	55·0	37·0	8·0
Rural	58·2	39·6	2·2	79·5	19·8	0·7
Total	53·5	42·1	4·4	75·8	22·4	1·8

Source: Census of 1961.

The Indonesians, however, point with pride to the fact that in all of Indonesia, 54·8 per cent of the primary age group, 7–13 years, were in school in 1961, 57·7 per cent of the boys and 51·7 per cent of the girls. Below ten years of age, the disparity in school attendance between sexes was even smaller, but above fifteen it was much greater. As might be expected, Djakarta had the highest percentage (69·4) in school, and Sumatra (60·2 per cent) exceeded all of Java (55·3 per cent) and the other islands (43·5–54·3 per cent). In all, 11·8 million young people, or about 15 per cent of the population aged five and above, were in school, a substantial achievement, since only 1·3 million were so reported in 1948–49 (see Table 13).

TABLE 13. *Number of Schools, Pupils and Teachers in Indonesia, 1937–38 to 1960–61*

Year	Schools	Pupils	Teachers
1937–38	20,983	2,192,304	47,492
1939–40	22,308	2,415,253	51,641
1948–49	9,331	1,309,630	26,533
1950–51	8,470	1,527,636	27,299
1951–52	17,741	4,394,662	62,360
1952–53	21,638	5,452,856	77,875
1953–54	26,828	5,812,190	112,676
1954–55	30,031	6,345,157	149,707
1955–56	31,237	6,360,977	172,470
1956–57	33,540	6,619,881	197,053
1957–58	32,339	6,404,460	201,992
1958–59	41,748	7,948,076	221,642
1959–60	44,087	8,991,334	254,424
1960–61	46,890	9,925,446	289,419

Source: *Statistical Pocketbook of Indonesia for 1957* and *1963*.

To cope with the bulge created by the fact that the baby boom of the fifties is now reaching school age, new schools have been built very rapidly, especially in the years between 1956 and 1960, when the number increased from 33·5 to 46·9 thousand. The ratio of pupils to teachers was still relatively high, 35–1, though not as high as the ratio of 50–1 in 1948–49. Although Indonesia was training over 30,000 new teachers a year in 1960–61, the greatest scarcity of qualified teaching personnel is still at the top.[24]

The educational pyramid had an unusually large base with 9·2 out of 9·9 million pupils and 236 out of 289 thousand teachers in primary schools in 1960–61. The evidence points to a continued growth in numbers of schools, pupils, and teachers, with increasing pressures by primary school graduates to push on to vocational school, or junior high, then senior high and the university. For example, in 1954–55, only 188,000 were in junior (up to third form) and senior high schools, (up to sixth form), but by 1960–61 the number had trebled to 542,000, although this was the hollow generation of the 1940s. In the same period, attendance at vocational schools, other than teacher training, increased from 64,000 to 150,000. In a speech in September 1965, President Sukarno reported 250,000 students enrolled in universities.[25]

To meet special training needs, many governmental departments and ministries have established courses, institutes, or academies. The armed forces have given a great deal of technical training to enlisted men, with special schools and staff colleges for their officers. Thousands of Indonesians have gone abroad for training or for academic courses. Private technical schools have sprung up, although they are not as numerous as in the Philippines. The oil companies have elaborate training programmes, the subjects ranging from industrial skills through advanced management. The shortage of trained and experienced managers has resulted in a number of courses in this field, one of the best known being run each year in the Puntjak by the Faculty of Economics of the University of Indonesia for a carefully selected group of managers in both private and public business firms.

In this, Indonesia is no different from most other Asian countries, which, with rising populations, are also faced with the problem of training sufficient numbers at higher levels each year to ensure some progress over the previous year. Often this can be done only at the cost of lowered standards;[26] certainly, the goal cannot be achieved overnight, nor even, perhaps, in a couple of generations. If, as seems likely from the labour force figures, Indonesia still has a surplus of unskilled labour and a scarcity of technical and entrepreneurial talent, vocational programmes, running the whole gamut from on-the-job training to technical schools, may become of particular importance in the years ahead, especially if the tempo of industrialization is increased.

II

PROBLEMS AND SOLUTIONS

Indonesia faces many problems in the political, economic, and social fields, a number of which have been touched upon in the foregoing presentation of some of the major demographic factors. In 1965, she had an already large population of 105 million, featuring a hollow generation, followed by a ten-year cohort of over twice as many people. Nothing can change that situation for some time—that is one of the 'givens'. The disparity between the concentration of population on Java, Madura, and Bali and the relatively low density in the Outer Islands intrigued the Dutch administrators and has been the basis of the population panacea for many Indonesian politicians. Some mobility is possible between islands and also between rural and urban areas. On the economic and industrial scene, high Indonesian officials and managers are gaining years of experience on the job, while the education and training of the labour force are being further extended and directed.

In the light of her recent growth and the high population projections, what are the possibilities of solution offered by transmigration, the reduction of fertility, or an increase in the tempo of economic activity?

Large Population Projections

All projections point to a continued and substantial increase in population. Prior to the Census of 1961, the United Nations, in its Population Study No. 30,[27] made several projections using various assumptions. Its conservative estimate, based on a crude birth rate of 43·8 per 1,000 in 1950–55, declining very slowly to 39·1 per 1,000 in 1975–80, with the corresponding death rates falling from 25·4 to 16, indicated that the population of Indonesia as a whole would rise from 90·7 million in 1960 to 138·5 million in 1980 (see Table 14)—a 53 per cent increase in twenty years, which is a more rapid rate than the rise from 1930 to 1961. If there were to be a moderate fertility decline to 35·3 per 1,000, the 1980 population figure would be 131 million, and with a rapid decline in fertility to 27·5 per 1,000, it would be 123·4 million in 1980. All three projections are probably much too low, since by the end of 1960, the population was 95·3 million instead of 90·7 million, and in 1965, 105 million instead of between 100·3 and 99·6 million.

TABLE 14. *UN Population Projections for Indonesia, 1950–80*

	1950	1955	1960	1965	1970	1975	1980
A Conservative Projections	75·0	82·2	90·7	100·4	111·0	123·4	138·5
B Low Mortality Projections	75·0	83·1	93·3	105·7	119·9	137·4	159·7
C Moderate Fertility Decline	—	—	—	100·0	109·4	119·5	131·0
D Rapid Fertility Decline	—	—	—	99·6	107·7	115·6	123·4
E Medium Population Projections	—	—	94·3	105·5	118·3	133·5	152·7

Source: UN *Population Studies*, No. 30, A pp. 114–15, B pp. 138–9, C and D p. 159, E ECAFE Asian Population Conference, *The Demographic Situation and Prospective Population Trends in Asia and the Far East*, 1963, p. 53.

On the other hand, the low mortality projection, which assumed mortality declining twice as fast as the conservative assumption up to 1975, indicated 93·3 million in 1960, 105·7 million in 1965, and 159·7 million in 1980. This is a bit higher than a later ECAFE medium population projection, showing 94·3 million in 1960, 105·5 million in 1965 and 152·7 million in 1980. The latter figures are based on an average annual increase of 2·3 per cent in the decade of the sixties and a 2·6 per cent increase in the seventies. The hollow generation will be reaching the marriageable age in the former, and the baby boom in the latter.

Possibilities of Transmigration from Java

The movement of people out of crowded Java to the frontier areas of the Outer Islands is the typical Indonesian answer to the population problem. Considerable research has gone into the various transmigration proposals.[28]

The conservative population projection made by the United Nations in the study referred to above estimated that in the period from 1950 to 1980, the population of Java would increase from 50 to 92·3 million, while in the same period the population of Sumatra would increase from 12 to 22·2 million.[29] This would mean an increase of population density in Java from 378 to 698 persons per square kilometre, while in Sumatra from only 25 to 47 persons. Using this projection, the United Nations estimated the effect on the population of Java of the migration of various numbers of households each year from 1950 to 1980:

'The successful transfer of 10,000 households in every five-year period gives rise to a settlement of population which numbers, at the end of thirty years, some 526,000 persons. It can be assumed that an annual transfer of 2,000 families results in 10,000 households being established in five years. Depending on the annual volume of transfers which can be achieved, population growth in Java will be diminished as follows, at the end of thirty years: by 2·6 million, with an annual transfer of 10,000 families; by 5·3 million with an annual transfer of 20,000 families; by 13·2 million with an annual transfer of 50,000 families; and by 42·1 million with an annual transfer of 160,000 families. In the latter event, population growth in Java, resulting from conservatively projected natural increase, would be completely neutralized, and Java's population would be maintained very near a constant level.'[30]

To stabilize the Javanese population even on the conservative projections would necessitate an expansion in Sumatra of 5·8 per cent a year, if all migrants went there. Furthermore, the 1961 census gave figures 2·2 million higher for Java than projected for 1960, and 1·3 million higher for Sumatra—almost as large as the number predicted for Sumatra in 1965. Actually, all these calculations now would have to be raised considerably, since during the first fifteen years the migrations have not even reached the level of 10,000 families a year, except in the post-war year of highest transmigration, 1960, when 11,439 families, comprising 46,096 individuals, moved. To this should be added those who were recruited for employment outside Java, amounting to 17,670 individuals (see

Table 15). Unfortunately, purely voluntary movements are not recorded.

Somewhat more recently, Professor Widjojo[31] made a number of projections for the thirty-year period 1960–90, starting with a population of 62·5 million in Java in 1960, a figure very closely in line with the 1961 census enumeration of 63 million. With constant fertility, a rapidly declining mortality rate, and no migration, he projected that Java would

TABLE 15. *Number of Transmigrants, and Workers and their Families Leaving Java to be Employed in Other Islands, 1938–62*

Year	Total number of transmigrants	Total number of workers and their families leaving Java for employment
1938	33,399	23,334
1939	44,694	25,347
1940	52,208	24,310
1951	2,864	18,415
1952	17,507	22,888
1953	39,427	5,463
1954	30,192	4,304
1955	21,389	12,228
1956	24,350	9,549
1957	23,230	2,755
1958	26,419	3,901
1959	46,096	5,236
1960	22,075	17,670
1961	19,609	16,662
1962	22,129	18,083

Source: *Statistical Pocketbook of Indonesia for 1963*, pp. 23 and 279.

have 104·1 million in 1980 and 146·2 million in 1990—more than doubling in thirty years. With an out-migration of one million persons each five years, the population projections for Java would be reduced to 99·1 million in 1980 and 137·1 in 1990. Using other less drastic combinations of fertility and mortality and an out-migration of one million in five years, the projections for 1980 ranged from 88·9 to 95·7 million and 108·6 to 123·6 million for 1990. He also projected that, with constant fertility, rapidly declining mortality, and an out-migration of 5 million young persons and their children every five years, the population of Java would rise by 1980 to only 76·2 million and 94·9 million by 1990—still more than a 50 per cent gain in thirty years.

All of these projections seem to indicate that, using any reasonable set of assumptions, migration will not solve Java's population problem, and even with overly optimistic assumptions, Java's population will still grow substantially. At a workshop held by the National Institute of

Economic and Social Research, led by Professor Kampto Utomo and Dr Kartomo Wirosuhardjo in 1963, transmigration was considered as a way to develop Sumatra and the other Outer Islands, rather than as a solution of the Javanese population problem. Specialized recruiting in Java and careful cost calculations would be required to determine whether this was the most efficient way to achieve economic development.[32] Such an approach might be a way to link older drives for transmigration with newer efforts to increase the level of production in the country. Any effect on Javanese population would not be harmful, but it should not be used as an intellectual crutch for forestalling more positive methods of meeting the population problem of Indonesia, and of Java in particular.

Possibilities for Decreasing Fertility

Interest in birth control is rising in Indonesia, but as might be expected, it is among upper-class, educated wives of government officials and professional personnel that interest is the greatest. A number of clinics have been established, and women's organizations have discussed various techniques. Unlike Japan, India, and Pakistan, where there have been varying degrees of official encouragement of birth control, President Sukarno has not given his approval—in fact, he has thus far stressed the rich resources of Indonesia and the desirability of increasing the population. Children are still considered a 'blessing', and big families are still 'in style'.

Although statistics are not available for all of Indonesia, the Greater Djakarta Census of 1961 showed that the average married woman fifteen years of age and over has had 3·33 births, with those thirty-five and over averaging from 4·48 to 4·88, depending on the age bracket. The average number of living children for married women over fifteen was only 2·33, with those aged 25–75 averaging from 2·55 to 3·18 living children at the time of the census. This means that, on the average, each of the 714,435 married women had lost one child. Out of 714,435 women, 1,850 had given birth to fifteen or more children, but only seventy-six of these women still had fifteen or more alive. About 40 per cent of the women twenty-five and over had given birth to five or more children; this figure rises to over 50 per cent for those aged forty-five and over.[33] These data show a high number of births per married woman, but they give no clue concerning fertility rates over time.

Other countries have reduced fertility as they industrialized, urbanized, provided more education, and raised levels of productivity and income. In other words, as many countries developed economically, social pressure for smaller families rose. A child no longer was an economic asset as help on the farm, but an expensive person that had to be fed, clothed, educated, and paid an allowance, with little prospect of net income to the family till after he or she had completed his or her education. People soon wanted to give their children more opportunities than they had had.

Thus far, Indonesia has experienced some rapid urbanization and growth in education. These two factors may slowly reduce average fertility rates. There is some increase in industrialization, but the pace is slow, and the Eight-Year Plan, 1961–68, has failed as yet to raise the economic tempo. The evidence does not suggest increases in productivity or per capita income. The record indicates that in the 1940's fertility declined and/or mortality rose because of the turmoil of war and revolution, creating a hollow generation. Obviously, no one would want to solve the population problem by returning to such conditions or by any of the Malthusian positive checks. The rapid inflation in the sixties may have some small effect on birth rates.

Possibilities for Increasing the Tempo of Economic Activity

Indonesians like to boast about their potential resources in oil, minerals, rich soils, and good growing climate, but after the reconstruction and recovery in the early 1950's from the war and the revolution against the Dutch, the country did not develop economically as rapidly as most of her neighbours. Indonesia turned to external drives, backed by military force plus large numbers of volunteers, to gain the return of West Irian and to mount a confrontation drive against Malaysia; she is trying to establish herself as a major power in the region and so looks to a large number of soldiers. These projects require large military budgets. At the same time billions of rupiah are spent to give Djakarta spectacular buildings, beautiful fountains, and imposing mosques. All of this is done in the cause of 'nation-building'. Fortunately, although inflation has raised the price of all foodstuffs, food shortages have been limited in area and in time; for example, the shortages before the first rice crop in 1964 were most severe in some of the areas of Central and East Java. The new slogan of '*Berdikari*'—self-reliance, 'stand on one's own feet'—is aimed at eliminating the need for rice imports, which in some years reached about a million tons. There is, therefore, a growing population pressure on the resource base, especially on the crowded islands of Java, Madura, and Bali, where landholdings are already very small and fragmented.[34]

Indonesia must increase her food supply in order to support her present population, let alone the two to three millions who are being added each year. As babies, their food consumption is well below the national average, but as they become teenagers the food demand will rise sharply. This food might be secured by gifts, loans, or purchases from abroad. If Indonesia could increase her exports of rubber, petroleum, tin, coffee, and other special tree crops, she might use the foreign exchange to buy rice and other staples. Some smaller neighbouring countries do this, but the magnitude of Indonesia's food requirements means that she would be spending a large share of her limited foreign exchange on food and not, therefore, on the capital goods, spare parts, and raw materials needed to expand her industries. Loans and gifts of food cannot be relied upon for long periods of time. Indonesia therefore seems faced with the necessity of raising her own food supply, even though marginal amounts may still come from abroad. She is increasing her supply of fertilizer through the Sriwidjaja fertilizer plant at Palembang and others. She is developing new strains of rice that respond to fertilizer, since some of the older types, when treated with fertilizer, only grew taller but had no higher yields. The huge Djatiluhur multi-purpose dam is about to be completed in West Java, which will make possible a second crop of rice in a large fertile area. Irrigation, better seeds, and fertilizer, coupled with better transportation facilities, on both land and sea, to move in the inputs and consumer goods and to move out the agricultural products, crops, livestock, forestry products, and fish, are high priority needs.

With an increasing number of high school and university graduates, Indonesia will have more trained personnel to fill important posts in government and business.[35] She has already encountered and will soon face more acutely the problem of the educated unemployed, which other Asian nations are experiencing, unless she can increase the tempo, not only of her agriculture, but of industry, mining, construction, transportation, commerce, and services. Most of these new jobs cannot be found in already intensively exploited agricultural areas, but must come from the opening up of new lands in the Outer Islands and from the development of new secondary and tertiary industries throughout the whole archipelago, especially in Java.

Conclusion

Greater mobility both to the cities and to the Outer Islands, even with greater education and faster agricultural and industrial development probably will not be sufficient to check the expansion of population here as it was checked in many Western countries as they developed. Indonesia, or more particularly Java, seems to be in a low income trap;[36] because of population growth, she cannot seem to increase her per capita income fast enough for a higher standard of living to check population increases. This suggests that the Government and various social institutions should take the leadership in pushing birth control measures. In a country where leadership is stressed, the Chief Bapak, President Sukarno, should be encouraged to add 'Guided Parenthood' to 'Guided Democracy'. Even with the most optimistic assumptions about all these possible solutions, Indonesia faces more difficult demographic problems in the second twenty years of her independence than in the first.

NOTES

1. The author acknowledges with thanks the assistance in the preparation of this chapter of Mrs Shanthi Wickramasinghe Radcliffe (MA Cambridge).
2. Republic of Indonesia, Central Bureau of Statistics, *Population Census 1961, Preliminary Figures, Series SP1*, 1963, 13 pp., Table 1. This figure was based upon a one per cent sample survey of the census returns for all islands except West Irian, where an estimate of 700,000 was used.
3. See, for example, Hildred Geertz, 'Indonesian Cultures and Communities', in Ruth McVey, ed., *Indonesia* (New Haven, HRAF Press, 1963), pp. 24–96. One of the broadest threefold groupings she makes is 'the strongly Hinduized inland wet-rice areas; the trade oriented, deeply Islamic coastal peoples; and the mainly pagan tribal groups of the mountainous interior regions' (pp. 30–1).
4. Central Bureau of Statistics, *Sensus Penduduk 1961 D.C.I., Djakarta Raya* (angka angka tetap), 1963, 62 pp., mimeo. This is a complete census report, not a one per cent sample.
5. Nathan Keyfitz, 'Population Dynamics in Indonesia: Focus on Research', presented at the 17th Annual Meeting of the Association of Asian Studies, San Francisco, April 2–4, 1965, 16 pp. (photo-offset).
6. G. William Skinner, 'The Chinese Minority', in Ruth McVey, ed., *Indonesia, op. cit.*, pp. 97–117. He estimated that Java and Madura had the most Chinese, 1,230,000 (but only 2 per cent of the population of Java), while Sumatra had 690,000 (4·4 per cent) and Borneo 370,000 (a high 9 per cent). In the rest of the islands there may have been 160,000 Chinese in 1961, or only 1·2 per cent of the population of that area (p. 99).
7. *Statistical Pocketbook of Indonesia*, 1963, pp. 21–2.
8. 'Population in Indonesia—The Short and Long Run', a seminar paper, 12 pp. (mimeo), delivered in Djakarta in 1964 by Professor Nathan Keyfitz. Many of the ideas included in this chapter grew out of discussions with Professor Keyfitz when we were both consultants to the National Institute of Economic and Social Research in 1964. He has expanded this seminar paper into 'Age Distribution as a Challenge to Development', *The American Journal of Sociology*, Vol. LXX, No. 6 (May 1965), pp. 659–68.
9. The Census of 1961 used other groupings: 0–14, 15–24, 25–44, 45–64, 65– , which tended to show similar differences among Java, Sumatra, and the other islands, but did not reveal the hollow generation as clearly. See *The Population of Indonesia* (Djakarta, 1963), 41 pp., mimeo, Table 5.
10. 'The Population of Indonesia', *Ekonomi dan Keuangan Indonesia*, Vol. No. 2 (February 1956), pp. 3–5.
11. Vaino Kannisto, *Population Increase in Indonesia*, Central Bureau of Statistics (Djakarta, 1963), quoted in *The Population of Indonesia*, 1963, *op. cit.*, p. 31.
12. *Ibid.*, p. 33.
13. Central Bureau of Statistics, *Statistical Pocketbook of Indonesia, 1963*, p. 20. See pages 46–8, which indicate the increase in public health employees and facilities and the decline of plague and smallpox since 1951. Much has been done to try to eradicate malaria and yaws. These forces will continue to decrease mortality rates.
14. See, for example, 'Report on the Labor Force Sample Survey of the Greater District of Bandung', *Ekonomi dan Keuangan Indonesia*, Vol. 11 (1958), pp. 571–99.
15. The English edition of this survey was reprinted in *Ekonomi dan Keuangan Indonesia*, Vol. 16, No. 1 (1963), pp. 1–96.
16. Central Bureau of Statistics, *Census of 1961* (extended one per cent sample, All Indonesia), Table 7, pp. 30–1.
17. 'Labour Force Sample Survey—Java and Madura', *Ekonomi dan Keuangan Indonesia*, Vol. 16, No. 1 (1963), p. 21.
18. For this and other points on the labour force, see Everett D. Hawkins, 'Labor in Transition', in Ruth McVey, ed., *Indonesia, op. cit.*, pp. 248–71, especially pp. 251–2.

See also my preliminary report to the Bureau of Economic Research, Gadjah Mada University, *Consumer Finances in the Region of Jogjakarta* (Jogjakarta, 1960), mimeo.
19. U.S. Department of Labor, Bureau of Labor Statistics, *Summary of the Labor Situation in Indonesia* (Washington, July 1955). Also my chapter on 'Indonesia' in Walter Galenson, ed., *Labor in Developing Economics* (Berkeley, University of California Press, 1962), pp. 71–137, especially pp. 85–7.
20. *Statistical Pocketbook of Indonesia, 1963, op. cit.*, p. 40.
21. Consulate General of the Republic of Indonesia (New York), *News and Views*, 1965.
22. The percentage of literacy in Latin characters was only a very small amount lower, 42·9 as compared with 46·7 per cent. *Census of 1961, op. cit.*, Tables 12 and 13.
23. This number is considerably less than the total number of literate people in Indonesia, indicating the importance of the adult courses, the religious schools and other training devices which have been used in the drive for literacy.
24. On this and related points, see Bruce Glassburner, 'Heightened Manpower for Economic Development: The Indonesian Experience', in Frederick Harbison and Charles A. Myers, *Manpower and Education* (New York: McGraw-Hill, 1965), pp. 173–201.
25. *News and Views, op. cit.*, September 30, 1965, p. 20.
26 Hla Myint, 'The Universities of Southeast Asia and Economic Development', *Pacific Affairs*, XXXV, No. 2 (Summer 1962), pp. 116–27.
27. United Nations, Department of Economic and Social Affairs, *Future Population by Sex and Age. Report III. The Population of South-East Asia (including Ceylon and China: Taiwan), 1950–1980* (ST/SOA Series A/30, New York, 1958, 166 pp.).
28. The classic work in this field is Karl J. Pelzer, *Pioneer Settlement in the Asiatic Tropics: Studies in Land Utilization and Agricultural Colonization in Southeastern Asia* (New York, Institute of Pacific Relations and the American Geographical Society, 1945).
29. United Nations, *op. cit.*, Chapter VII.
30. *Ibid.*, p. 29.
31. Widjojo Nitisastro, *Migration, Population Growth, and Economic Development in Indonesia: A Study of the Economic Consequences of Alternative Patterns of Interisland Migration*, Ph.D. Thesis, The University of California, Berkeley, 1961. Professor Widjojo has revised the thesis in the light of the 1961 census data, and it will be published by Cornell University Press. I am indebted to him and his colleagues at the University of Indonesia, Faculty of Economics, who have been engaged in demographic research, particularly the studies on labour force projections for the National Institute of Economic and Social Research. Some of his tables are reproduced by Karl J. Pelzer in 'Physical and Human Resource Patterns', in Ruth McVey, ed., *Indonesia, op. cit.*, pp. 21–3.
32. National Institute of Economic and Social Research, 'Report on the Transmigration Seminar', *Warta Leknas*, Vol. 1, No. 5 (Djakarta, 1963), 10 pp.
33. *Sensus Pendriduk 1961 D.C. I Djakarta Raya*, pp. 61–2.
34. Clifford Geertz paints a most gloomy prospect in his *Agricultural Involution: The Process of Ecological Change in Indonesia* (Berkeley, University of California Press, 1963).
35. Keyfitz, 'Age Distribution', *op. cit.*, pp. 665–8.
36. Richard R. Nelson, 'A Theory of the Low-Level Equilibrium Trap in Underdeveloped Economies', *American Economic Review*, Vol. XLVI, No. 5 (December 1956), pp. 894–908.

BIBLIOGRAPHY

Department of Labour, 'Labour Force Sample Survey in Java and Madura', *Ekonomi dan Keuangan Indonesia*, Vol. XVI, No. 1 (1963).

Djoko Santoso and Ali Wardhana, 'Some Aspects of Spontaneous Transmigration in Indonesia', *Ekonomi dan Keuangan Indonesia*, Vol. X, No. 6 (June 1957).

Geertz, Clifford, *Agricultural Involution: The Process of Ecological Change in Indonesia* (Berkeley, University of California Press, 1963).

Geertz, Hildred, 'Indonesian Cultures and Communities', in Ruth McVey, ed., *Indonesia* (New Haven, HRAF Press, 1963).

Glassburner, Bruce, 'High Level Manpower for Economic Development: The Indonesian Experience', in Frederick Harbison and Charles A. Myers, eds., *Manpower and Education* (New York, McGraw-Hill, 1965).

Hawkins, Everett D., 'Labor in Transition', in Ruth McVey, ed., *op. cit.* 'Indonesia', in Walter Galenson, ed., *Labor in Developing Economies* (Berkeley, University of California Press, 1962).

Kannisto, Vaino, *Population Increase in Indonesia* (Djakarta, Central Bureau of Statistics, 1963).

Keyfitz, Nathan, 'Age Distribution as a Challenge to Development', *American Journal of Sociology*, Vol. LXX, No. 6 (May 1965), pp. 659–68. 'Population Dynamics in Indonesia: Focus on Research', presented at the 17th Annual Meeting of the Association of Asian Studies, San Francisco, April 2–4, 1965.

National Institute of Economic and Social Research, 'Laporan Seminar Transmigrasi', *Warta Leknas*, Djakarta, Vol. 1, No. 5 (1963).

Pelzer, Karl J., 'Physical and Human Resource Patterns', in Ruth McVey, ed., *op. cit.*, *Pioneer Settlement in the Asiatic Tropics: Studies in Land Utilization and Agricultural Colonization in Southeastern Asia* (New York, Institute of Pacific Relations and the American Geographical Society, 1945).

'The Population of Indonesia', *Ekonomi dan Keuangan Indonesia*, Vol. IX, No. 2 (February 1956).

The Population of Indonesia (Djakarta, 1963).

The Republic of Indonesia, Central Bureau of Statistics, *Population Census 1961. Preliminary Figures 1961, Series S.P. 1* (Djakarta, 1963).

Population Census 1961. Extended 1% Sample, Series S.P. 11 (Djakarta, 1963).

Sensus Penduduk 1961. D.C.1., Djakarta Raya (Djakarta, 1963).

Statistical Pocketbook of Indonesia (Djakarta, 1963 and earlier years).

Skinner, William G., 'The Chinese Minority', in Ruth McVey, ed., *op. cit.*

United Nations, Department of Economic and Social Affairs, *Future Population Estimates by Sex and Age. Report III. The Population of Southeast Asia (including Ceylon and China: Taiwan), 1950–1980* (ST/SOA Series A/30). (New York, 1958).

United Nations, Economic Commission for Asia and the Far East, *Domestic Analysis and Projection of the Indonesian Economy* (EGPT 4/WP.8) (Bangkok, 1964).

The Demographic Situation and Prospective Population Trends in Asia and the Far East (Asian Population Conference, New Delhi, 1963).

US Department of Labor, Bureau of Labor Statistics, *Summary of the Labor Situation in Indonesia* (Washington, July 1955, and later issues).

Widjojo Nitisastro, *Migration, Population Growth, and Economic Development in Indonesia: A Study of the Economic Consequences of Alternative Patterns of Interisland Migration* (Ph.D. thesis, The University of California, Berkeley, 1961).

Widjojo Nitisastro and Nathan Keyfitz, *Soal Penduduk dan Pembangunan, Indonesia* (Djakarta, P.T. Pembangunan, 1954).

CHAPTER 6

PAKISTAN'S POPULATION PROBLEM

BY ANWAR IQBAL QUERISHI

THE ALARMING RATE at which the world population is increasing has been very appropriately, though not perhaps scientifically termed as 'population explosion'. Lately the population problem has been causing much anxiety to those who are interested in the welfare of the world, though the dangers with which unchecked growth of population is fraught had been indicated in unmistakable terms by Malthus a couple of centuries ago. If the present rate of growth is allowed to continue, it is doubtful if the underdeveloped countries like Pakistan, where living standards are precariously low and food supplies are lagging behind population growth, will even make any tangible progress and achieve a standard of living compatible with human dignity.

I

CHARACTERISTICS OF PAKISTAN'S POPULATION

Size of Population

The population of Pakistan, according to the latest decennial census of 1961, was 93·83 million. In 1961, only three Asian nations, namely Communist China, India and Indonesia had a larger population than Pakistan. The population of Japan, which in the past was larger, is now smaller than the population of Pakistan because of her low growth rate.

TABLE 1. *Population of Five Major Countries in Asia*

Country	Year (Latest census)	Population (in millions)
Asia total	1960	1,679·00
China (Mainland)	1960	646·53
India	1961	434·81
Indonesia	1961	95·19
Pakistan	1961	93·83
Japan	1960	93·42

Source: *United Nations Demographic Year Book, 1961.*

According to some agencies, estimates of Pakistan's population in

1961 made by the Census Office were on the low side. The Institute of Development Economics, Karachi, for instance, has concluded that the 1961 population figures were underestimated by about 8·25 per cent,[1] and the National Income Commission of Pakistan, on this basis, estimated Pakistan's population in 1959–60 at 98·88 million and in 1960–61 at 101·45 million.[2]

A rapidly increasing population generates a large number of economic and social problems. Some people hold the opinion that 'each new mouth to feed has also a new pair of hands to produce'. They, however, forget that considerable investment is needed to make a pair of hands productive, such as education in schools and colleges, public health services, housing, water supply, transportation, etc. Moreover, the hands, in order to feed the mouth, need work and it has been found that even in rich countries like the United States, unemployment is one of the most serious problems.

In order to improve the living levels of the population a good deal of investment is needed in underdeveloped countries, not only to ensure jobs for the growing labour force but also to remove existing unemployment and underemployment. With a high rate of population growth, the level of investment would have to be further increased.

The Rate of Increase

The increase in Pakistan's population from 1951 to 1961 exceeded most estimates. The official 1951 figure of 75·88 million was doubtless too low, as a result of admitted under-enumeration in the cities which was largely corrected in 1961. The extent of the previous under-enumeration in rural areas is less readily ascertainable. This factor certainly served to inflate somewhat the apparent ten-year increase. Nevertheless, the Census Commissioner commented in his report: 'Our observation and scrutiny of the actual enumeration and post-enumeration survey of selected localities, however, convince us that the increase in population between 1951 and 1961 was substantial and significantly larger than the moderate estimates made earlier.'[3]

Among these earlier estimates were the following:

TABLE 2. *Estimates of Pakistan's Population*

Agency	Pakistan's population (in millions)
Pakistan Planning Commission	88·9 (Mid-1960)
Mauldin and Hashmi	91·45
Rehman	90·41 (Mid-1961)
United Nations	92·51
Pakistan Census Office	89·00
Actual Count	93·83

The population of 93·83 million in 1961 indicates a growth rate of 23·7 per cent over about ten years, or 2·16 per cent per annum. If foreign residents are excluded, the apparent growth rate for Pakistan nationals is 23·8 per cent. It is strikingly higher than in previous decades of this century, as shown below:

TABLE 3. *Percentage Increase in Pakistan's Population by Decade 1901–61*

Decade	Pakistan	India	Pakistan and India sub-continents
1901–11	11·9	5·7	6·7
1911–21	6·7	0·4	0·9
1921–31	8·8	11·0	10·6
1931–41	18·8	13·5	15·0
1941–51	7·9	14·1	12·9
1951–61	23·7	21·5	22·9

Since the 1961 census there has been considerable speculation about the population growth rate. It is generally felt that the size of the population and its rate of growth as assessed in 1961, were on the low side and the present annual growth rate may be around 2·6 to 2·8 per cent or even higher.

As regards growth rate, the Institute of Development Economics has concluded from its study that the net rate of annual increase during recent years comes to about 2·6 per cent in both West and East Pakistan.[4]

Density

This increase of population is placing a considerable pressure on the limited resources of Pakistan. In 1961, the area of Pakistan was 365,529 square miles, and the population, excluding foreign nationals, 93,720,613 or 256 persons per square mile. The population per square mile in East Pakistan (area 55,126 square miles, population 50,840,235) was 922 and in West Pakistan (area 310,403 square miles, population 42,880,378) 138. If the river areas of 3,205 square miles in East Pakistan are excluded, the population density there goes up to 979 per square mile. The table below gives the population distribution in Asia and Pakistan.[5]

TABLE 4. *Population Distribution and Density in Asia and Pakistan*

Area	Land area in sq. km.	Land area Per cent distribution	Population Number (millions)	Population Per cent distribution	Persons per sq. km.
Asia	26,930,000	—	1,679·61	—	63
Pakistan	946,719	100·0	93·83	100·0	99
East Pakistan	142,776	15·1	50·85	54·2	356
West Pakistan	803,943	84·9	42·98	45·8	53

The above table shows the high density of Pakistan, particularly of East Pakistan, compared to the average density of Asia's population as a whole.

In East Pakistan the maximum density of 1,281 persons per square mile is in Dacca Division and the minimum, 786 per square mile, in Khulna Division. In West Pakistan the maximum density of 724 is in Lahore Division and minimum of 7 in Kalat Division.

The density of 356 per square kilometre in East Pakistan is more than six times the density (53) in West Pakistan. East Pakistan alone if compared with other countries or territories (leaving aside Hong Kong, Singapore and other small islands and places) is the most densely settled area in Asia (except adjacent districts of West Bengal and parts of South India) and the world. Taiwan (295) in 1960 and Japan (252) in 1960, which are the most densely settled countries in Asia, are now much below the density level of East Pakistan.

If the estimates of the Institute of Development Economics are accepted, the density of the two provinces rises further and in the case of East Pakistan it becomes alarming as shown below:[6]

TABLE 5. *Density of Population in Pakistan: 1963–64*

Area	Area (sq. miles)	Population (millions)	Density (per sq. mile)
Pakistan	365,529	109·56	291
East Pakistan	55,126	69·67	1,082
West Pakistan	310,403	49·89	161

Distribution by Age Groups

The age distribution of the population has an important effect upon the number of workers and the ratio of workers to dependants and to total population. In Pakistan, the 'Active' population is generally defined to include all between the ages of fifteen and fifty-nine.

Between 1951 and 1961 there were significant changes in the age structure of the population of Pakistan. The ratio of children up to four years increased from 14·2 to 17·4 per cent of total population, the increase being more pronounced in East Pakistan, where the ratio rose from 14·6 per cent to 18·2 per cent, than in West Pakistan, where the corresponding figures were 13·7 per cent and 16·4 per cent. The next age group, 5–9 years, accounted for a still larger proportion of total population, increasing from 14·9 per cent to 18·7 per cent in East Pakistan and from 13·1 per cent to 16·4 per cent in West Pakistan, or, for Pakistan as a whole, from 14·1 per cent to 17·7 per cent According to some demographers the relative importance of the 5–9 year age group was greater in Pakistan in 1961 than anywhere else in Asia, or indeed in the world.

There was a corresponding decrease in the proportion of the population in the 10–59 year age group, from which most of the working population is drawn, from 66·67 per cent in 1951 to 58·89 per cent in 1961. In East Pakistan the decline was from 66·10 per cent to 57·81 per cent and in West Pakistan from 67·43 per cent to 60·29 per cent.

The population in the 59 years and over group rose from 4·97 per cent in 1951 to 5·97 per cent in 1961. In East Pakistan the increase was from 4·43 per cent to 5·22 per cent, and in West Pakistan from 5·69 per cent to 6·93 per cent.

Sex Composition

In Pakistan, the age distribution by sex is very important, as most of the economically-active people are drawn from the male population, and only a fraction of the female population is gainfully employed. In 1961, 49·62 per cent of the total male population was in the 15–59 age group, compared to 52·94 per cent in 1951.

The female population in the 15–59 age group, expressed as a percentage of the total female population, declined more slowly from 51·91 in 1951 to 49·43 in 1961 than the corresponding percentage for either the total population (both sexes) or the male population.

The female population of Pakistan appears to have increased more rapidly than the male population. In 1961, the ratio to females was 111 to 100; in 1951, 113 to 100. The ratio declined in East Pakistan from 110:100 to 108:100 and in West Pakistan from 116:100 to 115:100.

The masculinity ratio in Pakistan is higher than in any other large population. The following four reasons apparently explain this abnormal situation.

1. Females have a somewhat higher mortality rate than males;
2. In a purdah-observing society females are more likely to be under-enumerated than males;
3. The number of males has been over-estimated, and
4. There is a higher masculinity ratio at birth.

Rural–Urban Population Distribution

The definition of urban population used in the 1961 census was different from that adopted in 1951. In 1961, it included all cities and towns with a population of 5,000 and above, plus all Incorporated Municipalities, and towns managed by Notified Area Committees irrespective of their population size. In 1961, the Provincial Directors of Census were empowered to use their discretion in treating a continuous collection of houses inhabited by not less than 5,000 persons as urban if the area had pronounced urban characteristics and especially if the population was largely non-agricultural.

If intricacies of definition are left out of account, the urban population of Pakistan increased by 57·4 per cent between 1951 and 1961. If all the new areas with less than 5,000 population which were added to the urban areas in 1961 are excluded, the growth rate for the urban population would be 57·7 per cent, and the proportion of urban population to total population in 1961 would be 12·8 per cent (instead of 13·1 per cent).

The growth rate of the urban population between 1951 and 1961 was almost three times as large as that of the rural population. The proportion of urban population to total population increased from 10·4 per cent to 13·1 per cent. Rural population increased by 20 per cent and urban population by 57·4 per cent.

The increase of urban population in 1961 was in part a consequence of the increase in the number of cities and towns of which there were 282 in 1951, and 393 in 1961. In East Pakistan there were fourteen places and in West Pakistan 103, which were rural in 1951 but classified as urban in 1961.

The past decade has witnessed an accelerated trend towards urbanization. Rates of economic development and opportunities for employment have varied widely, as between different localities inducing large-scale movement of population within the country. The major shift is from rural areas to urban centres of rapid industrial growth. Thus a number of urban areas have gained population far in excess of their natural increase, while certain rural districts have been consistently losing population.

About the turn of the century, Pakistan was mainly a rural country. By 1961, a semi-industrial pattern was emerging, especially in West Pakistan. The trend is summarized below:

TABLE 6. *Rural and Urban Population*

Year	Rural percentage	Urban percentage
1901	94·9	5·1
1911	95·1	4·9
1921	94·6	5·4
1931	93·5	6·5
1941	92·1	7·9
1951	89·6	10·4
1961	86·9	13·1

Marital Status of Women

In a modern society, the marital status of woman is important from the point of view of the labour force and fertility. A woman can take up any occupation if she is educated and moulds her career according to the requirements of that occupation. Further, the period of her potential employment depends largely upon the period a woman normally remains unmarried.

In some cases, even married women take up jobs in various occupations. Their chance of employment, however, depends upon the number of children they bear. With a large number of children, it is difficult for a woman to get rid of her domestic commitments. Further, as the number of her children increases, the scope of employment for a woman decreases.

In Pakistan, rural women rarely take up profitable employment, although the assistance they give to the male members of their families in various functions pertaining to agriculture is very useful. With the growth of industrialization and urbanization the scope for the increased participation of women in gainful employment is increasing. The number of women workers increased from 13·17 lakhs in 1951 to 37·62 lakhs in 1961—an increase of about 186 per cent. It is relevant to note that during the same period total population increased by 23·7 per cent and the civilian labour force by 31·35 per cent.

The Census of 1961 shows that there was a slight change in the marital status of women over the last decade. In 1961, 46·20 per cent of females were unmarried as compared to 45·14 per cent in 1951. Of the total number of women 43·92 per cent were married as compared to 44·84 per cent in 1951.

The average number of children per married woman increased between 1951 and 1961 by 20·04 per cent.

Pakistan's broad age groups if compared with some selected countries of Asia show that Pakistan has the highest proportion of children[7] and the highest proportion of older persons. The range of children extends from a minimum of 41·1 per cent in South Korea to a maximum of 44·5 per cent in Pakistan and of older persons from a minimum of 2·5 per cent in Formosa to a maximum of 4 per cent in Pakistan. The favourable structure of the females of reproductive age in Pakistan produced more births during the intercensal period, which increased the proportion of population in ages under ten. The age structure of the females of reproductive age during the current decade is not going to be as favourable as it was in the last decade.

Dependency Ratio

The dependency ratios of Pakistan show that the dependency load is highest in Pakistan but its Eastern province has a higher dependency load than its Western province. In a population in which the age structure is loaded with large proportions of children, women and older persons who have little potential of productive work, the true burden is higher than is shown by the dependency ratio.

In the broader perspective, the dependency ratio roughly signifies that Pakistani working age population is carrying a larger burden of dependency than any other Asian country.

Marital Status

In the 1961 Census, the population according to marital status at the time of enumeration was classified into four categories: (1) single, persons who were never married; (2) married persons who were married and habitually living together as man and wife, also persons who though married were living apart and were not widowed or divorced; (3) widowed, a person whose husband/wife was dead and who did not remarry; (4) divorced, persons who were either divorced or divorcees who did not remarry. From these definitions it is implied that the category of 'separated' was merged into the category of 'married'.

Ever Married

The proportion of males and females ever married is quite high in Pakistan but the proportion of females ever married is higher than the proportion of males ever married at all ages above ten. The overall proportion of ever married is higher in East Pakistan. A higher proportion of females in East Pakistan marry at early ages than in West Pakistan, but males in West Pakistan marry earlier than males in East Pakistan. At older ages, the spinsters are fewer than male celibates but the rate of celibacy is higher in West Pakistan, most probably due to greater shortage of females in West Pakistan than in East Pakistan.

Married

The proportion of those who were married at the time of the 1961 Census enumeration among the ever married was 87 per cent (92 per cent for males and 82 per cent for females) in Pakistan, 86 per cent in East Pakistan (95 per cent for males and 80 per cent for females) and 88 per cent in West Pakistan (90 per cent for males and 87 per cent for females). The lower proportion of married females than that of married males is due to lower remarriage rate of females than males. The proportion married among the ever married declined with age both for males and females. This conforms to the expected pattern: as the proportion of widowed persons increases with age it affects the proportion of married persons in the same manner.

As the proportion of married persons is an important factor in the study of changes in fertility patterns, a comparison between the 1951 and 1961 proportions would throw some light on the broader base of the population in 1961. The comparison shows that the proportion of married males and females has increased over the decade both in East Pakistan and West Pakistan.

The increase in the proportion of married females especially in the highly-reproductive period has affected the total number of married females exposed to risk of childbearing. It appears that the broader base of the population in 1961 than in 1951 is attributable to a large extent to the increase in early female marriage which of course accelerated the number of births.

Widowed

The overall proportion of widowed females is higher than that of widowed males both in East Pakistan and West Pakistan. This reflects an almost universally lower remarriage practice of widows than of widowers. In addition, the widowers tend to marry virgins rather than widows which keeps the proportion of widows high. The higher proportion of widowed persons in West Pakistan than in East Pakistan is noteworthy. The higher proportion of widowers in West Pakistan could be caused by higher mortality of females and lower remarriage practices of widowers or both. Apparently the female mortality in West Pakistan is more pronounced than in the Eastern wing which partially accounts for the higher masculinity ratio in West Pakistan.

The widowed increase with age both for males and females. The proportions of widowers, aged 10–14 and 25–9, are higher in West Pakistan than East Pakistan at all ages with a few exceptions. It has already been noted that a higher proportion of males in West Pakistan than in East Pakistan marry at early ages.

Divorced

The proportion of divorced persons in Pakistan is very low (0·4 per cent for males and 0·8 per cent for females) and it is lower in West Pakistan than East Pakistan. The higher proportion of divorced females than of males is a universal phenomenon.

The available data show that Pakistan is one of the low-divorce-rate areas of the world. This does not imply that the Pakistan population is one of the best maritally-adjusted populations. In Pakistan divorce is still a one-way traffic. Divorce is mostly a male prerogative. The Pakistani society is not tolerant to divorce. It has no favourable built-in attitude towards divorce. In some cases tension may exist but the males may not divorce their wives just to safeguard their prestige and honour. Thus, it is apprehended that the low-divorce rate observed for Pakistan may, in fact, be at the cost of marital or family adjustment.

Education

During the decade 1951–61, there was considerable progress in literacy and education. In the 1961 census, a person was considered to be literate if he or she could read with understanding a short statement on everyday life in any language. The condition of literacy in Pakistan as assessed in 1961 is shown in the following table. The literacy percentage was higher in East Pakistan than in West Pakistan, in urban areas than in rural areas, and among males than among females.

TABLE 7. *Literacy in Pakistan*

Area	Number of literates			Per cent of total population			Per cent of population 5 years and over		
	Both sexes	Males	Females	Both sexes	Males	Females	Both sexes	Males	Females
Pakistan	14,335,809	11,106,646	3,229,163	15·9	23·4	7·6	19·2	28·0	9·3
East Pakistan	8,955,501	6,846,060	2,109,441	17·6	26·0	8·6	21·5	31·5	10·7
West Pakistan	5,380,308	4,260,586	1,119,722	13·6	20·1	6·1	16·3	23·9	7·4
Urban									
Pakistan	3,702,921	2,670,334	1,032,587	30·2	38·7	19·3	35·8	45·0	23·3
East Pakistan	1,022,906	738,910	283,996	38·7	47·7	26·1	47·7	54·8	31·9
West Pakistan	2,680,015	1,931,424	748,591	27·9	36·1	17·6	33·0	42·2	21·2
Rural									
Pakistan	10,632,888	8,436,312	2,196,576	13·6	20·8	5·9	16·6	25·0	7·2
East Pakistan	7,932,595	6,107,150	1,825,445	16·5	24·6	7·8	20·2	29·9	9·7
West Pakistan	2,700,293	2,329,162	371,131	9·1	14·7	2·6	10·9	17·5	3·2

Source: *1961 Census of Pakistan, 1961 Bulletin, No. 4 Statement.*

Economic Characteristics of the Population

For the 1961 census any person of ten years or above was considered to be in the civilian labour force if he or she:

(1) was working for profit or earning wages or salary;
(2) was helping any member of his or her family on a farm, etc.;
(3) was not working but looking for work (during the week preceding the date of enumeration of a non-agricultural worker; no reference period for an agricultural worker).

The class excluded from the civilian labour force were students, housewives, beggars, and all other persons who were neither working nor helping nor looking for work. Most of the civilian labour force thus consisted of persons in age groups of ten and above who were either employed or unpaid family workers or were unemployed and looking for work. According to this definition, there was a civilian labour force in 1961 of 30·21 million persons of whom 17·44 million were in East Pakistan and 12·66 million in West Pakistan. As many as 22·44 million were engaged in agricultural and 7·76 million in non-agricultural activities. Agriculture was relatively more important in East Pakistan than in West Pakistan. In East Pakistan agricultural labour totalled 14·87 million, and non-agricultural 2·57 million. In West Pakistan, the number of agricultural workers was 7·57 million, while 5·19 million were engaged in non-agricultural professions.

The ratio of civilian labour to total population was greater in 1961 than in 1951. For this comparison people twelve years and above are regarded as members of the civilian labour force. The ratio rose from 30·68 per cent in 1951 to 32·58 per cent in 1961. This movement and the slight decline in the ratio of dependents to total population are shown in the following table.

TABLE 8. *Percentage Distribution of Population by Economic Categories, Pakistan and Provinces, 1951 and 1961*

	Pakistan		East Pakistan		West Pakistan	
Economic categories	1951	1961	1951	1961	1951	1961
Total population	100·0	100·0	100·0	100·0	100·0	100·0
Civilian labour force	30·68	32·58	30·73	33·16	30·61	31·83
of which:						
Agriculture	23·16	24·09	25·55	28·20	19·92	18·79
Non-agriculturists	7·52	8·49	5·18	4·96	10·69	13·04
Others, including dependents	69·32	67·42	69·27	66·84	69·39	68·17

Note: Civilian labour force including persons 12 years and over ensure comparability between the censuses.

II

PROBLEM

The rapid growth of population brings in its wake a number of socio-economic problems. A rapidly-increasing population, particularly in an underdeveloped country, is of poor quality and is a drain on national resources. The present population growth rate of 2·6 per cent arrived at by the Institute of Development Economics (Karachi) and accepted by the National Income Commission (Pakistan) is one of the highest in the world. There is no doubt that the rate of population increase is substantially higher in some of the Latin American countries, but it should be remembered that the density of population in those areas is much lower than in Pakistan. The pressure on the national resources is tremendous, which is reducing the capacity to save and invest and is retarding the pace of development.

During the 1950s the GNP is estimated to have increased at an annual rate of 2·5, while the population increased at a rate of 2·3 per cent, with the result that practically the entire increase in GNP was offset by population growth.

During the Second Plan period, the position has improved as the growth rate is estimated to have gone up to 5·2 per cent. In spite of an increase in production, both agricultural and manufacturing, most of the domestic production, is being consumed internally, necessitating even imports, which in the case of food grains alone now exceed Rs 500 million a year. Tea, once an important foreign exchange earner, has almost disappeared from the export list.

Because of high growth rate of population the per capita income of the people is rising rather slowly. The per capita income, at factor cost of 1959–60 on the basis of 1961 population census, works out to only Rs 359 ($75) in 1964–65—a miserably low figure which becomes more so if it is calculated on the basis of higher growth rate of population estimated by some agencies. Due to the rapid population growth the country is faced with the serious problem of food shortage which has assumed serious proportions. Before independence Pakistan, particularly its Western part, was known as the granary of the East and besides, meeting the demand of the deficit areas of the Indo-Pakistan sub-continent, it was a substantial exporter of food grains to other countries. The table on p. 158 shows the production of food grains in the country.

It will be seen that the production of food grains in the country has risen from an average of 12·65 million tons a decade ago to 17·25 million tons in 1964–65 or by nearly 13·6 per cent. But due to the increase in population, the situation has become unsatisfactory and in most of

TABLE 9. *Production of Food Crops in Pakistan: 1950–51 to 1964–65*

(Thousand tons)

Crop	Average 1950–51 to 1954–55	1963–64	(Preliminary) 1964–65
Rice	8,334	11,629	11,515†
Wheat	3,220	4,118	4,357*
Bajra	345	356	439
Jowar	235	234	288
Maize	389	522	523
Barley	126	122	132‡
Total	12,649	16,981	17,254

* Second estimate.
† Third estimate plus previous three years' average production.
‡ Previous three years' average.

the years the country has been deficient in food grains necessitating large imports to meet the demands of the country. These imports have been rising sharply as shown in the table below.

TABLE 10. *Imports of Wheat and Rice: 1952–53 to 1964–65*

(Quantity in tons)

Year (July–June)	Wheat	Rice
1952–53	649,125	—
1953–54	783,037	—
1954–55	3,970	—
1955–56	48,157	200
1956–57	648,490	515,456
1957–58	692,272	393,817
1958–59 (15 months)	903,818	218,718
1959–60	962,612	360,957
1960–61	1,350,007	382,207
1961–62	859,000	206,000
1962–63	1,611,610	236,490
1963–64	1,512,269	142,720
1964–65 (July–March)	1,260,858	58,340

Source: Ministry of Agriculture and Works.

In spite of increase in local production and imports, the per capita consumption of food grains has remained almost static as shown in this table below:

TABLE 11. *Per Capita Availability of Food Grains: 1947–48 to 1963–64*

Year (July–June)	Available for consumption (lakh tons)	Population* (in lakhs)	Per capita availability (ounces per day)
1947–48	105·31	752·8	14
1948–49	123·61	770·1	16
1949–50	120·14	787·8	15
1950–51	116·45	805·9	14
1951–52	104·66	824·4	13
1952–53	111·29	843·4	13
1953–54	132·93	862·8	15
1954–55	112·87	882·6	13
1955–56	107·16	902·9	12
1956–57	138·02	923·7	15
1957–58	130·10	944·9	14
1958–59	123·74	966·5	13
1959–60	143·01	988·8	14
1960–61	155·01	1,014·5	15
1961–62	152·86	1,040·9	14
1962–63	145·58	1,067·9	13
1963–64	166·43	1,095·6	15

* Population figures are based on estimates of the Planning Commission.
Source: Central Statistical Office.

Relentless efforts should, therefore, be made to invest and increase national income compared to the growth rate of population if the living standards are to be improved. This would also necessitate launching of mass-scale family planning measures to slow down the pace of increase in population.

III

POLICY

The Government of Pakistan, recognizing the fundamental importance of the population problem, is attacking it along several different lines. The Third Five-Year Plan, in its objectives, indicates the different measures which would be taken for rapid economic growth of the country as well as measures for creating new job opportunities and restraining the growth of population. Some of these are:

(1) To attain a rapid growth of the national economy with a view to ensuring a breakthrough to self-sustained growth in the shortest possible time. It is proposed to achieve a minimum increase of 37 per cent in gross national product at constant prices over the Third Plan, as compared to 29 per cent in the Second Plan. The annual rate of increase is projected at 6·5 per cent per annum in the Third Plan as against 5·2 per cent in the Second Plan.

(2) To reduce the degree of inter-regional and intra-regional disparity, it is proposed to reduce the existing level of disparity in income per head between East and West Pakistan by increasing total income by 40 per cent in the former and by 35 per cent in the latter province.

(3) To provide at least 5·5 million new job opportunities to absorb the entire increase in the labour force during the next five years as well as to reduce the existing level of employment by over one sixth.

(4) To accelerate the transformation in agriculture, now taking place, by placing the highest priority on measures to increase water availability and use of fertilizer, by maintaining strong farm incentives, and by supporting the entire range of agricultural programmes.

(5) To arrest the menacing growth of population by taking decisive steps towards population control.

(6) To provide better housing, more health services, and greater facilities for education, especially for lower income groups.

(7) To make substantial progress towards achieving certain specific objectives such as diminishing inequalities in the distribution of income, wealth and economic power, providing a measure of social security and promoting social and cultural change conducive to accelerated economic expansion.

Development Under the Third Five-Year Plan

The development programme for the Third Five-Year Plan proposes an expenditure of Rs 52,000 million, of which Rs 30,000 million is in the public sector and Rs 22,000 million in the private sector. Of the total plan size of Rs 52,000 million, Rs 27,000 million has been allocated to East Pakistan and Rs 25,000 million to West Pakistan. Greater allocation to East Pakistan has been made in view of greater pressure of population there and also with a view to bringing about parity in the per capita income of the two Provinces in as short a period as possible. The following table gives the sectoral allocation during the Third Five-Year Plan.

Of the total allocation of Rs 52,000 million, 26 per cent is earmarked for industry, 15 per cent for agriculture, 33 per cent for economic infrastructure and 26 per cent for social services and other sectors.

As agriculture accounts for nearly 80 per cent of the civilian labour force and 50 per cent of the GNP, the Third Plan lays great stress on this sector by allocating 15 per cent of the proposed expenditure to it. Large allocation to this sector has also been made because investment in agriculture brings about greater employment than in other sectors. The agricultural growth target has been raised from 3 per cent per annum to 5 per cent and the allocation has been increased by 128 per cent over the Second Plan expenditure compared to an acceleration of 87 per cent in industries, fuels and minerals.

TABLE 12. *Sectoral Allocation of the Third Plan*

(in million rupees)

	Public sector	Private sector	Total
Agriculture	4,670	4,000	8,670
Water and Power	8,420	650	9,070
Industry	4,580	8,300	12,880
Fuels and Minerals	700	750	1,450
Transportation and Communications	6,300	3,900	10,200
Physical Planning—Housing	3,030	4,000	7,030
Education	2,730	300	3,030
Health	1,330	40	1,370
Social Welfare	125	40	165
Manpower	115	20	135
Works programme	2,500	—	2,500
Total	34,500	22,000	56,500
Less expected shortfall	−4,500	—	−4,500
Total Programme	30,000	22,000	52,000

The Third Plan aims at a major breakthrough in agriculture. Food grain production is to be increased by 4·7 million tons. This represents an increase of 28 per cent compared to 14 per cent increase in population. The imported food grains are likely to decrease from 15 per cent of total national consumption in 1965 to 5 per cent in 1970 if this target is achieved.

In addition, the agriculture programme envisages irrigation of five million acres for the first time, besides improvement of another 21·7 million acres through drainage, protection against waterlogging and salinity, and flood control.

Family Planning Measures

Considering the high growth rate of population and the dangers which it entails, the Government of Pakistan has taken a number of measures to keep its growth under check. During the Second Plan (1960–65), so far 2,945 Family Planning Clinics have been established throughout the country—1,784 in West Pakistan and 1,161 in East Pakistan. Over 1,270 doctors and 1,280 health visitors, nurses, midwives and compounders have been trained in family planning. In addition, 5,614 Basic Democrats and social workers have been imparted orientation training on the subject during the period.

In 1964, about 500,000 people visited the various Family Planning Clinics as against 367,000 in 1963, 238,000 in 1962, 224,000 in 1961 and 92,000 in 1960.

Family Planning under the Third Plan

The Government of Pakistan has chalked out an ambitious programme of family planning for implementation during the Third Five-Year Plan. A sum of Rs 166 million has been earmarked for the implementation of the proposed programme. The main object of this programme is to bring down the birth rate from 55 per 1,000 to 45 per 1,000. In order to achieve this objective, 20 million couples, who represent almost all the women in reproductive age in 1970, will be induced to practise family planning in one form or another. The scheme will be applied during the Third Five-Year Plan to thirty-six districts of West Pakistan and sixteen districts of East Pakistan. Two thirds of the districts will be covered in the first two years of the Plan, and one third in subsequent years.

For the successful implementation of the programme, a strong organization is being created in the country. There will be a Family Planning Council at the Central and Family Planning Boards at the Provincial and district levels. All the Union Councils in West Pakistan and Thana Councils in East Pakistan will be associated with the programme. The work at these levels will be looked after by a Family Planning Supervisor (one for three Union Councils) in West Pakistan and Thana Family Planning Officer (one for each Thana) in East Pakistan. At the bottom of the hierarchy will be the village *dai* (midwife). She will perform such functions as motivating the people and distributing contraceptives.

The programme provides for 1,000 Family Planning Supervisors in West Pakistan who will work in collaboration with the Union Council Secretaries. In East Pakistan, 400 Thana Family Planning Officers have been provided. One general assistant, one female assistant and one male assistant will be attached to each Thana Family Planning Officer. A total of 50,000 village *dais* will be employed—30,000 in East Pakistan and 20,000 in West Pakistan at the rate of one *dai* for two villages of 1,600 people in East Pakistan and one *dai* for two villages in West Pakistan. About 2,400 part-time Family Planning Doctors—at the rate of six for each Tehsil in West Pakistan and three for each Thana in East Pakistan will be registered and appointed for the purpose of IUD insertions and clinical sterilization.

The programme envisages the establishment of thirty-seven whole-time urban clinics and 718 part-time clinics, as shown below:

	East Pakistan	West Pakistan
(1) Part-time clinics	400	318
(2) Whole-time clinics	16	21

The clinics will concentrate mainly on IUD insertions. The part-time clinics will be housed in existing health institutions and are meant for the use of family planning doctors. Each whole-time urban clinic will have one lady doctor, one health visitor, one family planning councillor and one female medical attendant. The objectives of the scheme include 1·5 million IUD insertions and 90,000 vasectomies during the Third Plan period.

Training of personnel will include the following:

(1) Under the scheme, 150 lady doctors, lady health visitors and trained midwives from each Province will be imparted ten days' training in family planning techniques and motivational aspects. These medical and paramedical personnel will then train the lady doctors, lady health visitors and midwives in their respective Tehsil/Thanas.

(2) A fourteen-day training course has been prescribed for Family Planning Supervisors in West Pakistan and Thana Family Planning Officers in East Pakistan. In West Pakistan Family Planning Supervisors will be trained at district headquarters and in East Pakistan six training centres will be opened at suitable places.

(3) Thana Family Planning Officers in East Pakistan will train their male and female assistants and Family Planning Supervisors in West Pakistan will impart training to Union Council Secretaries in a period of two weeks at Thana and Union Council respectively.

(4) A training course of three weeks' duration will be conducted for village *dais* (midwives) at each Thana and Union Council.

NOTES

1. *National Income Commission of Pakistan Interim Report* (Karachi, Government of Pakistan, 1964), p. 39.
2. *National Income Commission of Pakistan Interim Report, op. cit.*, p. 40.
3. *Census of Pakistan, 1961*, Vol. 1 (Karachi, Government of Pakistan, 1962).
4. *National Income Commission—Interim Report, op. cit.*, p. 39.
5. Sultan Shah Hashmi, *Country Background paper of Pakistan*, presented to the Asian Population Conference, held at New Delhi, December 1963, p. 11.
6. *National Income Commission Interim Report, op. cit.*, p. 40.
7. Sultan Shah Hashmi, *Country Background paper of Pakistan*, presented to the Asian Population Conference, held at New Delhi, December 1963.

BIBLIOGRAPHY

Ahmad, Nazir and Karol, J. Krotki, 'Simultaneous Estimation of Population Growth', *Pakistan Development Review*, vol. III, No. 1, Spring 1963.

Ahmed, Mohiuddin, 'An Estimate of Pakistan's 1951 Vital Rates', *Pakistan Economic Journal* (Dacca), September 1963.

'Vital Rates of East Pakistan Muslims', *Proceedings of the International Population Conference*, Ottawa, 1963 (Liege, 1964).

'Rates and Levels of Mortality and Fertility in Pakistan', *Population Review* (Madras), January, 1966.

Census of Pakistan 1951, Vol. I, Pakistan, Report and tables 1955 (Karachi, Government of Pakistan, 1955).

Census of Pakistan 1961, *Census Bulletin No. 2* (Karachi, Government of Pakistan, Ministry of Home Affairs, 1961).
Economic Survey (Karachi, Ministry of Finance, Government of Pakistan, 1964–65).
Economic Survey (Karachi, Ministry of Finance, Government of Pakistan, 1963–64).
Family Planning Scheme for Pakistan—During the Third Five-Year Plan Period, 1965–70 (Karachi, Government of Pakistan, Ministry of Health).
Hashmi, Sultan S., *The People of Karachi, Demographic Characteristics of the Population* (Karachi, Institute of Development Economics, 1964).
Interim Report, September 1964, National Income Commission (Karachi, Government of Pakistan, 1964).
Krotki, Karol J., 'Population Size, Growth and Age Distribution, 4th Release from the 1961 Census of Pakistan', *Pakistan Development Review*, vol. III, No. 2, Summer, 1963, pp. 279–305.
Kux, Dennis, 'Growth and Characteristics of Pakistan's Population', *Population Review*, January 1962.
Main Features of the Demographic Conditions in Pakistan (Country Background Paper presented to the Asian Population Conference) (New Delhi, 1963).
Qureshi, Anwar Iqbal, *Pakistan Marches on Road to Prosperity* (Karachi, 1965).
Qureshi, M. L. (Ed.), *Population Growth and Economic Development*, Institute of Development Economics (Karachi, 1959).
Second Five Year Plan of Pakistan (Karachi, Government of Pakistan, 1961).
The Second Five-Year Plan, Revised Estimates (Government of Pakistan, 1961).
Third Five Year Plan of Pakistan (Karachi, Government of Pakistan, 1965).
United Nations, *Demographic Yearbook* (New York, 1961).
The Population of Asia and the Far East, 1950–80, Future Population Estimates by Sex and Age, Report *IV* (New York, 1960).

CHAPTER 7

MALAYSIA'S POPULATION PROBLEM

BY J. C. CALDWELL

I

THE POPULATION OF MALAYSIA

The Formation of Malaysia

SOUTH-EAST ASIA's newest nation, the Federation of Malaysia, came into existence on September 16, 1963. The political stir, which that event has aroused, may tend to blind us to the small size of the country's population in Asian terms. The most recent estimate[2] credits Malaysia with 10,310,000 inhabitants or not much less than the population of Australia. Nevertheless, this number represents only 4·5 per cent and 0·6 per cent of the total populations of south-east Asia and the whole of Asia respectively. Even its neighbours of the Malay Archipelago dwarf it, for the population of Indonesia is nearly ten times as great and that of the suggested Malindophil Federation more than thirteen times larger.

Malaysia is split into two by the South China Sea. On the mainland of Asia lie the Federation of Malaya and Singapore, both relatively densely populated and economically advanced. Each has acquired since the Second World War considerable experience in the art of government. Some hundreds of miles to the east on the north-west coast of the island of Borneo are situated Malaysia's other two components, Sarawak and Sabah. Each has until recently been a British colony, and neither has enjoyed sufficient economic development or self-government to make its passage into independence at all simple.

The basic fact of Malaysia is its dichotomy into these two distinct parts. The two halves have some common features, such as the experience of British colonization, the use of English as an administrative language, and a mixture of Asian peoples of diverse origin resulting from the needs of a colonial economy. Nevertheless, the contrasts are many. The demographic difference is thrown into perspective by the fact that whilst 60 per cent of the area of Malaysia lies on Borneo, the two mainland territories, commonly referred to as Malaya, contain 88 per cent of the population. The average density of settlement of the former is sixteen persons per square mile compared with almost 180 persons per square mile in the latter. Much of this study will have to confine the detailed examination to the eight-ninths of the country's inhabitants living in

Malaya, for the lack of successive censuses and of adequate vital registration systems renders impossible at this stage a detailed demographic analysis of the Borneo territories.

TABLE 1. *Population and Area of Malaysian Territories*

	Latest census	Population	Population, mid-1962 estimate (in thousands)	Area (sq. miles)	Population density, mid-1962 (persons per sq. mile)
Federation of Malaya	1957	6,278,758	7,330	50,700	—
Singapore	1957	1,445,929	1,740	224	—
Sarawak	1960*	744,529	770	48,342	—
Sabah	1960*	454,421	470	29,388	—
Total, Malaya	1957	7,724,687	9,070	50,924	178
Total, Borneo territories	1960	1,198,950	1,240	77,730	16
Malaysia	—	—	10,310	128,654	80

* Census dates were actually two months apart.

The People of Malaysia

In spite of what has just been said about the small fraction that Malaysia's population forms of that of the whole of Asia, the study of this population is important. At a time when 'north–south' contrasts in economic development are causing concern, it should be noted that equatorial Malaya enjoys, not only one of the highest standards of living in the tropical world, but also one third only to that of Japan and Israel in the whole of Asia.

This relative prosperity has owed little, except for the occurrence of tin-ore deposits, to superior natural resources. It is largely a product of historical circumstance. The single most important economic resource in Malaya is a demographic one, namely a predominantly immigrant population aggressively determined upon its own economic betterment.

Immigration has also brought problems. Table 2 shows that the so-called *immigrant* races make up the majority of the population of Malaysia. In fact, the effect of immigration has been very much more marked than the table appears to suggest. Much of the Malaysian population is not really *indigenous*, but is descended from people of Indonesian stock who went to Malaya during much the same period as did the Chinese and Indians and with much the same economic motive. This is especially the case in the States of Selangor, Negri Sembilan Perak and Johore on the west coast of Malaya.

Malaysia is the case *par excellence* of the *plural society*. The racial division is apparent in the occupational structure of the country, in residence especially along rural–urban lines and in its effect upon politics. The creation of Malaysia can be explained largely by the fact that the Malays of the Federation of Malaya would only agree to federation with predominantly Chinese Singapore if the counterweight

TABLE 2. *Percentage Population of Malaysian Territories, by Ethnic Groups, 1960*

	'Indigenous' Malaysians	Chinese	Indians	Others
Federation of Malaya	50	37	11	2
Singapore	14	75	9	2
Sarawak	68	31	—*	1
Sabah	76	23	—*	1
Malaya	43	44	11	2
Borneo territories	71	28	—	1
Malaysia	46	43	9*	2

* The small number of Indians in Sarawak and Sabah are included in 'Others'. The percentage of Indians calculated for the whole of Malaysia is based only on those enumerated in Malaya.

of the Borneo territories, with their smaller proportions of Chinese, were also to be included. Even so, Malaysians do not make up as much as half of the population of the country, although at present they do possess the majority of the votes.

Other aspects of the situation are also more complex than the table might imply. The *Malaysian* population contains almost two thirds of a million people mostly in Borneo, who are neither *Malay* nor Muslim. Thus what may be regarded as a homogenous Malay block forms only two fifths of the population. Nor are the Chinese the only major *immigrant* race. Over five sixths of the remainder of the population of Malaysia belong to the Indian communities of the Federation of Malaya and Singapore. Thus, in racial terms, as well as in those of cultural influences Malaya is a meeting point for the three great ethnic groups of its part of Asia.

The conditions which originally formed the *plural society* have now passed. The colonial economy type of population has been largely transformed. With the passing of massive immigration, now restricted severely by legislation, the population is no longer characterized by a large number of newly-arrived immigrants, a great surplus of males and a concentration of the population in the adult age groups. Between the 1921 and 1957 censuses of Malaya the foreign-born population fell from 47 per cent to 17 per cent, the sex ratios from 159 to 107 males per 100 females and the proportion of the community made up by males in the 15–54 years of age range from 42 per cent to 26 per cent.[3]

Since the Second World War, Malaya has been on balance an emigrant land. But population growth has not slowed down. In the decade between the 1947 and 1957 censuses population increase reached almost 2 millions, or 25 per cent more than the increment added during the previous sixteen years. Natural increase was more than making up for the cut in migration, and, indeed, by 1957 had reached 3·5 per cent per annum, one of the highest rates in the world.

One of the reasons for the rise in the natural growth rate has been the better balance between the numbers of the sexes. More important, however, has been the very substantial fall in mortality which has occurred since the end of the War. For Malay's relative wealth has allowed it to achieve the lowest death rate in south-east Asia. An examination of this phenomenon will form part of the next section of this chapter, where population change is discussed, and necessarily the limitations of the data will confine the discussion to Malaya. Most trends discerned, however, will probably also be followed in the Borneo territories of Malaysia within the next few years.

Population Change in Malaya

It has been suggested that the greatest single benefit that the Industrial Revolution and subsequent economic growth has conferred upon mankind has been the guarantee that the vast majority of people in countries so affected will be able to live until old age. This benefit has only very recently been conferred upon most of the developing countries and with such speed as to raise the fear that the other benefits of economic modernization may be jeopardized. The reason for this difference between the developed and developing world is that the lowering of mortality in the former depended upon the slow growth of medical knowledge and technology, each advance based laboriously upon the previous one, and all advances depending upon economic growth creating a surplus of wealth to pay for scientific research. The developing countries in contrast have merely had to raise their national incomes to the point where they could afford to import existing medical technology and apply it to their populations. Furthermore, medical science has yielded increasing returns. The last generation has witnessed a great increase in the discovery and mass production of such materials as antibiotics and insecticides, which together with such prophylactics as vaccines, have been able to reduce mortality rates very dramatically and at relatively low cost in the poorer countries.

Available evidence indicates that the crude death rate in Malaya was above 40 per 1,000 prior to the First World War. Official figures for the period since the Second World War show declines between the 1945–49 period and 1961 of 17·5 to 9·2 in the Federation of Malaya and 12·5 to 6 in Singapore. Part of the explanation lies in a weakness of the crude death rate as a measure of true mortality levels, for some of the decline in the rate can be attributed to a change in the age structure of the community from one dominated by immigrant adults at a relatively high risk of death to one with a large proportion of children resulting from a high rate of natural increase. Nevertheless, most of the apparent fall in mortality was real, as the estimates of expectation of life at birth in Table 3 show.

TABLE 3. *Estimates of Expectation of Life at Birth,* Malaya, by Race and Sex, 1947 and 1957 (all numbers in years)*

		1947	1957	1947–57 increase
Malays:	males	38·6	53·2	14·6
	females	39·3	53·9	14·6
Chinese:	males	51·9	60·0	8·1
	females	62·5	67·8	5·3
Indians:	males	54·3	60·1	5·8
	females	45·0	56·2	11·2

* These calculations are based upon a study of available data and the correction of its defects as set out in *The Population of Malaya.*

An examination of demographic literature published up to about 1950 shows that no one expected the steep fall in mortality that has subsequently taken place in most of the developing world. The advances against mortality achieved in the 1947–57 decade in Malaya would have needed twenty-five years if the pre-World War II experience had still been applicable.[4]

The application of 1947 age-specific death rates to the 1957 population of Malaya provides a measure of the type of change that has occurred and of what it portends for the future. If 1947 mortality levels had prevailed, the number of deaths occurring in 1957 would have been 55,000 greater than the 89,000 actually recorded. Thus, a very substantial improvement in the populace's welfare had taken place. This saving of extra lives was not distributed evenly throughout the population by either race or age. The Malay share of the saving was 60 per cent, and it is this disproportionate improvement which has helped to stabilize the racial balance of the country, for the Malay rate of natural increase is now as great as that of the Chinese and Indians.

Perhaps more significant is the fact that over half the reduction in mortality occurred amongst children of less than five years. Thus the fall in mortality has achieved some of the same effect that would have resulted from an increase in fertility. It has given rise to a wave of population sweeping upwards through the age structure of the community, with as yet no sign of the far side of the wave. In Malaya, as in other developing countries, this wave is only now beginning to reach adulthood. Thus the economy has not yet been fully tested by the rapid mortality decline.

The gap between the levels of fertility and mortality is now much greater in Malaya than has ever been the case in any country which has succeeded in industrializing. In 1961 the crude birth rate was 40·7 per 1,000, the crude death rate 8·6 per 1,000, and the annual rate of increase almost 3¼ per cent per annum. If that rate of population growth were to be sustained, the population would double every twenty-two years and would reach 30 million by the end of the century.

However, in spite of exhibiting a crude birth rate in excess of 40 per 1,000, Malaya is now attracting wide interest, not only because of high fertility, but because of falling fertility. In the past few years Singapore's birth rate has fallen more rapidly than has been the case elsewhere in Africa or Asia or, with the exception of Puerto Rico, anywhere else in the developing world. The crude birth rate in the Federation of Malaya has been falling since 1957 and between that year and 1961 fell from 46·2 to 41·9 per 1,000, a fall of over 9 per cent. Singapore's birth rate has been falling since 1954 but the decline has become much steeper in recent years. Between 1954 and 1962 it fell from 45·7 to 35·5 per 1,000, a fall of over 22 per cent. In the five years following 1956 annual drops in the crude birth rate of 2·3, 3·2, 4·1, 4 and 8·3 per cent respectively were experienced. However, newly-published figures show the decline between 1961 and 1962 to have been only 1·2 per cent, thus bringing the crude birth rate to 35·1 per 1,000.

An analysis of all available data for the 1947–57 intercensal decade showed no definite evidence of any movement in Malay fertility during the ten-year period. Chinese fertility may have declined by approximately 4 per cent, about half of which can be explained by later female marriage if change in widowhood within marriage is ignored. There is some evidence of a greater fertility decline in the Indian community but the data for the earlier period is not sufficiently good for this to be certain. As a result of the study, the estimates of total fertility rates shown in Table 4 were computed by applying adjustments to the published data for the three-year period centring on the 1957 Census.

TABLE 4. *Total Fertility Rates by Race, Malaya, 1956–58*

	Malays	Chinese	Indians
Federation of Malaya	6·4	6·7	7·3
Singapore	6·4	6·5	7·1

These total fertility rates are amongst the highest in the world. Those of the Indians and Chinese are almost certainly above those prevailing in India and China, although not, it should be remarked, Taiwan. They may show the results of frontier conditions where high birth rates did not exert the same economic pressure, and a parallel may be drawn between this relationship and that between America and Europe in the eighteenth and early nineteenth centuries. The shortage of females in an immigrant society may also have played its part, especially in ensuring their early marriage. It might be noted that this situation has now passed, probably for ever.

Nevertheless, the study even of the 1947–57 period produced sufficient evidence of the possibility of a fertility decline to permit the prediction that one was perhaps already under way and to ensure that all population projections constructed incorporated such a phenomenon. Subsequent events have justified this view.

The two chief sources of evidence suggesting the likelihood of some decline in fertility were provided by the development of a rural–urban fertility differential and by the increase in the average age of females at marriage.

Singapore's fertility around 1957 has been seen to have been a little below that of the Federation of Malaya in the Chinese and Indian communities. A comparison between urban and rural fertility in the Federation taken as a whole is affected by regional fertility differentials, which are significant in the case of the Malays. However, a study of the urban–rural fertility differential made for each separate State suggested that for the Federation as a whole the level of urban fertility was about 17, 7·5 and 2·75 per cent respectively below that of the rural areas for Chinese, Indians and Malays respectively.[5]

The proportions of females married in the younger female marriageable age groups fell between 1947 and 1957 in each ethnic group. It has been argued that this arose at least partly from an increasing shortage of potential husbands.[6] Such a condition might seem to be unlikely in a country which has been until recent years subjected to a predominantly male immigrant stream. This is, however, not the case. The remaining unmarried immigrants are now mostly old men. The age groups in which most marriages take place exhibit normal sex ratios. But the customary age difference between married partners in Malaya is of the order of five years or even more in each ethnic group. In a rapidly-growing community each age group is larger than the next oldest group, and consequently a five-year age gap between spouses in a monogamous society increasing at 3·5 per cent per annum will result in at least one sixth of all women being an unmarriageable surplus. This phenomenon does tend to provide a brake on very high rates of natural increase once this marked difference between the size of successive age groups reaches the adult population, something that is only now resulting from the post-Second World War mortality decline.

This pressure upon the female marriage market is likely at this stage to be strongest in the Chinese community, for, in spite of popular legends, polygamy has not the importance in Chinese society that polygamy and the institution of unstable marriage have amongst the Malays. Nor is the Indian community as much affected, for a more marked surplus of immigrant males still exists in it. In fact the changes between 1947 and 1957 in the proportions of females ever married was greatest amongst the Chinese where considerable falls occurred in the 15–19, 20–24 and 25–9 years of age groups. The proportion married in the first age group was nearly halved. By 1957 fewer females of 20–24 years of age were married in the Malayan Chinese community than was the case in Australia, and many fewer were married than amongst females in the United States. The postponement of marriage in the younger and more fertile age groups would be expected to have a marked effect on fertility. The application of Chinese age-specific married fertility rates to the proportions of females married in the Malay community suggests that such postponement should have reduced Chinese fertility by about a quarter. The fact that Chinese fertility is of the same order as Malay and Indian fertility is explained by much higher fertility rates succeeding marriage, a phenomenon which admittedly may not be totally unrelated to the marriage postponement itself.

Apart from the question of the level of fertility within marriage, external changes to the married state which might be expected to affect the level of fertility were not confined to changes in the age at marriage. More important was the decline in mortality, which resulted in the breaking up of many fewer marriages by the death of one of the partners. Given constant age-specific married fertility rates, Table 5 shows

TABLE 5. *Effect on Total Fertility Rate of Changes in Proportions Married and of Mortality within Marriage, by Race, Malaya, 1947–57**

	Malays	Chinese	Indians
Change in female proportions married	−1·6%	−1·6%	−1·0%
Change in break-up of marriage by death of spouse(s)	+2·1%	+3·6%	+4·8%
Net effect	+0·5%	+2·0%	+3·8%
Maximum future possible change by elimination of death of spouse(s) during wife's reproductive span	+3·7%	+3·9%	+3·7%

*Assuming constant age-specific married fertility.

the effects that these two types of change could be expected to have had upon fertility levels between 1947 and 1957. The final line of the table shows the total further rise in fertility which would occur should mortality within marriage be reduced to zero during the wife's fertile span. It is apparent that future reductions in mortality, which are unlikely to approach the limiting case posited in the table, will not exert such contrary effects to rises in the female age at marriage or of reductions in married fertility as has hitherto been the case. The comparatively large Chinese gains from declining mortality compared with those of the Malays are explained by the relative concentration of Chinese fertility in the older age groups. The table makes it clear that greater falls in fertility may have occurred within marriage than changes in birth rates have indicated.

The most significant aspect of Malayan fertility is the great size of the surplus population left over from reproduction after the needs of community replacement and premature death have been met. The net reproduction rates of the Malay, Chinese and Indian communities were for the 1956–58 period 2·5, 2·9 and 3·1 respectively. The fact that the surplus indicated by this index is several times that found in Australia or the United States and dozens of times that found in some European countries is a measure of the population problems that the country will have to face in the years ahead.

Thus, the characteristics of Malaya's population have been fashioned by an immigration stream so substantial that it outnumbered the original inhabitants of the country. The stream was composed of three quite different types of people, only one of which had close cultural affinity with the inhabitants of the country. The days of the great migration streams are now over. The nature of the population has also been determined by the fact that previously very high death and birth rates have given way to a much lower and still falling death rate accompanied by a birth rate which remains very high, even though it has fallen significantly recently.

The resulting rapid rate of natural growth has produced, in the younger age groups at least, the characteristic age structure of a high-growth-rate population, in that each age group is considerably larger than the next older group. This structure prevails throughout the Malay population becoming only more intensified in the younger age groups. The same is true of the Chinese population under thirty-five years of age and of Indian children. At older ages population pyramids show the typical age bulge caused by the remnants of past immigration. The average age of the population has necessarily fallen. Nearly 45 per cent of the Malay and Chinese populations are under fifteen years of age, and even in the Indian community the proportion now exceeds 40 per cent. In the Chinese and Indian cases the relative size of this age group is more than double what it was a third of a century ago. Necessarily the dependency burden has grown and the labour force forms a smaller part of the community. The fraction of the community made up by males, 15–54 years of age, fell between the 1921 and 1957 censuses from 28 to 24 per cent, 58 to 24 per cent and 59 to 34 per cent in the case of Malays, Chinese and Indians respectively.

With the virtual cessation of immigration, sex ratios have become more normal. Ratios are close to parity for the Malays at all ages and the Chinese under fifty years of age. Even in the Indian community ratios are not extreme until after thirty years of age, and by 1967 will not be particularly abnormal in any of the main marriageable age groups.

For the first time in modern Malaya's history major change in the racial balance is neither taking place nor threatening to do so unless major internal strife were to occur along communal lines. Otherwise, the great majority of those now living in Malaya intend to stay, even if some of them sometimes wish it otherwise. The Malay and Chinese proportions of the population have become settled at about four ninths each, and the Indian proportion at about one ninth. Because of the relatively smaller populations of the Borneo territories, their addition to Malaya makes surprisingly little difference to the racial composition of the country. The immigrant races account for only 29 per cent of the combined population of the Borneo territories. But whereas these groups make up 57 per cent of the population of Malaya, they form no less than 54 per cent of that of Malaysia.

Little need be said on the religious division of the country except that it broadly follows the racial division of the country, although some Chinese are Christian and a few Indians Moslem. It might be emphasized that the division between the Malays and the *immigrant* communities is more a religious division than anything else.

Other social and economic characteristics have demographic implications. An examination of the *joint* or *extended family* established that perhaps a third of the Chinese in Malaya, who live within the bounds of normal family life, are to be found in such families. The proportion is very much less in the case of Malays and Indians, but much the same function may be served by the *kampongs* or by housing on the rubber estates. The most ramifying aspect of *extended family* relations in south-east Asia is not, however, the physical proximity in which large numbers of relatives live, but the financial responsibility that each has for others.

The stream of immigrants, which for over half a century went to the tin diggings, rubber plantations and commercial centres of the west coast of Malaya, and whose members were for the most part forbidden by law from acquiring cultivable land, has created distinctive occupational and settlement patterns in Malaya. As in other immigrant lands, such as Australia or the United States, one effect has been to accelerate the growth of non-agricultural industries and of urban population. There seems to be evidence from the recent history of Malaya and some other parts of south-east Asia that the tendency towards urbanization can also be accentuated by high rates of natural growth and by civil strife or military action in rural areas. In this way rapid population growth may assist in the development of the modernized section of the economy.

Table 6 reveals that by the time of the 1957 census less than half the economically-active population of Malaya were engaged in such rural pursuits as agriculture, forestry, hunting and fishing. In contrast the 1960 censuses of Sarawak and Sabah showed that over 75 per cent of the work force of the former and over 80 per cent of that of the latter were engaged in such activities. A smaller proportion still of Malaya's population are engaged in the typically peasant activities of south-east Asia, for more than half the rural work force is employed in the cultivation of such tree crops as rubber and oil palm. Where such activities are carried out on estates, they may be regarded as part of the modernized economy. In these circumstances working and living conditions are often imposed upon employees similar in many respects to those of urban, secondary industry.

TABLE 6. *Percentage of Economically-Active Population Engaged in Rural Occupations, by Race, Malaya, 1957*

	Malays	Chinese	Indians	Total population
Agriculture, forestry, hunting and fishing	70	33	47	49
As above, but excluding estate industries	43	12	1	23

The racial occupational differential is also reflected in resulting individual incomes. It has been estimated that the Chinese earn about three fifths of the total of such incomes, while the Malays receive only a little over one fifth.[7] For 1957, Chinese, Indian and Malay average individual incomes were estimated to be about M$916, M$747 and M$408 respectively. Nor was there much sign that this differential had lessened in the previous ten years, although it is possible that there had been a slight relative improvement in the Malay position. The importance of the export of estate-type products was clearly demonstrated by the fact that the rural incomes still exceed urban incomes in Malaya, by M$2,256 to M$1,930, even though urban areas now contain the majority of the population.

Observing the rather generous census definition of an urban area, Malaya's urban population can be said to have risen from 35 to 51 per cent between the 1947 and 1957 censuses. With 30 per cent of its population in towns with more than 20,000 inhabitants and 21 per cent in cities with more than 100,000 inhabitants, Malaya's level of urbanization is well above that of most of developing Asia and of the tropics throughout the world. The pattern is, in fact, similar to that of modern France and Sweden and to that of the United States in the 1920s. Four urban centres contain more than 100,000 people and one has now passed the million mark. This position may be contrasted with that in the Borneo territories, where Sarawak's largest town contains a little more than 50,000 people and Sabah's largest town about 12,000 inhabitants.

A more significant point still is that, of the unprecedented population increase in Malaya between 1947 and 1957, 98·3 per cent were absorbed by the towns and only 1·7 per cent augmented rural population growth. Part of the reason lay in the compulsory and voluntary population transfers associated with the Emergency. But the analysis of population change in a densely settled rural area, little affected by military activity, such as the Kelantan Delta, shows that movement from areas of rapid rural population growth has also been an important factor.

In demographic and economic terms, Malaysia falls into three quite distinct divisions. The first is the strip along the west coast of Malaya stretching from Penang to Singapore, sometimes known as *New Malaya*, which has borne the brunt of the immigrations, and in which the modernized estate, mining and urban economies have developed. Here the *plural society* is to be found. The rest of the peninsula, which may be termed *Old Malaya*, is still largely a Malay preserve. It has, however, been affected by the economic development of the west coast to a degree that the Borneo territories have not, and so, in density of settlement, spread of education and medical services, and probably in income earned, it may be regarded as standing somewhere between the two more contrasting areas. This is not the case, however, in terms of immigrant population.

In Table 7 it can be seen that, although *New Malaya* occupies only about one sixth of the area of Malaysia, it contains two thirds of its population. Furthermore, the process of population concentration is continuing. In 1911 *New Malaya* contained 68 per cent of the people of Malaya, by 1957 it contained 76 per cent of them. The contrast between the *plural society* of *New Malaya* and the largely Malay preserve of *Old Malaya* often obscures the fact that even most Malays live in *New Malaya*, 57 per cent of them doing so.[8]

TABLE 7. *Selected Characteristics of New Malaya,* Old Malaya, and Borneo Territories, 1962*

	New Malaya	Old Malaya	Borneo Territories
% of total area of Malaysia	17	22	61
% of total population of Malaysia	66	22	12
Density of settlement (persons per square mile)	307	78	16
% 'indigenous' Malaysians form of all population	32	77	71

* Penang, Perak, Selangor, Negri Sembilan, Malacca, Johore and Singapore.

The process of population concentration cannot be fully appreciated if attention is paid merely to *New Malaya*, for it only approximates to the area of dense settlement, and two of Malaya's most densely settled areas, in Kedah and Kelantan, lie outside it. It is possible to delineate an area of Malaya which contained in 1957 90 per cent of the population in 40·8 per cent of the area. What is more significant is that the area of dense settlement did not expand between the 1947 and 1957 censuses, and that its proportion of the country's population rose from 90·6 to 90·9 per cent, as it absorbed 91·9 per cent of the total intercensal increase. Although by 1957 the densely settled area exhibited a population density of 341 persons per square mile compared with twenty-three persons per square mile in the remaining three fifths of the country, there was no evidence that the frontier of dense settlement was expanding and little evidence that the sparsely settled area formed a kind of reserve of land ready to absorb future expansion as is so commonly believed in Malaya.

II

IS THERE A POPULATION PROBLEM IN MALAYA?

The Basic Population Problems

There are four basic problems, the nature of the *plural society* itself, impending changes in population resulting from new irreversible demographic processes, the continuation of a high rate of population growth, and the contrast between the two antithetical divisions of Malaya or even of the three divisions of Malaysia.

The *plural society* is a never-forgotten fact of life in Malaya. This does not mean that the possibility of communal conflict is particularly great. But it does mean that society is rent fairly deeply by differences in origin, religion and custom. And these differences are accentuated by the rural–urban division and above all by the awareness of the relative wealth of one group compared to the other. Common customs may eventually begin to evolve, although the religious barrier is a formidable one, but a blending of the ethnic stocks may not be achieved in the generations to come. If the trend towards births of inter-racial parentage continues at the same rate as it has since the War, it will take over a thousand years to cleave off even half of each of the major ethnic blocks into some kind of common Malayan blend.

The population projections show that, with the cessation of large-scale migration, the normalizing of the immigrant groups' sex ratios and the fall of the high Malay mortality rates, there is unlikely to be any significant change in the racial balance within the next generation. This is not, however, the case in terms of the age structures of the different

M

communities. One important implication of this qualification can be seen in the political field. Defining the potential electorate, as distinct from those actually enfranchised, as those twenty-one years of age or over, the Malay proportion of this body in Malaya was 48·4 per cent in 1957, but would fall to about 43 per cent by 1982. By that date the 'indigenous' Malaysian population of the whole of Malaysia will not account for more than about 46 per cent of the potential electorate, which, because of the enfranchisement of those actually born in Malaysia, will become ever more closely synonymous with the enfranchised population. Perhaps such a near balance will prove to be the happiest outcome to the situation.

There appears to be little likelihood that the plural society will spread evenly throughout the country, although it is probable that the Malay proportion will rise somewhat in *New Malaya* and fall to a limited extent in *Old Malaya*. The real changes will occur in the towns. High population growth rates, together with the inability of the rural Malayan economy to absorb extra population increments at this rate, ensure a continuing massive rural–urban migration stream. The exodus of Chinese from the rural areas during the Emergency means that in future the greater part of this stream must be made up of Malays. Between 1947 and 1957 the Malay proportion of the urban population rose from 17 per cent to 19 per cent, but a much more substantial rise will undoubtedly occur in the next two decades. In the past communal friction has been witnessed most commonly in rural areas; in the future, especially if urban employment cannot cope with the influx to the towns, this may no longer be the case.[9]

Perhaps the most important aspect of the population picture of contemporary Malaya is that the first waves of post-war births, less shrunk by infant and childhood mortality than any previous increments to the population, are now reaching adulthood. The apprehension about the ability of countries to employ and house the extra population produced by recent rises in the rate of natural increase has usually been premature, because, as we have seen earlier, such a large proportion of the extra lives saved were those of children. The real testing time is only just beginning. We shall glance at various aspects of the Malayan population and economy to note what the effects will be.

One of the most significant features of this increment of young people is that the ranks of potential mothers will swell very rapidly, and the first additions will be precisely to those age groups which are normally the most fertile. For many years now, the female reproductive age group, roughly those between fifteen and forty-four years of age, has been increasing in size at a considerably slower rate than has the whole population. Henceforth, exactly the opposite will be the case. Most mothers of the next generation have already been born, and so it can be stated that the female reproductive group will during the next twenty years increase in size at a rate that will never fall below 3·7 per cent per annum and will probably eventually reach 4 per cent. It is for this reason that it is unlikely that declining individual fertility in Malaya will result in further steep falls in the crude birth rate. It seems very probable that the crude birth rate will begin to rise again and that there will be quite a sharp upturn in the number of babies born each year. Thus, the Medium Projection postulated a fall in fertility of a sixth between 1957 and 1982, reaching in the case of the Chinese and Indian communities 18 per cent, which was shown to result not in a fall in the annual rate of increase but in a continued rise reaching 3·7 per cent per annum by the end of the period.[10] Recent declines in the crude birth rate suggest that the decline in individual fertility might exceed the amount postulated, but it would be a rash prophet who would predict a rate of natural increase falling below 3 per cent per annum during the next quarter of a century.

A change, even greater than that experienced by the ranks of motherhood, will be felt by the employment market as the work force is augmented by large numbers of youthful recruits. It is many years since the Malayan labour market was subject to the pressure of sudden substantial additions to the work force, because of the long ebb from the immigrant-dominated labour force of the boom-time colonial economy of the earlier years of this century. In the twenty-six years from 1931 to 1957 the population increased 78 per cent at an average annual rate of 2·2 per cent, but males of labour force age increased by only 11 per cent at an average annual rate of 0·4 per cent. Even in the last few years the size of this group has grown at little more than half the rate of the total population, but from the mid-1960's it will expand as rapidly as the total population, at a rate in excess of 3 per cent per year. In the last fifteen years Malaya has had to provide almost half a million male jobs. In the next fifteen years it will have to provide three times as many.

One effect of the fall in the infant and child mortality rates has been the disproportionate increase in the number of children. This has probably been felt more by the individual family than by the nation except in the provision of schooling. Between 1921 and 1957 a comparison of the numbers of children and of women from whom their mothers were probably drawn showed an increase in child dependency of about 64 per cent. From the national point of view, if we compare the increase in the number of children relative to the economically-active population, the increase in dependency has been more tban three times as great.

The greatest strains involved in the very great increase in child dependency have already passed. No further increase will take place in the Chinese community, and amongst the Malays and Indians only limited rises will occur between now and a final levelling off in the early

1970's. There will still be strains involved in the provision of schooling. Dependency ratios for primary schoolchildren do not level off until the late 1960's and those for secondary schoolchildren until the early 1970's. After that date the extension of schooling will merely have to cope with a general population growth rate in excess of 3 per cent per annum, the extension of schooling facilities to those not already covered, and certain provision for depreciation.

In the long run, however, the fundamental problem of Malayan demography, and indeed of the Malayan economy, is that of the very high rate of population growth. If Malayan population growth were to maintain anything like its present rate, it would be by no means impossible that it would outstrip economic growth and frustrate plans to create a modern economy with high living standards. If the capital-output ratio in Malayan conditions is around 3·5 : 1, an annual rate of population increase of 3·25 per cent will necessitate the reinvestment of 11·5 per cent of the national income merely to maintain living standards, even if depreciation of the present capital stock is not taken into account. Malaya has apparently managed to reach this level of investment in recent years. But in order to achieve such a modest rise in per capita incomes as 2 per cent per year, the investment rate would have to surpass 18·5 per cent per year, a very much more difficult task for an economy neither affluent nor subject to dictatorial control.

The real problem is not that of living space. Malaya may be able to accommodate a lot more poor people than it does now, and *Lebensraum* is not likely to become critical in our lifetime. The real problem is that of alleviating poverty and of raising living standards. In some economies it is possible to argue that a growth rate of 1·5 per cent per annum stimulates the economy more than one of 0·5 per cent per annum. The argument may well not apply to developing countries, and is, in any case, irrelevant to Malaya. The immediate need is to reduce a natural growth rate of 3–3·5 per cent per year to 2·5 per cent or perhaps 2 per cent. Even at the latter figure, the rate of population growth would still be double that obtaining in any country in Europe during the periods of maximum population growth accompanying the early stages of industrialization. High population growth rates not only mean wasteful duplication of economic assets, the so-called demographic investment, but often entail relatively inefficient expenditure because of the haste with which work must be carried out.

Finally, it should not be overlooked that Malayan society is geographically rift into two very different divisions. *New Malaya* contains 76 per cent of the population of Malaya and 81 per cent of its urban population. All towns with more than 40,000 inhabitants are found there. Of the population living in towns with more than 20,000 inhabitants, 96 per cent of such people in Malaya and 95 per cent in the whole of Malaysia live there. It is there where the modernized economy has been developing, and this is emphasized by the fact that all existing and planned *Industrial Estates* are to be found within its borders. For half a century, the proportion of Malaya's population living in *New Malaya* has risen by about two percentage points each decade. Population projections indicate that over the next twenty years, the average annual rate of population increase is likely to be about 3·9 per cent in *New Malaya*, as contrasted with 2·7 per cent in *Old Malaya*, resulting in an increase of its population density from 262 persons per square mile in 1957 to 670 in 1982. This is a density reached by few areas in the world at the present time. Even the rural population density in *New Malaya* is likely to amount to about 175 persons per square mile by that time. Still, if *New Malaya* is to be no more crowded than this by 1982, *Old Malaya* will then have to support almost ninety persons per square mile an in area, much of which will always remain rather inhospitable to close settlement. There is in fact little evidence that the area of *New Malaya* is expanding, or that its borders can be regarded as a frontier of settlement.

These contrasts have their brighter as well as darker sides. The concentration of capital, *immigrant* enterprise and urban population may help to create a manufacturing economy more rapidly than would otherwise be the case. But in a multi-racial society it has its dangers. The contrast between the wealth, and, even more, the apparent wealth, of the west coast and the poverty of the east coast can be construed in racial terms. Ninety-one per cent of the Chinese and 88 per cent of the Indians live in *New Malaya*, but only 57 per cent of the Malays do so.

Rather similar problems arise from the division of the community along urban–rural lines, for there is a racial differential in urban residence as can be seen in Table 8, and to the peasant cultivator the town

TABLE 8. *Percentage Ethnic Composition of Urban and Rural Population,* Malaya, 1957*

	Malays	Chinese	Indians
Urban population	19	68	10
Rural population	70	17	11

* All Singapore population has been classified as 'urban'.

can appear as a magnet attracting the country's wealth and even squandering it. As argued before, the Malay proportion of urban population will inevitably rise. One of the reasons for devoting increasing attention to racial relations in the towns is that a greater proportion of the country's population must in the future be found there. Between

1947 and 1957, almost two thirds of urban growth arose from rural–urban migration. And such migration must continue. Even if between 1957 and 1982 rural Malaya succeeds in absorbing extra population at an annual rate of 2 per cent, so that it takes in an increment of 2·5 million people compared with a third as many in the previous quarter of a century, the urban population of Malaya will still have to grow at an average annual rate of 4·75 per cent and by 8·5 million people for the whole period. By 1982 two thirds of all Malayans, instead of half, should live in towns or cities.

III

QUESTIONS OF POLICY

One might expect the attitude of the Government of the Federation of Malaya towards family planning to be more one of *laissez-faire* than that of the Indian Government for instance in that its attitude towards economic development is inspired less by ideas of governmental intervention. In 1961 the Federation of Malaya and Singapore embarked on five-year development plans. The former Government's policy is to lay the foundations where necessary for industrial development by undertaking ancillary works and offering favourable conditions such as limited taxation exemptions without undertaking manufacturing itself. On the other hand, it is intervening much more directly in the field of rural development, not because investment on the large scale envisaged is necessarily the way to maximize national economic growth, and the evidence suggests that it is not, but in order to try to alleviate the relative poverty of the Malay peasantry. Singapore's Plan goes further in the direction of participation in manufacturing through the Economic Development Board. Neither Sarawak nor Sabah have yet undertaken such economic planning, but it is possible that they will henceforth do so within the framework of Malaysia.

Neither Malayan Government accepted the responsibility for population planning in its Plan. In fact the Malayan authorities have stated that Malaya has no population problem. By this is meant that four fifths of Malaya is virtually uninhabited. The vision of empty land is dangerously attractive in Malaysia, and in Indonesia as well, for it obscures the fact that failure to modernize the economy is much more likely to be dependent upon failing to invest enough to outstrip population growth than merely being able to settle the excess population. The empty land may in fact be an Achilles' heel, for it may well drain away too much of the limited investment funds for its development.

This does not mean that Malayan authorities are not alive to the high rate of population growth. The Federation of Malaya Plan[11] pays considerable attention to the economic race against population growth. The Singapore report states, 'Population control is only one of the long-term solutions to the economic problems of Singapore. In the short term and particularly for the Plan period under consideration any possible decline in fertility would not make significant difference to the problems that have to be solved.'[12] The Federation of Malaya did support the resolution on 'Population Growth and Economic Development' at the Seventeenth Session (1962–63) of the United Nations but was not one of its Asian sponsors. However, there is no evidence that Malaysia is considering any governmental intervention in favour of birth control though voluntary efforts in the promotion of family planning are not wanting.

Yet it may be quite true that, even apart from the question of available unused land, Malaya's population problems are less serious than those of say India, though at the moment growth rates are more spectacular. Thoroughgoing economic modernization may require the development of a small family system in which care can afford to be lavished on the training and further education of children to take their place in technologically complex societies. Such a system cannot develop until there can be a guarantee that the children resulting from a limited number of births to each mother will almost certainly survive to grow up, and the care devoted to training will amost certainly be greater if the likelihood of capricious death during childhood can be reduced almost to vanishing point. Thus, the first step towards demographic and economic modernization must be the type of fall in mortality that Malaya has experienced and is continuing to experience, no matter what portents of economic disaster it may suggest. The real point at issue is whether the long-run dilemma can be solved by a subsequent fall in fertility. No matter how soon or how fast that fall comes, there will in a country with Malaya's demographic history be a considerable period when high population growth rates exert very great economic and social pressures.

It is true that major fertility transition has not occurred previously in a country with the type of economic structure now existing in Malaya. But in none of these countries has fertility been under such sudden pressure from rapidly declining mortality as has been the case in Malaya. In none have the child dependency ratios risen as rapidly or as far as in modern Malaya. In the West a close relation seems to have existed between the enforcement of compulsory school Acts, with their attendant costs to parents in the form of the extra expenditure necessary on schoolchildren and the deprivation of some of the children's earnings and the beginning of the trend towards the small family system. The spread of education in Malaya must be exerting similar pressures.

Other features of the society also suggest the possibility of greater numbers of individual decisions to limit family size. By Asian standards, educational, literary and urbanization rates are high. The Chinese, Indians and many of the Malays have broken with settled traditional backgrounds through migration and have necessarily adjusted themselves to the more empirical and experimental culture that must develop in immigrant lands. The Chinese have suffered a period of insecurity and uncertainty about the future, not unlike that felt by the Japanese in the late 1940's. They were the chief Japanese enemy during the wartime occupation and later a suspect minority during the Emergency. In addition, the Singapore Chinese have experienced some feelings of uncertainty both during Singapore's isolation as a separate state and while Malaysia was being set up. Moreover, Singapore does involve its population in a city way of life, subject to the qualification that an Asian city is a somewhat different phenomenon from a Western industrial city. Whilst Chinese culture has long extolled high fertility, there is little inherent in it that opposes specific methods for limiting the number of births.

That some of these arguments are correct has probably been borne out by the recent falls in fertility in Malaya and especially in Singapore. Western experience would lead us to expect such a decline in fertility to begin there first, for Singapore is not so much one of the two territories of Malaya, as its metropolis. In terms of a more general movement in fertility it is important to note that the birth rate has also declined, although to a lesser degree, in the Federation of Malaya, and that available evidence indicates that the fertility decline is not confined to the Chinese population but affects to some extent each of the three major races.

If governmental intervention to curb fertility is eventually decided upon in Malaya, the chances of its success will be greater than in most Asian countries. The nation is rich and can afford the investment. The greatest economic returns will not be immediate, but any government that can plan large-scale forest clearance for the planting of tree crops can think in terms of the necessary long-term perspectives. More importantly, government medical services and rural health centres have been and are being developed of the type, on to which base Swedish experience in Ceylon has shown an effective and relatively cheap birth control programme can be built.[13] It has been shown that the considerable falls in fertility in the last decade have all been achieved in countries where some form of governmental intervention has taken place.[14] Evidence seems to be accumulating in Asia that such intervention can be successful, even in countries where social conditions were previously thought to be unpropitious, if an existing universal health service network is employed.

More important for the demographer seeking hints as to likely future trends in fertility, and more unusual in the south-east Asia scene, is a well-entrenched system of family planning clinics.[15] The Singapore Family Planning Association was formed as long ago as 1949, and since 1955 has had governmental financial support amounting to about 0·5 per cent of the Singapore's Government's budget. By 1959 it was operating twenty-four clinics, many of them in conjunction with governmental or semi-governmental health services. In the Federation of Malaya, the Selangor Family Planning Association was formed in Kuala Lumpur in 1954 and by 1958 such bodies existed in five states as members of a Federation of Family Planning Associations. A little local governmental financial help had been secured in Kuala Lumpur. The most interesting aspect of the Perak Association's work was its use of mobile clinics to tour rural areas. These were manned by a female staff of two, one a social worker who put the case for family planning and the other a nurse to undertake the clinical work.

Not all Malayans who practise contraception go to family planning clinics. Many of them use the facilities of chemist shops or doctors. It is of interest, however, to examine the statistics of those who do attend. By the end of 1958 over 26,000 different women had used the Singapore clinics, representing 9 per cent of women aged 15–44 or 13 per cent of women aged 20–39 enumerated at the 1957 census. Probably these figures are very high compared with the attendance at the early English clinics for instance. The Chinese are somewhat more prone and the Malays somewhat less prone to use the clinics than their numbers in the community would warrant. A further investigation of attendance at Selangor clinics suggest that as high a proportion of Malays tend to attend clinics as Chinese when problems of more remote residence from clinics do not enter the situation.

Analyses of attendance at the Singapore clinics show no marked differential by family income. There is certainly evidence to show that the clinics are still used more as a method of calling a halt to large families than as a way of family planning throughout marriage. The average age at first attendance at both Singapore and Selangor clinics is twenty-nine years, and the average delay between marriage and first attendance is about ten years for each of the three major ethnic groups compared with five years for Europeans. At the time of first attendance at the clinics the average number of pregnancies already experienced by Malays, Chinese and Indians is 5·6, 5 and 5·1 respectively, compared with 2·4 in the case of Europeans. Over two thirds of those attending clinics claim to have first been advised to do so by doctors, nurses, social welfare workers and people of similar status. Finally, it might be remarked that the Family Planning Associations' emphasis is very strongly one of economic betterment. The cover of the Singapore Association's report pictorially contrasts large families, poor living conditions and parental exhaustion with small families, modern housing and livelier, better-dressed parents.

Malaysia is, then, one of the world's most significant test cases for students of the interrelation between demographic and economic problems. It is a comparatively rich country with a vigorous population. Yet so rapid is population increase that in the Five-Year Plans commencing in 1961 the Government of the Federation of Malaya has faced the fact that per capita net national income would still fall slightly even if the Plan were completely fulfilled,[16] and Singapore could imagine the level being maintained only if a very great increase in private investment occurred.[17]

Against this background, the recent falls in fertility are of very great interest. But it should be remembered that fertility is still very high and that population problems will be the major concern of economic planners for at least another generation. It would seem to be a reasonable surmise to predict that increasing governmental intervention will take place in the field of family planning in the years ahead, perhaps at first in the form of increased financial assistance for private organizations, and that the chances of the success of such intervention is considerably greater than in most Asian countries.

Inevitably, most of this study has had to be confined to the 88 per cent of the population of Malaysia who live in Malaya. Its chief theme is the problem of economic growth in a society exhibiting very high rates of natural increase, and the possibility of augmenting that growth by curbing fertility. Malaya is, in terms of economic development and demographic transition, by far the most developed segment of Malaysia, and it is there that important changes will occur first, if they occur at all. Such a concentration of the study has allowed the use of much more detailed and accurate population data and so has permitted a deeper analysis.

NOTES

1. During 1959–61 the author undertook a study of the population of Malaya, including a period spent in Malaya during 1959–60. The full study is held by the Australian National University as a Ph.D. thesis entitled, 'The Population of Malaya'. It is to aspects of this work that reference is made when mention is made of the findings of more detailed analysis, population projections, etc. Some of these findings have been published elsewhere (see Bibliography).

   In this paper the terms *Malaya* and *Malayan* are used to refer to the combined areas of the Federation of Malaya and Singapore, while Sarawak and Sabah are sometimes grouped together as the *Borneo territories*. The term *Malay* is used to refer to any of the inhabitants of Malaya who belong to one of the indigenous ethnic groups of the Malay Archipelago (essentially in this case Malaysia and Indonesia). When reference is made to such indigenous groups in the whole of Malaysia, the term *indigenous Malaysians* is employed. In common with normal usage in Malaysia, the term *Indian* also embraces the small number of Pakistanis also found there.

   A considerable amount of the population data employed has been drawn from the

1947 and 1957 censuses of the Federation of Malaya and Singapore and the 1960 censuses of Sarawak and Sabah.

2. I.e. mid-1962 (from official sources as compiled by the United Nations).
3. In subsequent discussion of the potential labour force the 15–54 years of age range will be used, as this is the only form in which the data are available from the earlier censuses.
4. I.e. as compiled in life tables based on mortality experience in various parts of the world between 1909 and 1950 and published in United Nations, *Methods for Population Projections by Sex and Age* (*Manuals on methods of estimating population:* Manual III) (New York, 1956).
5. Fertility as measured by child–woman ratios.
6. J. C. Caldwell, 'Fertility Decline and Female Chances of Marriage in Malaya', *Population Studies*, 17, 1, July 1963, pp. 20–32.
7. The material in this paragraph was drawn from T. H. Silcock, 'Appendix A: Approximate Racial Division of National Income', in T. H. Silcock and E. K. Fisk (eds.), *The Political Economy of Independent Malaya: a case study in development* (Canberra, The Australian National University, 1963), pp. 276–81. M$1 = 2s 4d sterling.
8. For a more detailed study of the contrasts between the two areas see J. C. Caldwell, '*New* and *Old Malaya:* Aspects of Demographic Change in a High Growth Rate, Multiracial Society', *Population Review*, July 1965.
9. A more detailed discussion of the analysis of urban growth and rural–urban migration is to be found in J. C. Caldwell, 'Urban Growth in Malaya: Trends and Implications', *Population Review*, Vol. 7, No. 1, January 1963, pp. 39–50. Further discussion of the racial aspects of urban employment can be found in E. L. Wheelwright, 'Industrialization in Malaya', in Silcock and Fisk, *op. cit.*, especially pp. 235–6.
10. The reductions in fertility were applied to the age-specific fertility rates.
11. The two development plans are set out in (i) Federation of Malaya, *Second Five-Year Plan, 1961–1965* (Kuala Lumpur, Government Press, 1961); (ii) State of Singapore, *Development Plan, 1961–1964* (Singapore, Government Printer, 1961).
12. Singapore Plan, *op. cit.*, p. 2.
13. Report given to the United Nations Asian Population Conference in Delhi, December 10–20, 1963, by Dr Arne Kinch. See also earlier reports: (i) Arne Kinch, 'A Preliminary Report from the Sweden–Ceylon Family Planning Pilot Project', in C. Kiser (ed.), *Research in Family Planning*, Princeton University Press, 1962, pp. 85–102; (ii) The Population Council, *Studies in Family Planning*, No. 2, December 1963, pp. 9–12.
14. Frank Lorimer, 'Issues of Population Policy', in Philip M. Hauser (ed.), *The Population Dilemma*, American Assembly (Columbia University), 1963, p. 149.
15. The material analysed on the family planning movements was obtained largely from their annual reports up to 1960.
16. Federation of Malaya, *Second Five-Year Plan, op. cit.*, p. 62.
17. Singapore, *Development Plan, op. cit.*, p. 54.

BIBLIOGRAPHY

Caldwell, J. C., 'The Demographic Background', in T. H. Silcock and E. K. Fisk (eds.), *The Political Economy of Independent Malaya: a case study in development* (Canberra, Australian National University, 1963).

'Fertility Decline and Female Chances of Marriage in Malaya', *Population Studies*, July 1963.

'Some Implications of Past Population Growth and Likely Future Trends in Malaya', *Population Review*, July 1963.

'Urban Growth in Malaya: trends and implications', *Population Review*, January 1963.

'New and Old Malaya: aspects of demographic change in a high growth rate, multiracial society', *Population Review*, July 1965.

Djamour, Judith, *Malay Kinship and Marriage in Singapore* (London, Athlone Press, 1959).

Etienne, Gilbert, 'La grande Malaisie: vues sur l'économie et la population de Singapour, de la Fédération de Malaisie et de Bornéo du Nord', *Population*, 18, 1.

Federation of Malaya, *Second Five-Year Plan*, 1961–1965 (Kuala Lumpur, Government Printer, 1961).

Freedman, Maurice, *Chinese Family and Marriage in Singapore* (London, H.M.S.O., 1957).

'The Growth of a Plural Society in Malaya', *Pacific Affairs*, June 1960.

Hodder, B. W., *Man in Malaya* (London, University of London Press Ltd., 1959).

International Bank Mission, *The Economic Development of Malaya: Report of a Mission Organised by the International Bank for Reconstruction and Development* (Baltimore, Johns Hopkins University Press, 1955).

Jones, L. W., *Sarawak: report on the census of population taken on 15th June, 1960* (Kuching, Government Printer, 1962).

Ma, Ronald and You Poh Seng, 'The Economic Characteristics of the Population of the Federation of Malaya, 1957', *The Malayan Economic Review*, October 1960.

Purcell, Victor, *The Chinese in Modern Malaya* (Singapore, 1956).

Silcock, T. H. and Fisk, E. K. (eds.), *The Political Economy of Independent Malaya: a case study in development* (Canberra, Australian National University, 1963).

Singapore, *Development Plan, 1961–1964* (Kuala Lumpur, Government Printer, 1961).

Smith, T. E., *Population Growth in Malaya: an analysis of recent trends* (London, Royal Institute of International Affairs, 1952).

You Poh Seng, 'Fertility and the Increase of Population in Singapore', *Proceedings of the World Population Conference* (New York, United Nations, 1954) Vol. 1.

CHAPTER 8

TAIWAN'S POPULATION PROBLEM[a]

BY WILLIAM PETERSEN

WHILE IN TERMS of its size and worldwide importance, Taiwan obviously does not rank with the giant countries analysed in other chapters of this work, from the point of view of a demographer this small country is in some ways more interesting. There is an abundance of accurate and up-to-date statistics that can be usefully analysed from a distance. Since Taiwan and Mainland China are to some degree parts of one cultural unit, one can hope to use these better data to enhance our understanding of Communist China. 'Taiwan is the only place where it is possible to study the processes of change of a Chinese population over a substantial period of time on the basis of excellent data.'[1] And since among under-developed nations Taiwan is relatively favoured, it offers a good laboratory to test the widespread notion that economic progress and social change in themselves bring a solution to the problems associated with population growth. For the statistics are excellent also on agricultural and industrial production, administration, communication and transportation, and in fact virtually every measurable element of the society. In 1895, when the Japanese first occupied Taiwan, it and Hainan each had a population of 2·5 million. Over the next half century, while the population of Hainan remained nearly constant, that of Taiwan increased to two and a half times its base figure. 'The reason for the remarkable contrast between these two islands is an interesting and significant problem,'[2] that is, the relation between economic development and population growth. Finally, Taiwan has recently become the focus of family planners' interest, and the initially great success of efforts to reduce the island's fertility has been subjected to much analysis.

Economic Development

The Taiwan that Japan took over in 1895 was notorious as a malarial deathtrap, with more rainfall than any part of Mainland China and in the lowlands a sub-tropical climate throughout the year. In area, with 13,885 square miles, this island is larger than the Netherlands, slightly smaller than Switzerland, about equal to Puerto Rico, Jamaica, and Hawaii combined. In general, the soils lack important minerals, because of inherent infertility, erosion, or the results of intensive monoculture.

With much labour and generous use of fertilizers, the total of arable land has been gradually increased, but still is scarcely a third of the whole island. Except for some coal at the northern end, the mountains that cover much of the land are deficient in minerals.[3] Taiwan was poor in agriculture and almost without other economic activities, truly an inauspicious first colony in Japan's new empire.

The Japanese administrators, however, set up what an American analyst has termed 'one of the most successful colonial programmes in the world'.[4] Within a few years, the island's new rulers conducted its first systematic land survey and on the basis of its results reformed the land taxes; they introduced the gold standard, established schools, standardized weights and measures, constructed roads and railroads, improved irrigation and encouraged the use of fertilizers, set up a research institute on sugar production and introduced improved strains of rice. From 1915–19 to 1940–42, the annual average in total production increased from 263 to 1,388 million yen, and in the production of agricultural commodities (mostly rice and sugar) from 145 to 576 million yen.[5]

To exercise its authority, the new regime restored the moribund *pao-chia*, or village mutual-aid group, and integrated it with a modern police force. As elements of their efficient system of zealous control, the Japanese established a population register, which still exists, collected vital statistics of generally great accuracy, and conducted a series of seven censuses that in important respects 'ranked in quality well above the more advanced censuses of the Western world'.[6] Taiwan's demographic data, in other words, are close to unique for a country at its stage of development. The accurate count was interrupted during the Second World War and the immediate post-war years,[7] but by 1952 the population register was again functioning well, and four years later a new census was taken.

Much besides the statistical record deteriorated during the war. Most heavy industry was destroyed by air bombardment, and other capital stock declined because of poor maintenance and the lack of parts. From 1938, a peak year, to 1944, production of rice in units of weight fell off by 58 per cent, and of sugar by 94 per cent.

After the defeat of the Kuomintang on the mainland, some two million Mainlanders retreated to Taiwan, where in 1947 they put down a revolt by the 'Taiwanese'—that is, persons of Chinese stock who had lived on the island before and during the Japanese rule. 'In the process they killed an estimated 10,000 Taiwanese, including a large percentage of the leadership class.'[8] The Mainlanders control China's shadow government, which is maintained in continued anticipation that it will be able to regain power from the Communists, and hold a large proportion of the higher posts in the army, Taiwan's 'provincial' administration, and the universities. The Taiwanese are important in the civil administration and dominant in the economic system. Neither group is satisfied with this division of power. In general, the Mainlanders regard their salaries, perquisites, and prospects as woefully inadequate, while many Taiwanese have felt that they must support an unproductive elite, who deny them access to many positions of high status. All post-war problems, in short, have been aggravated by the troubled Taiwanese–Mainlander relations—which, however, have probably improved in recent years.[9]

Notwithstanding the political and military problems derivative from Taiwan's status as the seat of China's aspirant government, the island has enjoyed an enormous economic progress. Much of this was brought about through the Joint Commission on Rural Reconstruction (JCRR), an American–Chinese agency through which monetary aid and technical assistance have been channelled.[10] Merely a list of its successful projects is impressive: improvement of seeds, introduction of better fertilizers and pesticides, island-wide rat control, mechanized farming, improved irrigation and flood control, virtual elimination of hog cholera and erysipelas, introduction of hybrid breeds of hogs, after an aerial survey an island-wide programme of reforestation, re-establishment of peasants' organizations and their co-operation with a newly-formed agricultural extension in educational programmes related to land use, rural health, home economics, and similar matters. Perhaps the most striking feature was a massive land reform, effected in three stages over five years, through which 78 per cent of the tenants received title as full or part owners of the land they worked.[11] In fifty-seven demonstration villages throughout Taiwan, these technical and social programmes were integrated into an overall improvement of rural life.[12]

From a modest base, the development of industry has also been rapid, especially in branches most closely related to the available resources (food-processing, cement, chemicals), though also in some cases in those based primarily on the market (textiles, fertilizers, machinery).[13] There has been a moderate shift of persons out of agriculture, which still remains dominant (Table 1). In mid-1965, the Taiwanese economy was adjudged to be at the take-off point, and in a 'graduation' ceremony American economic aid was discontinued. Since 1951, the United States had furnished \$1·5 billion in economic assistance (plus \$2·5 billion in military aid, which was to continue); and over that period, industrial production quadrupled and the number of industrial plants went from 10,000 to 25,000; agricultural production increased by 70 per cent; exports almost tripled and imports doubled; the illiteracy rate fell from 45 to 24 per cent, while enrolments in high schools tripled and in colleges quadrupled.[14] This rapid progress was possible because of American aid, but in the case of Taiwan—contrary to many other underdeveloped areas—the dollars were used with energy and skill. The Taiwanese entrepreneurs in both government agencies and private firms have taken full advantage of whatever opportunities there developed to advance the economy.

TABLE 1. *Percentage Distribution of Economically-Active Persons Aged Twelve and Over, Taiwan, 1952 and 1963*

	1952	1963
Agriculture	61·0	54·5
Industry	9·3	11·7
Commerce	8·5	8·9
Transportation	2·2	3·2
Personal services	7·7	9·2
Professions	2·5	3·8
Government services	6·0	7·4
Other	2·8	1·2
Total	100·0	100·0
	(2,936,000)	(3,617,000)

Sources: China (National), Council for International Economic Co-operation and Development, *Taiwan Statistical Data Book, 1964* (Taipei, 1964).

In part as a concomitant of this economic development, there has been a fairly rapid urbanization. Before the Second World War, about two thirds of the resident Japanese lived in cities, including the almost 30 per cent of the total in Taipei. These were the centres of administrative and commercial activity, as well as the places where those who could afford it were able to live most comfortably. Most of the small number of Mainlander merchants or labourers that the Japanese admitted, often temporarily, also were urban residents. For the Taiwanese themselves the towns represented the only escape from agriculture, and between 1920 and 1940 the number living in them more than doubled, reaching almost 15 per cent of all Taiwanese by the latter date.[15] In the post-war period urbanization has continued at an accelerated rate. While the island's total population increased by 42·9 per cent between 1950 and 1960, that of the five cities administered by the central government grew by 67·3 per cent, and that of the seven prefectural cities by 59·4 per cent. It has become appropriate to speak of one metropolitan area on Taiwan: up to 1954 the growth of Taipei City was at a higher rate than the rest of Taipei Prefecture, but then, after two years of fluctuation, the trend was reversed, with the faster growth in suburbs and satellite towns.[16]

From 1895 to 1965, in summary, two somewhat oppressive regimes succeeded in transforming the economy and to some extent the social structure of Taiwan, so that from a level of primitive poverty the island has now reached the stage of presumed self-generating economic growth. Two factors only can be denoted as important hindrances to future progress—the relations with Communist China, a matter we shall not consider here, and the rapid growth of the population, which is our main topic.

Population Growth

Having accepted the statement that Taiwan's population statistics are of excellent quality, an analyst who begins to use them in that spirit will often find a surprisingly great variation in the most fundamental data. The reason is not inaccuracy in the count but differences in the definition of which elements of the total number are to be included.[17] About a quarter million aborigines, of different racial stock from the Chinese, are divided into two classes: the large majority live on reservations, essentially cut off from the main society, and are excluded from most population compilations; the more or less sinicized minority that lives off the reservations is included. The Japanese, who grew rapidly from about 10,000 in 1896 to almost 400,000 in 1943 and then all returned to Japan after the war, and the Mainlanders, who supplanted them as the political elite, are, of course, part of the population as this is ordinarily compiled: since in formal terms Taiwan was a province of Japan and today is a province of China, neither group can be deemed aliens. However, for various purposes it is convenient, as we have seen, to separate out the Taiwanese, that is, persons of Chinese stock who had Japanese nationality before the war. Since the Japanese administration inhibited migration in either direction between Taiwan and Mainland China, the Taiwanese constitute virtually a closed population, whose rapid growth is due almost entirely to the excess of births over deaths.

As soon as the Japanese occupied Taiwan, before even its subjugation was complete, they began a survey of the population. The count in 1896, certainly incomplete but apparently not grossly inaccurate, was 2,588,000. By 1905, when the first census was taken, the enumerated population had grown by a fifth.

From 1905 to 1964, the population of Taiwan increased from slightly over 3 million to well over 12 million (Table 2). On the whole area of roughly 14,000 square miles, the density quadrupled, reaching figures that are among the highest in the world; and on the settled lowland areas the density recorded for any date has generally been more than double that given in the table. During the two inter-war decades, 1920 to 1940, the number of Taiwanese increased by 60·4 per cent. In a comparison with other countries, Shao-hsing Chen noted only four whose population had increased by a larger proportion during this period (Malaya, Honduras, the Dominican Republic, and the settled population of Palestine), but in every case the reason was a sizable immigration. The percentage natural increase of the Taiwanese was the highest in the world.[18] In the period immediately following the defeat of the Kuomintang on the mainland, the population increase, including

TABLE 2. *Population and Demographic Rates, Taiwan, 1905–64*

Year*	Population (thousands)	Persons per sq. mile		Uncorrected crude rates (unweighted averages) Birth	Death	Natural increase
1905	3,040	220	1906–10	41·7	33·4	8·3
1910	3,480	251	1911–15	42·9	28·6	14·3
1920	3,655	264	1916–20	40·4	31·0	9·4
1925	3,993	287	1921–25	42·8	25·0	17·8
1930	4,593	332	1926–30	45·0	22·1	22·9
1935	5,212	376	1931–35	46·0	21·2	24·8
1940	5,872	422	1936–40	45·4	20·6	24·8
1952	8,128	585	1952–53	45·9	9·6	36·3
1955	9,078	653	1954–56	44·9	8·2	36·7
1958	10,039	723	1957–59	41·4	7·7	33·7
1961	11,149	803	1960–61	38·9	6·9	32·0
1962	11,512	829	1962	37·4	6·4	31·0
1963	11,884	857	1963	36·2	6·1	30·1
1964	12,257	883				

* Census figures as of October 1st from 1905 to 1940; thereafter estimates as of December 31st based on household registrations.

Sources: George W. Barclay, *Colonial Development and Population in Taiwan* (Princeton University Press, 1954); China (National), Council for International Economic Co-operation and Development, *Taiwan Statistical Data Book, 1964* (Taipei, 1964); *Industry of Free China* (Taipei), 33:2 (February 1965).

immigration, was by more than 4 per cent a year; and the annual average for 1953–64, mostly a natural increase, was 3·5 per cent, or one of the world's highest rates.

Mortality

The principal dynamic element in this population growth, in Taiwan as typically in underdeveloped areas, has been the dramatic decline in mortality. The crude death rate in the nineteenth century, though unrecorded, was certainly well above forty, possibly closer to fifty; in 1963, it had fallen to a recorded 6·1, or almost the lowest in the world.

The conditions in the nineteenth century can be suggested by the record of the Japanese expeditionary forces.[19] Of the 6,190 Japanese soldiers that were sent to the Pescadores in March 1895, within two months 1,945 were sick with cholera and 1,247 were dead. Another army landed on Taiwan about the same time, and by the end of September four out of five were either sick or dead of cholera, malaria, dysentery, typhus, pneumonia, or beri-beri.

In 1896, the plague spread to Taiwan from Hong Kong, and over the next twenty-two years 30,000 persons were stricken and 24,000 died of it. It was wiped out largely by harsh but effective police power, through the isolation of patients, burning of contaminated houses, extermination of rats, and quarantine at ports. Serious outbreaks of cholera occurred in 1902, 1912, 1913, and 1920, but by the last of these years, the public-health system was sufficiently developed to bring it under close control. Compulsory vaccination, initiated in 1903, reduced the incidence of smallpox, of which the last serious outbreak was in 1918–20. By 1920, thus, the three major epidemics—the plague, cholera, and smallpox—were under effective control. In that year also the growing number of Western-style physicians exceeded for the first time the declining number of Chinese herbalists.

The most troublesome remaining problem was malaria, which had ranked as the first or second cause of death each year from the beginning of the century to 1916, after which date the Japanese controls began to pay off. They eventually set up as many as 200 anti-malaria stations equipped to analyse the blood of local populations, and persons found to be infected were given free a compulsory treatment with quinine and mepacrine. When this costly programme broke down during the Second World War, malaria epidemics again swept the island.[20] Beginning in 1951, the new government has undertaken a continuous anti-malaria programme using the pesticides developed during the war and concentrating its efforts in areas that periodic checks of the school population indicate as the most seriously affected. The incidence of malaria has been reduced to a few dozen cases, and it has all but disappeared as a cause of death.[21] Since malaria typically debilitates those it does not kill, the control of this disease has contributed also to the improvement in general health and the reduction of mortality from other causes.

How well-based is the remarkably low recorded death rate of 6·1? While apart from the war period registration has in general been reasonably complete and accurate, the reporting of infant deaths has been deficient, in part because of the effect of folk beliefs that persist in rural areas. To speak of a dead child is a bad omen for the living ones. Parents should not grieve for a child that dies before the age of twelve, for whom neither a coffin nor a funeral service is appropriate by traditional usage.[22] According to Barclay's estimate, in the late 1940's and early 1950's between half and two thirds of infant deaths may have gone unregistered;[23] but his calculation was based on the assumptions, apparently unrealistic, that at that time birth registrations and estimates of the population under the age of one were completely accurate.[24] According to field studies in three townships, in the late 1950's the corrected infant mortality rate was of the order of 50 per 1,000 live births, and up to 30 per cent of the infant deaths might not have been registered. In that case, the corrected crude death rate would be about one tenth higher than the official one, or still a very low figure. In 1963, excluding live-born infants that died before the registration of their births, the official infant mortality rate was 26·4.

Based on life tables for several recent years, the expectation of life from birth has gone up remarkably, from 38·8 (male) and 43·1 (female) in 1926–31 to 61·3 (male) and 65·6 (female) in 1959–60. The latter figures are slightly higher than the comparable ones in the United States for 1930–39. The improvement at higher ages, while of course smaller, was significant (Table 3).

TABLE 3. *Expectation of Life from Various Ages, Taiwan, 1936–40, 1959–60*

	1936–40		1956–58		1959–60	
Age	Male	Female	Male	Female	Male	Female
0	41·1	45·7	60·5	65·0	61·3	65·6
10	45·6	50·8	55·7	60·6	56·6	61·0
20	37·2	42·4	46·3	51·2	47·2	51·5
40	22·7	27·7	28·7	33·3	29·3	33·5
60	11·3	14·2	13·5	17·1	13·9	16·9

Sources: Lien-pin Chow and Shih-chu Hsu, 'Statistical Studies on Mortality in Taiwan during the Last Decade', *Industry of Free China* (Taipei), 14:2 (August 1960), 24; United Nations, *Demographic Yearbook, 1963* (New York, 1964), Table 26.

Fertility

In contrast with the dramatic decline in mortality, the pattern of change in fertility has been more complex, as indicated by the birth rates listed in Table 2. Shao-hsing Chen has divided the Japanese period of Taiwanese population growth into five periods, based mainly on the conditions affecting mortality.[25] During the first four of these periods, the birth rate rose:

1906–09	40·25
1910–20	41·40
1921–25	42·08
1926–40	45·24
1941–43	41·10

This rise was apparently real, not solely the spurious consequence of improving registration. It was the consequence, that is to say, of a rise in the average number of offspring per completed family or of a change in population structure that favoured the formation of more families.

Before considering these factors, we should note that there was a rise in the age at marriage over this period. Of females aged 15–19, 43 per cent were ever married in 1905 as against only 28 per cent in 1935; and of those aged 20–24, the comparable percentages were 92 and 83. Since this change by itself would have resulted in a decline in fertility, the actual rise all the more demands an explanation.

According to an intensive analysis of a sample of the registration records in one rural township,[26] the recorded mean number of children ever born increased significantly with the cohorts that began their reproductive period after 1905, when the Japanese administration improved the accuracy of the system. The indicated rise in fertility, thus in part a consequence of the improved registration, was also by this analysis in part real, effected by the decline in adult male mortality. Of females aged 40–44, 30·2 per cent were widows in 1905, but only 15 per cent in 1935; and among women of any younger age group, the decline in widowhood by about half also held. If we assume that all husbands were five years older than their wives and that no widows remarried (the second assumption in particular is not wholly valid for Taiwan), their husbands' deaths deprived women born before 1882 of 2·9 more years of their reproductive period than those born between 1903 and 1907, and this difference increased the completed family size by about one more birth. This rather neat analysis demonstrates one way that a decline in mortality increases fertility, but the possible effect is not limited to this particular relation. Since fecundity is in part a function of good health, it increases as morbidity is brought under control, though in many instances it would be difficult to prove this. For example, a population suffering from endemic malaria is relatively weak and listless, and one would expect the incidence of marital coitus to rise when this cause of lassitude is removed.

Another reason that the birth rate increased is that past high fertility had generated a population structure conducive to a continuing rise, with a higher proportion of the population in the most fecund age groups. The best measure of fertility independent of age structure is the average family size, and we have such data from a 1957 survey by Shao-hsing Chen and his associates.[27] Data on the completed family size of various cohorts were collected from a sample of the populations of Taipei and one of its satellite towns, and from the whole populations of a fishing village and a farming village. Respondents were classified also according to whether the family was Taiwanese or Mainlander. The results (Table 4) validated the hypothesis that fertility was highest in the fishing village, but in other respects were somewhat puzzling. In both villages completed family size fell over the ten-year period, but in both Taipei and the smaller town it rose considerably. That the completed family size of Mainlanders also rose from a lower level is difficult to interpret, for most of the births had been before the migration to Taiwan and thus under these respondents' different and probably quite varied conditions of life on the mainland. More generally, there is a good possibility—which Chen does not consider—that both the decline in the villages and the rise in urban areas partly reflected the common practice by which relatively well-to-do city people adopt the children of the rural poor.

TABLE 4. *Completed Family Size, by Cohort and Area, Taiwan, 1957*

	Birth cohorts 1898–1902	1903–07	1908–12
Taiwanese			
Taipei	4·9	5·3	5·4
Town	4·8	5·9	5·9
Fishing village	8·7	8·1	8·1
Farming village	7·5	6·6	6·3
Mainlanders	4·0	5·0	4·7

Source: Shao-hsing Chen, Yao-tung Wang, and Frederic J. Foley, 'Pattern of Fertility in Taiwan', *Journal of Social Sciences* (Taipei), 13 (1963), 209–94, at p. 220.

That the birth rate fell from its high point in 1926–40 to a slightly lower figure in 1941–3 was the consequence, one would suppose, of the privations occasioned by the war, but the supposition is not well based. The real reason—or at least the main reason—was the smaller size of the cohorts in the prime breeding years. Those aged 20–24 in 1940 had been born in 1915–19, when malaria and influenza reduced the number of births and increased infant mortality.[28]

By 1952–3 the birth rate was up again to 45·9, close to the highest figure since data were first collected (Table 2). The more substantial decline since the mid-1950s has been partly in response to an intensive effort to disseminate contraceptives, which showed an encouraging initial success. The analysis of these data, however, is so closely linked with theories concerning Taiwan's probable future population growth that it is convenient to postpone our discussion of them to that section of the paper.

Population Structure and Projections

In 1930, Taiwan had a relatively squat population pyramid, typical of a country with a rapidly growing population. Both the slight rise in fertility indicated by several studies and particularly the great decline in mortality, which especially affected infants and children, increased the proportion in the younger age groups. Net migration, though one cannot determine it precisely, had the contrary effect. The Japanese and the Koreans and other aliens enumerated in the census, almost all of whom subsequently left Taiwan, constituted only 6·1 per cent of the total population in 1930; and the Mainland Chinese who subsequently immigrated were both more numerous and probably of a higher average age. Nevertheless, over one generation the base of the population pyramid broadened considerably, as can be seen from the shift in size of the three broad age groups:[29]

	1930	1963
0–14	40·3%	46·0%
15–49	48·9	44·0
50+	10·7	10·1

With the large proportion of the population moving up to the age at marriage, even if the number of children per family were to decline, the fertility of the whole population would fall less, or might even remain constant.

The burden of dependency, the consequence mainly of this increase in the proportion of infants and children, rose considerably in the post-war period (Table 5). The rapid increase in the number of school-age

TABLE 5. *Burden of Dependency, Taiwan, 1952 and 1963*

		1952	1963
A	Persons under 15	3,442,000	5,446,000
B	Persons 60 and over	334,000	512,000
A+B	Dependent persons	3,776,000	5,958,000
C	Persons aged 15–59	4,352,000	5,926,000
$\frac{A+B}{C} \times 100$	Dependency ratio	86·8	100·5

Source: China (National), Council for International Economic Co-operation and Development, *Taiwan Statistical Data Book, 1964* (Taipei, 1964).

children means that the cost of education will rise greatly,[30] and some years later it will be difficult to absorb these large cohorts into the labour force.[31]

Two projections of Taiwan's population are reproduced in Table 6. From 1960 to 1961 and again the following year, the actual population grew by 3·3 per cent; from 1962 to 1963, the increase was by 3·2 per cent, and the following year by 3·1 per cent. If we extrapolate the population growth by the lowest of these percentages, or even by 3 per cent, the 1965 figure is considerably higher than any of the three United Nations projections, and a bit higher than the lowest of the 1967 figures of Liu and Lung. On the basis of this very rough check, then, even the rather large projected populations are too small.

The main unknown is the future trend of Taiwan's birth rate, and as we noted many recent articles have discussed what will happen to the island's fertility. In 1962 a fertility survey was conducted in Taichung under the joint supervision of the Taiwan Population Studies Centre and the University of Michigan Population Studies Centre, with financial aid from the Population Council. This indicated that with the spread of

TABLE 6. *Two Projections of Taiwan's Population (thousands), 1960–82*

		United Nations (1959)†			Liu and Lung (1960)‡		
	Actual population*	Constant fertility	Gradual fertility decline	Rapid fertility decline	Constant fertility	Gradual fertility decline	Rapid fertility decline
1960	10,792	10,591	10,591	10,591			
1961	11,149						
1962	11,512				11,637	11,637	11,529
1963	11,884						
1964	12,257						
1965		12,552	12,495	12,438			
1967					13,735	13,675	13,347
1970		14,838	14,586	14,334			
1972					16,202	15,939	15,047
1975		17,670	17,023	16,376			
1977					19,220	18,200	16,751
1980		21,272	19,931	18,590			
1982					22,981	20,703	18,395

* Sources as in Table 2.

† United Nations, Department of Economic and Social Affairs, *The Population of Asia and the Far East, 1950–1980*, Population Studies No. 31 (New York, 1959), p. 30.

‡ Liu K'o-chih and Lung Tun-i, 'Projection of Taiwan's Population, 1957–1982' (in Chinese), 1960; quoted in Ramon H. Myers, 'Economic Growth and Population Change in Taiwan', *Malayan Economic Review* (Singapore), 8:2 (October 1963), pp. 104–117.

modern ideas many women might be willing to plan their families if given the opportunity.[32] On the basis of this hypothesis, an intensive programme was initiated in the same city to test the inhabitants' receptivity to family planning and to furnish contraceptives to those willing to use them.[33] In 1964, some 250 private physicians agreed to participate in a programme to expand family planning from Taichung to eighteen of the island's twenty-two counties and city districts. They inserted loops and gave after-care when necessary for the equivalent of $1.50 per patient, half ordinarily to be paid by her and half by the JCRR. During 1964, almost 50,000 were inserted, with the number rising rapidly from 516 in January to 6,822 in December. According to a follow-up survey, fewer than one per cent of the loops recorded had not been inserted (presumably the physicians had filled in the forms fraudulently in order to collect the 75 cents), 6·35 per cent of the patients had expelled the loop, and 12 per cent had had it removed for reasons other than a desire for pregnancy.[34] Taiwan's total fertility rate fell by 3·7 per cent in one year and from 1959 to 1964 the decline was by 11·5 per cent (Table 7).

TABLE 7. *Age–Specific Birth Rates, Married Women, Taiwan, 1959–64*

Age Group	Rate per 1,000 married women 1959	1962	1963	1964	Percentage change in rates 1962–3	1963–4	1959–64
15–19	373	375	374	360	−0·3	− 3·7	− 3·5
20–24	437	424	425	432	+0·2	+ 1·6	− 1·1
25–29	374	380	379	377	−0·3	− 0·5	+ 0·8
30–34	296	256	250	231	−2·3	− 7·6	−22·0
35–39	212	161	153	132	−5·0	−13·7	−27·8
40–44	100	76	70	60	−7·9	−14·3	−40·0
45–49	18	12	12	10	—	−16·7	−44·4
Total fertility rate	9,050	8,420	8,315	8,010	−1·2	− 3·7	−11·5

Source: Ronald Freedman, Lien-pin Chow, and Julia Ann Smith, 'The Accelerating Fertility Decline in Taiwan', *Population Index*, October 1965.

A number of analysts have extrapolated this downward trend with a greater enthusiasm than would seem to be warranted. The mounting euphoria is indicated by the very titles of the successive articles: 'Fertility Trends in Taiwan: Tradition and Change' (1963), 'A Study in Fertility Control' (1964), 'Fertility and Family Planning in Taiwan: A Case Study of the Demographic Transition' (1964), 'The Transition from High to Low Fertility: Challenge to Demographers' (1965), and 'The Accelerating Fertility Decline in Taiwan' (1965).[35] It may be that this optimism will prove to be well based, though I doubt it; it may even be that it is legitimate to generalize from such an experience as that in Taiwan to rules for reducing the world birth rate,[36] though I doubt that even more. Reasonable caution would suggest a more modest appraisal of our knowledge of what determines. a population's fertility—not to say how to intervene in order to control it. This criticism can be specified on a number of points.

1. *Public-opinion polls.* The spread of American sociology to other countries has often meant in particular the dissemination of survey research. Polling is fraught with methodological difficulties even in the United States, where fear of government oppression is minimal compared with a sizable proportion of the rest of the world, where access to homes and a view of domestic life are much less hampered even than in Continental Europe, and where communication across class or regional lines is less self-conscious even than in Britain. How shall we react to the export of these American methods to societies that in one way or another lack this degree of openness?

A Chinese proverb tells us that 'before a stranger it is better to express only a third of your opinion', and after quoting this Sheo-hsing Chen commented as follows:

'In a modern society, particularly one of the Western type, the individual citizen expresses his individual or even individualistic opinion quite freely. In a traditional folk society it is almost impossible to get a clear individual opinion on many problems. What are problems for the modern are not considered problems by these people, because they are connected with unquestionable mores. Some of our queries were considered just too foolish to answer. Other questions were looked on as impolite or of bad omen. Some knowledge of the social and cultural background is necessary to understand this attitude.'[37]

This stricture does not mean, of course, that polling ought not to be attempted in a country like Taiwan, but it does suggest that some special precautions might be appropriate. Should one expect useful responses, for instance, to a question on abortion (which is illegal in Taiwan), one of those included in the Taichung survey? Is a knowledge of survey methodology sufficient, or is a deep understanding of 'the social and cultural background' a prerequisite to effective research?

It is especially puzzling that demographers should make use of a somewhat dubious instrument when in Taiwan there exists, in the population register, an undoubtedly superior record on many of the relevant points. We have referred to one interesting analysis based on the register,[38] and a study by the Eberhards is directly comparable with the Taichung survey.[39] In 1959 and 1960, the Family Planning Association of China had conducted a survey in the T'ao-yüan district, a prosperous agricultural district including the non-industrial and typically provincial town of the same name. Of the 76,688 women approached in home visits, 18 per cent of those aged 20–44 expressed interest in birth control and 11 per cent of the same age group started using contraceptives. For every fourth ward of T'ao-yüan town, the women on file with the Family Planning Association were systematically compared with data in the population register on all females aged 15–50, in order to see how typical planners were of the general population. As in Chen's study, Mainlander women were found to be much more likely to use contraceptives, presumably because of their generally better education and higher status, but also because they had been brought up in a country more open to modernist ideas than pre-war Taiwan. (If the most receptive group is not native to Taiwan, what does this suggest about the future trends among Taiwanese; it is a question that does not arise from the Taichung survey, which did not differentiate the respondents by this characteristic.) Among Taiwanese women, in general those most similar to Mainlanders in their social background were also most likely to use contraceptives.

Of course, one cannot get information on attitudes from the population register, but it is especially difficult to judge what such data signify. 'Three boys and two girls,' according to the proverbial saying, constitute the ideal family. A 'large' family, thus, has six or more living children, and a 'small' one has four or fewer living children. Chen asked his respondents whether in their opinion a large family, so defined, is better, and he found it 'amazing' that so few answered in the affirmative. Except against a background of the myth that traditionally all Chinese want the maximum progeny, it is perhaps more amazing that 14·2 per cent of the Taipei sample and even 10·5 per cent of the Mainlanders, not to say 42·1 per cent of the fishing village, stated a preference for families with six or more children.[40] The modal 'ideal' family size among Chen's respondents was four to five children, but with a wide range by age and residence.[41] According to the Taichung survey, the modal number of children in the 'ideal' family was three to four,[42] or less than in the larger city of Taipei. Are such responses reliable; are they a valid index of probable behaviour?

2. *The Demographic Transition.* There is obviously some overall validity in the notion that demographic history can be summarized in the three stages of the demographic transition, but when one applies this theory to a specific locale the gross mechanics of change do not suffice.[43] There is no place in the theory, for example, for the rise in fertility that we have noted. Population growth is not, as the theory suggests, merely a dependent variable, which obediently follows the modernization of the economy and society, but is itself a powerful determinant of social change. The contrast between 'traditional' and 'modernist' is in any case less clear-cut than one might suppose from some analyses.[44]

To understand the effect of modern ideas on fertility, one must first judge their effect on traditional Taiwanese practices that limit family size.[45] Various modes of conscious birth control—coitus interruptus, several other contraceptive techniques, abortion—go back for centuries and might lead to the readier adoption of the more effective means now available. Intra-uterine devices are a novelty in the West, but some women were using a type introduced by the Japanese, the so-called Ota ring, more than twenty years ago, and today according to the Taichung survey the Margolies coil or Lippes loop is preferred over all other available contraceptives. Given this tradition, it is not quite appropriate to cite the 'fumbling experimentation with a variety of methods, including contraception, abortion, and sterilization', as part of 'a case study of the demographic transition'.[46] On the contrary, *one* effect of modern influences is to reduce the legitimacy of abortion and especially infanticide, which was traditionally quite common in Fukien province, the original homeland of most Taiwanese.

A potentially important limitation of family size in traditional Chinese society was the large number of days on which sexual intercourse was held to be inauspicious or even dangerous. There is a wide variety of overlapping and partly contradictory rules, spelled out in books that the Eberhards found in the stalls of street vendors, and astrological calendars summarizing such information are also widely circulated today. If all of these rules are followed, intercourse is permitted only about one hundred days during the year. To attack such beliefs as superstitions is, *ceteris paribus*, to encourage a higher fertility.

Nor are modernist influences unambiguously opposed to large families. Western attitudes towards contraception include the Catholic opposition to it, which in Taiwan was represented by the writings of Father A. R. O'Hara. Chiang Kai-shek, like most nationalist leaders of underdeveloped countries and in this case following the precept of Sun Yat-sen, was initially opposed to birth control. Even so, a family-planning association was established in 1954, and it won important support from Dr Chiang Mon-lin, chairman of the JCRR. In 1960 the government began to provide contraceptive information and devices in about a third of the island's 330 health stations,[47] and this effort has been followed, as we have seen, by a widely-publicized campaign financed by several American foundations. The religious and nationalist-military opposition to family planning has been overcome, but it would be too sanguine to suppose that it has been dissipated.

3. *Fertility analysis.* The decline in Taiwan's fertility has taken place over the past seven years, which is far too short a period to give more than a preliminary indication of what any generation of parents will do. A shift in the timing of births does not necessarily mean a reduction in the completed family size, and a part of the decline in fertility seems to be only that. The age at marriage has been going up, and married girls aged 15–19 are having few children (Table 7).[48] One can applaud both trends and yet recognize that the long-term effect on family size cannot be very great and may even be nil.

The major decline in fertility has been among women aged thirty and over and especially among those aged forty and over (Table 7). The implications of this fact are indicated in the report on the T'ao-yüan survey:

'In general women did not tend to become interested in family planning until they had already had a fairly large number of children. . . . Even the wives of people in higher-status occupations or those having more contact with modern ideas usually had four children when they took to family planning. In the occupationally lower and presumably poorer groups, interest in family planning did not start until there were more than four children. . . . Probably many mothers . . . were already close to the end of their child-bearing period.'[49]

If one extrapolates these results into the near future, one might hope that the developing family pattern will become general, so that the average completed family size will fall from something like six to something like four children. If this is realized, it will mean a solid achievement, but one that defines its own limits.

On the basis simply of common sense one anticipates that those most interested in using contraceptives will take advantage first of any birth-control programme available to them; and *a priori* this suggests that there is little warrant for extrapolating an initial high rate of success to the rest of the population. But if the principal decline in fertility has occurred among specific and limited population groups—Mainlanders and women over thirty with relatively large families—then there is even less reason to expect an 'accelerating fertility decline'. For women aged 20–29, which is the prime breeding period, age–specific birth rates have not changed significantly, whether the base is married women or all women (Table 7).

SUMMARY

Of all the world's underdeveloped countries, Taiwan is close to unique in its half century of excellent demographic statistics. The analysis of these data and of the sizable number of supplementary monographs is of greater interest, therefore, than Taiwan's small size and consequent slight world importance—apart from its relations to Communist China—might suggest. The growth of the island's population has accompanied a remarkably successful economic development, by which Taiwan has been transformed from a fever-ridden hellhole to a country on the brink of self-generating modernization. To the degree that one can generalize from this single case, Taiwan's history indicates that however successful the effort to stimulate the economic growth of underdeveloped countries, this will not solve the problems derivative from the concomitant rapid population increase.

From 1905, when the first census was taken, to 1964, Taiwan's population increased more than four times, and the current rate of growth is more than 3 per cent annually. In the latter year, population density on the whole of the island—hardly more than a third of which is arable—rose to 883 persons per square mile. It is anticipated that as the large cohorts at the bottom of the broad-based population pyramid move through life, they will disrupt the school system, make large-scale unemployment more probable, and increase the number of parents in the next generation. As always, this rapidly growing population has a structure that stimulates further rapid growth.

The growth of population has been mostly a natural increase. If we ignore the insignificant number of aboriginal Formosans, the main body of the island's population is relatively homogeneous. The Japanese administrators and their hangers-on, who began coming to Taiwan in the last years of the nineteenth century, left it to the man after Japan's defeat in the Second World War. They were replaced as the dominant class by Kuomintang military and civil administrators, who retreated to this bastion from the mainland. Taiwan is distinguished from most other countries of Asia, thus, by its lack of important ethnic fissures, such as have disrupted the economic and social progress not only of India–Pakistan or Malaysia–Singapore but also of such smaller nations as Ceylon or Thailand.

The decline in mortality has been extraordinarily rapid. Indeed, the remarkable crude death rate in 1963—only 6·1—may be spuriously low, in consequence of a slight under-registration of infant deaths. In the main, however, it is the result of the very successful mass attack on epidemic diseases; and in Taiwan, as also in other underdeveloped countries, this means that the decline in mortality has taken place largely without important change in the people's way of life. A third reason is the population structure: when childhood diseases are brought under effective control, so that ailments associated with old age become the main causes of death, a country with relatively few old persons is likely to have a lower death rate than even that in the most advanced nations.

The crucial question, in Taiwan as elsewhere, is the future of the island's fertility. The crude birth rate fell from a recorded high, forty-six in 1931–5, to 36·2 in 1963 to an estimated thirty-three in 1965; and a number of analysts have extrapolated this downward trend with a greater enthusiasm than would seem to be warranted. Western accounts, it is true, have probably exaggerated the propensity of the average member of traditional China's familistic society to undertake the responsibility for a very large family, so that in Taiwan (as also in India, Puerto Rico, or any other underdeveloped country where this type of research has been undertaken) the actual attitudes undoubtedly do not conform with this stereotype. On the other hand, one must not assume that public-opinion research is a neutral instrument, operating with the same efficiency—whatever that is—in the Western world and in a country like Taiwan, where people have been given little reason to abandon the cautious dissimulation a peasant uses in communicating with strangers or, worse, with persons somehow tied to the government. A research team looking for a particular attitude may well find it—because that is what it is looking for.

Yet, one might respond, a certain portion of the population has shown that it is willing to take advantage of the contraceptive facilities provided. The most important reason for supposing that from this beginning contraception will become a standard part of Taiwanese family life is that it can be effected with a simple, effective, and inoffensive means, the intra-uterine device. But can one sanguinely assume that both the country's rulers and most of its people have reversed their stand entirely, when only a few years ago national-military and family-social precepts apparently induced some hostility to population control? The success to date has been among women born and brought up on the mainland, and thus atypical of the Taiwanese population, and among women aged thirty and over with generally a large number of children. The success to date among married women in their twenties has been nil.

NOTES

a. A preliminary draft of this paper was read by Wolfram Eberhard, Alide Eberhard, Judith Davis, Reinhard Bendix, Ronald Freedman, and John Y. Takeshita. I am happy to acknowledge that I benefited greatly from their comments and criticisms.

1. Frank Notestein, Preface to George W. Barclay, *Colonial Development and Population in Taiwan* (Princeton, Princeton University Press, 1954).
2. Shao-hsing Chen, 'Population Growth and Social Change in Taiwan', *Bulletin of the Department of Archaeology and Anthropology*, National Taiwan University, Taipei, 5 (May 1955), pp. 76–103; 6 (November 1955), pp. 86–119, at 5, pp. 77–8.
3. Cheng-siang Chen, *Taiwan: An Economic and Social Geography*, Research Report No. 96, Fu-Min Geographical Institute of Economic Development (Taipei, 1963).
4. Barclay, *Colonial Development*, p. 7.
5. *Ibid.*, Ch. 2; Ramon H. Myers, 'Economic Growth and Population Change in Taiwan', *Malayan Economic Review* (Singapore), 8:2 (October 1963), pp. 104–17.
6. Barclay, *Colonial Development*, p. 10. The first of these—*The Population Census of Formosa*, 1905 (Tokyo, Imperial Printing Bureau, 1909)—begins with a detailed, confidence-inspiring account of how the census was organized. Even in this abridged English translation, it includes not only breakdowns by age, race, marital status, occupation, education, and so on, but chapters on opium addicts, who constituted some 4 per cent of the total population, and on bound feet, which virtually incapacitated two thirds of the females aged 5 and over. The low opinion that Japanese had of the natives is indicated in many ways; as one example, the literacy of these Chinese was measured only by whether they could read and write Japanese.
7. Estimated demographic rates for this period are given in George W. Barclay, *A Report on Taiwan's Population* (Princeton, Office of Population Research, 1954); L. P. Chow and S. C. Hsu, 'Taiwan's Population Problem', *Population Review* (Madras), 4:2 (July 1960), pp. 17–36.
8. Mark Mancall, ed., *Formosa Today* (New York, Praeger, 1964), p. 4. The figure of 10,000 is evidently a very loose approximation. Mancall adds in a footnote that 'an important Taiwanese leader in Taipei at the time . . . has estimated privately that at least 17,000 were killed', but Ong Joktik, a contributor to the same volume, states that over 10,000 were 'either executed or imprisoned' (p. 165).
9. Robert A. Scalapino, 'Communist China and Taiwan', U.S. Senate, *Congressional Record*, Proceedings and Debates of the 86th Congress, Second Session, January 19, 1960.
10. Its achievements have been recorded in a large body of writings, much of it technical

and detailed. For summary accounts, see Albert Ravenholt, 'Formosa's Rural Revolution', *American Universities Field Staff Report*, March 23, 1956; Joint Commission on Rural Reconstruction, *A Decade of Rural Progress, 1948–1958* (Taipei, 1958).

11. See Chen Chang, *Land Reform in Taiwan* (Taipei: China Publishing Co., 1961).
12. Joint Commission on Rural Reconstruction, *Intensive Village Improvement in Taiwan* (Taipei, 1960).
13. U.S. Bureau of Foreign Commerce, *Investment in Taiwan (Formosa): Basic Information for United States Businessmen* (Washington, D.C., U.S. Government Printing Office, 1959); various issues of *Industry of Free China* (Taipei).
14. *New York Times*, July 1, 1965.
15. Barclay, *Colonial Development*, Ch. 5.
16. Shao-hsing Chen, 'The Trend of Urbanization and the Formation of a Metropolitan Area in Taiwan during the Last Decade', *Journal of Sociology* (Taipei), 1 (1963), pp. 59–79.
17. Shao-hsing Chen, 'Population Growth', 5, pp. 78–9.
18. *Ibid.*, 5, p. 80.
19. *Ibid.*, 5, pp. 87–8.
20. Taiwan Provincial Malaria Research Institute, 'The Malaria Eradication Program in Taiwan', *Annual Report for Fiscal Year 1959* (Ch'ao Chow, 1959).
21. Among the millions of persons presently under surveillance, the few cases discovered often turn out to be persons who had travelled abroad and presumably brought the disease back with them. See, for example, Taiwan Provincial Malaria Research Institute, *Quarterly Report Covering April–June 1964* (Ch'ao Chow, 1964).
22. Shao-hsing Chen, Yao-tung Wang, and Frederic J. Foley, 'Pattern of Fertility in Taiwan', *Journal of Social Science* (Taipei), 13 (1963), pp. 209–94, at p. 267.
23. Barclay, *A Report*, p. 27.
24. Lien-pin Chow and Shih-chu Hsu, 'Statistical Studies on Mortality in Taiwan during the Last Decade', *Industry of Free China* (Taipei), 14:2 (August 1960), pp. 7–34, at pp. 20–23.
25. Shao-hsing Chen, 'Population Growth', 5, p. 83; *cf.*, *ibid.*, 6, pp. 86–7.
26. Chi-hsien Tuan, 'Reproductive Histories of Chinese Women in Rural Taiwan', *Population Studies*, 12:1 (July 1958), pp. 40–50.
27. Shao-hsing Chen, 'Pattern of Fertility'.
28. Shao-hsing Chen, 'Population Change', 6, p. 88.
29. Japan, Government-General of Taiwan, *Population Census, 1930* (in Japanese; Taipei, 1934), p. 30; United Nations, *Demographic Yearbook, 1963* (New York, 1964), Table 5.
30. Yung-jung Lee, 'Population Growth and the Problem of Education in Taiwan', *Economic Review* (Taipei), No. 101 (September–October 1964), pp. 11–23; Henry F. McCusker, Jr, and Harry J. Robinson, *Education and Development: The Role of Educational Planning in the Economic Development of the Republic of China*, prepared for the Minister of Education, Government of the Republic of China (Menlo Park, Calif., Stanford Research Institute, 1962).
31. Harry Weiss, 'Manpower Problems and Programs in Taiwan', *Labor Development Abroad* (Washington), August 1964, pp. 1–6.
32. For a concise statement of the findings, see John Y. Takeshita, 'Changing Fertility in Taiwan', paper read at Asia Studies Conference, San Francisco, April 2–4, 1965.
33. John Y. Takeshita and Ronald Freedman, 'Important Results of the 1963 Taichung Family Planning Study', paper read at first Western Pacific regional conference, International Planned Parenthood Federation, Seoul, May 26–9, 1965.
34. Robert W. Gillespie, *Family Planning on Taiwan, 1964–1965* (Taichung, Population Council, 1965).
35. Freedman, J. Y. Peng, J. Y. Takeshita, and T. H. Sun, 'Fertility Trends in Taiwan: Tradition and Change', *Population Studies*, 16:3 (March 1963), pp. 219–36; Bernard Berelson and Ronald Freedman, 'A Study in Fertility Control', *Scientific American*, 210:5 (May 1964), pp. 3–11; Ronald Freedman, John Y. Takeshita, and T. H. Sun, 'Fertility and Family Planning in Taiwan: A Case Study of the Demographic Transition', *American Journal of Sociology*, 70:1 (July 1964), pp. 16–27; Ronald Freedman, 'The Transition from High to Low Fertility: Challenge to Demographers', presidential address, Population Association of America, Chicago, April 23, 1965; Ronald Freed-

man, Lien-pin Chow, and Julia Ann Smith, 'The Accelerating Fertility Decline in Taiwan', *Population Index*, October 1965.
36. Donald Bogue, 'The Demographic Breakthrough: From Projection to Control', *Population Index*, 30:4 (October 1964), pp. 449–53.
37. Shao-hsing Chen, 'Pattern of Fertility', p. 266.
38. Tuan, 'Reproductive Histories'; see also Freedman, 'Fertility Trends in Taiwan'.
39. Wolfram and Alide Eberhard, 'Family Planning in a Taiwanese Town' (mimeographed; Berkeley, Calif., University of California Center for Chinese Studies [1961]).
40. Shao-hsing Chen, 'Pattern of Fertility', p. 273.
41. *Ibid.*, pp. 276–80.
42. Freedman, 'Fertility and Family Planning'.
43. For an elaboration of this argument, see William Peterson, 'The Demographic Transition in the Netherlands', *The Politics of Population* (Garden City, New York, Doubleday, 1964), pp. 166–92.
44. For example, a paper based on a master's essay at Michigan shows 'a systematic relationship between socio-economic development and fertility', based on ecological correlations and with no discussion of countertrends. Paul K. C. Liu, 'Socio-Economic Development and Fertility Levels in Taiwan', *Industry of Free China*, 24:2 (August 1965), pp. 2–17.
45. The following discussion is based largely on Eberhard, 'Family Planning', pp. 1–3.
46. Freedman, 'Fertility and Family Planning', p. 27.
47. Sheppard Glass, 'Some Aspects of Formosa's Economic Growth', in Mancall, *Formosa Today*, pp. 80–81. A study of a sample of the patients indicates that the programme was successful in reducing their fertility substantially; see John Y. Takeshita, J. Y. Peng, and Paul K. C. Liu, 'A Study of the Effectiveness of the Pregnancy Health Program in Taiwan', *Eugenics Quarterly*, 11:4 (December 1964), pp. 222–33.
48. The evidence is not consistent in two of Professor Freedman's papers. In one he states that the age-specific birth rate of the 15–19 age group *increased* by 5 per cent from 1958 to 1962 ('Fertility and Family Planning', p. 17); in another he gives these rates as 46 in 1959 and 45 in 1962 ('The Accelerating Fertility Decline', Table 1).
49. Eberhard, 'Family Planning', pp. 15–16. *Cf.* similar data in Takeshita, 'Important Results', Table 13.

BIBLIOGRAPHY

Barclay, George W., *A Report on Taiwan's Population* (Princeton, Office of Population Research, 1954).

Colonial Development and Population in Taiwan (Princeton, Princeton University Press, 1954).

Chen Cheng-siang, *Taiwan: An Economic and Social Geography*, Research Report No. 96, Fu-Min Geographical Institute of Economic Development (Taipei, 1963).

Chen Shao-hsing, 'Population Growth and Social Change in Taiwan', *Bulletin of the Department of Archeology and Anthropology*, National Taiwan University, Taipei, 5 (May 1955), 76–103; 6 (November 1955), 86–119.

Yao-tung Wang, and Frederic J. Foley, 'Pattern of Fertility in Taiwan', *Journal of Social Science* (Taipei), 13 (1963), 209–94.

Chow, Lien-pin, and Shih-chu Hsu, 'Statistical Studies on Mortality in Taiwan during the Last Decade', *Industry of Free China* (Taipei), 14:2 (August 1960), 7–34.

Eberhard, Wolfram and Alide, 'Family Planning in a Taiwanese Town', Mimeographed (Berkeley, Calif., University of California Centre for Chinese Studies, 1961).

Freedman, Ronald, John Y. Takeshita, and T. H. Sun, 'Fertility and Family Planning in Taiwan: A Case Study of the Demographic Transition', *American Journal of Sociology*, 70:1 (July 1964), 16–27.

—— and J. Y. Peng, 'Fertility Trends in Taiwan: Tradition and Change', *Population Studies*, 16:3 (March 1963), 219–36.
—— Lien-pin Chow, and Julia Ann Smith, 'The Accelerating Fertility Decline in Taiwan', *Population Index*, October 1965.
Gillespie, Robert W., *Family Planning on Taiwan, 1964–1965* (Taichung, Population Council, 1965).
Taiwan Provincial Civil Affairs Department, *1961 Taiwan Demographic Fact Book* (Taipei, 1963).
Tuan Chi-hsien, 'Reproductive Histories of Chinese Women in Rural Taiwan', *Population Studies*, 12:1 (July 1958), 40–50.

CHAPTER 9

AUSTRALIA'S POPULATION

BY ROBERT V. HORN

I

INTRODUCTION

Australian Environment

AUSTRALIA, in terms of the white man's settlement, is a 'young country', its history dating back to Captain Cook's discovery of the fertile coast in 1770 and the founding of European settlement in 1788. Or, we might go back a little earlier, to the seventeenth century when Dutch, Spanish and Portuguese sailing the Indian and Pacific Oceans sighted the Australian coastline. The Dutch mapped some of the coast of 'Terra Australis' but they did not persist with exploration or settlement; for what they found on landfall was a barren coast, far off the rich trading routes to the North. Or, earlier still, it is likely that Asians sighted Australia: Chinese, Indians, Malays, Arabs and Polynesians sailed far to the South and West, and they brought back the stories of the Great Southland that later inspired European explorers; however, little is known about the Asian voyagers, except for the evidence of Malay trepang fishers visiting the north-west coast in the eighteenth century and perhaps earlier.

But the 'young and empty' country had a history of settlement going back to the mists of time, perhaps to the Ice Ages, 30,000 years ago, when land bridges still connected the Australian mainland with Asia to the north and Tasmania to the south. The earliest settlers are thought to have been a negroid people that crossed the continent and settled in Tasmania. There they numbered a few thousand at the coming of the white man—a peaceable people that fell victim to the barbarities of the newcomers and became extinct by the 1880's.

The aboriginals on the mainland are of different ethnic origin, linked with the Dravidians of Malaya and Southern India, or perhaps even with pre-Dravidian tribes that came originally from the Mediterranean region and are related to European stock. There were some 200,000 to 300,000 of them, spread thinly across the continent, when the white man came; now only about 40,000 remain, living mainly in the northern parts. These 'Stone Age' people in general are of medium height, long-limbed with high, narrow heads, heavy eyebrow ridges and broad, flat noses. Their dark-brown skin and dark, wavy hair set them apart from the black skin and 'woolly' hair of negritos.

On the mainland, as in Tasmania, relations of the early white settlers to the aboriginals were typical of the impact of an advanced technical civilization on primitive tribal communities; it is a story of dispossession and depopulation which forced withdrawal from the coast to the interior where the whites did not follow. A period of well-intended but inept policies of civilization, pacification and christianization was followed by negative protective measures. Only in this century have Australians become aware that the aboriginals have a complex social organization, an intricate family system and a highly-developed culture of myths and art manifestations. Sentimental sympathy with the 'dying race' is gradually turning into a more resolute policy of fitting aboriginals into white society. Resistance by the aboriginal population did not become—as it did in Africa and New Zealand—a factor in the development of white settlement. The limits were, and are, rather set by the geography of the continent. Australia has an area of 2,971,000 square miles, measuring about 2,400 miles from east to west and 2,000 miles from north to south with 12,000 miles of coastline. It lacks high mountain chains and substantial rivers and is much more arid than the great land masses of Europe and North America, which are more distant from the Equator. The climate ranges from the tropical north, which occupies 39 per cent of the continent and includes the Northern Territory and over one half of the areas of the States of Queensland and Western Australia, to the temperate south-eastern regions where the higher mountains carry snow in winter. About one third of Australia in the centre and north-west, has an average annual rainfall of less than ten inches and is mainly unoccupied desert. A further third, to the north, has its rainfall concentrated in the summer and climate suitable only for the sparse grazing of stock. The remainder, mainly to the south and east, is suitable for agriculture and intensive stock-raising, but only about half a million square miles have the benefit of a fairly uniform rainfall distribution throughout the year.[1]

Climate, water resources and topography have determined the extent of settlement, its dispersion across the continent and the frequent concentration of land-ownership in large holdings. Irrigation and soil improvement (e.g. sown pastures and fertilizers) are being used to increase yields and to extend the boundaries. The present land use is estimated as follows:[2]

	Million acres	Per cent of total
Natural pasture, rough grazing	1,086	57·1
Crops, orchards, sown pasture	71	3·7
Forest reserves	33	1·7
Urban areas	4	0·2
Other areas	710	37·3

Captain Cook made the first systematic exploration of the east coast and proclaimed British sovereignty in 1770. His expedition reported favourably on the potential of the area but this did not result in immediate settlement. The stimulus to colonization came a little later, partly from the need to find a place for the disposal of criminals after the War of Independence had halted transportation of British convicts to America. The First Fleet, carrying about 700 convicts, landed at Sydney Cove in 1788, and this source of 'colonists' did not end for New South Wales until 1841, for Tasmania until 1853 and for Western Australia until 1863, when the three States had received 80,000, 70,000 and 10,000 convicts respectively. Original settlement in Victoria and South Australia was mainly based on free immigration.

Until 1850, when the total population had reached 400,000, the greater part were still convicts, released convicts (emancipists) or their descendants. There has been much argument about the character of these first pioneers who 'left their country for their country's good',[3] and we can here only quote one view: 'The truth is that most of them were habitual criminals, whether great or small. It is also true that the economic and social conditions in Britain were such as to drive a great many people to crime.'[4]

It might also be noted that most of the convicts and first free settlers were labourers from the cities, that many of them came from Ireland, then described as 'a nation of paupers', and that the background of early settlement favoured the qualities of individual resourcefulness, comradely 'mateship', class solidarity and egalitarianism which have permeated the subsequent history of Australia—as manifested in the strong trade-union movement or the exploits of Australian soldiers in the World Wars. Two further features of the early settlement were: a high rate of urbanization, with major concentrations first in Sydney and later also in the other State capitals near the seaboard, and a high rate of masculinity which persisted until the second decade of the present century.

The arrival of free immigrants gathered momentum after the 1840's. By then Britain's narrow purpose of a penal settlement under military rule had expanded into the prospect of a useful colonial addition to the Empire. Early experiments in agriculture had been disappointing but the progressive exploration of the hinterland had shown its pastoral potential, and fostered by a rising demand from England, wool growing became the predominant industry. The opening up of the inland, the inflow of British capital, free immigration and the growth of national consciousness received a major impetus from the discovery of large gold deposits in New South Wales and Victoria in 1851 (1882 in Western Australia). A rapid inflow of migrants trebled the population within ten years and lifted it above the million mark in 1858. The early riches of alluvial gold soon dried up but the migrant flow, at a lesser rate, was maintained. Rural development extended from sheep to cattle raising and large-scale wheat farming, while commerce and manufactures offered increasing opportunities in the towns.

The migratory ways of the gold seekers seemed to fit in with the nomadic life of the bush workers, and the European and American migrants of the period quickly merged into the Australian environment. The main groups of non-white immigrants were some 50,000 Chinese on the goldfields and later some 57,000 South Sea Islanders ('Kanakas') indentured for work on the sugar and cotton fields of northern New South Wales and Queensland; and it was fear of low-wage competition combined with racial prejudice which eventually led to national policies of exclusion of non-white immigrants.

Responsible government was granted to the colonies in the second half of the nineteenth century, and they were federated as States to form the Commonwealth of Australia in 1901. In relation to Britain, Australia advanced from colonial status to that of a dominion, 'an autonomous community within the British Empire' (Imperial Conference, 1926) and to equal status as a member of the British Commonwealth. The role of immigration in growth receded until the Second World War. Rural development slowed down, but exports of primary produce (mainly wool, wheat, meat, butter, minerals) and the inflow of British capital remained the main determinants of the Australian economy and tied it to the fluctuations of international trade cycles.

TABLE 1. *Growth of Australia's Population by Successive Millions*

Year	Population (millions)	Interval in years	Rate of increase annual average (per cent)	Notes
1788	0			
1858	1	70·0		
1877	2	19·0	3·5	
1889	3	11·75	3·5	Boom of 1880's
1905	4	16·0	1·7	Depression of 1890's
1918	5	12·75	1·8	World War I
1925	6	7·75	2·4	Post-War Growth
1939	7	14·0	1·1	Depression Period
1949	8	9·75	1·4	World War II
1954	9	4·75	2·5	Post-war Immigration
1959	10	4·75	2·2	,,
1964	11	4·75	2·0	

The Second World War and the subsequently accelerated pace of immigration and Anglo-American capital imports have since brought diversification and expansion of commerce and manufacturing, without as yet obliterating altogether the basic features imposed by the earlier history: a population of predominantly British origin concentrated in coastal centres and spread thinly over vast inland areas; allegiance to the British Crown and adherence to Commonwealth policies and an economy largely dependent on oversea earnings from exports of rural produce and thus on the vagaries of international markets.

We can sum up Australia's history in steps of successive million increments to the population (excluding aboriginals), Table 1.

II

THE AUSTRALIAN POPULATION

The Australian Aboriginals

The Australian Constitution provides that 'in reckoning the numbers of the people of the Commonwealth . . . aboriginal natives shall not be counted'. They are therefore excluded from the Census and other statistics quoted here in subsequent sections (except Table 8). A separate enumeration at the time of the 1961 Census puts their number at 40,100 of whom 17,400 lived in the Northern Territory, 10,100 in Western Australia and 8,700 in Queensland; this is only about one fifth to one eighth of their estimated number at the time of the first white settlement. Precise figures are still not available because some aboriginals continue to lead a nomadic life in remote areas, but it appears that the decline in numbers has been halted in recent years. There has been a steady rise in the number of mixed-bloods who are included in the Census; the number of persons with one aboriginal and one European parent increased from 31,300 in 1954 to 39,200 in 1961, and there has been a process of progressive dilution for the descendants of earlier 'mixed' unions.

Only a few demographic details about the full-blood aboriginals are available. Some of them live in large tribal reserves in the centre and north with no more than occasional contact with 'white' civilization, although development for mining and military purposes is making intrusions into these areas. A further portion is under the care of religious missions or government agencies who provide some food, education and other welfare services. Some are in employment but only a small proportion have become more fully absorbed into the white environment. Most of those employed are probably in unskilled or semi-skilled occupations, such as stockmen in the large northern cattle stations or in other farm and labouring jobs. Conditions vary, but often they receive less pay than white workers while getting some protection from exploitation through standards laid down by regulation. Many work only intermittently and rely heavily on public welfare services for sustenance. Much goodwill and effort, and a little more money, are now being expended on their educational and social advancement but so far only a few have reached any higher standard in this respect.

Population by States and Urbanization

Australia's population at June 30, 1965, was estimated at 11,359,500 or 3·8 persons per square mile. The density varied from thirty-six in Victoria and thirteen in New South Wales, the two most populous States, and fourteen in the island State of Tasmania down to about 2·5 in Queensland and South Australia and one in Western Australia which occupies one third of the continent but carries only 7 per cent of its population. The two mainland territories, which are administered by the Commonwealth, present a contrast: the Australian Capital Territory, designated in 1909 as the seat of Government, occupies only 0·03 per cent of the total area but carries 0·8 per cent of the population, making a density of ninety-four per square mile, while the Northern Territory with its vast arid regions occupies one sixth of the continent but carries only one person per fifteen square miles.

Two thirds of Australia's population is concentrated in two States, New South Wales and Victoria, and nearly 40 per cent in their capitals, Sydney and Melbourne; they have been the most populous States for over one hundred years, with Victoria only temporarily leading New South Wales during the second half of the last century. The other mainland States have gone through major phases of expansion—Queensland in the 1880s, Western Australia in the 1890s and South Australia in the 1950s, but in absolute terms their growth could not match that of the two larger States. In the period 1947 to 1965 the population rose by 1·2 million each in New South Wales and Victoria, by 500,000 in Queensland, 400,000 in South Australia, 300,000 in Western Australia and 100,000 each in Tasmania and the Territories, making a total increment of 3·8 million in the eighteen years. The annual growth rates in that period were about 2·5 per cent in Victoria, South Australia and Western Australia, 2 per cent in New South Wales, Queensland and Tasmania and 8 per cent in the Territories, with an Australian average of 2·3 per cent.

All States show a high and rising concentration in their capital cities which are situated near the seaboard. About 57 per cent of Australia's population now live in the capitals and about three quarters in centres classed as urban. Outside the metropoles there are no very large towns; only three have a population of more than 60,000 (Newcastle 220,000 and Wollongong 150,000 in New South Wales and Geelong 100,000 in Victoria). The population living in areas classified as rural has steadily declined from one half to one fifth of the Australian total during the past fifty years. This drift reflects the increasing industrialization and

TABLE 2. *Population by States and Capital Cities—Australia—June 1965*

		Area	Population—persons				Population
State or Territory	Capital city	Sq. miles	Capital city	Rest of State	Total State	Per sq. mile	Capital city as per cent of State
New South Wales	Sydney	309,400	2,349,600	1,843,000	4,192,600	13·5	56
Victoria	Melbourne	87,900	2,121,900	1,086,200	3,208,100	36·5	66
Queensland	Brisbane	667,000	677,000	933,700	1,610,700	2·4	42
South Australia	Adelaide	380,100	614,600	439,600	1,054,200	2·8	58
Western Australia	Perth	975,900	465,000	339,500	804,500	0·8	58
Tasmania	Hobart	26,200	124,000	242,000	366,000	13·9	34
Northern Territory	Darwin	520,300	16,900	17,900	34,800	0·1	48
Australian Capital Territory	Canberra	900	85,800	2,800	88,600	94·3	97
Total—Australia		2,967,700	6,454,800	4,904,700	11,359,500	3·8	57

prosperity which are attracting to the cities the surplus rural population of working age as well as the bulk of the immigrants.

Age Distribution and Conjugal Condition

Australia, like the United States, Canada and Japan, occupies an intermediate position between the more aged populations of Europe and the younger, but shorter-lived, populations of continental Asia. If we take three groups—those aged under nineteen, 19–64 and over sixty-five, Australia had about 38 per cent in the young group (1963–65), as against proportions of between 25 and 33 per cent in Europe and over 50 per cent in south-east Asian countries, while for the group over sixty-five the Australian ratio of 8·5 per cent was less than the 10–12 per cent applying in Europe but much higher than the 2–3 per cent rate applying to most Asian countries. The middle (working age) group share was greater proportionally in Europe at around 60 per cent than in Australia at 53 per cent but at the expense of there being fewer children, and it was less in Asia (40–50 per cent) as the effect of there being more children.

Table 3 gives a more detailed age grouping of the Australian population. Post-war immigration partly compensated for the short-fall in births during the 1930's and contributed a large part of the rise in the

TABLE 3. *Population in Age Groups—Australia*

	Males	Females	Persons	Per cent of population, as at June				
Age last birthday	As at June 1965			1933	1947	1954	1961	1965
0– 1	231,900	219,600	451,500	3·20	4·35	4·32	4·25	3·97
2–15	1,378,500	1,314,100	2,692,600	22·51	19·32	22·81	23·94	23·70
14–20	723,300	686,000	1,409,300	12·88	10·70	9·21	11·10	12·41
0–20	2,333,700	2,219,700	4,553,400	38·59	34·37	36·34	39·29	40·08
21–44	1,857,800	1,743,900	3,601,700	36·33	36·31	35·32	32·31	31·71
45–64	1,134,000	1,113,400	2,247,400	18·60	21·27	20·04	19·89	19·78
65 and over	402,100	554,900	957,000	6·48	8·05	8·30	8·51	8·43
Total	5,727,600	5,631,900	11,359,500	100%	100%	100%	100%	100%

21–64 age group of 1·4 million (to 5·8 million) between 1947 and 1965. However, as a proportion of total population this group fell from 58 per cent to 51 per cent, mainly because of the upswing in births during and since the war which is now slowing down, as presaged by the fall in the 0–1 year group. Increasing longevity and declining masculinity (i.e. greater longevity of women) raised the mean age of the population from 24·5 years in 1891 to 32·5 in 1947, while the upturn in births and immigration reduced it to thirty-one years in 1965 (median age twenty-seven years).

The absolute and relative increase in the number of children during the post-war period has boosted the demand for educational facilities, and this has been strengthened by the raising of the minimum school-leaving age from fourteen to fifteen (or sixteen) in some States, as well as by the trend for more children to stay on to reach higher grades at school and to go on to Universities. School enrolments in 1964 totalled 2·4 million and University enrolments for full-time studies 45,000; in addition, there were 32,000 part-time or external University students.[5]

Census tabulations for Conjugal Condition show a relatively high level of marriage rates. The Nuptial Rate (number of married to 1,000 unmarried) for the population aged twenty and over reached 2,841 in 1961, and the proportion of 'ever-married' to total population reveals a trend to earlier marriages: for the ages 20–24 it rose for men from 13 per cent in 1933 to 24 per cent in 1947 and 27 per cent in 1961, and for women from 31 to 49 and 61 per cent respectively; or for ages 45–54 (indicating the ultimately married proportion) it rose in this period from 85 to 87 and 90 per cent respectively for men and from 86 to 87 and 92 per cent respectively for women.

One might also mention here a slight rise in ex-nuptiality in recent years. In 1963 ex-nuptial births totalled 13,500 or 5·7 per cent of all births. In addition, there has been some rise in the number of nuptial first births to marriages of less than eight months' duration; in 1963 they totalled 17,600 or one quarter of total nuptial first births.

Population Growth Trends

Table 4 summarizes the growth of the Australian population during the past forty years, divided into eight-year periods which roughly delineate major changes. The relative prosperity of the 1920's was followed by the economic depression of the 1930's when both migration and births were low. The rate of natural increase recovered from 0·8 to 1·1 per cent during the War and subsequently rose to 1·4 per cent in the 1948–55 period when the gain from migration also reached the high rate of 1·2 per cent per annum. The net migration peak was 150,000 persons in both 1949 and 1950, but more recently the number has been between 61,000 (1961) and 105,000 (1965). In the 1956–63 period immigration provided one third of the total population increment, but in 1964 and 1965 it contributed again nearly one half of the increment. In the long run (forty years) migration has contributed three tenths and natural increase seven tenths of the population growth.

As to the future, simple arithmetic suggests that at the 1963–64 rate of 2 per cent increase per annum the Australian population would double to 22 million by the end of the century, or at the possible rate of 2·2 per cent per annum it might reach 25 million by then. This projection, however, assumes normality of political and economic factors and is rendered doubtful by uncertainty about future fertility rates and the availability of migrants.

TABLE 4. *Australia's Population Growth: 1924–63*

Eight years	Population at end of period	Elements of increase: Natural increase	Migration	Total	Annual percentage rate of increase: Natural increase	Migration	Total
1924–31	6,552,600	591,100	205,500	796,600	1·2	0·5	1·7
1932–39	7,004,900	415,800	36,500	452,300	0·8	0·1	0·9
1940–47	7,638,000	604,800	28,300	633,100	1·1	—	1·1
1948–55	9,311,800	919,200	754,600	1,673,800	1·4	1·2	2·6
1956–63	11,022,800	1,115,600	595,400	1,711,000	1·4	0·7	2·1
1924–63		3,646,500	1,620,300	5,266,800	1·1	0·5	1·6

Natural Increase of the Population

Conditions in Australia, since its emergence to nationhood, might be considered as favourable to rapid indigenous population growth. Already in the 1880s (crude) birth rates were appreciably higher and death rates lower than in Britain. Life expectancy has been relatively high, as has been the marriage rate (7·5 per 1,000 mean population in the long run), while the average age of women at marriage remained comparatively low (twenty-three years in 1881–90 and twenty-five years more recently). Compared with crowded Europe, living conditions have been favourable for the raising of large families, which, at least in the past, were regarded as natural and desirable objectives.

However, economic and social factors in Australia, as elsewhere, have partly countered this development. Commercial depressions in the 1890's and 1930's drastically reduced marriage and births (and immigration), and this was not fully offset in subsequent prosperous periods. The world wars inhibited growth through reduced births and war casualties, although the effect in Australia was less severe than in the countries which became battlefields. Yet, in 1914–18 Australia despatched 340,000 soldiers abroad and of those 59,000 were killed and in 1939–45 nearly a million personnel were enlisted and 34,000 killed. Attendant factors in the reduction of family size were the disruption of family life, the impetus towards greater emancipation of women and accelerated urbanization as a result of greater industrialization.

Trends in fertility bear some resemblance to the European pattern. Already sixty years ago a decline in the birth rate led to a Royal Commission of Enquiry in New South Wales which found the cause to be a fall in average issue (i.e. not in age composition or marriage rates), as evidenced by a decline in the rate of fecund marriages, a tendency for fertility to cease at earlier ages and a decline in fertility at all ages. It recognized, and disapproved of, the growth of voluntary family limitation which coincided with the spread of improved contraceptive devices, although it did not perceive that this was not so much the cause as the means of giving effect to the emerging trend of Neo-Malthusian doctrines as well as of economic–social advancement.

Some of these trends have prevailed in the long run: a high rate of marriage at an early age, coupled with deliberate limitation of family size in the context of growing industrialization and affluence, and, more recently, a shift towards early completion of families. As short-hand indicators we may quote the figures of average issue of wives aged 45–9 (taken as roughly equivalent to married women with completed families) which fell from five in 1911 to 2·4 in 1964; or the distribution of the number of children in this group which in the category 'none' rose from 11·4 to 18·5 per cent and for 'one or two' rose from 18·2 to 40·8 per cent with corresponding relative falls in the larger family sizes.[6]

Table 5 sums up the more recent trends. The crude birth rate fell from a post-war peak of 24 per 1,000 of mean population to 20·6 in 1964, which is still high compared with that of the more aged populations of Europe and Japan but less than that in most African, Asian and American countries. If we allow for age distribution, by expressing fertility as the ratio of births per 1,000 women of child-bearing age, the long-term downward trend from 1880–1933, which reduced the rate for married women from 321 to 131, was only partly reversed after the war and the rate fell from 160 in 1946–48 to 149 in more recent years. A similar trend is evident in age-specific fertility rates (not shown here). As an index of the reproductive propensity of the population, the Gross Reproduction Rate (or the Net Reproduction Rate which allows for mortality) was down to about one in 1933, rose to 1·7 in 1961 and then fell slightly to 1·5 in 1964. This again is high by European or Japanese standards but less than in other parts of the world. The seventh column of the table relates births to the marriages from which they could have resulted and estimates the number of children a marriage of that year is likely to produce. Because of the incidence of migrant marriages there might be some progressive overstatement in this series (estimated at 8 per cent for 1963), but again there is the typical trend of an early post-war rise which has been halted or reversed in the past three years.

It is difficult to assess the effects of the various demographic factors involved but it is possible that the recent downturn in fertility is at least in part connected with the introduction and popularization of oral contraceptives. As in Europe and North America the use of 'the pill' has spread quickly in Australia. It is too early yet to be definite about its final effects on births and family formation, but it appears that if it were to become generally accepted, in particular among Catholics who raise relatively large families, it might act as some check on fertility rates.

TABLE 5. *Birth, Death and Fertility Rates—Australia*

Year	(1) Birth rate	(2) Death rate	(3) Fertility rates Women aged 15–44 Total	(4) Married women	(5) Reproduction rates Gross	(6) Net	(7) Fertility of marriages Nuptial confinements per marriage
1881	35·3	14·7	170	321	2·65	1·88	
1891	34·5	14·8	159	332	2·30	1·73	
1901	27·2	12·2	117	235	1·74	1·39	
1911	27·2	10·7	117	236	1·71	1·42	
1921	25·0	9·9	107	197	1·51	1·31	
1933	16·8	8·6	71	131	1·05	0·96	
1947	24·1	7·3	104	160	1·49	1·42	2·55
1954	22·5	6·9	109	149	1·56	1·50	2·66
1961	22·8	6·3	112	154	1·72	1·66	3·05
1963	21·6	n.a.	106	149	1·62	1·56	2·92
1964	20·6	n.a.	101	n.a.	1·53	1·47	2·78

(1) Births per 1,000 of mean population. (2) Deaths per 1,000 mean population; from 1933 on 'standardized' rates. (3) Births per 1,000 women. (4) Nuptial births per 1,000 married women. (5) and (6) Based on age-specific fertility; net rate also on life expectancy. (7) Number of children per marriage that can be expected from ruling fertility conditions in year shown.

Immigration

The chart of immigration into Australia has been marked in the past by steep peaks and troughs, and a statistician (C. H. Wickens in 1928) has used for migrant absorption the simile of the boa constrictor whose huge meals are followed by long periods of digestion. Since the War the level has been sustained but the effects of economic recessions were still felt in temporary falls during 1953, 1958 and 1961.

Traditionally Britain has been the major source of migration, and the lesser inflow from other countries has been absorbed into the British-Australian mould. With a view to easy assimilation, migrant planning has given first preference to the British, then to migrants from north-western Europe and lastly to southern Europeans. The main instruments of the policy have been assisted passage schemes, in particular since 1947 when they were extended from British migrants to apply also to nationals from other selected European countries. Since 1860, and in particular since 1900, the greater part of migrants have come out under such schemes.

At times Australia has provided a haven for refugees from political and religious persecution. Already among the convicts there were Irish rebels, Scottish 'martyrs' and English Chartists. From Germany came Lutheran refugees in the 1830's and a hundred years later 9,000 Jewish refugees. The Second World War brought in its aftermath some 200,000 refugees from Eastern Europe. However, the greater number of migrants came by their own choice from Britain and Western Europe, attracted by the economic opportunities of a new and rapidly developing country.

Table 6 gives some data on the post-war inflow. It should be noted that the classification is based on stated intention and includes some who eventually leave again. So, while 'permanent and long-term arrivals' in

TABLE 6. *Permanent and Long-term Arrivals, Australia, October 1945 to June 1965*

Nationalities	Assisted arrivals Persons	% Total	Other arrivals Persons	% Total	Total arrivals Persons	% Total
British	653,500	56·0	579,400	48·7	1,232,900	52·3
North-Western Europe	194,100	16·6	102,100	8·6	296,200	12·6
Southern Europe	92,900	8·0	351,200	29·5	444,100	18·8
Eastern Europe	216,800	18·6	83,300	7·0	300,100	12·7
United States of America	7,900	0·7	28,400	2·4	36,300	1·6
Lebanese	—	—	9,800	0·8	9,800	0·4
Chinese	—	—	11,200	0·9	11,200	0·5
Others	1,300	0·1	24,700	2·1	26,000	1·1
Total	1,166,500	100%	1,190,100	100%	2,356,600	100%

Age groups—all arrivals, October 1945–June 1965	Males		Females		Total	
0–14	301,800	24·0%	278,000	26·3%	579,800	25·0%
15–59	924,600	73·4%	726,300	68·6%	1,650,900	71·3%
60 and over	32,400	2·6%	53,800	5·1%	86,200	3·7%
Total	1,258,800	100%	1,058,100	100%	2,316,900	100%

Source: *Australian Immigration*, Quarterly Statistical Bulletin issued by Department of Immigration, Canberra, Vol. 2, No. 18, January 1966.

the nineteen years totalled 2·4 million, the net population gain from migration was only 1·6 million. And among the departures the British element outweighed the rest. The classification is based on nationality, and it includes among the British also Maltese, Cypriots and some Asians, as well as naturalized persons of foreign birth. The table indicates that about one half of the migrant arrivals were British, as defined, and also that about one half of the total were assisted with free or reduced passages. The rate of masculinity was 119; however, because of a more even sex distribution in departures, it was 127 for net migration (125 for the foreign-born population in 1961, see Table 7). The male surplus is relatively high for migrants from Italy and eastern Europe, but it has been reduced since the 1950's. In general, foreign-born single female migrants have tended to marry foreign-born males, while some of the excess of the latter have married Australians.[7] A feature of post-war policy has been the sponsoring of young family groups as migrants, in particular from Britain, and, in general, migration has been heavily concentrated in the younger age groups.

Between 1945 and June 1965, 465,000 aliens (i.e. non-British) were naturalized in Australia, but in June 1965 there remained 400,000 unnaturalized aliens who were either unable (i.e. not yet eligible) or unwilling to take out naturalization papers.

Birthplace and Race

'Australia's immigration policy is directed towards maintaining a predominantly homogeneous population. It is hoped in this way to avoid difficult social and economic problems. It is regarded as fundamental to

TABLE 7. *Australian Population by Birthplace, June 1961*

	Males	Females	Persons	Per cent total
United Kingdom and Eire*	400,400	355,000	755,400	7·2
New Zealand, Canada, South Africa	30,700	30,100	60,800	0·6
Italy	134,600	93,700	228,300	2·2
Germany	57,600	51,700	109,300	1·0
Netherlands	56,800	45,300	102,100	1·0
Greece	43,600	33,700	77,300	0·7
Poland	36,400	23,600	60,000	0·6
Malta and Cyprus	27,700	20,200	47,900	0·5
USSR, Ukraine, Baltic States	32,200	27,500	59,700	0·6
Hungary, Yugoslavia, Bulgaria, Czechoslovakia, Rumania	63,000	36,700	99,700	0·9
Other European countries	39,100	26,100	65,200	0·6
America (excluding Canada)	7,500	5,500	13,000	0·1
Europe and America‡	929,600	749,100	1,678,700	16·0
Asia (excluding Cyprus)	42,200	28,400	70,600	0·7
Africa (excluding South Africa)	11,000	9,700	20,700	0·2
Pacific Islands (excluding New Zealand)	4,400	4,400	8,800	0·1
Born outside of Australia	987,200	791,600	1,778,800	17·0
Born in Australia	4,325,000	4,404,400	8,729,400	83·0
Total	5,312,200	5,196,000	10,508,200	100%

* England and Wales, 572,300; Scotland, 132,800; Ireland, 50,200.

‡ Includes New Zealand, Cyprus, South Africa.

this policy that people coming to Australia for permanent residence should be capable, both economically and socially, of ready integration into the community. Consequently, preference is given to persons of European origin. The Australian practice is not one of the total exclusion of persons of other than European origin. The immigration laws governing residence in Australia permit the Minister to exercise discretion.The policy so administered takes into account the qualifications of persons wishing to settle here and the merits of each case, including considerations of a humanitarian nature and broad national interest.'—*Yearbook of the Commonwealth of Australia* (Canberra, 1964), pp. 303–4.

Tables 7 and 8 reflect Australia's immigration policy as stated above. Out of 1,779,000 residents in 1961 who were not born in Australia, about one half were born in British countries (755,000 in the British Isles, 47,000 in New Zealand, 39,000 in Malta, 6,000 in Canada) and most of the others came from continental Europe, in particular from Italy, Germany, the Netherlands, Greece and Eastern European countries. The European predominance was maintained in the context of post-war migration which lifted the proportion of the population born outside of Australia from 10 per cent (744,200) in 1947 to 17 per cent in 1961.

Table 7 shows that in mid-1961 there were in Australia about 100,000

TABLE 8. *Australian Population of Non-European Origin: 1961*

	Non-European		European and non-European (One half each)		Total
	Persons	Males per 100 females	Persons	Males per 100 females	Persons
(1) Australian Aboriginal	40,100	not available	39,200	101	79,300
(2) Torres Strait Islander	5,000	97	200	120	5,200
Sub-total: (1) and (2)	45,100	not available	39,400	101	84,500
(3) Chinese	20,400	232	3,200	107	23,600
(4) Indian, Pakistani	3,500	494	500	122	4,000
(5) Syrian, Lebanese	3,200	130	200	100	3,400
(6) Japanese	1,700	123	1,000	109	2,700
(7) Malay, Indonesian	1,600	267	800	98	2,400
(8) Other Asian	3,100	180	1,000	93	4,100
(9) Other	3,100	129	1,700	100	4,800
Sub-total: (3) to (9)	36,600	211	8,400	103	45,000
out of which:					
Australian-born	10,300	111	6,900	102	17,200
Born outside of Australia	26,300	282	1,500	109	27,800
Total (1) to (9)	81,700		47,800		129,500

persons who were born in Asia, Africa or the Pacific Islands. This includes Europeans born in these parts but excludes Australian-born descendants of non-whites. Classification by 'race', which is broadly based on ethnic origin, in Table 8 indicates that in 1961 there were about 130,000 persons, or 1·2 per cent of the Australian population, who were wholly or partly (one half) of non-European origin. About two thirds of these were descendants of original inhabitants, that is, Australian aboriginals (about 40,100 full-blood and 39,200 half-caste) or Torres Strait islanders (5,200); the latter live mainly in Thursday Island and other parts of Queensland.

Apart from those there were 36,000 other non-Europeans and a further 8,400 with one European and one non-European parent. These two groups were mainly of Asian descent: about one half (23,600) of the total of 45,000 were Chinese, 4,000 were Indians or Pakistani, 3,400 Syrians or Lebanese and smaller numbers came from Japan, Malaya, etc. More than a quarter of the people of full non-European descent (other than aboriginals, etc.) were born in Australia. The other 26,300 included a large portion of temporary residents, i.e. 10,500 students (by 1964 their number had risen to 12,000) from Malaysia (5,300, apparently mostly of Chinese 'race'), Hong Kong (2,900) and the Pacific Islands plus a few hundred each from Indonesia, Thailand, and the Philippines (in 1964 also 200 from African countries); and there were several thousand others on temporary permits, such as businessmen (8,000 in 1964), as well as ships' crews in Australian ports on Census day, numbering perhaps several hundred. This leaves only a few thousand non-Europeans who were admitted for permanent residence. In March 1966 the regulations governing admittance of non-Europeans were eased to allow the entry of 'well-qualified people . . . considered on the basis of their suitability as settlers, their ability to integrate readily, and their possession of qualifications which are in fact positively useful to Australia'. At the same time it was made easier for non-European migrants admitted into Australia to qualify for permanent residence and naturalization and to bring their immediate families to Australia, but these concessions do not apply to Asian students, now numbering 12,000, who are admitted for limited periods only. A minor, rather than a major rise in the admission of Asians into Australia is expected to follow these reforms which in time will also lead to a better balance of males and females; in 1961 there had been twice as many male as female Asians in Australia.

Religion

Statement of religion is not obligatory for the Australian Census and in 1961 about one tenth of the population did not answer the relevant question. Of those who did, 99 per cent professed to be Christians; this included 3·7 million or 39 per cent Anglican (Church of England in Australia), 2·6 million or 28 per cent Catholics, 1·1 million or 12 per cent Methodists, 1 million or 10 per cent Presbyterians and 900,000 members of other Christian denominations. Adherents to non-Christian faiths consisted of 59,000 Jews and 9,000 'others'.

Thus Australia professes to be an overwhelmingly Christian country although, as in Europe and America, religion has been a waning influence in the social and cultural development of the country. The Church of England, to which 35 per cent of the population claim adherence, is not now formally dependent on the Mother Church but it furnishes a strong spiritual link with England, and the Australian branch is the largest outside of England. However, in proportion to other faiths, it has lost some ground since the War, due mainly to the partial shift in immigration from Britain to Central Europe which has brought in large numbers of Catholics, Greek Orthodox and Lutherans. This relative loss also applies to the major Nonconformist faiths of British origin (Methodist, Presbyterian, Congregational, Baptist); between 1947 and 1961 the number of adherents to these and the Anglican faiths rose from 4·7 million to 6 million but fell as a proportion of total population from 62 to 57 per cent.

Between 1947 and 1961 the number of Catholics in Australia rose by a million, from 21 to 25 per cent of the population, due to the inflow of migrants from Italy, Poland, the Netherlands and Germany and also to the relatively high marriage fertility of this group. Out of the 704,000 Christians in Australia in 1961 who were born in continental Europe, two thirds were Catholics; or, to put it another way, 23 per cent of all Catholics in Australia were immigrants as against a rate of 15 per cent for all other denominations (including 'unstated'). There is some parallel in the influx of Irish Catholics which played a major part in Australia's early history; actually, the present proportion of Catholics in New South Wales (26 per cent) remains less than it was 110 years ago (30 per cent). The present Catholic congregation in Australia is nearly as large as that in Eire. It is larger than in any African or Asian country, excepting India, and as a proportion of total population it is about twice as high as in the United Kingdom. Nor do the numbers fully measure the importance of this group because it has a stronger hold over its adherents than the major Protestant denominations. This is evident in its separate education system, embracing one fifth of all Australian schoolchildren, and in the bias its support has given to politics of the moderate left and centre in particular in New South Wales and Queensland where its position is relatively strong.

Work Force

The relatively low pre-war birth rates and the extension of education tended to reduce the proportion of the population available for jobs in the post-war period, though this was largely compensated by immigration and also by the greater participation of women in the work force. It is evident that from now on the number of adolescents available for work will be rising, both in absolute numbers and relative to the population, and that this will require a high economic growth rate to provide sufficient job opportunities.[8] During most of the post-war period, as at present, full employment has prevailed in Australia, and some minor recessions only briefly raised the number of job seekers to above 100,000 or a maximum of 3 per cent of the work force.

The progress of Australia's industrial development is reflected in the shift from primary to secondary and tertiary industries. The proportion of the work force in the primary group (rural and mining) has declined from about one third at the turn of the century and a quarter in the 1920's and 1930's to 18 per cent in 1947 and 12 per cent in 1961. Not only has there been a relative decline but the actual number in this group, which had tended to be static at 560,000 between 1947 and 1954 fell to 513,000 in 1961. Mechanization has reduced manpower requirements on the land and in the mine, or shifted it to some extent to the manufacture and maintenance of equipment and to its operation by contract workers. While becoming less labour intensive, the output of the primary industries has continued to expand, as indicated by an increase of 58 per cent in the quantum index for all farm production for the fifteen years ended 1963–64 and by the rise of 81 per cent in black coal output in this period and substantial rises also in the production of major base metals (iron, lead, zinc, copper).

However, the rural and mining expansion cannot compare with the faster growth in manufacturing which raised its work force by one third and more than doubled overall output in the fifteen years, led by rises of some 300 per cent in steel production, 250 per cent in electricity generation and 220 per cent in cement output. Manufacturing now employs some 1·14 million people or 30 per cent of the work force (1961), as against only 20 per cent in 1933. Within manufacturing the post-war period has seen major expansion in iron and steel, motor and other engineering works, chemicals, plastics, paper and printing industries. Power generation and distribution, water supply, and building and construction are also growing rapidly to keep pace with demand from the rising population and industries.

It has been estimated[9] that for every additional 100 persons in Australian factories there is a complementary requirement of about eighty in service industries, but the latter have expanded even faster than that, in particular in the categories of commerce, finance, and community, business and professional services, and this reflects the increasing sophistication of the Australian economy. Tertiary industries as a whole (i.e. industries not classified to the primary and secondary groups) now employ about one half of the total work force.

Using a classification by occupation, 55 per cent of the work force in 1961 were in what might be termed manual classes (farmers, miners, transport workers, craftsmen, process workers, labourers); 8 per cent were professional or technical workers (e.g. 100,000 teachers, 12,000 medical practitioners) and most of the balance were also in 'white-collar' occupations (e.g. clerks, salesmen). As regards occupational status, there has been a post-war decline of employers and the self-employed relative to employees, due largely to the reduced importance of farming and the general trend towards larger business units in trade and industry. About one quarter of the wage and salary earners are employed by governmental authorities, which include the postal, railway and urban transport services as well as government schools, hospitals and administrative services. Civilian employment in these government services now totals about 900,000, and the defence forces comprised approximately 50,000 in 1964.

Because of the relatively high labour intensity of the service industries the work force distribution between primary, secondary and tertiary industries of 12, 38 and 50 per cent respectively in 1961 does not accurately measure their contribution to the Gross National Product. This totalled £7,266 million in 1960–61 and was distributed over these three groups in proportion of 15, 40 and 45 per cent respectively; or, if rental value of dwellings is excluded, in the proportions of 15, 42 and 43 per cent respectively.

The trend towards a relative fall in the agricultural work force has been worldwide; and the present Australian proportion of 11 per cent is similar to that applying in Canada, Belgium, Holland or Switzerland, although well above the rates of 7 per cent applying in the United States or 5 per cent in Britain. However, the relatively minor place of agriculture in Australian employment is shown when this rate of 11 per cent is compared with the 33 per cent for Japan (now falling rapidly), approximately 40 per cent for the Eastern European countries, or 50 to 75 per cent for many parts of South America, Africa, and Asia (e.g. India 70 per cent). The distribution of the Australian work force between the secondary and tertiary industries stands in the proportion of 45:55, which is about the same as in Japan; in the United States and Canada this ratio is 40:60.

The increasing participation of women has been a feature in the development of the Australian work force. In 1961 they made up one quarter of the total, as against 22 per cent in 1947. The rise has been most significant for married women, in particular in the age groups 35–55, that is after the main family formation period: in 1961, four out of every ten women workers were married, as against two out of ten in

TABLE 9. *Population and Living Standards*

	Year	AUSTRALASIA Australia	New Zealand	AMERICA United States	Colombia	EUROPE United Kingdom	Switzerland	Greece	AFRICA United Arab Republic	ASIA Japan	Thailand	India
Population (millions)	(1965)	11·4	2·6	194·6	17·8	54·5	6·0	8·5	29·0	98·0	30·6	472·0
Birth rate (crude), per 1,000 of population	(1964)	20·6	24·1	21·0	(44)	18·8	19·2	20·8a	(42)	17·7	(35)	(38)
Death rate (crude), per 1,000 of population	(1963)	9·0	8·8	9·4	(12)	11·3	9·4	9·4a	(15)	6·9	(8)	(13)
Fertility rate per 1,000 females aged 10–49	(1963)	80	100	81	125	68	64	76a	—	51	121	137
Life expectation at birth for males—No. of years	(1950/62)	67	68	67	(44)	68	69	67	52	67	(49)	42
Gross domestic product $ per head (estimated) parity)	(1963)	1,680	1,924	2,790	189	1,497	1,951	412	156	628	112	74
Gross domestic product % rise p.a. per head †	(1954/60)	1·6	1·9	1·2	2·0	2·1	2·9	5·3	(2·1)	9·1	1·4	1·4
Food supply:												
Calories per day, per head	(1962/63)	3,140	3,510	3,090	2,070	3,290	3,170	2,910	2,890	2,280	2,000b	2,000
Protein, grams per day, per head	(1962/63)	90	112	91	46	89	88	94	86	70	42b	51

Production:												
Electricity, 000 kWh per head	(1964)	3,050	3,700	5,600	250	3,300	3,900	435	(175)	1,850	28	70
Cement, tons (metric) per 1,000 of population	(1964)	325	300	335	110	310	735	310	90	340	36	21
Domestic use: Steel, tons (metric) per 1,000 of population	(1963)	389	201	540	31	368	355	78	16	258	13	16
Motor vehicles in use, No. per 1,000 of population	(1963)	307	294	430	14	167	144	13	4	43	5	1
Telephones in use, No. per head	(1963)	234	355	447	25	177	347	49	9	88	2	1
Letters posted per year, No. per head	(1963)	197	207	361	(7)	204	305	28	11	88	2	10
Newspapers sold per year, copies per 1,000 of population	(1963)	375	400	301	56	490	365	(121)	17	420	(11)	1
Doctors, inhabitants per physician	(1962)	880	690	760	2,400	960	750	790	2,600	900	10,000	6,000
University students, No. per 10,000 of population	(1962)	101	140	203	49	81	58	35	62	91	23	27
Dwellings: average No. of persons per room	(1962)	0·7	0·7	0·7	(1·9)	0·7	0·7	1·5	1·6	1·4	2·2b	2·6

* In a few cases the previous year was substituted. Bracketed figures refer to more remote periods. † Real terms. (a) Yugoslavia, (b) Ceylon.

Sources: United Nations, *Monthly Bulletin of Statistics* (January 1966), *Statistical Yearbook* (1964), *Yearbook of National Accounts Statistics* (1964), *Demographic Yearbook* (1964), *Compendium of Social Statistics* (1963).

1947, and one out of ten in 1933. Factors in the increasing employment of women include the rise in job opportunities, in particular in the tertiary industries where three quarters of them work, the shortening of working hours, the greater use of labour-saving devices in the home, the desire to lift the living standard of the family, and the trends towards earlier marriage and earlier completion of families. There has also been a change in social attitudes towards working women, and the trend has been strengthened by the migrants who have a greater rate of female work force participation than the Australian-born population. The present Australian ratio of one quarter for the female portion of the work force remains still well below the ratio of one third that applies in India, the United States, the United Kingdom and some Western European countries or ratios of between 40 per cent to 50 per cent for Japan and Eastern Europe. Much lower ratios (10–20 per cent) apply in many Muslim and Latin American countries.

III

AUSTRALIA AND THE WORLD

Summing up, we find that Australia's population is about 11 million or about the same as that of Ceylon, Taiwan, the Netherlands or Hungary. By European or Japanese standards it is a young and fertile population, and immigration adds stimulus to growth. Much of Australia's population is concentrated on the coast, as the vast, arid inland and the north will support only light settlement. In overall density of population, Australia ranks very low in the world.

Ethnically Australia has a European population in which the aboriginals and other non-white groups form only tiny minorities. British stock predominates, and it determines political, social and cultural attitudes as much as it does in New Zealand, and more so than in North America which has moved further away from the colonial past. People born in continental Europe now make up one tenth of the Australian population, but selection and assimilation policies are aimed at absorbing them, or their children, into the British-Australian pattern. However, this pattern is being gradually modified by political and economic associations with the United States and south-east Asia. Economically, Australia benefits from the interaction of population growth, stability, and capital inflow from Europe and America. A sound base of agricultural and mining resources, of skilled manpower and adequate investment funds, supports an industry structure of increasing sophistication.

A comparison of Australia with some of the wealthier and poorer countries shows that levels of consumption and general living standards in Australia and New Zealand are very close to those in the United Kingdom and the United States. In many respects Japan is beginning to rival Australia, while both are far ahead of most of the other independent countries of Asia, Africa, Latin America or Southern and Eastern Europe.[10]

NOTES

1. For details see: John Andrews, *Australia's Resources and Their Utilisation* (Sydney, University of Sydney, 1964). Another estimate by Professor T. Griffith Taylor in *Australia, A Study of Warm Environments and Their Effect on British Settlement* (London, Methuen, 1959) regards 42 per cent of the continent as arid, of which about one half is fair pastoral country except during droughts; 34 per cent good pastoral country under 'normal' conditions; 21 per cent fair temperate-climate farming country suitable for close settlement but a quarter receiving less than 20 inches of rain; and 3 per cent tropical with uniform rainfall and suitable for agricultural development.
2. Based on Sir Samuel Wadham, R. Kent Wilson and Joyce Wood, *Land Utilization in Australia* (Melbourne, Melbourne University Press, 1964), p. 5.
3. Henry Carter in *Barrington Prologue* (1796); see *Australian Encyclopaedia*, ed. A. H. Chisholm (Sydney, Angus and Robertson, 1958).
4. Russel Ward, *The Australian Legend* (Melbourne, Oxford University Press, 1958), p. 19
5. School participation rates and university enrolments are as follows:

		Males		Females	
		1954	1964	1954	1964
School population	Total	823,000	1,225,000	782,000	1,142,000
Per cent total	aged 14	81%	94%	79%	94%
population:	aged 15	45%	69%	41%	62%
	aged 16	21%	42%	18%	34%
University	Full-time	15,000	32,000	4,000	12,000
enrolments:	Part-time	8,000	25,000	3,000	7,000

6. W. D. Borrie and Geraldine Spencer, *Australia's Population Structure and Growth* (Melbourne, Committee for Economic Development, 1964), p. 49, points to the post-war trend of increasing average size of completed families as being due to fewer one- and two-child families, more three-child and, to some extent, more four-child families, but fewer families with five or more children.
7. C. A. Price and J. Zubrzycki, 'Immigration Marriage Patterns in Australia', *Population Studies*, Vol. 16, No. 2, November 1962. R. V. Horn, 'Marriages of Migrants in Australia', *Economic Record*, Vol. 38, No. 84, December 1962.
8. W. D. Borrie, see reference (6) above, estimates, with certain stated assumptions, that work force may rise at the rate of 2·5 per cent per annum in the 1961–76 period, as compared with 2·2 per cent in 1947–61.
9. Burgess Cameron, 'The Anatomy of High Employment', *Economic Record*, Vol. 36, No. 76, December 1960.
10. A thorough comparative study of production and trade in many countries has been published recently by A. Maizels, *Industrial Growth and World Trade* (London, Cambridge University Press, 1963).

BIBLIOGRAPHY

Andrews, J., *Australia's Resources and their Utilisation* (Sydney, University of Sydney, 1964).

Atlas of Australian Resources (Canberra, Department of National Development, 1953–61).

Borrie, W. D., *Population Trends and Policies* (Sydney, Australasian Publishing Co., 1948).

and G. Spencer, *Australia's Population Sturcture and Growth* (Melbourne, Committee for Economic Development of Australia, 1964).

Census of Australia, 1961 (and for earlier years).

Chisholm, A. H. (ed.), *Australian Encyclopaedia* (Sydney, Angus and Robertson, 1958).

Crawford, R. M., *Ourselves and the Pacific* (Melbourne, Melbourne University Press, 1961).

Australia (London, Hutchinsons University Library, 1952).

Crisp, L. F., *The Parliamentary Government of the Commonwealth of Australia* (London, Longmans, 1961).

Demography Bulletin, Commonwealth Bureau of Census and Statistics, Canberra.

Elkin, A. P., *The Australian Aboriginals: How to Understand Them* (Sydney, Angus and Robertson, 1961).

Fitzpatrick, B., *The Australian People—1788–1945* (Melbourne, Melbourne University Press, 1964).

Grattan, C. Hartley (ed.), *Australia* (Berkeley, University of California Press, 1947).

Greenwood, G. (ed.), *Australia: a social and political history* (Sydney, Angus and Robertson, 1960).

Hancock, K., *Australia* (Brisbane, Australian University Paperbacks, 1961).

Harper, N. D. and D. Sissons, *Australia and the United Nations* (New York, Manhattan Publishing Company, 1959).

Laserson, C. F., *The Face of Australia* (Sydney, Angus and Robertson, 1964).

Miller, J. D. B., *Australian Government and Politics* (London, Duckworth, 1959).

Nankervis, F. T., *Descriptive Economics* (Melbourne, Longmans, 1961).

Sawer, G., *Australian Government To-day* (Melbourne, Melbourne University Press, 1961).

Shann, E. O. G., *An Economic History of Australia* (Melbourne, Georgian House, 1948).

Shaw, A. G. L., *Economic Development of Australia* (Melbourne, Longmans, 1960).

The Story of Australia (London, Faber, 1961).

Taylor, T. G., *Australia: a study of warm environments and their effect on British settlement* (London, Methuen, 1959).

Wadham, S. H., Wilson R. Kent, and J. Wood, *Land Utilization in Australia* (Melbourne, Melbourne University Press, 1957).

Ward, R. B., *The Australian Legend* (Melbourne, Oxford University Press, 1960).

Year Book of the Commonwealth of Australia (Canberra, 1965).

Zubrzycki, J., *Immigrants in Australia* (Melbourne, Melbourne University Press, 1960).

CHAPTER 10

ASIAN MIGRATION—AN AUSTRALIAN FAILURE?

BY ANTHONY CLUNIES ROSS

HAVE STATES THE RIGHT to limit immigration at their discretion? Legally they have this right, but have they morally? And if there are moral limits to their freedom to do as they like in this matter, what are those limits, and how do they apply to Australia's case? This essay will provide material directed to the answering of these questions.

The Australian immigration policy is not unique as its overseas critics often imply. Australia is peculiar mainly in this: that seventy or more years ago its immigration policy was exalted into an ideology, so that attempts at rational thought and argument on the subject have been bedevilled to this day. Different generations might provide different submissions in its defence, but 'White Australia' continued for many years to be an integral part of the idea of nationhood. When a policy has become an ideology, the practice of it may be altered to some extent, but canny politicians may feel obliged to insist that the alterations are matters of detail and that the fabric remains as before. Hence Australian statesmen and administrators who have had to give excuses for the policy in recent years have behaved rather like dogs with experimental neuroses who turn frenzied somersaults as a result of trying to fulfil two mutually contradictory requirements. On the one hand, official sources will tell you that they know of no such thing as a 'White Australian Policy', and indeed the policy is no longer so referred to in official statements. On the other hand, no Minister for Immigration has yet claimed that the 'established policy' is at an end, notwithstanding recent important moves towards liberalization.

Despite this confusion, two assertions seem incontrovertible. First, the number of non-Europeans admitted to permanent residence in Australia has so far been very small. Secondly, the motives which originally inspired the policy were at least in part racialist; that is to say, they depended on a belief in 'white' superiority and a fear of racial admixture. These two assertions must be clearly distinguished. The former is a statement of how things are at the moment; the latter, of how they were at the beginning of the century. It is, however, true that, though public sentiment has to a large extent lost its racialist content, the policy as administered today has features which can only be explained by its racialist history.

The present writer believes that there are good reasons why, in the near future, non-European immigrants should enter in numbers which are small in relation to the total population. On the other hand, he believes that entry might well be less restrictive than it has been hitherto, and that racialist relics in its regulation should be completely eradicated.

In admitting only very small numbers of non-Europeans to permanent residence, Australia resembles the United States, Canada and New Zealand. The policies of these countries have attracted less opprobrium than Australia's, probably because they have not been erected into great national principles, because Canada and the United States have never aimed at total exclusion of any ethnic group, and because Canada, particularly, has been prepared in recent years to adjust its policy in the interests of humanity and international good manners. But North America and New Zealand would seem on the face of it as eligible as Australia to be candidates for alleviating the population problems of Asia, and all four nations have apparently declined the honour.

Should they do otherwise? Can they feed the hungry by opening their doors? This question will be discussed as it bears on Australia, but most of the same considerations apply to the other prosperous areas of white settlement.

How Empty is Australia?

Australia is not as wastefully empty as it appears on the map. Dr Horn has given two estimates of its capacity for human settlement. About 37·6 per cent of the area of the Commonwealth has less than ten inches of annual rainfall and is therefore drier than any part of Japan, China (south of a line from Tientsin to Chengtu), Korea, south-east Asia (apart perhaps from a minute area in the rain-shadow of the Chiri Hills), or the Indian subcontinent east of a line from Ahmedabad to Amritsar. In most of the dry and moderately dry parts of Australia the rainfall is erratic. Furthermore there are none of the immensely fertile pockets in which most of the population of Asia lives: no Gangetic Plain or Mekong Delta; no North China Plain, Yangtse Valley or Szechuan; nothing comparable to the Coromandel Coast or the volcanic areas of Java and Bali. Much of Australia is empty as much of Tibet is empty, or the Mindanao and Kalimantan highlands, or the Rajasthan desert. Even with the application of such technical developments as can now be foreseen, much of the land could not support agriculture or more than the sparsest pastoral use. Desert Australia has next to no permanent rivers, so that irrigation demands either the tapping of the limited water supply available from bores, or the turning westward of east-coast streams at fantastic expense before dams and irrigation channels can usefully be built. Much, too, of the wettest parts of the continent and of Tasmania is either barren mountain or rainfall-jungle.[1]

All this is not to say that Australia is incapable of closer settlement. The area under wheat has shown considerable responsiveness over five-to-ten-year periods to sustained price-changes and has been rising steadily since 1956. The total crop area is now at roughly double its size of 1943–4. Undoubtedly a larger urban market or more favourable overseas prices would give us opportunities of making a more intensive yet profitable use of some areas of what is now grazing land by growing vegetables, fruit and grain. Butter, cheese and sugar might in those circumstances change from highly protected to free-market products. With increasing prices, more and more irrigation would presumably become worthwhile. The small wheat-sheep farmers and orchardists might find it easier to attract suitable labour and therefore to increase the area they cultivated. The purchase for grain-farming of blocks of pastoral land would become a more secure investment. Tropical agriculture—rice, peanuts and the now subsidized cotton—is also capable of extension. There is little doubt that, if purchasing power in the food-deficit countries increased at a rate sufficiently faster than that of the increase in their own food output, then the quantity of agricultural produce from Australia, North America and New Zealand would also increase through the application of more labour or capital even independently of technical advances. The same could happen if the total population of Australia itself increased sufficiently. All this might well occur without disturbing high Australian wages and living standards and without creating artificially a group of rural labourers with depressed wages.

Australian farm output has not by any means been stagnant, though over the last decade its increase has been accompanied by technical improvements that have reduced the farm work force. The forecast index for the quantity of Australian farm production in 1964–5 is very nearly double the average for the years 1941–2 to 1946–7 and is about 45 per cent higher than the average for the years 1952–3 to 1956–7. At the same time, according to census returns, the farm work force fell by about 7 per cent from 1954 to 1961.[2]

Three Ways of Developing Australia as Supplier

Apart from the continual development and extension of techniques that are profitable under present economic conditions, there are three ways in which Australian land might be further developed to provide food for some of the underfed people in Asia.

One is simply to increase the general purchasing power of the people concerned, whether by gifts from abroad for current consumer use, or by any of the many forms of investment that would raise the industrial or agrarian productivity of the Asian populations.

A second way is to allow unlimited Asian immigration into Australia, or even to assist such immigration financially, and to allow the immigrants to enter freely into Australian economic life.

A third is to admit or assist selected impoverished people under certain occupational restrictions. We might bring in low-wage labourers from abroad and confine them to specific pursuits in certain parts of the country. (This was done in the Queensland sugar industry at the end of the nineteenth century by private contract with indentured Pacific Islanders. It was also done by the Australian Government after the Second World War with many assisted European migrants, who were obliged to work as directed for the first two years of their stay.) Or we might bring in families prepared to grow food for their own use and very little else, and we might endow them with small plots of land, expecting them to work these more intensively, with less expectation of profit, and with less dependence on the market, than would have been the case with the alternative Australian owners. We could, in other words, introduce impoverished peasants as subsistence farmers. Again it would be necessary to confine them by law to farming if we wanted them to stick at it. The attraction of much higher earnings to be obtained as urban employees would otherwise almost certainly divert large numbers to the cities.

The first of these three paths, that of aid in goods and services, is the only one by which Australia is likely to contribute significantly to the economic progress of Asian peoples.

One argument in favour of the 'aid in goods' solution is that it is easier to transfer capital than to transfer the corresponding amount of labour. ('Capital' means, in the last analysis, goods to work with, or goods that can be used to meet the consumer needs of workers before their final product becomes available.) If it is to be done with humanity, transferring labour means shipping not only the labourer but also his wife—or someone likely to be willing to be his wife—and his children.

The business of supporting the rising populations of low-income countries is essentially a matter of providing them, directly or indirectly, with goods they can work with, and skills with which to use the goods. So long as there are parts of the world capable of more intensive agricultural development, increasing the food supply of the impoverished populations does not necessarily entail providing them with more land or even increasing their own food output. It is enough that they should develop their industrial sectors so that they are able to make the extra goods with which to pay for food produced overseas and for storing and shipping it. If that part of their purchasing power which they spend on food tends to increase faster than the food supply available to them, world food prices will tend to rise—and this in turn will lead to a greater output of food.

The assertion that it is easier to transfer capital than to transfer the corresponding quantity of labour may be correct in some cases, but it is not obviously true and it does not tell the whole story. A sounder argument derives from the presumption that low-income countries, with their smaller wages and higher ratios of labour to capital, can provide extra employment more cheaply than can those with higher incomes. If the criterion of success in alleviating poverty is the number of new jobs created that are remunerative by local standards, we might reasonably compare the costs of providing such jobs in an 'over-populated' country such as India with the costs of providing them in Australia. In India (or Pakistan or Indonesia or the Philippines) the scope for expansion of remunerative employment is chiefly in manufacturing, mining, transport and communication, since rural industry is already over-supplied with labour and capital investment in agriculture is likely to diminish rather than increase the demand for workers. In Australia too, unless extraordinary measures are taken, the urban sector will continue to provide most of the growth in employment. Therefore it is realistic to assume in each case a considerable capital cost in providing the employment.

One very rough limiting estimate (explained in a footnote)[3] suggests that it would take on average no more than £A1,900 (Rs. 20,000; $4,300) to use Australian supplies in order to allow for the creation of an extra job in India in the context of current planning in that country; but that it would take at least £A3,300 (Rs. 35,000; $7,400) on average to transport a family of four from Bombay to Melbourne and to provide a job for the breadwinner of the family at roughly Australian levels of productivity. The figures are little more than guesses, but the comparison is fairly certain to be of this order, whether it is India or some other low-income country of emigration that is taken as the instance. The family that migrates will certainly be better off materially in Australia than if the breadwinner had filled the extra job in the emigrant country; but closely associated with this is the fact that work will on average be cheaper to create in the low-income country and that the same outlay is therefore likely to provide a larger number of remunerative jobs there than in Australia. If the number of such jobs provided is taken as the measure of success, as on humane grounds it may well be, the aid-in-goods policy is more efficient than the policy of aid through migration.

Thus the transferring of families would appear to be a socially wasteful way of linking the capital goods with the work force. If Australia is concerned to assist in alleviating India's low living standards, she will do this most economically, not by subsidizing Indian migrants to come to Australia, but by providing tied grants which the Indian government would be free to devote to the import of expert services; or to the import of capital goods; or to the so-called 'maintenance' imports of industrial materials and components; or even to imports of consumer goods in order to allow, without inflation, for the employment of larger numbers of people in productive and remunerative work.

It is worth adding that emigration tends to benefit the emigrants and their immediate relations exclusively, whereas development expenditure involving the same outlay within the low-income country tends rather to spread its advantages and also to foster the extra benefits described as external economies of growth. If there really were a choice between on the one hand immense emigration without developmental expenditure, and on the other hand developmental expenditure at home providing *even the same number* of people with gainful employment as the emigration, there is little doubt that the government of a low-income country like India would choose the latter. The economic task of India could not be forgotten simply because there were relatively rich Indians who had settled abroad.

It is wrong, furthermore, to think that large-scale migration to Australia could in any sense 'solve' the population problems of Asia or of any of the large Asian countries. The annual population increase of the ECAFE area is about 35 million. When we look at the great sea migrations of the last hundred or so years, we find their rates quite trivial by comparison. Australia is one of the leading immigrant recipients today, and yet the average annual net immigration for the years 1960 to 1964 was only 77,000. It was only in 1882, in 1921 and at the peak of her immigrant boom in 1903–14, that the United States took in more than 750,000 per year, and only in six of those years did the number exceed a million.[4] The total number of *arrivals* in Australia in 1964 was 452,400, the highest annual figure until that date. Clearly shipping space alone would set a relevant limit to the number that could be shifted in any period of time. The number of Indians who went abroad in the 104 years between 1834 and 1937 is estimated by Kingsley Davis to have been around 30 million, and four fifths of this number were ultimately to return.[5] The number of persons of Chinese descent in south-east Asia is estimated to be around fourteen million in 1965.[6] A migration of a million people *a year* is immense, even by the standards of these notable movements.

If we supposed that Australia might receive an extra million permanent settlers a year from Asia, we should be imagining something truly extraordinary; for this would raise the rate of migration to Australia more than tenfold, and the total number of arrivals in Australia more than threefold. It would be extraordinary as a sheer feat of uprooting people and moving them by sea, and the effect on Australian society would be immense. The immigrants would somehow have to be accommodated. To imagine that they would share the existing housing is to imagine an invasion, not a peaceful migration, and it is no good thinking that, because the migrants would be poor, they would be able to sleep in the streets or in shanties on unoccupied ground. Urban Australia would reject the latter solution, for health reasons if for no other.

Limitations of Asian Immigration

If conservatively we were to assume that a quarter of the migrants would aspire to enter the Australian work force, this would initially mean raising, to well over three times its present value, the rate of net job creation if old and new Australians were to be gainfully occupied. Unless a substitute for real capital were to be secured by turning huge numbers of families loose as subsistence peasants on unimproved small plots of land, the provision of work for the immigrants would require considerable extra real investment. To make a closely related point, the maintenance of current levels of real income per head for the people already in Australia would, in these circumstances, demand an immense increase in additions to real capital, financed by extra taxes or private saving at home or else from overseas. If we wanted to create an extra £A250 of income a year for each of the immigrants (well under half the current national income per head), and were to finance it entirely from home resources, and if the value ratio between the extra capital and the extra real income it made possible were three to one, then we should need an extra £750 million reduction in annual consumption, quite apart from the cost of transporting the immigrants. This would mean that we should have to be taxed or cajoled to a point at which we would reduce our consumer spending by at least an eighth. Living standards would certainly run lower *than they would have done without the extra migration*. Unless the average productivity of natural and artificial capital assets were simultaneously to rise in quite extraordinary measure (an unlikely event at a time when the work force was being swollen by poor and presumably largely unskilled immigrants), living standards would also be lower than *before the migration programme had begun*.

These economic difficulties no doubt seem trifling beside those currently faced by Pakistan or India. It is true that the average level of consumption in Australia, even under the constraints induced by these changes, would still be princely by the standards of most Asian countries, and with careful organization and current sacrifices might continue to be so as each million of the new migrants rolled in. But Australians, like any other people, will judge their sacrifices not by the norms of countries which most of them have never seen, but by what they are used to themselves. Even admitting that Australians *should* be prepared to make such sacrifices, one has the greatest difficulty in imagining their willingly doing so. Furthermore the sacrifices would be likely to bear specially hard on particular groups. The maintenance of full employment under these conditions would be a feat of organization of a type to which Australian governments in peacetime are unaccustomed, and, without drastic corrective measures, the flood of poor immigrants would be likely to make a section of relatively rich Australians, with valuable assets or skills, richer, while the majority who lacked these things would grow poorer.

Moreover, let it be repeated that this hypothetical million Asian immigrants a year, so fantastically high for an alien influx to a nation of only eleven millions, would make only marginal differences to Asian population pressure. The million would be no more than a tenth of the natural increase of the Indian population alone within the same period. The £A75 a head (£A300 for a family of four) which we have imagined (see footnote 2) as required for transport, plus a cost equivalent to the much greater economic sacrifices incurred by Australians in accommodating the immigrants, would almost certainly be better used in providing extra capital goods, training and extension work in the underdeveloped countries. Moreover, the objects of this expenditure could include the control of conception. For a million migrants transport alone would probably cost £A75 million. Where a relatively cheap method such as vasectomy is available to reduce conceptions by perhaps two or three per operation, it is almost certain that an annual expenditure of this amount over ten years on the reduction of conception would induce a much larger retardation of population growth than an equal investment in emigration. This would be far more each year than was allocated to family planning *over the whole period* of the Indian Third Five-Year Plan. Likewise, any additional sacrifices such as a potential recipient country would have to be prepared to make in order to employ and accommodate the migrants should rather take the form of aid, thus contributing more directly and effectively to raising the living standards of the population remaining in the potential emigrant country.

The figure of £A750 million per year as the extent of the sacrifice available from Australia is, no doubt, fantastic, as has been admitted earlier. But it is still only 12–15 per cent of Australian personal consumption expenditure. Less remote from reality would be a sacrifice of 5 per cent of Australian personal consumption expenditure for the use of low-income countries, and this would amount to about £A275 million ($616 million; Rs. 2,933 million); a sum which, distributed from Australia between any two or three of the largest Asian countries that are developing to the limit of their foreign exchange resources, would serve as useful assistance, even if it took the form of tied grants. A sum as large as this may also be remote from political possibility at the moment, but, if there is to be agitation for Australian help, this is the appropriate form in which to ask for it. And perhaps an extra annual contribution of, say, £A100 million in aid (which, with the existing annual £A50–60 million, would raise total Australian aid to low-income areas to about 1·75 per cent of current Australian net national income) is a reasonable goal.

The narrowly economic difficulties of large-scale Asian migration to Australia pale before the social tensions that they are likely to bring with them. Suppose that the unskilled Australian workman in every city notices a sudden influx of people physically and culturally different from himself. Along with this phenomenon he experiences, at best, a revival of controls and restraints on enjoyment that are uncomfortably reminiscent of wartime, and, at worst, a widespread loss of jobs, probably coupled with rising prices and in particular with acute shortage and dearness of housing. Neither outcome is likely to favour inter-racial harmony. It is worth comparing our suggested million annual intake with the numbers of West Indians that had been entering Britain before their entry was restricted. The peak years 1961 and 1962 taken together saw a net intake of 116,000 West Indians and 78,000 'other Commonwealth Citizens' to mix with a settled population four to five times the size of Australia's, while before the time of the Nottingham and West London disturbances of 1958 less than 200,000 West Indians altogether had settled in the United Kingdom.[7] Obviously rates of intake very much smaller than our imaginary annual million can cause inter-racial trouble in certain circumstances. With as great a flow of immigrants as we have discussed, it would be very hard not to give the impression that one ethnic group was being impoverished by the presence of the other.

This impression would be avoided if the immigrants were bound either to tropical agriculture as labourers or to smallholdings as near-subsistence peasants. These measures have a superficial attractiveness on purely economic grounds, and the writer has heard them proposed by non-Europeans. The experiment of small peasant settlement could in principle establish a partly separate economy at a lower standard of living, in incomplete communication with the larger Australian economy. The number of rural workers displaced by a very wide expropriation of land suitable for this purpose would still be only a small part of the work force, and, with some increase in the demand for the products of Australian secondary industry, there should be no particular difficulty in maintaining full employment. Export earnings would probably fall because more land would be devoted to producing for domestic consumption, and devaluations or heavy import restraint would probably be necessary to deal with international payments; but the Australian industrial worker might well be compensated for the corresponding price rises by an improvement in his bargaining position that would spring from the new, albeit poor, consumers who were added to the domestic market. On the other hand, there might well be difficulties, even with the most ruthless expropriation policy, in finding enough watered, arable land to sustain an annual inflow of a million rural settlers.

Yet speculation on these points is idle. Australian social ideals and values would present overwhelming obstacles to the whole scheme. One of the less regrettable strains in support for the 'White Australia Policy' was egalitarianism, the aversion to a helot-state of first and second class citizens. Social equality is part of the national legend, and conditions have brought it much closer to reality than in many of the more traditional societies of Europe and Asia. Binding immigrants to the land or to certain industries for life would be repugnant, and in Australian conditions it would soon become unenforceable. Restricting foreigners to one occupation is practised on a small scale with pearl-diving in the north-west of Australia, but public feeling as shown by the reaction to the proposed deportation of two Malay divers in 1961, is likely to be openly hostile to the enforcement of such a restriction. Furthermore, world opinion would almost certainly condemn it, especially if there were serious opposition within Australia. The Universal Declaration of Human Rights declares that everyone has the right 'to freedom of movement and residence within the borders of each state (Article 13(1)), 'to free choice of employment' (Article 23(1)), 'to equal pay for equal work' (Article 23(2)). Apartheid is not acceptable in Australia or in the world at large.

Thus there are various arguments, of differing moral status, for keeping the flow of Asian migrants to Australia well below the hypothetical million a year. That admitting such large numbers of migrants from any country would drastically lower the Australian standard of living may be an argument of narrow self-interest. That this would be an uneconomical way of using whatever sacrifices Australians are prepared to make for the benefit of low-income populations is an argument of a more respectable kind. That admitting people who are aliens in culture and appearance, under conditions of acute economic strain, is likely to rouse racial opposition and ill-feeling is a very telling argument indeed, which neither nationalist nor internationalist is entitled to neglect.

But why not set the sights rather lower? Why not divide Australia's annual intake of migrants between Europeans and Asians and take 50,000 of each? The country has shown that it can sustain an annual net intake sometimes exceeding 100,000 (and indeed an average annual net long-term intake of 78,104 from 1946–60) without overt social tension. More than half the post-war migrants have not spoken English as a native language, and a considerable proportion have come from communities with living standards markedly lower than Australia's.

In spite of these facts, one answer which (the writer predicts) will continue to be given for at least the next decade is that even such a rate of admission of Asians (or other non-Europeans) would bring a risk of social conflict much greater than the risk attending an equal rate of admission of Europeans. The risk is not necessarily great provided the immigrants are suitably selected, but the writer does not believe that the post-war Australian experiment entitles us to ignore it. For of the 2,136,200 immigrants who *arrived* between October 1945 and June 1964, about 1,270,000 came from the British Isles, north-western Europe or the 'white' dominions. All of these would be indistinguishable physically from familiar Australian types, and they have displayed no noticeable tendency to congregate in particular parts of cities. About 240,000 were migrants from central and eastern Europe, who might be slightly more remote physically and linguistically but would still not be readily distinguishable. For better or for worse, few relics of alien cultures are likely to persist in the lives of Australian-born descendants of these 1,510,000. Southern Europeans—Greeks, Italians, Maltese, Cypriots, Spaniards and Portuguese—who are somewhat more likely to be distinguished by appearance, who have sometimes tended to congregate in particular suburbs, and who have church affiliations or other cultural characteristics that may give a peculiar stamp to the children, numbered only 470,000.[8]

The total *net* migration from southern Europe and the Middle East from 1947 to 1962 was slightly over 400,000 (about 25,000 a year),[9] but it was still much smaller than (in fact, about a half as great as) the number of Asians who would have entered over the same sixteen-year period if we had allowed the entry of 50,000 a year. In spite of the very favourable record of acceptance, fears are still expressed that the Italian community may inspire hostility if there should be any serious economic recession. The latent forces of prejudice are evident in the fact that judges and magistrates in their sermons to convicted migrants regularly imply that crime is a property of less happier lands and alien to the 'Australian way of life'.

In appearance, South and East Asians differ much more from the usual Australian spectrum than do Southern Europeans. If the likelihood that any minority will be used as a scapegoat increases both with its numbers and with its distinctness from the majority, then it would seem that, to be safe, we should begin by admitting smaller annual numbers of Asians than the numbers of Southern Europeans admitted at present. If the general desirability of some Asian immigration is accepted, it might be reasonable to experiment with a maximum annual intake of 5,000 which might be cut if trouble seemed likely. The occupational and educational composition of the newcomers would, of course, be relevant, and it may well be thought that the higher the accomplishments of the immigrants the larger the group might be allowed to be.

To argue in this way does not involve any assumptions of racial or cultural superiority. It merely recognizes an unfortunate tendency of human beings to channel their hostility onto aliens, and it nevertheless aspires to stifle this tendency by experience of inter-racial living under favourable conditions. That the experiment is worth making is suggested by the examples of comfortably harmonious inter-racial relations in such areas as Hawaii and Brazil. That it must be made with care and with due attention to eliminating the sources of prejudice is suggested by a number of other instances where racial mixture has worked less happily, though the newsworthiness of 'incidents' and gross discrimination may lead us to exaggerate their frequency.

The writer therefore suggests that to admit relatively small numbers of non-Europeans to Australia is a prudent and defensible policy for the immediate future while conceding that the arguments for it assume the possibility of a truly human naughtiness, niggardliness and mistrust among the Australian populace.

Background to Present Policy

Australia's non-European immigration policy is now one of admitting relatively small numbers. But the original principle was one of total exclusion from permanent residence, and so it remained, without wavering, until at least 1950. 'In pursuance of established policy', says the official *Yearbook of the Commonwealth of Australia* as recently as 1963,[10] 'the general practice is not to permit persons of non-European descent to enter Australia for the purpose of settling permanently, but exceptions are made . . .'. The sentence has been dropped from the latest edition of the *Yearbook*, but no ending of this rule has been declared. Despite the valuable changes of March 1966, it is still not the practice that any Asian who is reasonably certain to be absorbed without friction is admitted. There is a *prima facie* exclusion of all non-Europeans, modified by exceptions in certain defined cases.

This approach, which is what makes the restrictions understandably obnoxious to those non-Europeans who are aware of them, can only be properly explained from the policy's history.

In the later nineteenth century feeling against coloured migration developed mainly from experience with two groups: Chinese, whose competition was felt principally in alluvial gold-mining, pastoral employment and furniture making; and indentured Pacific Islanders, who formed a cheap substitute for white labour on Queensland canefields. Near the turn of the century, political fear of Japan provided another ground of objection. By 1900 these diverse considerations were commonly rationalized by convenient, and at that time widely accepted, beliefs about race. The report of the debates on the Immigration Restriction Bill in 1901 (one of the first to be considered by the Parliament of the new Australian Commonwealth) is a museum of the racial beliefs and prejudices that could be entertained by educated and uneducated Anglo-Saxons sixty years ago. The view that racial mixture is disastrous for the whites was almost universal. Thus a member of Queensland talked of 'maintenance of the purity of the race, which is more than threatened',[11] and another described the presence of mixed-race children (or a mixture of races) in Queensland schools as evidence of 'contamination and deterioration',[12] while the able and sophisticated Barton, in introducing the Bill, quoted with approval the radical Professor Pearson:

'The fear of Chinese immigration which the Australia democracy cherishes . . . is, in fact, the instinct of self-preservation, quickened by experience. We know that coloured and white labour cannot exist side by side; we are well aware that China can swamp us with a single year's surplus of population; and we know that if national existence is sacrificed to the working of a few mines and sugar plantations, it is not the Englishman in Australia alone, but the whole civilized world, that will be the losers. . . . We are guarding the last part of the world in which the higher races can live and increase truly for the higher civilization.'[13]

There was a sense of nobility about the cause, a sense of defying vested interests for the sake of high principle. Economic considerations, the effect of Chinese or Japanese immigration in lowering wage-levels, were certainly mentioned, for example by W. M. Hughes, but it would not be true to say that these occupied a great part of the attention of speakers; nor was the fear of open discord in a mixed-race state the principal theme that it has since become of those supporting 'White Australia'. Higgins and Deakin, high-minded intellectual radicals, were inclined to stress the disadvantages of cultural, rather than mere ethnic, diversity within the nation, but the two were never fully distinguished, even though Higgins was 'quite willing to admit that in their own associations the Chinese are as good as we are'.[14] And Deakin believed that 'it is not necessary to reflect upon them [the other races] even by implication. It is only necessary to say that they do not and cannot blend with us; that we do not, cannot, and ought not to blend with them.'[15]

Wrapped in the aura of promoting national purity and integrity there were certainly some more specific motives. One was fear of intervention by Japan if a colony of Japanese nationals should develop in Australia.[16] Another was a humanitarian dislike of the conditions in which Pacific Islanders were recruited for labour in Queensland. There were also vested interests on the side of exclusion as there were vested interests opposed to it. Yet it is likely that most Australians of the day would have agreed with Deakin's words: 'We here find ourselves touching the profoundest instinct of individual or nation—the instinct of self-preservation—for it is nothing less than the national manhood, the national character, and the national future that are at stake.'[17] Deakin went on to say that 'the desire that we should be one people and remain one people without the admixture of other races' had been as universal and powerful a motive as any in inducing the Australian colonies to federate.

The Immigration Restriction Act of 1901 made no reference to race. It enabled the government to exclude non-Europeans—or indeed anyone else the government might choose to exclude—by describing as a prohibited immigrant 'any person who when asked to do so by an officer fails to write out at dictation and sign in the presence of the officer a passage of fifty words in length in any European language directed by the officer'. (Clause 3(a).)[18]

The Courts at first raised various difficulties for the government in administering the test, and in one famous later case even went so far as to rule that Scots Gaelic was not a language within the meaning of the Act, but generally the legislation was quite sufficient for its purposes. It was at first administered liberally, apparently so as to admit anyone who was proficient in English,[19] but from 1903 exclusion of Asians, Africans and Islanders was pursued with full rigour. The dictation test, changed in 1905 (under Japanese pressure) to refer to 'any prescribed language', remained in force until removed by the Migration Act, 1958.

Section 3(n) of the 1901 Act prevented the exclusion of anyone who had been 'domiciled' in Australia, and Section 3(m), which was in force until suspended by proclamation in 1903, prevented the exclusion of 'a wife accompanying her husband if he is not a prohibited immigrant, and all children apparently under the age of eighteen years accompanying their father or mother if the father or mother is not a prohibited immigrant'. After 1903, however, a man could actually be lawfully domiciled in Australia but be prevented by law from bringing his wife or children to reside with him. This disability was removed in the 1920s for the wives and children of Indians resident in Australia, but even after the Second World War it was possible for a Filipino married to an Australian to be excluded and compulsorily repatriated. Members of the armed forces of the Crown, diplomatic and official missions, crews of government ships, and (under rigid restrictions) the crews of other ships temporarily in Australian ports, were specifically exempted from the category of prohibited immigrants, and certificates of exemption could be issued to others. Generally students, tourists and merchants, and in some cases wives of residents, were given temporary exemption, but the readiness to grant it varied with the nationality involved. The Chinese, who were the largest non-European immigrant group, the one against whom the demand for exclusion had first been generated, and the one most notable for evading the restrictions, were generally treated the most harshly.[20]

Apparently the exclusion policy was effective. The three major Asian groups present in 1901 were Chinese, Japanese and Indians (including Sinhalese). The numbers of all three groups, as recorded in the censuses, declined over the succeeding twenty years.[21] There were fewer Asians still at the census of 1954, when the total population who were not Europeans, Aborigines, Torres Islanders or mixed-bloods was about 23,000;[22] though by the Census of 1961 the number had grown.[23]

From the early years of the policy public protest was sometimes made over the harsh impact of its administration on particular individuals. Yarwood[24] cites the case of Poon Gooey, a greengrocer of Horsham in Victoria, whose wife the Department compulsorily repatriated after she had come to visit him on a temporary certificate of exemption. In spite of the consensus in favour of White Australia at the time (1912–13), there was widespread though unavailing protest over the Department's action. Another instance from the same writer[25] is that of the petition signed in 1912 by 101 European residents of Broome, asking for a three-year extension of the exemption given to a Japanese doctor, Suzuki. This apparent conflict between mistrust of the group and the goodwill towards particular individuals is present with some of the staunchest supporters of the policy today. The present Leader of the Opposition, Mr Calwell, who as Minister for Immigration in the 1940s was one of the harshest administrators of the policy, is reputed to have learnt Mandarin Chinese and (without any real political need to do so) to take a considerable interest in his Chinese constituents in the City of Melbourne. A former President of the Australian Natives' Association and persistent public champion of the policy prided himself on having part-Asian teachers at the school of which he was head and spoke of them warmly.

The near-consensus in favour of 'White Australia' began to break visibly during the Second World War. Once this had happened, the protests about individual cases became more significant. Ministers for Immigration could no longer comfort themselves with the thought that protesters were being inconsistent. Thus it is natural that the Liberal–Country Party coalition governments that have been in power from 1949 to the present day should have made important changes in the administration of the policy while pretending to maintain its fundamental purposes. The expressions of these purposes and of the assumptions which buttress them have subtly changed nonetheless to accord with the very different climate of opinion. There are still, of course, racialist cranks, but a man would certainly be recognized as a crank today if he were to aver, as Isaac Isaacs (later to become Governor-

General) did in 1901, that he would willingly say that 'the colour line is that which shall bar inferior races from entering Australia'.[26]

The precise degree of liberalization achieved by 1964 can be described in the words of the current *Yearbook*. 'The present immigration policy provides *inter alia*—

(*a*) that non-Europeans who are the spouses, unmarried minor children or aged parents of Australian citizens, or of British subjects permanently permanently resident here, may be admitted for permanent residence;

(*b*) that a European British subject proceeding from overseas to Australia for permanent residence may be accompanied by his non-European spouse and unmarried minor children;

(*c*) that non-Europeans who have been admitted for temporary residence may qualify, on residential and other grounds, for permanent resident status and subsequently for naturalization;

(*d*) in addition to those non-Europeans admitted for temporary residence for commerce and trade, for the admission, on a selective basis for indefinite stay, of highly qualified and distinguished people who seek to reside here (including those non-Europeans who have taken educational courses at the tertiary level in Australia, who have spent at least five years in their own countries after having completed their courses, and who have qualifications from which the Australian community would benefit); and

(*e*) that those non-Europeans whose continued residence in Australia was induced by political events in their own countries, may be permitted to remain here indefinitely.[26]

The current expression of the older and till recently dominant politicians can be given in the words of Mr Downer, speaking in 1960 as Minister for Immigration:

'. . . I believe that both Australia's national growth and our international relations will best be served by continuing our present policies. For they observe well-tried principles: homogeneity, readiness of absorption, familiarity of religion, the same fundamental attitudes to living. Above all, the thought process of the people we seek to attract are, if not the same, at least in tune with ours.'[28]

Yet these supposedly self-evident truths are widely questioned. In 1943–5, the national bodies of the Presbyterian and Methodist Churches and one of the Roman Catholic Archbishops expressed their dissent from the policy. They have been joined in course of time by at least six of the sixteen metropolitan daily newspapers, by the representative and influential Australian Council of Churches, the National Missionary Council, the Australian Student Christian Movement and the National Youth Council and by various conferences of the Methodist Church, the Presbyterian Church, the Churches of Christ and the Society of Friends. The National Union of Australian University Students conducted an opinion poll which showed that the great majority of students in every University were for change. The Democratic Labour Party, which is fourth in popular vote, has stood since 1961 for considerable liberalization of Asian entry, based on 'reciprocal arrangements with specific countries', while its Victorian branch has in 1964 asked in addition that 'the basis of selection of individual migrants' should be 'personal worth and their suitability in relation to the overall migration programme'.[30] The Australian Labour Party, traditionally the strongest supporter of the policy, decided at its Federal Conference in August 1965 to delete the words 'White Australia' from its platform and to substitute a statement of the criteria on which Australia's immigration policy should be based. These criteria include 'the welfare and integration of all its citizens'.[27] More significantly, Mr Daly, MP, parliamentary spokesman of the Labour Party on immigration matters, endorsed the reforms of March 1966, while making certain stipulations that were unexceptionable.[28] The fact that these changes were received throughout Australia with almost no adverse comment is the most striking measure of how opinion has moved.

Prior to the changes, a number of public opinion polls had been held on the subject. Not all have asked the same question, but the general import of the answers seems to be that a higher and higher proportion since 1954, comprising a growing majority since 1959, have been prepared to support some form of liberalization of permanent entry for non-Europeans.[29] In 1965 6 per cent of those questioned wanted Asians admitted without restriction, 71 per cent wanted selective admission and only 16 per cent wanted all Asians excluded. The number of Asian settlers proposed by those favouring selective admission 'centred at about 1,250 a year'.[30]

What do these various dissenters want? No doubt the answer is 'a variety of different things', and no doubt many have not fully faced the issues. Yet it is fairly clear that more and more people, even a majority, reject the mystique, the ideology, of White Australia. However cautious they may be about change, it would appear that they do not believe as their ancestors did in this fundamental dividing line of colour. Until the changes of March 1966 the White Australia policy was one of the topics most discussed in school debates and essays, and it will probably remain so. This is understandable because it poses for Australians one of the few fundamental issues of social values with which they are confronted. The issue is not whether 500 or 5,000 non-Europeans are admitted, important though that may be. It is whether we aspire to separateness or to togetherness.

The rule on non-European immigration today is that certain exceptions are made to a policy of total exclusion. 'Race' is the main dividing-line, though assimilability is at last starting to play a part. The history of the policy, the fact that it is still *principally* racial in the distinctions which it makes, and the fact that its official description as 'established policy' stresses the continuity with the past: these things give it a racialist image and render it objectionable. Because it is unnecessarily offensive, because it ostensibly declares false values, it is in the opinion of the present writer immoral. Australian statesmen will have to decide whether it is really what they want.

NOTES

The author of this chapter wishes to thank his fellow-contributors: Dr Robert Horn for some apt advice, and Dr Kenneth Rivett for advice and extensive editorial assistance.

The text of this chapter was prepared before Australia's conversion to decimal currency and before the Indian devaluation of 1966. Consequently Australian currency is expressed in pounds (£A1 = $A2). The rough conversions of sums into Indian rupees are made at the pre-1966 exchange-rate (£A1 — Rs.10.67). Since June 1966, the exchange value of the Indian rupee has been reduced in terms of other currencies by 36·8 per cent at par.

1. An estimate made by a UN study group in 1954 of the world's potential cropland put it at 4,000 million acres, of which four fifths was considered to be already cultivated. 'Of the final uncultivated fifth, F A O has suggested that a third lies in Asia, a quarter in North and central America (mainly in Canada), and a quarter in Africa, and little elsewhere. The remaining cultivable land requires special exertion for its use.' (Quotation and reference from: 'Political and Economic Planning', *World Population and Resources* (London, George Allen and Unwin, 1955), p. 32.
2. The figures on which these estimates are based were kindly supplied by Professor F. H. G. Gruen.
3. As a very rough approximation we can say that it is expected to take on average an investment of £A1,200 to provide an extra remunerative job in India. This figure is the broadest guess, made with the aim of erring on the high side. Rather than postulate purely hypothetical jobs that could be provided for a capital expenditure of £A250 each (which we could describe by supposing that each job would provide a family of four with an income of £A25 per head and that the incremental capital-output ratio was 2·5), I have used an estimate that has at least been drawn up with the intention of showing what is likely to happen in the actual development process. The 'cost per job' has been reached by taking the public and private development outlays projected under India's Third Five-Year Plan (Government of India, Planning Commission, *Third Five-Year Plan* (New Delhi, 1961), p. 56, and adding to them the sum of Rs. 5,300 crores, which appears from figures on the Second Plan period to be the approximate amount by which the sum of net investment and government consumption exceeded the planned public and private developmental expenditures for the five-year period (*Ibid.*, pp. 58 and 59. Compared with: UN, *Economic Survey for Asia and the Far East* (Bangkok, ECAFE), several issues, statistical tables on national accounts.) I have interpreted the public figure (generously) as 8,100 crores of rupees, and divided the sum (about 17,500 crores) by the number of jobs (14 million) that were expected to be created in the Plan period other than by special programmes in the rural sector. The quotient of the division is Rs. 12,500 per job. This calculation assumes that (*a*) the Third Plan estimates were broadly realistic; (*b*) the mix of capital and current public developmental expenditures projected in the Plan, and the expected private investment expenditure, represented

between them the social investment necessary (given the socio-political context) to produce the planned increase in income and employment; (*c*) certain approximate relations between planned developmental expenditures and national accounting aggregates were maintained from the Second Plan and (*d*) the marginal relations between social investment and employment for future development do not differ greatly from these less strictly marginal ones relating to conditions now past.

If Australia were to contribute to development in India and did so by means of 'tied' grants (that is, by gifts of Australian goods and services), the cost to be imputed per job would be somewhat greater, not only because of the costs of transport of the goods and 'experts', but also because some excess cost is likely to follow from the high salary payments that would have to be made if Australian technical or educational services were used and from the very limitations involved in tying to one source of procurement. An addition of 50 per cent to the price of buying the goods and services in India would probably be generous. Hence we might take £A1,900 as the cost of providing the extra job from Australian resources.

If, instead of building up the capital at the disposal of the Indian population, we decided to provide for their needs by transporting a certain proportion of the population to Australia, we should find that a family of a husband and wife and two children between three and twelve years old would require about £A300 in fares from Bombay to Melbourne. When they arrived they would have to be provided with equipment for the breadwinner to work with, and indeed with housing, which would probably have to be far more costly than what they had left. This plant and accommodation would have to be paid for in some way or other by the pre-existing Australian economy, either through government expenditure or because private individuals were able to invest enough capital in Australia to house and employ the newcomers. (Training might be involved in either case and therefore need not be considered, and I assume that the inflow of overseas capital would not be affected either way by the extra migration.) What is it likely to cost in new investment to support each immigrant family at near-minimal Australian standards? Suppose each migrant family's breadwinner were to earn £A1,000 a year. It is unlikely, judging from such data as exists on other industrial countries, that the amount of extra capital needed to produce this extra income would be on average less than three times the value of the extra income. As a conservative estimate we should probably have to add £A1,000 for housing to the cost of the enterprise per family, and we should be lucky if each migrant family were able to occupy housing whose cost of replacement was not much more than that. The migrants would admittedly have left some form of housing behind them, but none whose value was likely to be recoverable by the authorities to offset the cost of the migration project.

Even ignoring housing we are thus left with a cost of £A1,900 per family incurred in providing remunerative work in India by means of aid-grants tied to Australian purchases, and on the other hand a cost of £A3,300 incurred in transporting a family of four and providing remunerative work in Australia. Housing costs might well add £A1,000 or more to the latter figure.

4. United States, Bureau of the Census, *Historical Statistics of the United States, 1789–1945* (Washington, D.C., 1949), p. 33.
5. K. Davis, *The Population of India and Pakistan* (Princeton, Princeton University Press, 1951), p. 99.
6. S. Chandrasekhar, *Red China: An Asian View* (New York, Praeger, 1964), Fourth Impression, p. 167.
7. United Kingdom, Central Office of Information, *Britain, An Official Handbook* (London, H.M.S.O., 1964).
8. This breakdown of gross arrivals of people intending to stay for a year or more is (unavoidably, I think) compiled from the official figures in a way which lacks strict logical consistency and is therefore only a rough approximation. To suggest this, I have expressed the component numbers to the nearest 10,000. From the figures cited by Dr Horn (pp. 211–232, above) for arrivals of people who are British or North-western European *by nationality* I have deducted the approximate numbers of arrivals of people who gave Malta or Cyprus *as their place of last permanent residence* (65,000), and I have added the same number (65,000) to the corresponding figure for arrivals of people who are Southern European by nationality. In each case 'long-term' and 'permanent'

arrivals only have been counted. Maltese and Cypriots appear to be the only groups to immigrate in significant numbers who were British by nationality but un-British for purposes of racial prejudice and not native speakers of English. The relative importance of Southern European immigrants may be somewhat understated by this comparison because of their comparatively low rate of re-emigration. The figure in the sentence following that to which this note refers—of *net* immigration of Southern Europeans and Middle Easterners—implies that their number has been about a third of total net immigration. The breakdown of arrivals by country of last permanent residence is taken from: Commonwealth of Australia, Commonwealth Bureau of Census and Statistics, *Demography* (Canberra, Commonwealth Government Printer), various issues.

9. This figure is derived from permanent and long-term migration figures (by country of last and intended next permanent residence) given in various issues of: Commonwealth of Australia, Commonwealth Bureau of Census and Statistics, *Demography* (Canberra, Commonwealth Government Printer).
10. Commonwealth of Australia, Commonwealth Bureau of Census and Statistics, *Year Book of the Commonwealth of Australia*, No. 49 (Canberra, Commonwealth Government Printer, 1963) p.348
11. Commonwealth of Australia, Parliament, *Debates* (Canberra, Commonwealth Government Printer), IV, 4646. Speech by Wilkinson, September 6, 1901.
12. *Ibid.*, IV, 4631. Speech by Mauger, September 6, 1901.
13. *Ibid.*, IV, 3503. Quoted in speech by Barton, August 7, 1901.
14. *Ibid.*, IV, 4658. Speech by Higgins, September 6, 1901.
15. *Ibid.*, IV, 4804. Speech by Deakin, September 12, 1901.
16. This is discussed in A. T. Yarwood, *Asian Migration to Australia* (Melbourne, Melbourne University Press, 1964), Ch. 1.
17. Commonwealth of Australia, Parliament, *Debates*, IV, 4804. Speech by Deakin, September 12, 1901.
18. Reproduced from Yarwood, *op. cit.*, p. 157.
19. *Ibid.*, p. 48.
20. *Ibid.*, Ch. 6 *et passim.*
21. *Ibid.*, p. 163.
22. Immigration Reform Group, *Immigration: Control or Colour Bar?*, ed. K. Rivett Melbourne University Press, 1962), p. 38.
23. See the chapter by Dr R. V. Horn above, pp. 211–232.
24. *Op. cit.*, p. 80.
25. *Ibid.*, p. 102.
26. Melbourne *Age*, August 17, 1964.
27. *Ibid.*, August 3, 1965.
28. *Sydney Morning Herald*, March 25, 1966.
29. The results are given in more detail and discussed in Immigration Reform Group, *op. cit.*, pp. 117–20.
30. *Hobart Mercury*, November 27, 1965.

BIBLIOGRAPHY

Australia, Commonwealth of, Commonwealth Bureau of Census and Statistics *Year Book of the Commonwealth of Australia* (Canberra, Commonwealth Government Printer), various years.

Australia, Commonwealth of, Parliament, *Debates* (Canberra, Commonwealth Government Printer).

Borrie, W. D., 'Australia', in B. Thomas (ed.), *Economics of International Migrations: proceedings of a conference held by the International Economic Association* (London, Macmillan, 1958).

Chandrasekhar, S., *Red China: An Asian View* (New York, Frederick Praeger, 1964), Fourth edition.

Corden, W. M., 'The Economic Limits to Population Increase', *Economic Record* (Melbourne), November 1955.

Davis, K., *The Population of India and Pakistan* (Princeton, Princeton University Press, 1951).

Ellis, H. S., 'Are there Preferable Alternatives to International Migration as an Aid to Economic Development?' and discussion in Thomas, *op. cit.*

Forsyth, W. D., *The Myth of Open Spaces* (Melbourne, Melbourne University Press, 1942).

Higgins, B., *Economic Development* (London, Constable, 1959).

Immigration Reform Group, *Immigration: Control or Colour Bar?*, ed. K. Rivett, with a historical chapter by D. Johanson (Melbourne, Melbourne University Press, 1962), esp. Chs. 1, 8.

India, Government of, Planning Commission, *Third Five Year Plan* (Delhi, Government Printer, 1961).

Isaac, J., *Economics of Migration* (London, Kegan Paul, 1947).

Karmel, P. H., 'The Economic Effects of Immigration', in H. W. Arndt and W. M. Corden (eds.), *The Australian Economy: a volume of Readings* (Melbourne, Cheshire, 1963).

United Kingdom, Central Office of Information, *Britain: an Official Handbook* (London, H.M.S.O., 1964).

United States, Bureau of the Census, *Historical Statistics of the United States, 1789–1945* (Washington, D.C., 1949).

Willard, M., *History of the White Australia Policy* (Melbourne, Melbourne University Press, 1923).

Yarwood, A. T., *Asian Migration to Australia* (Melbourne, Melbourne University Press, 1964).

CHAPTER 11

A PROPOSAL FOR CHANGE IN AUSTRALIA'S IMMIGRATION POLICY

BY KENNETH RIVETT

IN THE YEARS since the Second World War, Australian Governments have actively encouraged immigration from Europe. During the same period, only a very few non-Europeans have been allowed to settle here. The country's immigration policy can still be described, more or less accurately, as one of maintaining a 'White Australia', even though that phrase is no longer used officially.

It is always significant when a once-popular slogan is publicly rejected. Even if the rejection is due solely to a wish to propitiate world opinion (and the rejection of the words 'White Australia' reflects more than this), it still shows that the old attitude is accepted less confidently; and in the case of Australia's immigration policy, there have been not only a change of name but also important changes in the policy itself.

Today non-Europeans can ordinarily become permanent residents if they are spouses, minor unmarried children or aged parents of Australian citizens, or of other British nationals who have obtained the right of permanent residence. (Brothers, sisters and adult children are seldom eligible unless they qualify on some other ground.) Thanks to a policy change announced in March 1966, non-Europeans can acquire the right of permanent residence, which in practice is quickly followed by citizenship, if they have been here for five years on the kind of temporary permit which is given to traders and to persons allowed to enter for the purpose of working in Chinese cafés or laundries. Since European immigrants who are not British subjects must also wait five years for citizenship, the delay is not unreasonable.

A few 'distinguished and highly qualified' non-Europeans—the approximate number in 1964 was fifteen—have been allowed to settle annually. In March 1966 this category was widened to include well-qualified persons who are likely to be useful to the Australian economy, and there were added two further sub-categories of 'persons who have been of particular and lasting help to Australia's interest abroad in trade, or in other ways' and 'persons who by former residence in Australia or by association with us have demonstrated an interest in or identification with Australia that should make their future residence here feasible'. It should also be mentioned that about 800 Asian evacuees who had been brought here during the Second World War were permitted to stay, and that the same right has been extended to Asians who were in Australia when their countries came under Communist rule.[1]

It is not easy to find out the number of non-Europeans who are being allowed to settle, partly because the Department of Immigration's statistics are in process of being rebased. Official policy distinguishes between Australian citizens, persons who have been granted or allowed to acquire a right of permanent residence but who are not citizens, and persons who are given temporary permission to live here. The test of how far there is still a policy of 'White Australia' is the number of non-Europeans obtaining a right of permanent residence, whether they have been here previously on temporary permits or are entering the country for the first time. During 1963 about a thousand non-Europeans obtained this right and a similar number did so in the following year.[2]

Part of the increase is due to intermarriage between permanent residents and non-European spouses, many of them Asian students, of whom there are more than 12,000 in Australia at present. Some inflow from this cause will continue, but much of the recent rise in the number of non-Europeans obtaining the right to stay is due to those who have been here for the necessary period on temporary permits acquiring permanent resident status and also the right to bring in close relatives. The number of non-Europeans who are here on temporary permits is falling, chiefly because the Government is understandably reluctant to continue the practice of admitting Asians conditionally on their performing manual work for particular non-white employers. Some widening of categories such as occurred early in 1966 was probably needed even to maintain the present low intake, but the Minister has stated definitely that the number of non-Europeans entering will be 'somehat greater than previously'.

Thus the concessions made so far involve a significant though modest break with the old policy. Public opinion was certainly ready for it: the last opinion conducted on the subject, held in 1965, showed that a substantial majority of Australians supported at least a measure of immigration reform. An even larger majority might have done so if it were not that until fairly recently, the case for change was urged at times on what were rather dubious grounds.

One such ground, suggesting itself, naturally enough, to many Asians and to some people in Europe, is that Australia has vast resources, which needy people could use. As Mr Clunies Ross has shown, Australia's resources are not so exceptional, and there are sound economic and non-economic reasons why her help to the underdeveloped world should not take the form of allowing mass immigration.

A second questionable criticism of the policy of 'White Australia' has been the simple statement that it is wrong to discriminate on grounds of colour. One hardly answers this contention by pointing out that the non-European countries themselves limit immigration, and that in doing so, they sometimes pay explicit regard to the nationality (and where the admission of ethnic Chinese is concerned, the race) of the would-be immigrant. It could be argued that they are wrong to do so, that Australia should not be guilty of the same mistake, and that in any case our policy is distinctive in that Australia, at the same time as she excludes almost all non-white immigrants, openly encourages the immigration of whites. Yet objectionable though some of us believe that policy to be, there are grave difficulties about opposing it *merely* on the ground that it involves racial discrimination.

In the year 1964–65 Australia admitted 140,000 Europeans.[3] The net intake of permanent settlers will be appreciably less; still, if immigration is to continue on this scale, and if there is to be *any* control of non-European migration, then some discrimination against non-Europeans is unavoidable. It will be argued below that though the admission of highly-skilled immigrants could be controlled without racial discrimination, a measure of discrimination is desirable at present, while in the case of unskilled immigrants, Australia could only control their entry without differential treatment if she were prepared for her intake of persons of European race to be cut back drastically.

One feels some sympathy with those Australians who reject the kind of criticism which has stopped at saying that the present policy is discriminatory. They may reasonably point out that the phrase 'discrimination' has irrelevant connotations, that it is used most frequently of situations where a majority or minority is denied equal citizenship, and that no such denial results from the Australian policy. Australia's position, they might add, is exceptional. Neither the United States, nor Canada, nor any South American country, nor any country in which most of the population are non-European is seeking today to recruit unskilled immigrants. None of these countries has been as successful as Australia in controlling unemployment, and no other country—not even New Zealand—is as anxious as Australia to increase its European population. It is unfair that we should be condemned so harshly because, as an incidental result of the welcome we extend to European migrants, we are forced to discriminate so explicitly against would-be settlers who are non-European.

What Australians who reason in this way are apt to overlook is that differential treatment according to race is a matter of degree. Australia's policy is less injurious to human dignity than the discrimination in South Africa or in the Deep South of the United States; even so, it produces harmful effects, which a new policy can mitigate in proportion as it is more liberal.

For the sake of internal harmony, it is prudent for Australia to pay some regard to race in deciding which applicants shall be allowed to settle. Human beings the world over are liable—though in differing degree—to racial prejudice; and so long as they are, the control of immigration will remain one of the most effective means of preventing such prejudice from causing conflict. However, the part which race plays in the selection of Australia's immigrants has until recently been excessive and there is reason to fear that it may remain so. Our policy would only be defensible if a mere handful of non-Europeans were all who could live here without friction. This is certainly not the case, and even if it were, a rigid policy of exclusion intensifies the very prejudice against the effects of which it is meant to guard.

If a country promotes immigration on the present Australian scale, and if it pushes the racial element in its choice of migrants beyond the point that prudence justifies, then its reputation in the outside world is bound to suffer. Of the harm done to our good name, at least until the changes of March 1966, more and more Australians were becoming aware, if only from the cabled comments that appeared in our press. But if the recent policy had really been needed to avert racial conflict, it would have been dubious wisdom to change it merely because it was criticized overseas. In fact it is only likely to be modified appreciably when more Australians realize that there are other reasons also why a larger number of non-Europeans should be admitted.

Can a policy be framed which improves substantially on the present one, yet guards against the dangers of racial friction? That claim has been made for the proposals put forward by the Immigration Reform Group, a research body which has largely influenced the thought of the Associations for Immigration Reform that exist in most of the Australian states. In 1962 the Group published a book, *Immigration: Control or Colour Bar?*, from which the arguments and suggestions below are partly drawn. Recent discussion, however, has brought out the great importance of paying regard, when selecting immigrants, to the type of occupation that they would follow on getting here, and to their circumstances in their country of origin. Hence these aspects will be dealt with at some length.

The Economic Case for Change

For various reasons, persons of Asian, African or Polynesian race may wish to settle in Australia. One of the reasons most frequently encountered is the desire for economic betterment—including the desire to send money home to poorer relatives. This motive is so strong and so ubiquitous that the strength of other motives said to be present along with it is often hard to assess; but another perfectly genuine reason for wanting to come here may be the wish to be reunited with family members now in Australia. A third reason is the need to escape political persecution, ranging from the threat of execution to much milder forms of discrimination. A fourth reason which influences some Asians who have studied in Australia is one of which, from its nature, they seldom talk: they have seen at first hand a society where marriage is based on mutual attraction, not parental choice, and they are reluctant to return to communities where their freedom to marry will often, in practice, be narrowed greatly by social pressures.

Some of Australia's critics have urged that her immigration policy is simply redundant, seeing that few non-Europeans would want to come here anyway. That view runs counter to the experience of all rich countries in the years just *before* they have limited immigration. Moreover, even if the past suggested otherwise, it is clear that the desire for higher living standards, and the willingness to move in order to obtain them, are spreading and intensifying. We must assume that until Asians and Africans, West Indians and Pacific Islanders achieve higher levels of real income, a number of them will want to go to any rich and non-Communist country that is prepared to admit them.

Even where the genuineness of other motives besides the economic is beyond doubt, the question whether would-be immigrants should be allowed to move should be decided partly—except in extreme cases—by the economic effects on their countries of origin and on Australia, such effects in this country having some importance in themselves, and even more so far as they determine whether racial antagonism will be stirred up by the migrants' presence.

As Mr Clunies Ross shows in the previous chapter, massive immigration from almost any non-European country would be sure to depress the average standard of living in Australia. The low proportion of non-Europeans who possess skills usable in an industrialized economy would mean that if immigration were unrestricted, the non-Europeans who came to Australia would almost all fill jobs that were unskilled. They would compete with unskilled Australians, whose material interests would suffer more than those of any other section of the host community. Help from rich to underdeveloped countries should take the form of allowing large-scale immigration, rather than sending capital, when the underdeveloped countries cannot use more capital through lack of personnel with the necessary training and experience. But the point is hardly relevant, since as things are the underdeveloped countries get much less capital than they can use effectively. Meanwhile the case for preferring 'aid in goods' is greatly strengthened by the probability of internal friction if massive immigration were both cause and accompaniment of economic hardship to the host community. There are, no doubt, economic grounds for allowing extensive immigration from Hong Kong, where geographic factors may eventually limit the productivity of capital; but this situation, while important and relevant in the present context,[4] is obviously exceptional.

Such is the core of the Australian case (and of the American, British and Canadian cases) for limiting non-white immigration, while somewhat similar reasons justify restriction of the immigration of whites. Indeed, on a cool view of the economics of population movement, one may wonder that Australia should admit as many immigrants as it does. It is hard honestly to commend the present level of immigration as tending to raise the living standards of people *now in Australia* or of their descendants. Our intake since the war may even have been economically harmful to persons previously in Australia, not of course in the sense that real income per head has fallen or will fall, but in the sense that it has not risen and will not rise as much as it would have done otherwise. The immigrants have not brought with them much capital, hence their entry has tended to mean that the people here before them have less capital per head to work with, and produce less in consequence. To set against this is the important point that the growth in population, and the expectation of further growth, have helped to attract capital from abroad. But the net effects, current and long term, of an inflow of overseas investment are complex, especially so far as uncertainty exists about the possibility of expanding earnings from our traditional exports.

It can be said with confidence that Australia would never have admitted migrants on the present scale if it were not for the hope that a larger population, and the resultant economic growth, would add to the country's military potential. Leaving aside the morals and politics of this reason for encouraging immigration, it seems rather questionable strategically. What is even more questionable is that hitherto only Europeans should have been thought of as military assets. The Asian settler has been treated, if anything, as a wartime liability, it being felt that his possible contribution would be more than offset by the risk of his engaging in 'Fifth Column' activity. In recent years the 'Fifth Column' argument against Asian immigration has not been used much —it is obviously irrelevant as regards a small inflow of well-chosen immigrants. But the political future of most of Asia remains so uncertain that there is still a slight doubt as to the ultimate allegiance of Asian settlers. At all events no politician has yet been prepared to support Asian immigration on military grounds.

Australia, it must be conceded, is in the unsavoury position of basing its immigration policy chiefly on fear. Partly because of fear, it seeks only Europeans, even though, by and large, Europeans have less to gain from coming here than any other racial group. To that extent the national attitude is self-referenced. Yet in fairness, many Australians also feel that in an overpopulated world, our natural resources *ought* to be used more intensively. It is a rather vague feeling, the product of unfocused guilt rather than conscious purpose; but it is one factor motivating our current immigration programme, nor should it be regarded as non-existent because as yet, in this century, it has not issued in an open offer to would-be migrants who are non-European.

What is required now is for Australia's growing sense of international responsibility to influence, more directly, her choice of immigrants. A major consideration should be that the economic gain to any migrant allowed to settle here will patently be greater, the worse his opportunities in the country he leaves. Hence the desirability, *prima facie*, of some of Australia's immigrants being non-European. However, the effects of their being able to come will differ considerably from case to case.

For present purposes let us assume—though matters are not quite so simple—that an intake of migrants *much the same in occupational composition as the host community* will tend, on balance, to lower real income per head. Consistently with this assumption, a small intake consisting of migrants with particular skills may have the opposite effect. This is particularly clear as regards the very small category of trained and experienced personnel who, by reason of Australian circumstances, can make a special contribution to this country.

For instance, Australia may only be able to sell some types of goods to Asia when her manufacturers have continual guidance from those with expert knowledge of the market concerned. In the case of producer goods, especially, it is scarcely enough to rely on second-hand or even first-hand impressions of what the buyer is likely to want. Rather must the Australian producer find out the buyer's production problems and help him to solve them. The surprising fact that Australia exports relatively little agricultural equipment to Asia or Africa (other than South Africa)[5] may be due partly to the absence in Australia of enough people with an intimate knowledge of Asian or African farming problems—a knowledge that can be applied during the vital phase when products are being 'developed', *before* they are put on the market. Such people were not likely to make careers in Australia unless they knew that they could stay here for as long as they wished, and the Government's recent decision to allow them to apply for resident status and citizenship after the usual five-year waiting period was absurdly overdue.

In the past our immigration policy must also have impeded the production of goods intended for the Australian consumer. There are fields where Japanese producers lead the world, yet where it may be appropriate, even so, for the product to be made in Australia, and where this cannot be done efficiently unless Japanese experts are able and willing to work here for a considerable time. As other non-European countries develop, there will be more and more spheres in which Asians and Africans have something to teach the world. Australia—so anxious to obtain know-how from Europe and America—has now wisely decided not to cut itself off from this experience in the way that it would do if the non-European expert were not permitted to live here for as long as he liked.

At the moment, the number of non-Europeans who can make a special contribution to the Australian economy may not be large. However, the admission of other non-Europeans with special qualifications—indeed, with any qualification that a Western-type economy can use—has understandably raised the question of whether they could be of greater service by staying at home.

It is a sign of the times that this argument against freer migration should be used widely within Australia, and that it should, in general, be used sincerely. Nor can it be doubted that it has considerable force. The underdeveloped countries are all short of capital, some are exceptionally short of natural resources, and all are peculiarly short of the various kinds of trained personnel who played such a vital part in raising levels of income in the rich economies. Moreover, in any economy—partly by accident, but increasingly by design—economic life is so arranged that an able applied scientist or entrepreneur or salaried administrator is almost always a net benefactor of his fellows. The value of his contribution, direct and indirect, is usually greater than what he is paid; and even if it is not, an appreciable part of his earnings return to the State as direct and indirect taxes.

Whether in these circumstances a highly-qualified Asian or African will be more use here or in his country of origin turns on several conflicting considerations. The one resource in which his country is almost sure to be rich is unskilled, underemployed labour. If he stays at home, he should be able to make this resource more productive. Moreover, the fact that few of his fellow countrymen possess similar qualifications to his means that the indirect effects of his work in raising standards of efficiency etc. are more important than they would be in a developed economy. To set against this is the consideration that in an underdeveloped economy, there is less capital per worker, so that a given amount of effort, skilled or unskilled, yields less than it would if expended in a context where capital was more plentiful.

A century ago, it was widely thought that the allocation of qualified or other manpower should be left to the free play of the market. Entrepreneurs and professional men, it was pointed out, would go where they were paid most, or, if they did not, it would be because they were not offered enough to offset the disadvantages connected with the move. They would be paid most in the country where they contributed most to the value of world production, and should therefore be allowed to go where they wished. This argument undoubtedly contains an important truth. It must be qualified, however, mainly for the reason that market value is an inadequate measure of social contribution. In the present context, the principal reason why the two diverge is that the gain from exceptional performance accrues as a rule to the country where the performance occurs; hence if skilled Asians settle in Australia, it is chiefly Australia that gains from their presence. The rest of the world will only benefit if they send part of their earnings to relatives at home, or if their efforts cheapen the products that Australia sells overseas. There are problems about comparing the usefulness of any type of work in one economy and in another if the comparison is based solely on the market values to which the work contributes, directly or indirectly. But even to the extent that the two contributions can be compared, it may still be held that, since need in the poorer countries is more urgent, a given contribution in a poor country will do more good than a contribution valued more highly in the market but made in a rich country.

In any case, market values are 'rigged' by governments. There are good reasons why, in the underdeveloped world, the earnings which skilled personnel are able to obtain and retain after tax should be less than the earnings which rightly or wrongly they are allowed to retain in developed economies. For one thing, the shortage of well-qualified people in the underdeveloped countries causes them to earn much more than the unqualified; it is essential, and on the whole likely, that the shortage will be steadily eased; and as Professor Silcock has remarked, it may therefore be unwise to fix salaries on a basis that will be inappropriate later. 'If specialist salaries were raised to the world level, only inflation could remove the future income-differentials problem for the governments of backward areas when more specialists were available.'[6] Yet if salaries are below the world level, the specialists will tend to emigrate.

This is indeed a powerful reason why the movement of well-qualified people from poorer parts of the world should not be quite unrestricted. But if restriction is justified by the needs of the countries which migrants would otherwise leave, it is surely for the governments of those countries to impose the restriction and incur the resultant criticism. Moreover, there are certain classes of skilled migrant whose departure does not involve their countries of origin in appreciable loss. Some scientists, most mathematicians, many artists and almost all philosophers produce for a world market; and the world, which includes their countries of birth, will benefit most if they are allowed to work in whichever environment seems most likely to promote creation.

A larger category of would-be migrant whose country may profit little from his staying are the members of non-European minorities who suffer racial discrimination at home and are therefore unable to use their skills fully. Such is often the position of Indian and Chinese minorities, and even majorities, outside India and China. A measure of discrimination against them in some fields may be justified on the same ground as the privileges offered to Indian harijans and New Zealand Maoris, viz. that it helps the less advanced group (Malays, Africans or Fijians) to progress more rapidly. But where a majority discriminates against a minority, the process is likely to be pushed too far, even from the standpoint of the economic interests of those imposing the restriction. In general, the indigenous peoples of Asia and Africa are not allowing themselves to gain all they might, in either the short term or the long term, from the enterprise and industry of the Indians and Chinese in their midst. It can even be wasteful to dispense too completely with the services of Europeans! The European, however, can always get out—he is welcome in a number of countries with full or nearly full employment —whereas the same escape is not open to the ethnic Chinese and Indians of South-East Asia, Africa or Fiji.

If differential treatment is taken to the point where some citizens have no chance of filling the kind of job that they could hold elsewhere, they should be given the chance to leave. Australia should sometimes be willing to receive them even if they could be of *some* use to the countries which treat them as second-class citizens. For if they can be of some use, the government discriminating against them may want to keep them, and if in addition they are able to emigrate, it may be forced to modify its policy. If it insists on keeping them yet still discriminates against them, it will expose itself to world censure.

A further reason why some qualified persons can leave their countries of origin without loss to the latter is that these countries may contain more people with a particular qualification than the countries concerned have a use for. Arts, Law and Commerce graduates cost little to train, unless they are trained well. The lower the standards of the degree-conferring body, the cheaper it is to turn out students who meet its requirements, the harder such graduates find it to obtain suitable employment, and the more they multiply themselves through coaching colleges that prepare students for external examinations. The final result can be a situation where a degree becomes a condition of getting even a clerk's job, though the job could be filled equally well by someone with less training. Understandably, these graduates often wish to emigrate, even though clerical work might be all they could get elsewhere unless they improved their qualifications. True, they can usually find employment in their own countries as rural schoolteachers, if they will accept the very low salary, the cultural isolation and much physical discomfort. But if a few graduates were enabled to emigrate, it would make little difference to the supply of teachers. The number of men and women who were still being pressured towards that vocation would remain large.

It cannot be pleaded for this type of would-be migrant that his training will be better used in a place like Australia. On the contrary: here as in other rich countries the ability to read and write is now so widespread that clerical labour as such has ceased to be skilled, though particular clerical skills and experience may still, of course, command a premium. It might therefore seem that the Asian Arts or Commerce graduate who cannot use his knowledge within his own country has no stronger claim for admission to Australia than has an Asian without skill. There is, however, the difference that he is likely to fit into the Australian setting with less personal stress and less chance of engendering friction. The policy announced by the Australian Government in March 1966 leaves insufficient scope for the entry of migrants in this category.

Here as in a second respect, Hong Kong presents a situation where the case for providing opportunities to emigrate is unusually strong. The huge inflow of refugees before and since the Second World War has included many with some tertiary education and a good knowledge of English: some of them are graduates with degrees acquired on the Mainland but not recognized in Hong Kong itself. If these people obtain work in an Australian office or factory (and perhaps, if they wish, study part-time for a qualification recognized in Australia), the effect in Hong Kong will not be to hold back its development but simply to ease somewhat its acute problem of population. In Hong Kong the pressure on space and especially on present and potential water supply[7] is creating conditions where it will become harder and harder for the effects of population to be offset by further investment. In such circumstances the case for helping a relatively poor community by injecting capital, rather than by allowing freer migration, is obviously weakened.

This short discussion of the economics of admitting particular categories of migrant may be summed up as follows: granted that mass immigration may impose a heavy cost on the receiving nation, and granted also that immigration is not as a rule the most appropriate way for rich nations to help poor ones, it must still be conceded (i) that some immigrants are notable assets to their host communities, (ii) that some skilled non-Europeans cannot use their skills in their own countries, and (iii) that at least one economy—Hong Kong's—is reaching a point where the effects of further population growth can best be offset by emigration. It follows that migration has a part to play, now as in the nineteenth century, in the effort to raise world living standards.

Non-economic Arguments

The case for permitting freer migration is clearly strengthened if there are also non-economic reasons why an immigrant should move. These reasons are peculiarly strong in the case of close relatives of persons who reside permanently in the immigrant country—including sisters, brothers, and adult children, who are now excluded from Australia, unless they qualify for entry on other grounds. The reasons are even stronger in the extreme case of refugees whose lives and liberty are in danger (and whose training and talents will certainly *not* be used at home if they are kept out). We should also remember the indirect ways in which a non-European nation may benefit if it has some gifted expatriates abroad—especially as a few of them will choose, like Jinnah and Hastings Banda, to return eventually to their own countries. If non-European migrants can be absorbed harmoniously, retaining as much as they wish of their original cultures but also participating as fully as they wish in all aspects of Australian life, there will be valuable long-term fruits. We cannot know the exact nature of those fruits unless and until they are given a chance to materialize; no one at the start of the century could foresee the immense effects of the years Gandhi was to spend in England and South Africa. But if the fruits could be foreseen, they might appear highly relevant to the political and even the economic problems of the next fifty and a hundred years.

Certainly, the presence of an immigrant minority, happily integrated with the host community but not wholly merged in it, can contribute to mutual understanding in the same way as do student training, cultural exchanges, talks between businessmen, and visits from politicians. Moreover, if these latter links are to be more than superficial, they will be followed sometimes by requests to settle—or at any rate, to stay longer than was originally intended, with the possibility of a further stay should this be desired. Students at Australian universities will often wish to return to Asia in due course. Frequently, they ought to do so; but the wider purposes of their visits would be served more fully if right from the start they were not virtually certain that later on they would have to go.

The way in which a more liberal policy could contribute to Australia's relations with other countries is shown vividly by the experience of Britain. Every part of the British Commonwealth, 'white' or non-white, contains professional and business folk who have studied in Britain,a smaller number who have earned their livings in Britain, and a number whose wealth or qualifications are such that, under the current legislation, they *can* live in Britain if they choose. Even under this legislation, a Commonwealth visitor's stay is seldom overshadowed by the knowledge that he will be unable to return permanently to Britain, whatever opportunities unfold for him. The fact that Asian students and other visitors to Australia are eventually under pressure to leave, and have little chance either of staying or of coming back as settlers, works more powerfully than Australians realize against the formation of closer and deeper ties between Asia and Australia.

It remains to add two further and consequential arguments to the above critique.

If it is established that for both economic and non-economic reasons, there is a *prima facie* case for allowing more non-Europeans to settle than have been allowed to do so hitherto, then the recent decision to allow a 'somewhat greater' number to do so should be interpreted very liberally, unless one is extremely pessimistic about the possibility of their integrating harmoniously with other Australians. If the pessimism is justified, if the problems of non-Europeans much exceed what is normal for other first generation immigrants, if the trouble is due to their skin colour and so will still be there for the next few generations, even where there is intermarriage, then the outlook for Australia's aborigines and her small Chinese community (descendants of some of the Chinese who were here before immigration restriction) is a grim one. If almost all ginger-haired people are excluded from Australia, on the ground that they will not get on with other Australians, then either they are excluded wrongly or the outlook for ginger-haired children born in Australia is unhappy. A rigid policy of excluding these folk would proclaim clearly, to ginger and non-ginger alike, that the ginger-haired are not and never can be accepted fully as citizens. Such a policy might not be intended to keep the ginger-haired away from fellow Australians, or to foster anti-ginger feeling, but it would have both those effects. Not surprisingly, some leading Australian Chinese and some persons active on behalf of aborigines are also members of the Associations for Immigration Reform.

In the whole pattern of relations between developed and underdeveloped countries, the role of immigration should probably be fairly small. If one concedes, however, that it has a role—and a larger one than Australian policy may be prepared to assign it, even now—then refusal to allow it to fill that role must continue to expose Australia to strong and widespread criticism. Immigration restrictions are the ugliest of all restrictions imposed by rich nations to maintain their privileges. They are partly imposed also in the interests of social peace, but they can only be enforced by hunting down the men and women who attempt illegal entry, who stow away in ships at the risk of dying from thirst or suffocation, and who usually face these hazards for the sole purpose of securing a chance to live decently by their own efforts. On balance, it is doubtless wise to restrict the right of free movement, thereby averting the evils that unlimited entry would bring with it; but it is wrong to push restriction even fractionally further than seems to be needed for that purpose. The offence against morality is all the graver if the criterion for rejection is racial; for misuse of that criterion implicitly endorses the view that any attempt to unite whites and non-whites in a common citizenship is doomed to failure. In so many words, supporters of *apartheid* have cited Australia's immigration policy as implying a belief that no democracy can flourish if more than one racial group is included in the electorate.

The mere fact that Australia's name is used to excuse internal policies distinct from, and less excusable than, the White Australia policy was itself a reason for changing it—to which could be added the policy's effect in making Australia disliked, mildly or heartily, throughout the non-European world. True, if it were not for the policy's traditional name, it would never have attracted so much attention. But the damage is now done; no mere change of label would have placated Australia's critics; and there are, besides, independent reasons why a more liberal approach is timely. The organized agitation of the sixties in favour of relaxation began with an effort to spell out these reasons; and the Associations for Immigration Reform would collapse overnight if their members did not believe that there are other grounds for change besides the self-interest of Australia's whites.

The Bases of a New Policy

Can Australia frame a migration policy which is superior to her past one, and yet involves enough control to avoid internal racial friction? Would such a policy be regarded by non-Europeans as superior to the almost rigid barrier that Australia has raised until very recently?

Our official spokesmen used to argue that immigration was an internal matter, which international agencies should not debate. Indeed our vote has been cast more than once on the side of those countries that wish to limit the issues discussed in world forums and at conferences of the Commonwealth Prime Ministers. It has been so cast from a pathetic fear that otherwise the Australian policy on non-European migration will be criticized in turn.

That approach is defeatist and, in the present day, self-defeating. Australia's response to overseas criticism should rather be, first, that we have declared our intention to change our policy and to review even the new policy at a later date, and secondly, that we are often judged too severely, if only because few non-Europeans, in public life or out of it, have given much thought to the sort of policy that they want Australia to follow. Only when Asians and Africans have clarified their views about the kind of issues that *ought* to determine Australia's stand on migration will there be a true meeting of minds, and with it, a chance of removing 'White Australia' from the sufficiently long list of contentious inter-racial issues. It will be far better if this can occur *before* UN or ILO debates the matter and *before* Australian or other governments take up defiant attitudes from which they may find it embarrassing to retreat.

For two reasons, agreement between Australia and her critics may be more readily attainable than is generally realized:

1. The governments of the underdeveloped countries are anxious not to lose too many highly-trained persons. It seems that the Indian, Pakistani, Ceylonese and perhaps other governments take steps now to stop qualified people from emigrating. As we have seen, the question whether such personnel should leave the underdeveloped countries is not simple: even if it seems clear that their own nations will be losers, there is still a conflict between personal freedom and net public advantage. It should be Australia's conscious aim to bring the conflict into the open. To resolve it is not Australia's duty, nor that of any other country whose immigration policy is in question, and it is not fair that the onus of resolving it should be thrown on the countries of immigration.

Australia should therefore welcome any debate in any world body that has the indirect result of forcing the countries of potential *emigration* to decide what they want. Their governments are likely, though not certain, to favour fairly close restriction—at least so long as the shortage of qualified people remains so acute.

2. The governments of underdeveloped countries would be likely to deplore a situation where a high proportion of their emigrants were drifting into jobs at the base of Australia's social ladder. Significantly, the Indian Government has prohibited the emigration of unskilled labour to Malaya.[8] 'Pakistan', said a Trade Commissioner in Australia, 'has no intention of encouraging members of the coolie class to emigrate.'[9] These attitudes are continuous with the opposition of pre-Independence Indian nationalists (and of the British-controlled Government of India) to indentured labour, despite the economic gains that the emigrant often secured. Official circles in the West Indies appear to think differently, but their attitude is exceptional.

From Australia's point of view, it is equally important that no racial group, physically different from the host community, shall be found predominantly in jobs with low status. The result could only be to fan the race prejudice which is latent here as in all other countries, white or non-white. Snobbery is a fact of life, including Australian life. The fact that Australia has a relatively high degree of social mobility does not mean, necessarily, that people at the bottom of the scale are viewed with more respect than they would be in a more rigid society. Indeed, in Australia today, they perhaps enjoy less respect than they did in the less mobile Australia of thirty years ago. Regret it as we may, we must take it as a datum that if yellow-skinned or black-skinned people gravitate disproportionately to work which is poorly regarded, their racial group will not be much respected by other Australians.

From here the argument need only be taken a stage further. Suppose that the governments of all non-European countries come to share the viewpoint of India and Pakistan and to oppose emigration that is predominantly unskilled. Suppose, in addition, that they will only release a few of their skilled nationals. The two attitudes, taken together, amount to asking that Australia and similar countries shall permit only small intakes, balanced as between the skilled and unskilled. Such is precisely the kind of intake that Australia can absorb harmoniously at the present time.

The Immigration Reform Group, in *Immigration: Control or Colour Bar?*, has suggested that, for an experimental period, 1,500 non-Europeans a year should be granted the right to settle permanently, and that a number of those now here on temporary permits should be allowed to remain.[10] If the experiment succeeded—i.e. if there were no friction to speak of—the figure would be raised, though it may well be that for the next decade or so, an annual intake as low as 5,000 would be a suitable target. One can imagine internal or international crises in Asia so serious that Australia, along with other democracies, would have a duty to take more immigrants than it could easily absorb; but barring such contingencies, the wise course may be to hasten slowly. Later on it may be safe to raise our intake much higher; for if it is chosen on the lines proposed, it will have a very different impact from the unrestricted inflows of population—free, indentured and enslaved—that laid the basis for racial friction in other parts of the world.

Any intake should be so chosen that on arrival, the immigrants would fill jobs at each occupational level. Part of the intake should comprise close relatives, including the categories now excluded. Sooner or later Australia might ask the governments of non-European countries—starting with those with whom Australia has the closest links—to frame agreements that would state the numbers and occupational categories of the migrants who were to be admitted. (It would be essential that these agreements should not restrict in any way the right to admit political refugees.) This method of control could, in practice, be highly flexible—unlike quotas imposed by statute or regulation.

Under international law legal control over immigration appears to rest almost wholly with the immigrant country, hence it would be disingenuous to deny that Australia would have more influence in deciding who should be admitted than would the countries of emigration. However, if one of these were to break off negotiations for what the world considered adequate reasons, it would be embarrassing for Australia; so that in practice both parties would have some bargaining power. Sometimes, negotiations might fall through; but the Australian Government, by embarking on them, would show that it was anxious to give due weight to the wishes of non-European governments in determining the numbers and types of emigrant who were allowed to come here.

If non-European immigration to Australia were regulated along these lines, and if, at the same time, we continued to promote large-scale immigration from Europe, our policy would still involve a measure of discrimination based on race.

We discriminate now as between migrants from various parts of Europe; while in addition, our immigration programme takes account of the occupations that would-be immigrants are likely to follow when they get here—as indeed it must do, if the programme is not to destroy full employment, nor impose an undue burden on any group of Australians. Suppose that occupational and educational criteria were the only ones used. Suppose that no regard were paid to the race or country of origin of the would-be immigrant.

One of two courses could then be followed. The educational standard for entry could be set high, so that few non-Europeans would qualify. In that case, few Europeans would qualify either, and Australia's whole intake of immigrants would be cut back drastically. As a less extreme step, all workers without skills that were marketable here would be excluded, in which case also our intake would fall considerably.

Alternatively, European immigration could continue on its present scale, and an effort could be made, as now, to strike a balance between unskilled breadwinners and breadwinners with various types of usable skill. If this were done, some non-Europeans would get in as professional people, along with the current intake of European professionals. An uncertain number would get in as clerks. In the case of the unskilled category, there can be little doubt that as word of the new policy spread, the number of non-European applicants would become so large that there could be no question of accepting all of them, along with those European applicants who were likewise prepared to accept unskilled jobs when they got here. Hence the only way to avoid discrimination would be to choose applicants by lot, or by taking the same *proportion* of applicants from each country. Whichever course were followed, the intake of unskilled labour would be overwhelmingly non-white. That would mean that in each non-white group, racial or national, there would be a far higher proportion of unskilled workers than among European immigrants or among the host community. An essential condition for the successful integration of non-whites would be violated.

There is no escaping the conclusion that if Australia were to maintain her present level of immigration and at the same time to avoid differentiation based on race, the non-European intake would be of such a kind and on such a scale that race friction would be almost inevitable. It follows that for the time, anyway, race should play *some* part in determining our choice of immigrants. Nor can one see why this should be objected to, especially in an era when non-European governments themselves restrict immigration, and do so sometimes on a basis of race or nationality. The road to internal harmony is to be colour blind as between residents, but to pay some regard to colour in deciding which would-be immigrants should be accepted.

It is understandable that in Britain and elsewhere, some internationalists should want immigration to be uncontrolled, or else to be controlled in a way that pays no regard to the would-be immigrant's race. But differentiation at the point of entry is not to be rejected merely because white racialists may also want it. The racialist is wrong both in his reasons for seeking control ('the non-whites matter less than we do') and in the degree of discrimination that he is therefore prepared to practise. Given, however, the *fact* of race prejudice, actual and latent, a statesman has a positive moral duty to avoid creating conditions on which such prejudice will feed and strengthen.

The mistake of those who oppose all differentiation is the mirror image of the mistake of those Australians who used to treat the danger of racial friction as adequate ground for maintaining a colour bar. The fact of an almost rigid White Australia policy tended to make Australians exaggerate the importance of racial difference. By contrast, an immigration policy which pays some regard to race drives home the fact that new arrivals who are marked off physically from the host community, and may also differ from it culturally, will not integrate harmoniously unless there is an effort at mutual adjustment on the part *both* of the immigration minority *and* of the host community.

Before the policy changes of March 1966, it was rumoured more than once that when the Afro-Asian countries had expelled South Africa from the United Nations, or otherwise 'dealt with' her, they would turn their attention to the racial aspect of Australia's immigration policy. Such a move is less likely now, but if it is ever made, and if resolutions are passed implying that race should be wholly disregarded when choosing immigrants, then some of the governments supporting the resolution will be acting hypocritically. It will be direct hypocrisy if the government concerned imposes quotas based on the race or nationality of the would-be migrant. It will border on hypocrisy even if the government concerned excludes *all* unskilled workers and admits any worker possessing certain skills, irrespective of race; for in an underdeveloped country, a policy of that kind is almost sure to have the effect of drastically limiting immigration from all sources, and probably of giving a decided racial slant to whatever intake there is.

Australia, however, must not be content to stay on the defensive. She must show that in the implementation of her new policy on non-European migration, she is giving due weight to the various purposes, local and external, that immigration can serve. She must establish beyond doubt that her policy consciously challenges the prejudices of some Australians, even while it is restrained by a reasoned judgment as to the number of non-whites whom the nation can now absorb without friction.

Efforts within Australia to ensure the adoption of such a policy will not be impeded, and could be aided, if UN or ILO would appoint a committee to state the principles that acceptable immigration and emigration policies must satisfy—a committee whose findings might later be the basis of resolutions at the political level. The Asians and Africans who served on it would bring to its deliberations a knowledge of why their own countries restricted immigration. They would be asked to furnish definite suggestions as to the policies on emigration that they thought their own countries should follow. Of necessity, the committee's recommendations would apply universally. They would, therefore, be addressed to Malaya and Nigeria, as much as to Australia and the USA. One would hope that they would challenge all racialism—white, yellow, brown or black. If they did, they would strengthen those elements in each nation which are concerned lest the nation may fall short, and be seen to fall short, when its policies are judged by an impartial standard.

For the restriction of immigration does not just touch the dignity and interests of the groups excluded. It affects, even more closely, the pride and self-respect of the excluding nation. Most Australians came to feel that they were demeaning themselves by retaining an immigration policy which until recently ignored so utterly the ties that unite us to our non-white neighbours. Our own self-respect has suffered when, for inadequate reason, we rejected a fellow democrat from Ceylon, when we excluded a fellow Protestant from southern India or Ghana, or a fellow Catholic from Vietnam or the Philippines.

The ignorance, the insensitivity, the lack of international conscience that permitted the old rigidity are now disappearing. Prior to the changes of March 1966, more and more of our people were asking for an immigration policy that reflected our political pragmatism and moderation. Back in the 1920s, a visiting English Bishop could say of 'White Australia' that it was 'not so much a policy as a passion'.[11] Today it is no longer a passion, and as a policy persists only in modified form. Change is bound to be gradual. It would have gone further by this time were it not that some members of the generation now disappearing from political life were slow to realize that reform was possible without surrendering any valid aim of a reasonable policy of control.

NOTES

1. These facts are drawn from a statement to the Australian House of Representatives by Hon. Hubert Opperman, Minister for Immigration, on March 9, 1966; a speech by Hon. A. R. Downer, then Minister for Immigration on December 4, 1959, quoted in Immigration Reform Group, *Immigration: Control or Colour Bar?* (Melbourne, Melbourne University Press, 1962), pp. 33–4; and information supplied by the Department of Immigration.
2. Information supplied by the Department of Immigration.

3. Melbourne *Age*, May 8, 1965.
4. See p. 266, below.
5. M. Bernasek and Z. M. Kubinski, 'Agricultural Machinery and Implements' in A. Hunter (ed.), *The Economics of Australian Industry* (Melbourne, Melbourne University Press, 1963), pp. 486–8.
6. Discussion on a paper by T. H. Silcock, 'Migration Problems of the Far East' in B. Thomas (ed.), *Economics of International Migration: proceedings of a conference held by the International Economic Association* (London, Macmillan, 1958), p. 387. See especially the comments of Professor Ellis, Mr Turvey and Professor Timlin.
7. 'When this (current) programme is complete, conventional sources of supply which can be tapped economically will be practically exhausted and the hope must be that, if further supplies are necessary, the use of nuclear power to distil sea water will by that time have become an economic proposition.' *Hong Kong: Report for the Year 1960* (Hong Kong, Government Press, 1961), p. 34.
8. Singapore *Straits Times*, September 10, 1958; Madras *Hindu*, August 21, 1949.
9. *Sydney Morning Herald*, March 5, 1948. Mr K. M. Kaiser, Pakistan's High Commissioner in Australia, went so far as to say that the White Australia policy 'was not causing any hard feelings in Pakistan'. This courteous statement conflicts, unfortunately, with the evidence, but Mr Kaiser's reasoning is revealing: 'The only two classes of Pakistanis Australia would need were the coolie class as labourers and trained workers. It would be a national indignity to allow the first to come out here and we cannot spare any trained people.' (Melbourne *Herald*, April 4, 1962.)
10. Immigration Reform Group, *op. cit.*, p. 135.
11. Melbourne *Herald*, July 5, 1927, quoted in C. Turnbull, 'White Australia: Policy and Passion', in R. J. Gilmore and D. Warner (eds.), *Near North* (Sydney, Angus and Robertson, 1948), p. 74.

BIBLIOGRAPHY

S. Chandrasekhar, 'Asian Migration and the Role of the Churches', Address before the International Migration Conference of the World Council of Churches, Leysin, Switzerland, *Population Review* July, 1961.

C. P. Fitzgerald, 'Overseas Chinese in South East Asia', *Australian Journal of Politics and History* (Brisbane), May 1962, Vol. 8, No. 1.

E. Hambro, *The Problem of Chinese Refugees in Hong Kong* (Leyden, Sijthoff, 1955).

L. W. Hollingsworth, *The Asians of East Africa* (London, Macmillan, 1960).

Hong Kong Annual Report, 1956, Ch. 1, 'Review: A Problem of People' (Hong Kong, Government Printer, 1957).

Hong Kong Report for the year 1960, Ch. 1, 'Hong Kong's Water Supplies: 1960, A Year of Decision' (Hong Kong, Government Press, 1961).

Immigration Reform Group, *Immigration: Control or Colour Bar?*, esp. Chs. 2, 3, 7, 9–12 (Melbourne, Melbourne University Press, 1962).

C. Kondapi, *Indians Overseas, 1839–1949* (New Delhi, Indian Council of World Affairs, 1951).

V. Purcell, *The Chinese in South-East Asia* (London, Royal Institute of International Affairs, 1951).

T. H. Silcock, 'Migration Problems of the Far East' and discussion in B. Thomas (ed.), *Economics of International Migration: Proceedings of a conference held by the International Economic Association* (London, Macmillan, 1958).

J. J. Spengler, 'Effects produced in Receiving Countries by Pre-1939 Immigration' and discussion, in Thomas, *op. cit.*

E. Szczepanik, *The Economic Growth of Hong Kong* (London, Oxford University Press, 1958).

A. E. S. Tay, 'The Chinese in South-East Asia', *Race* (London), November 1962, Vol. 4, No. 1.

V. Thompson and R. Adloff, *Minority Problems in Southeast Asia* (Stanford, Stanford University Press, 1955).
United Nations Department of Social Affairs, Population Division, *Elements of Immigration Policy* (New York, United Nations, 1954).
University of Sydney, Department of Tutorial Classes, 'White Australia—Today's Dilemma', *Current Affairs Bulletin*, October 7, 1957, Vol. 20, No. 12.
'White Australia—Reform?', *ibid.*, July 6, 1964, Vol. 34, No. 4.
J. M. Van Der Kroef, 'Asia's "Educated Unemployed" ', *Eastern World* (London), November 1961, Vol. 15, No. 11.
P. B. Westerway, 'Pressure Groups' and discussion, in *Forces in Australian Politics*, ed. J. Wilkes (Sydney, Angus and Robertson, 1963).

APPENDIX 1

DEMOGRAPHIC AND ECONOMIC DATA FOR ASIAN COUNTRIES

TABLE 1. *Percentage Distribution of Economically-Active Population**

Country and year	Agriculture†	All non-agriculture	Manu-facturing	Other
Nepal				
1952–54	93·5	6·5	1·9	4·5
Thailand				
1954	88·0	12·0	2·1	9·9
1960	82·3	17·7	3·4	14·3
Korea, Republic of				
1955	79·7	20·3	—	—
Pakistan				
1951	76·5	23·5	6·3	17·2
1961	75·0	25·0	8·1	16·9
India				
1951	72·1	27·9	9·1	18·8
1961	73·8	26·2	9·6	16·6
Philippines				
1956	58·5	41·5	12·4	29·1
1960	60·9	39·1	12·1	27·0
Malaya				
1947	64·9	35·1	8·0	27·1
1957	58·6	41·4	6·3	35·1
Iran				
1956	56·3	43·7	13·9	29·8
China (Taiwan)				
1940	63·9	36·1	9·9	26·2
1956	55·5	44·5	12·1	32·4
Ceylon				
1953	52·9	47·1	10·1	37·0
1963	53·0	47·0	7·3	39·7
Japan				
1955	41·0	59·0	17·6	41·4
1960	32·8	67·2	21·7	45·5
New Zealand				
1954	18·7	81·3	25·1	56·2
1961	16·1	83·9	26·0	57·9
Australia				
1954	13·5	86·5	28·0	58·5
1961	10·9	89·1	27·0	62·1
Singapore				
1947	8·1	91·9	19·0‡	72·9
1957	8·5	91·5	14·2	77·3
Hong Kong				
1961	7·4	92·6	39·9	52·7

* Economically active population comprising employers and workers on own account; salaried employees and wage earners; unpaid family workers; others and status unknown.

† Comprising agriculture, forestry, hunting and fishing.

‡ Including construction.

Source: International Labour Office, *Yearbook of Labour Statistics*, and national sources.

TABLE 2. *Food Consumption Per Person Per Day (average 1959–61)*

	Burma	Ceylon	China (Taiwan)	India	Indonesia	Japan	Malaysia (Malaya)	Pakistan	Philippines	Thailand	Weighted average	Australia	New Zealand
Calories per day:													
Cereal products	1,520	1,241	1,514	1,304	1,175	1,493	1,443	1,532	1,229	1,448	1,350	899	820
Starchy crops*	112	77	53	53	377	182	106	17	157	176	110	80	111
Sugar	91	225	127	168	104	157	279	134	137	86	150	419	513
Pulses†	112	305	179	271	155	140	127	109	109	152	210	40	42
Other fruits and vegetables	78	46	61	42	143	98	81	80	116	68	70	155	149
Fats and oils‡	123	101	99	87	142	118	167	85	98	65	100	449	528
Meat, fish, eggs	85	84	226	18	58	139	127	60	127	109	50	813	782
Milk, cheese	45	39	3	114	2	34	74	99	25	20	80	352	510
Total§	2,170	2,120	2,440	2,060	2,160	2,360	2,400	2,120	2,000	2,120	2,120	3,210	3,460
Protein per day (grammes):													
Animal	8·8	12·2	11·5	7·2	5·0	18·0	14·0	10·9	10·7	9·1	9·0	66·8	76·3
Pulse	4·5	5·7	11·1	14·4	7·6	12·1	5·6	6·2	3·7	4·5	11·2	1·3	1·3
Other	32·9	29·4	36·2	34·0	30·7	39·7	34·1	38·6	30·2	31·4	34·5	31·7	30·2
Total	46·2	47·3	58·8	55·6	43·3	69·8	53·7	55·7	44·6	45·0	54·7	99·8	107·8
Fats per day (grammes)	33·3	46·8	44·7	30·3	36·8	31·7	41·6	27·2	32·0	31·7	31·5	142·5	159·2

* Potatoes, sweet potatoes, yams, and cassava. Also includes bananas and plantains in producing countries.
† Includes nuts and cocoa.
‡ Includes butter and ghee.
§ Rounded to the nearest 10 calories.

Source: Foreign Regional Analysis Division, Economic Research Service, US Department of Agriculture, *Food Balances for 12 Countries in the Far East and Oceania*, 1959–61, p. 2. The data differ from national sources.

TABLE 3. *Urban Population as Percentage of Total Population*

Burma		
1921		9·8
1931		10·4
Ceylon		
1946		15·4
1953		15·3
1963		14·9
China:		
Mainland	1949	10·6
	1956	14·2
Taiwan	1947	50·7
	1955	56·0
India		
1941		12·8
1951		17·3
1961		18·0
Japan		
1946		30·4
1955		56·3
1960		63·4
Korea, Republic of		
1949		17·3
1955		24·5
1960		28·0
Malaysia: Malaya		
1947		26·5
1957		42·7
Pakistan		
1941		7·9
1951		10·4
1961		13·1
Philippines		
1948		24·1
1956		35·3
Thailand		
1947		9·9
1960		11·8

Source: United Nations, *Demographic Yearbook, 1960 and 1963*. For Republic of Korea and Pakistan, national sources.

Note: The concept underlying the urban/rural classification changes from country to country and even between censuses for the same country.

TABLE 4. *Relative Contribution of Women in Each Age Group to Gross Total Fertility in Selected Asian Countries: 1960 or most recent available date (per cent Distribution of age-specific Birth Rates)*

Region and country	Year	Total	Age of women (in years) 15–19	20–24	25–29	30–34	35–39	40–44	45–49
Asia									
Ceylon	1953	100	6·4	24·6	28·0	22·7	14·1	3·5	0·6
China (Taiwan)	1960	100	4·2	22·0	29·0	22·1	14·7	6·8	1·1
Cyprus	1960	100	4·5	26·0	29·8	19·0	15·1	4·6	1·0
Federation of Malaya	1956–58	100	9·1	24·7	25·5	19·6	13·4	6·0	1·7
India	1958–59	100	14·0	25·4	23·5	18·1	12·3	4·8	1·9
Israel: Jewish population	1960	100	6·8	30·1	30·4	19·2	9·9	3·0	0·6
Japan	1960	100	1·1	26·6	45·0	20·0	5·9	1·3	0·1
Philippines	1950–55	100	4·5	23·2	25·3	22·1	15·7	7·4	1·8
Ryukyu Islands	1960	100	1·6	18·2	30·2	25·2	17·3	6·7	0·8
Sarawak	1950–55	100	8·0	24·4	24·1	19·9	14·9	7·0	1·8
Singapore*	1957	100	6·0	23·0	27·0	22·1	14·8	6·2	0·9
Thailand	1950–55	100	4·0	20·2	24·4	21·2	18·5	9·1	2·5

* Excluding non-locally domiciled population.

Source: *Population Bulletin of the United Nations*, No. 7, 1963 (New York, 1965), p. 104.

TABLE 5. *Major Asian Cities and Their Population (1961–64)*

City	Country	Population
Ahmedabad	India	788,333
Baghdad	Iraq	1,541,734
Bandung	Indonesia	972,566
Bangalore	India	905,134
Bangkok	Thailand	1,773,318
Bombay	India	4,146,491
Calcutta	India	2,926,498
Canton	China	1,650,000
Changsha	China	700,000
Chengtu	China	1,135,000
Chungking	China	1,620,000

City	Country	Population
Dairen	China	1,054,000
Delhi	India	2,061,758
Fu-shun	China	1,019,000
Hangchow	China	600,000
Hankow	China	804,500
Harbin	China	1,552,000
Hyderabad	India	1,085,722
Istanbul	Turkey	1,459,528
Jakarta	Indonesia	2,906,533
Kanpur	India	881,177
Karachi	Pakistan	1,912,598
Kobe	Japan	1,113,977
Kowloon	Hong Kong	726,976
Kyoto	Japan	1,284,818
Lahore	Pakistan	1,296,477
Luta	China	1,590,000
Madras	India	1,416,056
Manila	Philippines	1,138,611
Mukden	China	2,423,000
Nagoya	Japan	1,591,935
Nanking	China	1,113,972
Osaka	Japan	3,011,563
Peking	China	4,140,000
Pusan	Korea	1,162,614
Rangoon	Burma	800,993
Saigon	Vietnam	1,336,000
Seoul	Korea	2,094,000
Shanghai	China	6,900,000
Sian	China	1,368,000
Singapore	Singapore	1,687,300
Surabaya	Indonesia	1,007,945
Taegu	Korea	698,277
Taipei	Taiwan	979,081
Tai-yuan	China	1,053,000
Teheran	Iran	1,512,082
Tientsin	China	3,220,000
Tokyo	Japan	8,813,939
Tsingtao	China	1,144,000
Victoria	Hong Kong	674,962
Wenchow	China	631,276
Wuhan	China	2,226,000
Yokohama	Japan	1,637,944

APPENDIX 2

THE MARRIAGE LAW OF THE PEOPLE'S REPUBLIC OF CHINA*

CHAPTER ONE

General Principles

Article 1. The arbitrary and compulsory feudal marriage system, which is based on the superiority of man over woman and which ignores the children's interests shall be abolished.

The New Democratic marriage system, which is based on free choice of partners, on monogamy, on equal rights for both sexes, and on protection of the lawful interests of women and children, shall be put into effect.

Article 2. Bigamy, concubinage, child betrothal, interference with the remarriage of widows and the exaction of money or gifts in connection with marriage shall be prohibited.

CHAPTER TWO

The Marriage Contract

Article 3. Marriage shall be based upon the complete willingness of the two parties. Neither party shall use compulsion and no third party shall be allowed to interfere.

Article 4. A marriage can be contracted only after the man has reached twenty years of age and the woman has reached eighteen years of age.

Article 5. No man or woman in any of the following instances shall be allowed to marry:

(*a*) Where the man and woman are lineal relatives by blood or where the man and woman are brother and sister born of the same parents or where the man and woman are half-brother and half-sister. The question of prohibiting marriage between collateral relatives by blood within the fifth degree of relationship is to be determined by custom.

(*b*) Where one party, because of certain physical defects, is sexually impotent.

(*c*) Where one party is suffering from venereal disease, mental disorder, leprosy or any other disease which is regarded by medical science as rendering a person unfit for marriage.

Article 6. In order to contract a marriage both the man and the woman shall register in person with the people's government of the sub-district or village in which they reside. If the marriage is found to be in conformity with the provisions of this Law, the local people's government shall, without delay, issue marriage certificates.

If the marriage is found not to be in conformity with the provisions of this Law, registration shall not be granted.

* (Peking, Foreign Languages Press, 1950.) Promulgated by the Central People's Government on May 1, 1950.

CHAPTER THREE

Rights and Duties of Husband and Wife

Article 7. Husband and wife are companions living together and shall enjoy equal status in the home.

Article 8. Husband and wife are in duty bound to love, respect, assist and look after each other, to live in harmony, to engage in production, to care for the children and to strive jointly for the welfare of the family and for the building up of a new society.

Article 9. Both husband and wife shall have the right to free choice of occupation and free participation in work or in social activities.

Article 10. Both husband and wife shall have equal rights in the possession and management of family property.

Article 11. Both husband and wife shall have the right to use his or her own family name.

Article 12. Both husband and wife shall have the right to inherit each other's property.

CHAPTER FOUR

Relations Between Parents and Children

Article 13. Parents have the duty to rear and to educate their children; the children have the duty to support and to assist their parents. Neither the parents nor the children shall maltreat or desert one another.

The foregoing provision also applies to step-parents and step-children. Infanticide by drowning and similar criminal acts are strictly prohibited.

Article 14. Parents and children shall have the right to inherit one another's property.

Article 15. Children born out of wedlock shall enjoy the same rights as children born in lawful wedlock. No person shall be allowed to harm or discriminate against children born out of wedlock.

Where the paternity of a child born out of wedlock is legally established by the mother of the child or by other witnesses or by other material evidence, the identified father must bear the whole or part of the cost of maintenance and education of the child until it has attained the age of eighteen.

With the consent of the natural mother, the natural father may have custody of the child.

With regard to the maintenance of a child whose natural mother marries, the provisions of Article 22 shall apply.

Article 16. A husband or wife shall not maltreat or discriminate against children born of a previous marriage.

CHAPTER FIVE

Divorce

Article 17. Divorce shall be granted when husband and wife both desire it. In the event of either the husband or the wife insisting upon divorce, it may be granted only when mediation by the sub-district people's government and the sub-district judicial organ has failed to bring about a reconciliation.

In cases where divorce is desired by both husband and wife, both parties shall register with the sub-district people's government in order to obtain divorce certificates. The sub-district government, after establishing that divorce is desired by both parties and that appropriate measures have been taken for the care of children and property, shall issue the divorce certificates without delay.

When only one party insists on divorce, the sub-district people's government may try to effect a reconciliation. If such mediation fails, it shall, without delay, refer the case to the district or city people's court for decision. The sub-district people's government shall not attempt to prevent or to obstruct either party from appealing to the district or city people's court. In dealing with a divorce case, the district or city people's court must, in the first instance, try to bring about a reconciliation between the parties. In case such mediation fails, the court shall render a verdict without delay.

In the case where after divorce, both husband and wife desire the resumption of matrimonial relations, they shall apply to the sub-district people's government for a registration of re-marriage. The sub-district people's government shall accept such a registration and issue a certificate of re-marriage.

Article 18. The husband shall not apply for a divorce when his wife is with child. He may apply for divorce only one year after the birth of the child. In the case of a woman applying for divorce, this restriction does not apply.

Article 19. The consent of a member of the revolutionary army on active service who maintains correspondence with his or her family must first be obtained before his or her spouse can apply for divorce.

As from the date of the promulgation of this Law, divorce may be granted to the spouse of a member of the revolutionary army who does not correspond with his or her family for a subsequent period of two years. Divorce may also be granted to the spouse of a member of the revolutionary army who had not maintained correspondence with his or her family for over two years prior to the promulgation of this Law and who fails to correspond with his or her family for a further period of one year subsequent to the promulgation of the present Law.

CHAPTER SIX

Maintenance and Education of Children After Divorce

Article 20. The blood ties between parents and children do not end with the divorce of the parents. No matter whether the father or the mother acts as guardian of the children, they still remain the children of both parties.

After divorce, both parents still have the duty to support and educate their children.

After divorce, the guiding principle is to allow the mother to have custody of a baby still being breast-fed. After the weaning of the child, if a dispute arises between the two parties over the guardianship and an agreement cannot be reached, the people's court shall render a decision in accordance with the interests of the child.

Article 21. After divorce, if the mother is given custody of a child, the father shall be responsible for the whole or part of the necessary cost of the maintenance and education of the child. Both parties shall reach an agreement regarding the amount and the duration of such maintenance and education. In the case where two parties fail to reach an agreement, the people's court shall render a decision.

Payment may be made in cash, in kind or by tilling land allocated to the child.

Such agreement reached between parents or a decision rendered by the people's court in connection with the maintenance and education of a child shall not prevent the child from requesting either parent to increase the amount decided upon by agreement or by judicial decision.

Article 22. In the case where a divorced woman re-marries and her husband is willing to pay the whole or part of the cost of maintenance and education for the child or children by her former husband, the father of the child or children is entitled to have such cost of maintenance and education reduced or is entitled to be exempted from bearing such cost in accordance with the circumstances.

CHAPTER SEVEN

Property and Maintenance After Divorce

Article 23. In case of divorce, the wife shall retain such property as belonged to her prior to her marriage. The disposal of other household properties shall be subject to agreement between the two parties. In cases where agreement cannot be reached, the people's court shall render a decision after taking into consideration the actual state of the family property, the interest of the wife and the child or children, and the principle of benefiting the development of production.

In cases where the property allocated to the wife and her child or children is sufficient for the maintenance and education of the child or children, the husband may be exempted from bearing further maintenance and education costs.

Article 24. After divorce, debts incurred during the period of marriage shall be paid out of the property acquired by husband and wife during this period. In cases where no such property has been acquired or in cases where such property is insufficient to pay off such debts, the husband shall be held responsible for paying these debts. Debts incurred separately by the husband or wife shall be paid off by the party responsible.

Article 25. After divorce, if one party has not re-married and has difficulties in maintenance, the other party shall render assistance. Both parties shall work out an agreement with regard to the method and duration of such assistance; in case an agreement cannot be reached, the people's court shall render a decision.

CHAPTER EIGHT

By-Laws

Article 26. Persons violating this Law shall be punished in accordance with

law. In cases where interference with the freedom of marriage has caused death or injury, the person guilty of such interference shall bear criminal responsibility before the law.
Article 27. This Law shall come into force from the date of its promulgation. In regions inhabited by national minorities, the People's Government (or Military and Administrative Committee) of the Administrative Area or the provincial People's Government may enact certain modifications or supplementary Articles in conformity with the actual conditions prevailing among national minorities in regard to marriage. But such measures must be submitted to the government Administration Council for ratification before enforcement.

APPENDIX 3

INDIA'S PLANNING COMMISSION ON FAMILY PLANNING

THE FIRST FIVE YEAR PLAN

The recent increase in the population of India and the pressure exercised on the limited resources of the country have brought to the forefront the urgency of the problem of family planning and population control. The application of medical knowledge and social care has lowered the death-rate, while the birth-rate remains fairly constant. This has led to the rapid increase in the growth of population. While a lowering of the birth-rate may occur as a result of improvements in the standards of living, such improvements are not likely to materialize if there is a concurrent increase of population. It is, therefore, apparent that population control can be achieved only by the reduction of the birth-rate to the extent necessary to stabilize the population at a level consistent with the requirements of national economy. This can be secured only by the realization of the need for family limitation on a wide scale by the people. The main appeal for family planning is based on considerations of the health and welfare of the family. Family limitation or spacing of the children is necessary and desirable in order to secure better health for the mother and better care and upbringing of children. Measures directed to this end should, therefore, form part of the public health programme.

All progress in this field depends first on creating a sufficiently strong motivation in favour of family planning in the minds of the people and, next, on providing the necessary advice and service based on acceptable, efficient, harmless and economic methods. But these presuppose (1) intensive studies about the attitudes and motivations affecting family size and techniques and procedures for the education of the public on family planning, and (2) field experiments on different methods of family planning as well as medical and technical research.

A programme for family limitation and population control should:

(*a*) obtain an accurate picture of the factors contributing to the rapid population increase in India;

(*b*) discover suitable techniques of family planning and devise methods by which knowledge of these techniques can be widely disseminated; and

(*c*) make advice on family planning an integral part of the service of Government hospitals and public health agencies.

A sum of Rs.65 lakhs has been allocated by the Central Government in the Plan of the Ministry of Health for a family planning programme.

This programme includes:

(1) The provision, in Government hospitals and health centres, of advice on methods of family planning for married persons who require such advice: Medical officers working at hospitals and health centres like maternity and child wel-

fare clinics should give advice to women regarding family planning when such advice is necessary for health reasons. If a doctor feels that a woman patient cannot undergo again the strain of pregnancy and parturition without danger to health, it is obviously the duty of the doctor to give such advice as is necessary to enable the person to prevent conception. In these circumstances the doctor would be justified in suggesting any chemical, mechanical or biological methods of contraception or sterilization as may be indicated for the individual case. The giving of advice on birth control has been a procedure allowed by the Ministry of Health in UK in medical centres maintained by the local authorities.

(2) Field experiments on different methods of family planning for the purpose of determining their suitability, acceptability and effectiveness in different sections of the population: If it can be demonstrated that our people, particularly those living in rural areas, can be educated to accept the rhythm method and use it as a practical method of limiting family growth, Governmental support should be extended to the propagation of this method. From the point of view of avoiding enormous expenditure as well as that of securing the ethical values that community life would gain by the self-imposed restraint which the rhythm method involves, it would seem desirable to try out this method fully and thus ascertain its practicability. Whether the rhythm method is capable of wide application in the community with adequate results or not, actual experimentation alone can tell. Research and experiments need not however be confined to a single method. There are numerous voluntary agencies which are currently propagating the spread of information on family planning and the use of chemical and mechanical contraceptives. Their activities would need support.

(3) Development of suitable procedures to educate the people on family planning methods: Inexpensive means of rapidly educating the public in matters relating to family size will have to be evolved if large-scale reduction in the national birth-rate is to be obtained. Scientific techniques are available to assess the effect of mass educational campaigns. These techniques should be used to develop educational programmes suitable for the different economic and social sections of the population.

(4) Collection, from representative sections of the population, of information on reproductive patterns, and on attitudes and motivations affecting the size of the family: The reproductive pattern in any population is largely determined by social and cultural factors which may differ from one area to another. A thorough investigation of the differences in attitudes and motivations towards family size and of the factors responsible for producing such differences is important. Research along these lines is necessary if we are to understand the particular sentiments and aspirations to which programmes of family limitation in various sections of the population should appeal.

(5) Study of the interrelationships between economic, social and population changes. The information obtained by such studies will form the necessary background for the formulation of a national population policy and the development of appropriate measures for population planning based on factual information.

(6) Collecting and studying information about different methods of family

planning (based on scientifically tested experience in India and abroad) and making such information available to professional workers.

(7) Research into the physiological and medical aspects of human fertility and its control.

It is considered that the problems of population and family planning may be divided into those relating to:

(1) policy and approach, and
(2) research and programmes.

Two committees have accordingly been constituted. It would also appear desirable to set up at a later date a population commission to assess the population problem, consider different views held on the subject of population control, appraise the results of experimental studies and recommend measures in the field of family planning to be adopted by the Government and the people.*

THE SECOND FIVE YEAR PLAN

The problem of regulating India's population from the dual standpoint of size and quality is of the utmost importance to national welfare and national planning. The objectives set out in the First Five Year Plan were:

(1) to obtain an accurate picture of the factors which contribute to rapid increase of population,
(2) to gain fuller understanding of human fertility and the means of regulating it,
(3) to devise speedy ways of education of the public, and
(4) to make family planning advice and service an integral part of the services in hospitals and health centres.

The family planning programme was primarily directed to the building up of an active public opinion in favour of family planning and the promotion of family planning advice and service on the basis of existing knowledge. At the same time demographic as well as medical and biological studies were taken up. Assistance in the shape of subsidies or grants was given to States, local authorities, voluntary organizations and scientific institutions for about 115 family planning clinics and for nineteen research schemes relating to biological and demographic problems. It is proposed to develop this programme further during the second plan.

The family planning programme has now gone far enough to call for its further development on systematic lines, for continuous study of population problems and for a suitable central board for family planning and population problems. Such an organization should be more or less autonomous in its working. The main constituents in the Central Board's programme will be:

(1) extension of family planning advice and service;

* *The First Five Year Plan* (New Delhi, Planning Commission, Government of India, 1953), pp. 522–4.

(2) establishment and maintenance of a sufficient number of centres for the training of personnel;

(3) development of a broad-based programme of education in family living, which should include within its scope, sex education, marriage counselling and child guidance;

(4) research into biological and medical aspects of reproduction and of population problems;

(5) demographic research, including investigations of motivation in regard to family limitation as well as studies of methods of communication;

(6) inspection and supervision of the work done by different agencies, governmental and non-governmental, to which grants are made by the Central Board;

(7) evaluation and reporting of progress; and

(8) establishment of a well-equipped central organization.

It is proposed to establish clinics, one for 50,000 population, in all big cities and major towns. As regards small towns and rural areas, clinics will be opened gradually, in association with primary health units. These clinics are intended to create a general awareness of the problem and to provide advice and service. The establishment of a central training and clinical institute and a rural training unit near Bangalore are under consideration. A contraceptive testing and evaluation centre is being developed at Bombay. It is necessary that training in family planning should be imparted to all medical and nursing students. All hospitals and an increasing number of dispensaries should develop in due course a family planning service. It is also proposed to promote actively medical, biological and demographic research. A provision of nearly Rs.5 crores has been made for family planning programmes. It is expected that about 300 urban and 2,000 rural clinics will be set up in the course of the second plan.*

THE THIRD FIVE YEAR PLAN

In recommending the programme of family planning, the First Five Year Plan stated:

'It is apparent that population control can be achieved only by the reduction of the birth-rate to the extent necessary to stabilize the population at a level consistent with the requirements of national economy. This can be secured only by the realization of the need for family limitation on a wide scale by the people. The main appeal for family planning is based on considerations of health and welfare of the family. Family limitation or spacing of the children is necessary and desirable in order to secure better health for the mother and better care and upbringing of children. Measures directed to this end should, therefore, form part of the public health programme.'

In pursuance of the policy outlined above, there has been a steady expansion

* *Second Five Year Plan* (New Delhi, Planning Commission, Government of India, 1956), pp. 553–4.

of activities in the field of family planning especially in the Second Plan. The programme for the Third Plan has been recently considered by a special committee appointed by the Ministry of Health and by the Planning Commission's Panel of Health.

In the Chapter on Long-term Economic Development, certain provisional estimates of increase in population over the next fifteen years have been cited, and it has been stated that the objective of stabilizing the growth of population over a reasonable period must be at the very centre of planned development. In this context, the greatest stress has to be placed in the Third and subsequent Five-Year Plans on the programme of family planning. This will involve intensive education, provision of facilities and advice on the largest scale possible and wide-spread popular effort in every rural and urban community. In the circumstances of the country, family planning has to be undertaken, not merely as a major development programme, but as a nation-wide movement which embodies a basic attitude towards a better life for the individual, the family and the community.

During the First Five Year Plan, 126 family planning clinics were set up in urban areas and twenty-one in rural areas. In the course of the Second Plan, the number of clinics increased to 549 in urban and 1,100 in rural areas. In addition to these clinics, family planning services are provided at 1,864 rural and 330 urban medical and health centres. A number of sterilization centres have also been established. The programme is guided by the Central and State Family Planning Boards. All States have set up special units for family planning work. Considerable amount of research work is in progress at the Contraceptive Testing Unit at Bombay and elsewhere under the guidance of the Indian Council of Medical Research and at the All-India Institute of Hygiene and Public Health, Calcutta. Demographic research centres have been set up in Bombay, Calcutta, Delhi and Trivandrum. A number of valuable field investigations have been carried out, such as the India–Harvard–Ludhiana population study and the studies undertaken at Ramanagaram in Mysore, in the Lodi Colony in Delhi, at Najafgarh near Delhi, and at Singur near Calcutta. A broad-based training programme has been developed which includes centres for training of instructors, a rural training demonstration and experimental centre, development of training clinics into regional training centres, touring training teams and *ad hoc* training courses. Family planning has also been incorporated in the normal training programme of a number of teaching institutions for doctors and medical auxiliaries. As against Rs.65 lakhs in the First Plan, a financial provision of Rs.5 crores was made in the Second Plan.

The programme for family planning in the Third Plan provides for (a) education and motivation for family planning, (b) provision of services, (c) training, (d) supplies, (e) communication and motivation research, (f) demographic research, and (g) medical and biological research. The programme as approved, involves a total outlay of Rs.50 crores. Clearly, the limitations of a programme of the nature of family planning arise not from finance, but essentially from considerations of organization, and personnel, which affect the scale and intensity at which the programme can be implemented.

Various studies suggest that there is already considerable awareness of the need for family limitation and desire for practical help and guidance. This does not mean that the difficult problems of communication and motivation have been overcome or that in terms of advice and organization much more than a beginning has been made, in particular, in approaching rural communities. It is to these aspects that much greater attention should be given in the Third Plan. The intensification of the educational programme is crucial to the success of the entire movement. Family planning education, being part of education for a better life, has to be interwoven with other constructive activities, especially the work of the primary health centres, community development blocks and voluntary organizations. Information has to be made available on the largest possible scale and conditions created in which individuals can freely resort to family planning.

Family planning services have to be made available much more widely than at present. In this, the central feature must be the integration of family planning with the normal medical and health services, specially those rendered through the primary health centres. To an extent such services might also be made available through centres maintained by voluntary agencies, mobile units and industrial and other establishments. According to the tentative programmes drawn up for the Third Plan, the number of family planning clinics is likely to increase from about 1,800 at the end of the Second Plan to about 8,200. Of the latter, about 6,100 clinics may be in rural areas and 2,100 in urban areas. Distribution of simple contraceptives and general advice could be entrusted in a much larger measure to voluntary organizations, to para-medical personnel and to *dais* specially trained in family planning work. The additional personnel and other expenditure required for enabling every primary health centre to provide family planning services is proposed to be incorporated in an integral manner into the programme for primary health centres. The main difficulty here is of securing the requisite trained personnel specially women workers. For expanding training facilities, it is essential to organize a large number of intensive short-term courses. In the urban areas, it is proposed that greater use should be made of private medical practitioners in providing advice, distributing supplies and, to the extent possible, in undertaking sterilization.

A large-scale family planning programme has to be supported necessarily by indigenous manufacture of contraceptives. In this respect, although there has been some progress, the situation cannot be said to be satisfactory. The estimates of supplies, which have been current hitherto, are based on a programme of very small dimensions. In view of the nature of the programme, it is considered that it will be necessary for the Government to take initiative in prescribing standards and specifications, determining prices, and also participating increasingly in production. In the early stages and for certain sections of the population, the provision of supplies free of cost and at subsidized rates will also be necessary. It is recommended that detailed plans for the production of contraceptives, both by Government and by private firms, should be drawn up as a matter of high priority, keeping in view the objective that, as rapidly as possible, supplies will in fact become available on the scale needed.

An expanded programme of research is to be undertaken in the Third Plan. Amongst others, the following aspects are being investigated:

(i) Development of studies of human genetics.
(ii) Studies in the physiology of reproduction.
(iii) Development of more effective local contraceptives.
(iv) Development of a suitable oral contraceptive.
(v) Follow-up of sterilization cases, both male and female, to investigate possible after-effects in such cases.

An expert committee on oral contraceptives has been appointed to review periodically the developments in this field and to make recommendations. A committee to guide communication, motivation and action-research in family planning has also been recently set up. Studies of the sociological problems involved in family planning need to be developed on more comprehensive lines than has been hitherto attempted.

Over the past five years, facilities for sterilization operations have been extended in several States and about 125,000 operations have been carried out. Within the programme of family planning, sterilization undertaken on the basis of voluntary choice has a valuable contribution to make. It is visualized that during the Third Plan facilities for sterilization will be extended to district hospitals, sub-divisional hospitals and to such primary health centres as have the necessary facilities for surgical work. With the help of mobile units, these facilities can be extended further.

The main task in the field of family planning in the Third Plan is to find effective solutions to certain basic problems and to mobilize all the available agencies for educational and extension work in support of family planning. Administrative arrangements at the Centre and in the States will need to be greatly strengthened. To equip thousands of primary health centres and in due course their sub-centres as well, with personnel and supplies, and to be able to reach out to the villages not merely with advice but more positively with the means to practise family planning, are tasks whose magnitude and complexity should not be underestimated. To utilize such diverse agencies as private medical practitioners, indigenous doctors and village *dais* for family planning work along with the family planning clinics and the primary health centres will call for most careful planning at the local level. The organization of production of contraceptives on the scale needed is another major undertaking. It is essential that the help of voluntary organizations, labour organizations and other associations in various fields of national life should be sought on as large a scale as possible and integrated into the practical programmes of work adopted in each area.

Finally, it should be added that besides the facilities which are undoubtedly needed, in any large-scale effort to limit families there should be the greatest emphasis on moral and psychological elements, on restraint and on such social policies as education of women, opening up of new employment opportunities for them and raising of the age of marriage. In addition to advice on birth control the family planning programme should include sex and family life education and advice on such other measures as may be necessary to promote the welfare of the family.*

* *Third Five Year Plan* (New Delhi, Planning Commission, Government of India, 1961), pp. 675–8.

THE FOURTH FIVE YEAR PLAN

Most of the programmes in this sector are of a continuing nature. Top priority is being given to family planning. Training facilities for different categories of medical personnel will be increased in order to overcome the shortage of qualified personnel. The campaigns against communicable diseases will be intensified.

It is proposed to increase the number of medical colleges from 87 at the end of the Third Plan to 112 at the end of the Fourth. It is estimated that during the Fourth Plan the outturn of doctors would be in the neighbourhood of 45,000 in addition to 86,000 expected to be available by the end of the Third Plan. This is expected to raise the doctor-population ratio to 1 : 4,600 as against 1 : 5,800 at the end of the Third Plan period. Training of nurses and nurse-midwives will be stepped up so that by 1970–71 an additional 42,000–45,000 nurses and 60,000 auxiliary nurse-midwives will be available as against 45,000 nurses and 35,000 auxiliary nurse-midwives at the end of the Third Plan. It is proposed to add 60,000 beds in the Fourth Plan in order to maintain the present bed-population ratio of 0·49 per thousand. Small-pox eradication programme will enter the maintenance phase during the Fourth Plan after achieving 100 per cent coverage of the population.

The basic objective of the family planning programme is to reduce the birth rate from 40 per thousand at present to 25 per thousand as expeditiously as possible. The operational goal for achieving this objective is to create facilities for 90 per cent of the married population of India for the adoption of family planning by: (i) group acceptance of a small-sized family, (ii) personal knowledge about family planning methods, and (iii) ready availability of supplies and services. It is intended to cover the whole country with about 5,500 rural family planning welfare centres, about 41,000 sub-centres and about 1,800 urban centres.

All conventional methods of contraception will be utilized with particular emphasis on the IUCD because of its efficacy, reversibility and acceptability. The target for IUCD insertions is 6 million 1966–67 rising up to 10·5 million by 1970–71. At present 30,000 loops are being produced daily in a public sector factory at Kanpur. To meet the entire need, production is being stepped up to 60,000 loops per day.

To meet the training needs of a large number of personnel engaged in this programme, the existing 16 family planning training centres will be up-graded and 28 new centres on the basis of one training centre per 10 million population will be established.

For the success of this programme, active association and participation of voluntary agencies, private medical practitioners, local leaders, local bodies, labour organizations and other associations is being secured.

The total outlay proposed for health and family planning is Rs. 587 crores. Of this, Rs. 95 crores have been earmarked for the family planning programme but any additional amount that this programme can usefully spend will be provided through the Annual Plans.

* * * * *

India's population according to the 1961 Census was 439·2 million. The estimated mid-year population of 1966 is 498·9 million. Improvement in public health has caused a sharp fall in the death rate without any significant change in the fertility rate. As a result, there has been a steady rise in the annual growth of population. It rose from 1·26 per cent per annum during the decade 1941–51 to 1·97 per cent per annum during 1951–61. The growth rate was estimated to be 2·4 per cent per annum during the period 1961–65. This rate of growth is expected to rise still further to 2·5 per cent per annum during the period 1966–70. Expectation of life at birth which used to be only 27 in the 1920's and nearly 32 in 1945 is now reckoned at 50 years. With the all-round improvement in health conditions, the death rate will fall still further and the expectation of life will increase. The rate of growth of population is bound to rise unless action is taken on a national scale to bring it down.

India's objective of attaining socio-economic betterment of the people can only be fulfilled if the rate of growth of population is controlled and human skill and resources are developed to the desired extent. The Government of India have recognized family planning as a key programme for the success of the country's Five Year Plans of development and have adopted a nation-wide programme with the objective of reducing the birth rate from 40 per thousand at present to 25 per thousand as expeditiously as possible. The operational goal for achieving this objective is to create facilities for 90 per cent of the married population of India, for the adoption of family planning by:

(i) Group acceptance of a small-sized family.
(ii) Personal knowledge about family planning methods; and
(iii) Ready availability of supplies and services.

India is one of the few countries which has taken up family planning as a national programme. In the First Plan, a modest beginning was made. During the Second Plan, an action-cum-research programme was initiated. The programme was intensified towards the middle of the Third Plan when the emphasis was shifted from the clinical approach to a more vigorous extension education approach for motivating the people to accept the norm of a small family. The programme involves various aspects of community life and social behaviour of the people. Its successful implementation requires (i) large numbers of trained staff such as doctors, nurses, midwives, health educators and other experts as well as non-technical administrative and executive personnel, (ii) training facilities on a very wide scale for training of all categories of staff, (iii) supplies of contraceptives, intra-uterine device (IUCD), equipment, transport, etc.

There were only 147 Family Planning centres at the end of the First Plan period. This number increased to 11,474 by the end of the Third Plan. In addition to these centres, nearly 9,329 centres for distribution of contraceptives have been located particularly in the rural areas. These centres provide supplies, services and advice on family planning. The programme has all along been integrated with the maternity and child health programme. All known methods of contraception are being followed with particular emphasis on the IUCD, which was introduced in the last year of the Third Plan. The response of the people has been encouraging both in urban and rural areas, particularly the response of women to the IUCD. Over 0·8 million IUCD were inserted and more than 1·5 million sterilization operations were performed by the end of the Third Plan.

Certain organizational changes have been introduced in order to facilitate speedy implementation of the programme. The Ministry of Health has been redesignated as the Ministry of Health and Family Planning. A Department of Family Planning has been created with a separate Secretary. A Commissioner of Family Planning has been appointed with Regional Directors for better liaison with the State Governments and State organizations for Family Planning. For technical support, a Central Family Planning Institute has been established as an autonomous organization. For giving advice on demography and communication research, two committees have been formed, viz. The Demographic Advisory Committee and the Communication Action Research Committee. For medical and biological research, an Advisory Committee has been formed under the auspices of the Indian Council of Medical Research. A Cabinet Committee has been constituted with the Minister for Planning as Chairman and the Ministers of Finance, Information and Broadcasting, Food and Agriculture and Health as Members. This committee will facilitate the taking of quick decisions and speeding up the implementation of the programme.

In keeping with the basic objective of reducing the birth rate from 40 to 25 per thousand as expeditiously as possible, the outlay of Family Planning has been stepped up from Rs. 27 crores in the Third Plan to Rs. 95 crores in the Fourth Plan. The programmes include the recruitment and training of doctors and other workers at various levels to implement the campaign and the provision of supplies and services that go with it. It is intended to cover all the 5,000 Community Development blocks as well as the urban areas where there are large concentrations of population. Provision is being made for audio-visual equipment, technical equipment, mobile units, etc. The Department of Family Planning has, since the preparation of this chapter, proposed an additional outlay of Rs. 144 crores in the Fourth Plan for further intensification of the programme. These proposals will be considered and any additional amount that this programme can usefully spend will be provided through the Annual Plans.

Although it is intended to promote all methods of contraception, emphasis is being laid on the IUCD because of its efficacy, reversibility and acceptability. Stress is also being laid on all other conventional methods. The successful implementation of this programme requires large numbers of women doctors and steps are being taken to ensure the availability for the purpose. A Central 'task force' of doctors has been created and special stipends are being given to women medical students who agree to serve in the family planning programme after their graduation. It is also intended to involve private medical practitioners in the programme.

The mass education and motivation programme will be intensified during the Fourth Plan. Steps have already been taken to make fuller use of various media like films, radio, press, etc., for promoting the acceptance of the family planning programme as a way of life. These include mobile audio-visual vans, transistorized radio sets for villages not having electricity and the production of a large number of feature films and short films on family planning.

As already mentioned, the programme will be implemented on a co-ordinated basis involving several Ministries. The most important is the professional work of doctors and other medical personnel under the Ministry of Health and Family Planning. Steps have already been taken to start the manufacture of loops for the IUCD programme and the manufacture of condoms, both in private and public sectors. The Ministry of Information and Broadcasting will play a major role in the mass education field. The Block staff of the Department of Community Development and the staff of the Ministries of Education, Local Self Government and Social Security and various industrial organizations will be utilized for the propagation of family planning programmes. The overall coordination will be done through the Committee of the Cabinet.

The active participation of Voluntary Agencies, Local Leaders, Local Bodies, Labour Organizations and other associations in various fields of national life is essential to the successful implementation of the programme. Since it involves mass contact with the people it is vital that representatives of the people themselves are fully associated with the programme. With this end in view, enhanced provision has been made for voluntary organizations and steps are being taken to associate local leadership both in the rural and urban areas.*

* *Fourth Five Year Plan—A Draft Outline* (New Delhi: Planning Commission, Government of India, 1965), pp 54–5, 346–9.

APPENDIX 4

EUGENIC PROTECTION LAW IN JAPAN (1948)

CHAPTER III

Protection of the Mother's Life and Health

A. Artificial interruption of pregnancy at physician's discretion
Article 14. The physician designated by the Medical Association which is a corporate juridical body established in the prefectural district as a unit (hereinafter called the 'designated physician'), may exercise artificial interruption of Pregnancy, at his discretion, to the person who falls under any of the following items, with the consent of the person in question or the spouse.

(1) A person or the spouse who has psychosis, mental deficiency, psychopathias, hereditary bodily disease or hereditary malformation;

(2) A relative in blood within the 4th degree of consanguinity of a person or the spouse who has hereditary psychosis, hereditary mental deficiency, hereditary psychopathias, hereditary bodily disease or hereditary malformation;

(3) A person or the spouse who is suffering from leprosy;

(4) A mother whose health may be affected seriously by continuation of pregnancy or by delivery from the physical or economic viewpoint;

(5) A person who has conceived by being fornicated by violence or threat or while incapacitated to resist or refuse.

2. With reference to the consent under the preceding paragraph, the sole consent of the person in question shall suffice if the spouse is unascertainable, or if the spouse fails to declare his or her intention, or if no spouse remains after conception.

3. If the person who shall undergo the operation for artificial interruption of pregnancy is insane or feebleminded, the consent of the person under obligation to protect another under Article 20 of the Mental Hygiene Law (where the guardian, the spouse, the person having parental power or the person under obligation to sustain another becomes the person under obligation to protect another) or under Article 21 of the same law (where the Mayor of city, town or village becomes the person under obligation to protect another) may be regarded as that of the person in question.

B. Practical Guidance in Contraception
Article 15. Practical guidance in contraception by means of contraceptive instruments designated by the Minister of Health and Welfare for the use of women shall not be given as vocation by a person other than a physician, unless he is not designated by the Metropolitan, Hokkaido or prefectural governor. However, the act of inserting a contraceptive instrument in the cavity of the uterus shall not be performed by any person other than a physician.

2. The person who may gain designation of the Metropolitan, Hokkaido or prefectural governor under the preceding paragraph shall be a midwife, a

public health nurse or a nurse who has completed the course sanctioned by the Metropolitan, Hokkaido or prefectural governor in accordance with the standards prescribed by the Minister of Health and Welfare.

3. In addition to matters provided for in the preceding two paragraphs, necessary matters in connection with the designation or sanction by the Metropolitan, Hokkaido or prefectural governor, shall be prescribed by cabinet order.

Article 25. (Notification) The physician or the designated physician who has carried out the eugenic operation or artificial interruption of pregnancy in accordance with the provisions of Article 3 paragraph 1, Article 10, Article 13 paragraph 2 or Article 14 paragraph 1, shall send to the Metropolitan, Hokkaido or prefectural governor the duly arranged records of such operation for the month accompanied by the statement of reasons.

THE PENAL CODE

(Law No. 45, April 24, 1907)

CHAPTER XXIX

Crimes of Abortion

(Abortion)

Article 212. When a pregnant woman procures an abortion on herself by the use of drugs or otherwise, she shall be punished with penal servitude for not more than one year.

(Consent to abortion)

Article 213. A person, who at the request of a woman or with her consent causes her abortion, shall be punished with penal servitude for not more than two years. If she is thereby killed or injured, the offender shall be punished with penal servitude for not less than three months nor more than five years.

(Abortion through professional conduct)

Article 214. A doctor, midwife, pharmacist, or druggist, who at the request of a woman or with her consent causes her abortion, shall be punished with penal servitude for not less than three months, nor more than five years. If she is thereby killed or injured, the offender shall be punished with penal servitude for not less than six months nor more than seven years.

(Abortion without consent)

Article 215. A person, who causes the abortion of a woman without her request or consent, shall be punished with penal servitude for not less than six months nor more than seven years.

2. Attempts of the crime mentioned in the preceding paragraph shall be punished.

(Death or injury through abortion without consent)

Article 216. A person, who commits the crime mentioned in the preceding Article and thereby kills or injures a woman, shall be punished with the penalties for the crimes of inflicting injury, if they be the graver.

APPENDIX 5

AUSTRALIA'S IMMIGRATION ACT

1. Powers and Legislation of the Commonwealth.—(i) *Constitutional.* Under section 51 (xxvii) and (xxviii) of the Commonwealth Constitution, the Parliament of the Commonwealth is empowered to make laws with respect to immigration, emigration, aliens and the influx of criminals.

(ii) *Legislation.* Immigration into Australia is regulated by the *Migration Act* 1958–1964 which came into force on June 1, 1959, and repealed the *Immigration Act* 1901–1949 and the *Aliens Deportation Act* 1948.

Any immigrant entering Australia after the commencement of the Act without having been granted an 'entry permit' or who is not within an exempted class is a prohibited immigrant. Exempted persons include diplomatic, consular and trade representatives of other countries, and seamen who enter on leave while their ships are in Australian ports. For the purposes of the Migration Act an immigrant includes a person entering for temporary stay.

An entry permit is normally granted at the port of entry by means of a stamp in the traveller's passport or equivalent travel document. There is no form of application involved. Temporary entry permits are granted to persons who have been authorized to enter for a limited period only. Persons eligible to enter for indefinite residence are granted permits of unrestricted validity. A person who is refused an entry permit must be kept on board the ship on which he arrives; otherwise the shipping company is liable to a fine of £500.

The Act abolished the 'Dictation Test' as a means of excluding or deporting ineligible persons. Other deportation powers which were contained in the repealed legislation were largely re-enacted, although with some revision.

The Act revised the law relating to the emigration of Aboriginals and children, repealing the *Emigration Act* 1910.

The Act does *not* affect passport or visa requirements for entry to Australia. All persons who, prior to the 1958 Act, had been required before embarkation to obtain visas or other kinds of authority to proceed to Australia, are still required to obtain them. Likewise, persons who have not had to obtain prior authority to proceed to Australia are not now required to obtain such authority solely as a result of the Act. Persons previously allowed to enter without production of passports—notably British people arriving from New Zealand—are still able to do so.

The *Aliens Act* 1947–1959 provides that a register of aliens shall be maintained for every State or mainland Territory of the Commonwealth. Unless exempted, aliens sixteen years of age and over are required to register with the Department of Immigration and to notify the Department of any change of address, occupation or employment, and of their marriage. The Act provides also that the consent of the Department must be obtained before an alien may change his surname.

The *Immigration* (*Guardianship of Children*) *Act* 1946–1952 provides that the Minister for Immigration becomes the legal guardian of every person under the age of twenty-one years who enters Australia (except for certain groups exempted) other than in charge of, or for the purpose of living in the care of, a parent or adult relative. It is primarily administered through the Child Welfare authorities in each State and mainland Territory who, as the Minister's delegates under the Act, supervise the welfare of each 'immigrant child'.

2. Conditions of Immigration into Australia.—(i) *Admission of Non-Europeans*. Australia's immigration policy is directed towards maintaining a predominantly homogeneous population. It is fundamental to this policy that people coming to Australia for permanent residence should be capable, both economically and socially, of ready integration into the community.

The Australian practice is not one of the total exclusion of persons of other than European origin. The immigration laws governing residence in Australia permit the Minister to exercise discretion. The policy so administered takes into account the qualifications of persons wishing to settle here and the merits of each case, including considerations of a humanitarian nature and broad national interest.

In addition to the indigenous people, there are in Australia some 37,300 non-Europeans. Of those 15,300 are Australian citizens (10,300 by birth and 5,000 by naturalization and registration), while 4,000 have permanent residence status but have not sought or qualified for citizenship.

The remaining 18,000 comprise 4,400 non-Europeans who have been admitted, in some instances with their families, on a temporary basis in a variety of categories, 1,200 visitors, and an Asian and other non-European student population of 12,400, including both government-sponsored and private students.

The present immigration policy provides, *inter alia*—

(*a*) that non-Europeans, who are the spouses, unmarried minor children or aged parents of Australian citizens, or of British subjects permanently resident here, may be admitted for permanent residence;

(*b*) that a European British subject proceeding from overseas to Australia for permanent residence may be accompanied by his non-European spouse and unmarried minor children;

(*c*) that non-Europeans who have been admitted for temporary residence may qualify, on residential and other grounds, for permanent resident status and subsequently for naturalization;

(*d*) that, in addition to those non-Europeans admitted for temporary residence for commerce and trade, highly qualified and distinguished people who seek to reside here (including those non-Europeans who have taken educational courses at the tertiary level in Australia, who have spent at least five years in their own countries after having completed their courses, and who have qualifications from which the Australian community would benefit) may be admitted on a selective basis for an indefinite stay.

Those non-Europeans, whose continued residence in Australia was induced by political events in their own countries, have been permitted to remain here indefinitely.

(ii) *Persons of European Race*. Maltese, Cypriots and aliens of European race desiring to settle permanently in Australia are required to obtain authority for admission from the Department of Immigration or an Australian overseas post. Their admission under the present policy is subject to their compliance with the Commonwealth's requirements with regard to health, character, freedom from security risk and general suitability as settlers.

(iii) *General Information*. General information as to conditions of entry into Australia may be obtained from the following officers:—

(*a*) In Australia—the Secretary, Department of Immigration, Canberra, Australian Capital Territory, and Commonwealth Directors of Migration in the capital cities of the various States;

(*b*) in oversea countries—from migration officers or from Australian diplomatic posts.

CITIZENSHIP AND NATURALIZATION

1. Commonwealth Legislation.—*The Nationality and Citizenship Act* 1948 commenced on Australia Day (January 26th), 1949, and repealed all previous Commonwealth legislation on this subject. The most significant effect of the Act was the creation for the first time of the status of 'Australian Citizen'. In this respect the Act was complementary to citizenship legislation passed or about to be passed by other countries of the British Commonwealth. All Australian citizens, and the citizens of other countries of the British Commonwealth, are declared to be British subjects. Australian citizenship was automatically acquired as from January 26, 1949, by persons who were British subjects at that date and who either (a) were born in Australia or New Guinea; or (b) were naturalized in Australia; or (c) had been residing in Australia during the five years immediately preceding January 26, 1949; or (d) were born outside Australia of fathers to whom (a) or (b) above applied (provided the persons concerned had entered Australia without being placed under any immigration restriction); or (e) were women who had been married to men who became Australian citizens under the above headings (provided that the women concerned had entered Australia without being placed under immigration restrictions). For the purposes of the Act, 'Australia' includes Norfolk Island and the Territory of Papua, and by an amendment of the Act in 1950 it was further provided that Nauru shall be treated in the same manner as New Guinea.

Citizenship may be acquired in the following ways:—(a) by birth in Australia; (b) by birth outside Australia, of a father who is an Australian citizen, provided that the birth is registered at an Australian Consulate; (c) by registration—Certificates of Registration as Australian citizens may be granted by the Minister to British subjects or Irish citizens who make application and satisfy the Minister that they can comply with specified requirements as to residence in Australia, good character and intention to reside permanently in Australia; (d) by naturalization—Certificates of Naturalization as Australian citizens may be granted by the Minister to aliens who make application and can comply with requirements somewhat similar to those previously required under the *Nationality Act* 1920–1946. Requirements for naturalization are—(i) as a rule five years' residence in Australia is required, but residence in other British countries or service under a British government may be accepted (special concessions in the matter of residence qualifications in respect of persons who have voluntarily enlisted in the armed forces were made by an amending Act of 1952); (ii) the applicants must have an adequate knowledge of the responsibilities and privileges of citizenship; (iii) Certificates do not take effect until the applicant takes the Oath of Allegiance. The oath is now taken, and citizenship is conferred, at public ceremonies held in the locality of the applicant's place of residence, and presided over by the mayor or equivalent head of the local government authority.

The Declaration of Intention to apply for naturalization, which was introduced by the original Act of 1948, is no longer compulsory, although it can still be made if an intending applicant so desires. This change was made by the amending Acts of 1955 and 1959 under the provisions of which aliens may lodge applications on completing four and a half years' residence, but may not be granted naturalization until five years' residence has been completed.

Under the Act, the independence of married women in nationality matters is recognized, and British nationality is restored to those women who had lost it through marriage to aliens. Marriage does not affect a woman's nationality. Alien women who marry Australian citizens may, however, be naturalized under somewhat easier conditions than those which apply to other aliens.

ABOUT THE CONTRIBUTORS

CALDWELL, JOHN CHARLES, M.A., PH.D.—Educated at Sydney, New England and the Australian National Universities. Has worked in Thailand, Malaya and West Africa. Directed population research programme in Ghana as Senior Research Fellow in Demography and Associate Professor of Sociology at the University of Ghana, 1962–64. Now, Fellow in Demography in the Institute of Advanced Studies of the Australian National University at Canberra. Has published various articles and chapters on the demography of Malaya, Ghana and Australia and is one of the authors of the forthcoming book, *Social and Economic Survey of Ghana.*

CHANDRASEKHAR, SRIPATI, M.A., PH.D., D.LITT.—Educated at the Madras Presidency College, University of Madras, Columbia and New York Universities and the London School of Economics; Professor and Chairman, Department of Economics, Annamalai University, 1947–51; Director of Demographic Research, UNESCO, Paris, 1948–49; Professor and Chairman, Department of Economics, Baroda University, 1951–55; Nuffield Foundation Fellow, London School of Economics, 1953–55; Director, Indian Institute for Population Studies, Madras, since 1950; Visiting Lecturer, University of Pennsylvania, 1944–45; Visiting Professor of Demography, University of Missouri, 1956–57; Visiting Professor of Population, University of Pittsburgh, 1961–62; Visiting Professor of Sociology, University of California, 1965–66; Gokhale Endowment Lecturer, University of Madras, 1951; McBride Trust Lecturer, Western Reserve University, 1954; Norwegian-India Fondet Lecturer, University of Oslo, 1955; Banaili Readership Lecturer, Patna University, 1959; Sir William Meyer Endowment Lecturer, University of Madras, 1962; Sir A. Ramaswamy Mudaliar Endowment Lecturer, Kerala University 1964; National Science Foundation Lecturer, University of California, Riverside, 1964; The Maharaja of Dharbanga Endowment Lecturer, Allahabad University, 1965; Delegate to more than twenty-five international conferences during the last two decades; has visited and lectured in more than seventy countries including Communist China and the Soviet Union; Member of several national and international academic and scientific bodies; elected member of the Upper House of the Indian Parliament; Member, Demographic Advisory Committee, Government of India; Member, Government of India Central Family Planning Council; he now divides his time between India and the United States of America; has contributed many articles to learned periodicals and general magazines; received the Watumull Award for distinguished work in Indian Demography, 1965; received honorary doctorate from the University of Redlands (USA); editor, *Population Review*, a journal of Asian Demography; among his books are *India's Population: Fact and Policy* (1946); *Census and Statistics in India* (1948); *Hungry People and Empty Lands* (1953); *Population and Planned Parenthood in India* (1955); *Infant Mortality in India* (1958); *China's Population* (1961); *Red China: An Asian View* (1964); *American Aid and India's Economic Development* (1965).

HAWKINS, EVERETT DAY, M.A., PH.D.—Educated at the Oberlin College and Princeton University; Instructor in Economics at Princeton University, 1934–35. Professor of Economics at Mount Holyoke College, 1947–63; Visiting Assistant Professor at the California Institute of Technology, 1940; Visiting Professor at Gadjah Mada University, Indonesia, 1958–60; Consultant to the National Economic and Social Research Institute, Djakarta, 1963–64. Now Professor of Economics, University of Wisconsin.

Also Director of Information, OWI, Chungking, Hankow and Mukden, 1942–46; Programme Planning Officer, ECA, Djakarta, 1951–52; Indonesia Desk Officer, TCA, 1952–53; Member of several American academic societies. Author of *Dismissal Compensation* (1940), contributor to *Indonesian Labour: A Management Survey* (1961) and *Indonesia* (Human Relations Area Files, 1963).

HORN, ROBERT VICTOR, M.A., D.PHIL.—Educated at Koeln and Sydney Universities. Worked in commercial and banking concerns in Germany and France. Resident in Australia since 1937; has worked as an economic analyst in Australian State and Commonwealth government departments. He is also qualified as an accountant and as an Associate of the Bankers' Institute of Australia. At present Lecturer in Economics at the University of New South Wales. Has contributed several articles to professional journals in the fields of immigration statistics and national regional income.

PETERSEN, WILLIAM, M.A., PH.D.—Educated at Columbia College, University of Paris, New School for Social Research and Columbia University. Henrik Willem Van Loon Fellow, 1951–52; National Science Foundation senior postdoctoral fellow, 1958–59; special consultant to the Governor of Colorado on the population of Colorado, 1958–59; Associate Editor, *American Sociological Review*, 1960–62; Member, Board of Directors, Population Association of America, 1962–65; Fellow of the Institute of International Studies, University of California, Berkeley, 1965–66. Now Professor, at the Institute of Human Sciences, Boston College, Boston; has contributed several articles to learned periodicals and general magazines. Author of *Planned Migration: The Social Determinants of the Dutch-Canadian Movement* (1955); co-author of *University Adult Education: A Guide to Policy* (1960); *Population* (1961); co-author of *Nevada's Changing Population* (1963) and the *Politics of Population* (1964).

QUERISHI, ANWAR IQBAL, M.SC.(ECON.), PH.D.—Educated at the Punjab University, the London School of Economics and Trinity College, Dublin. Professor and Chairman, Department of Economics, Osmania University, 1937–47; Deputy Economic Adviser to the Government of Pakistan, 1947–51; Adviser, International Monetary Fund, 1951–55; Financial and Economic Adviser to the Government of Saudi Arabia, 1955–59; now Economic Adviser to Pakistan Government, Ministry of Finance; has been a member of several Government Commissions; has represented his country at various international economic and statistical conferences. Author of *The Farmer and His Debt* (1934); *The State and Economic Life* (1937); *Islam and Theory of Interest* (1946); *Development of Pakistan's Economy since the Revolution* (1961); and *Pakistan Marches on the Road to Prosperity* (1965).

RIVETT, KENNETH DEAKIN, M.A., PH.D.—Educated at the University of Melbourne. Nuffield Foundation Dominion Travelling Fellow, 1957–58; Visiting Fellow, Research School of Social Sciences, Australian National University, 1965; now Senior Lecturer in Economics, University of New South Wales. Has contributed several articles to learned and popular periodicals. Author of *Economics and*

Economy (1958); a pamphlet on *The Economic Thought of Mahatma Gandhi* (1959); editor, *Immigration: Control or Colour Bar?* (1962); co-author, *Needs Among the Old: A Survey in Marrickville, N.S.W.* (1964).

ROSS, ANTHONY IAN CLUNIES, M.A.—Educated at Sydney, New South Wales, and at Melbourne and Cambridge Universities, and holds degrees in History and Economics respectively from the last two universities. Now Senior Lecturer in Economics at Monash University at Melbourne. Co-author of *One Per Cent: The Case for Greater Australian Foreign Aid* (1963); co-author, *Australia and Nuclear Weapons* (1966).

WILKINSON, THOMAS O., M.A., PH.D.—Educated at North Carolina, Duke and Columbia Universities. Served in Civil Information and Education Section of the Occupation of Japan, 1946–48; Research Associate, Bureau of Applied Social Research, Columbia University, 1950–53; Research Sociologist, University of California, Berkeley, 1957–58; Instructor to Professor of Sociology and Anthropology, University of Massachusetts, Amherst, 1953 to present. Has contributed several articles to professional journals. Author of *Korean Urbanization* (1953); *Demographic Indices of the World's Urban Population* (1954); contributing author, *The World's Metropolitan Areas* (1958); *The Urbanization of Japanese Labour: 1868–1955* (1965).

INDEX OF NAMES

Adloff, R., 275
Agarwala, S. N., 97
Ahmed, Mohiuddin, 163
Ahmad, Nazir, 163
Aird, John S., 70
Andrews, J., 233

Barclay, George W., 207, 208
Barnasek, M., 275
Beal, Edwin G., 117
Bendix, Reinhard, 207
Berelson, Bernard, 208
Bogue, Donald, 209
Borgstrom, Georg, 46, 70
Borrie, W. D., 223, 236, 254
Buss, Claude A., 46

Cameron, Burgess, 233
Carr-Saunders, A. M., 14
Carter, Henry, 233
Chandrasekhar, S., 8, 11, 46, 48, 54, 69, 70, 71, 97, 98, 99, 253, 254
Chen Chang, 208
Chen Cheng-siang, 207
Chen Shas-hsing, 197, 202, 208, 209
Chen Ta, 71
Chen Yi, 67
Chiang Kai-shek, 204
Chiang Mon-lin, 204
Chisholm, A. H., 234
Chou En-lai, 66
Chow, Lien-pin, 196, 201, 207, 208, 209
Coale, Ansley J., 19
Confucius, 59
Cook, Captain, 213
Corden, W. M., 254
Cowan, C. D., 46
Crawford, R. N., 234
Cressey, George B., 46, 71
Crisp, L. P., 234

Davis, Judith, 207
Davis, Kingsley, 46, 99, 253, 255
De Francis, John, 69
Djamour, Judith, 187
Downer, A. R., 250, 251, 274

Eberhard, Abide, 207, 209
Eberhard, Wolfram, 207, 209
Elkin, A. P., 234
Ellis, H. S., 255
Emerson, John Philip, 71
Enke, Stephen, 23, 46
Etienne, Gilbert, 188

Fisk, E. K., 187
Fitzpatrick, B., 234
Fitzgerald, C. P., 275
Foley, Frederic J., 208
Forsyth, W. D., 255
Freedman, Maurice, 188, 208, 209
Freedman, Ronald, 201

Gandhi, Mahatma, 42, 91
Geertz, Hildred, 144
Geertz, Clifford, 144
Gillespie, Robert W., 201
Gilmore, R. J., 275
Glass, Sheppard, 209
Glassburner, Bruce, 145
Gopalaswami, R. A., 98, 99
Grattan, C. Hartley, 234
Greenwood, G., 234
Gruen, F. H. G., 252

Hambro, E., 275
Hancock, K., 234
Harbison, Frederick, 144
Hardin, Garrett, 98
Harper, N. D., 234
Harrar, J. George, 46
Harrison, G. A., 97
Hashmi, Sultan S., 163, 164
Hauser, Philip, 46, 187
Hawkins, Everett D., 143, 145, 199
Higgins, B., 255
Ho Ping-ti, 71
Hoeber, Francis P., 69
Hollingsworth, L. W., 275
Horn, Robert V., 211, 254
Hoover, Edgar M., 98
Houston, Evelyn, 8
Hsu Shih-Chu, 196, 207, 209
Hu Chang-tu, 71
Hughes, W. M., 247
Hunser, A., 275
Hutton, J. H., 97
Huxley, Sir Julian, 96, 97

Isaac, J., 255
Ishii, Ryoshi, 118
Iyer, Sir P. S. Sivaswamy, 98

Jones, L. W., 188

Kaiser, K. M., 275
Kannisto, Vaino, 143
Karmel, P. H., 255
Kent, Wilson R., 234

Keyfitz, Nathan, 143, 144, 145
Kinch, Arne, 187
Kirby, E. Stuart, 60, 71
Kondapi, C., 275
Krishnamurty, G. B., 98
Krotki, Karol J., 164
Kubrinski, Z. M., 275
Kux, Dennis, 164

Lang, Robert, 8
Laserson, C. J., 234
Levy, M. J., 118
Lee Yung-jung, 208
Li Choh-Ming, 71
Lippert, Donna, 8
Liu Ko-chih, 200
Liu, Paul K. C., 209
Lorimer, Frank, 187

Ma, Ronald, 188
Maizels, A., 233
Ma-Yinchu, 64
Mancall, Mark, 207
Mao, Tse-tung, 63
Marx, Karl, 60
May, Jacques M., 46,
McCusker, Jr., Henry F., 208
Mcvey, Ruth, 143
Mencius, 59
Miller, J. D. B., 234
Moreland, W. H., 97
Muramatsu, M., 114, 115, 117
Myers, Charles A., 144
Myers, Darlene, 8
Myers, Raymon H., 200

Nankerbis, F. T., 234
Nehru, Jawaharlal, 92
Nelson, Richard R., 144
Nitisastro, Widjojo, 144, 145
Notestein, Frank W., 207

O'Hara, Father A. R., 204

Pai Chien-hau, 62, 70
Parsons, Talcott, 118
Payne, Anthony M. M., 46
Pelzer, Karl J , 145
Peng, J. Y., 208
Penrose, E. F., 118
Petersen, William, 8, 189, 209
Pisarev, I., 20
Pressat, Roland, 71
Price, C. A., 233
Purcell, Victor, 188, 275

Qureshi, Anwar Iqbal, 146, 164
Qureshi, M. L., 164

Radcliffe, Shanthi W., 143
Radhakrishnan, S., 98
Ramesam, Sir Vepa, 98
Reeder, L. G., 98
Reischaver, Edwin O., 109, 117
Rivett, Kenneth, 8, 38, 45, 256
Robbins, John, 46
Robinson, Harry J., 208
Robinson, Joan, 70
Ross, Anthony Clunies, 235, 257, 260

Santoso, Djoko, 144
Sauvy, Alfred, 177
Sawer, G., 234
Scalapino, Robert A., 207
Schumpeter, E. B., 118
Scott, J. C., 71
Shann, E. O. G., 234
Shao, Li-tzu, 62
Shaw, A. G. L., 234
Silcock, T. H., 187, 188, 275
Sissons, D., 234
Skinner, G. William, 143
Smith, Julia Ann, 201
Smith, E. E., 188
Snow, Edgar, 66, 67, 71
Spencer, Geraldine, 233
Spencer, Joseph E., 46
Spengler, J. J., 275
Stone, Abraham, 91, 98
Sun, T. H., 208
Sun Yat-sen, 204
Szczepanik, E., 275

Tai, S. K., 69
Taeuber, Irene, 117, 118
Takeshita, John Y., 208
Tanaka, Heikichi, 113, 117
Tay, A. E. S., 275
Taylor, T. Griffith, 233, 236
Thomas, Brinley, 254
Thompson, V., 275
Thompson, Warren S., 46
Tien, A. Y., 71
Tuan Chi-hsien, 210
Turnbull, C., 275

Ullman Morris B., 71

Van Der Kroef, J. M., 276

Wadham, Sir Samuel, 233, 234
Wang Ya-nan, 70
Wang Yao-tung, 208
Ward, Russell, 233, 234
Wardhana, Ali, 144
Warner, D., 275
Weiss, Harry, 208

Westerway, P. B., 276
Wilkinson, Thomas O., 100, 118
Willard, M., 255
Wilson, R. Kent, 233
Wint, Guy, 47
Wood, Joyce, 233, 234
Wu Yuan-li, 69, 71

Yang, C. K., 71
Yarwood, A. T., 249, 250
You Poh Seng, 188

Zubrzycki, J., 233, 234

INDEX OF SUBJECTS

Abortion, in China, 63; in India, 99; in Japan, 114, 299
Aden, 16
Afghanistan, 16, 48
Age composition, *see under* various countries
Agriculture, 33, 88, 131, 277, 278
Arctic circle, 11
Arid regions, 46, 212
Asia's population, growth, 13; density, 15; area, 16; diseases, 21; literacy, 20; *per capita* income, 20; age composition, 25; sex ratio, 26; problem, 32; policy, 33; migration, 35, 37; family planning, 40
Assimilation of immigrants, 257
Australia, environment, 211; population growth, 214; aboriginals, 215; urbanization, 216; age distribution, 218; natural increase, 220; immigration, 222; religions, 226; work force, 227; empty continent, 236; Asian immigration, 241; immigration policy, 246; new immigration policy, 269

Baby boom, 123
Bahrain, 16
Birth control, *see* Family Planning
Birth rates, 30
Birth registration system, 53
Bhutan, 16
Brunei, 16
Burma, 16, 279

Cambodia, 16
Canada, 261
Ceylon, 16, 279
China (communist) statistics, 49; density, 50; age composition, 51; sex ratio, 51; rural-urban ratio, 52; minorities, 53; vital statistics, 53; marriage reform 56; growth of population, 57; population policy, 59–62; birth control, 65
China (Nationalist), *see* Taiwan
Cities, 280
Communism, 49, 67
Contraception, *see* Family Planning
Cyprus, 16

Dead Sea, 11
Death rates, 30
Density, 16, 17
Diaphragm and jelly, 92
Divorce, 154, 283

Education, 76, 155

Epidemics, 73
Essay on The Principle of Population, 60
Expectation of life, 82, 196

Family, 27, 282
Family planning, 40, 65–7, 90–6, 161–3, 202–5, 281–97
Famine, 73
Fertility, 30, 54, 80, 103, 125, 201
Fiji, 265
Food, 278

Hong Kong, 16, 266

Immigration, 37, 89, 241, 269
Immigration: Control or Colour Bar?, 259, 279
Income, *per capita*, 24
India, boundaries, 72; population growth, 73; age and sex composition 74; rural-urban ratio, 77; occupations, 79; birth rate, 81; infant mortality, 81; expectation of life, 82; standard of living, 84; population policy, 87; agriculture 88; industralization, 89; family planning, 90
Indonesia, area, 119; regional disparities, 120; population growth, 121; baby boom, 123; fertility and morality, 124; labour force, 127; education, 133; population problem, 136; transmigration, 138
Infant mortality, 30, 81
Intra-uterine device, 94
Iran, 16
Iraq, 16
Israel, 16, 17

Japan, area and density, 16, 17, 100; population growth, 101; urbanization, 103; age structure, 106; occupations, 107; educational levels, 111; population policies, 114; cities, 279, 281
Jordan, 16

Korea, North, 16, 17, 279
Korea, South, 16, 17
Kuwait, 16, 17

Laos, 16, 17
Lebanon, 16, 17
Lebensraum, 69

Macau, 16, 17
Madhya Pradesh, 77

Malaria, 21, 82
Malaysia, formation, 165; people, 166; ethnic groups, 167; population problem, 177; population policy, 182
Malnutrition, 278
Marital status, 27, 28, 57, 75, 153
Medical care, 21, 23
Migration, 35, 37, 89, 90, 138, 222, 223, 241, 256–74
Mongolia, 17
Mount Everest, 11
Muscat and Oman, 17

Nepal, 17

Occupation, 79, 109, 110, 131, 156, 175, 192, 212, 277
Optimum size, 84

Pakistan, population size, 146; rate of increase, 147; density, 148; sex composition, 150; rural-urban ratio, 151; dependency ratio, 152; marital status, 153; education, 154; population problem, 157; population policy, 159; family planning, 161
Philippines, 16, 17, 279
Physicians, 23
Planned parenthood, *see* Family Planning
Population policy, 33, 59, 87, 114, 136, 159, 182, 205
Poverty, 24
Pressure of population, 16–17

Qatar, 17
Quality of population, 84

Race, 37, 225, 226
Report on World Social Situation, 32
Refugees, 39
Religion, 226
Rhythm method, 91–2
Ryukyu Islands, 17

Saudi Arabia, 17
Salpingectomy, 94–5
Sex ratio, 27, 52, 75, 150
Sikkim, 17
Singapore, 17
Soviet Union, 11
Standard of living, 84–5, 230
Sterilization, 66–7, 94–5, 115
Syria, 17

Thailand, 16–17, 279
Taiwan, economic development, 189; population growth, 193; mortality, 194; fertility, 196; population projections, 198; age-specific birth rates, 201; demographic transition, 203; fertility, 204

Trucial Oman, 17
Turkey, 17

United States of America, 21, 24, 25, 27, 48, 72, 261
Uttar Pradesh, 77

Vasectomy, 94–5, 115
Vietnam, North, 16–17
Vietnam, South, 16–17, 24

Widows and widowers, 27–8, 56–7, 153

Yemen, 17

For Product Safety Concerns and Information please contact our EU representative GPSR@taylorandfrancis.com
Taylor & Francis Verlag GmbH, Kaufingerstraße 24, 80331 München, Germany

www.ingramcontent.com/pod-product-compliance
Ingram Content Group UK Ltd.
Pitfield, Milton Keynes, MK11 3LW, UK
UKHW022218190926
475702UK00003B/419
* 9 7 8 1 0 3 2 3 6 7 2 9 3 *